MARKETING FOR BANKERS

MARY ANN PEZZULLO

EDUCATION POLICY & DEVELOPMENT

 AMERICAN
BANKERS
ASSOCIATION

1120 Connecticut Avenue, N.W.
Washington, D.C. 20036

Library of Congress Cataloging-in-Publication Data

Pezzullo, Mary Ann.
  Marketing for bankers.

  (Education policy & development)
  Includes index.
  1. Bank marketing.   I. Title.   II. Series.
HG1616.M3P49   1988   332.1′068′8   88-6372
ISBN 0-89982-354-8

Printed in the United States of America
1989 Printing

CONTENTS

PREFACE

The accelerating pace of change in the banking industry is supported by the fact that this edition of *Marketing for Bankers* is the fifth ABA text dealing with that subject in the past 32 years, yet it has been only 6 years since its predecessor. The genealogy of this book reflects the evolution of marketing awareness in the banking industry.

Background

The first of these books was *Public Relations for Your Bank,* published in 1956. At that time, marketing consisted primarily of community relations and publicity, and 16 of the 18 chapters dealt with these topics. In 1967, its successor, *Bank Public Relations and Marketing,* included more detail on selling and business development. Then in 1975, Leonard L. Berry and James H. Donnelly, Jr. wrote the first edition of *Marketing for Bankers*. By this time, commercial banks held less than two-thirds of the deposits in financial institutions in the United States, compared with about 80 percent in the early 1950s. The industry was facing stiffer competition than it had ever known and, like many industries before it, banking became increasingly aware of the need to use the more sophisticated marketing techniques of marketing research and marketing planning.

However, as Berry and Donnelly explained so well in that text, markets change as their environments change, and as markets change, so does the perception of the field of marketing. By the early 1980s, there had been dramatic changes in the technological, legislative, economic, social, and especially the competitive environment for banking. So the 1982 text presented a broader role for marketing than did its predecessor, reflecting the higher level of marketing awareness called for by the realities of banking in the 1980s. The new text was organized around, and placed greater emphasis on, the process of planning, from development of the situation analysis to performance monitoring and evaluation.

In the six years since the publication of that text, not only has competition intensified, but the deregulation of deposit interest rates has brought about major changes in banking products, pricing, and promotional tactics. In light of all these changes, marketing has taken on an increasingly important role in many banking organizations, and the need to think and plan more strategically has been recognized. Rather than taking a short-term, tactical approach to marketing problems, today's managers must take a long-term, strategic view of where they want their banks to be in several years. The organization and content of this edition of *Marketing for Bankers* reflect these changes.

Changes in the Third Edition

The third edition of *Marketing for Bankers* has been reorganized and rewritten to reflect the need for more strategic marketing, for careful target market selection and segmentation, and to place more emphasis on the implementation stage of marketing planning, as even the best planned marketing strategy can fail if it is not implemented effectively. The text has also been revised to spend less time on abstract marketing theory and philosophy and more time on the strategic issues of objective setting and target market selection. Of the 16 original chapters, 13 have been updated and retained. The 2 chapters on marketing as an organizational philosophy and as a managerial process have been distilled into one, providing an introduction to marketing and its key concepts. The chapter on strategy formulation has been replaced with chapters on the strategic marketing process, objective setting, and target market selection. The new text, therefore, has 17 chapters, and they are organized into 5 parts.

Organization

Part 1: What is Marketing? introduces the main topic and presents key marketing concepts. *Part 2: Strategic Marketing* consists of four chapters on the basics of marketing planning, the strategic marketing process, and the first two steps in marketing planning: development of the situation analysis and objective setting. *Part 3: Understanding the Market* presents the tools for evaluating markets as well as the end result: target market selection. The tools, of course, are an understanding of consumer and organizational buying behavior and marketing information and research. *Part 5: Marketing Mix Strategies* contains chapters on product, pricing, distribution, and promotion strategy formulation. The last section of the book, *Part 5: Other Topics in Bank Marketing*, deals with the important steps of organizing for the marketing function and implementing and evaluating marketing plans. A chapter is devoted to the topic of public relations and communications, an important element in the development of the bank's image and personality but one which, because its audiences are different, falls outside the scope of bank marketing as the text defines it. Since the earlier chapters deal largely with examples from consumer bank marketing, a chapter is included on the application of marketing strategy to the commercial, institutional, and trust businesses of a bank.

The text concludes with a chapter on the future of bank marketing and the challenges that lie ahead. Developments are already underway in the social, economic, technological, political-legal, and competitive environments that will affect bank products, pricing, promotion, and distribution strategies in the years to come.

Audience

This book is written for two audiences. First, it is directed toward bank employees who are pursuing formal studies in banking. Second, and no less important, it is for staff at all levels who want to learn to apply marketing principles to the banking industry. It is my hope that many chief executive and senior officers will read *Marketing for Bankers*, because their understanding and support of marketing's efforts are critical to the successful implementation of marketing plans. One of the messages of this text is that the marketing effort cannot function in isolation within a bank. It must communicate with, and have the cooperation of, staff at all levels. The more clearly senior management understands what marketing is, or can be, the more likely it is that marketing efforts will succeed.

Acknowledgments

I am grateful to many individuals who contributed to the development of this and the previous edition of *Marketing for Bankers*. The scholarly review and critique by Darlene Brannigan Smith, Ph.D., George Washington University, were instrumental in reorganizing and sharpening the focus of this edition. Michael P. Sullivan's careful review, suggestions, and input for the chapter on public relations and communications were invaluable. Individuals who provided a sounding board and expert advice and comments are Jerry Nussbaum, Mary Lee King, Michael Rappeport, and Patricia Labaw.

I am also grateful for the experience and knowledge that I have acquired in my current affiliation with the marketing staff of Fidelity Bank. Work done by Geralyn Higgins in product development, and Andrea Vayda in marketing research, formed the foundation for two of the case studies. The cooperation of my former associates at United Jersey Banks, especially Lenore Smith, marketing director, and Gary Simmerman, president of United Jersey Bank/South, contributed to the development of two other cases.

Frederick G. Schwartz, senior vice president of public relations at Norstar Bank in Syracuse, New York, and Steve Pugh of the Richmond, Virginia, AIB chapter brought to their reviews of this text the unique perspective of banking professionals who also teach from the book. Their comments were very helpful.

My thanks go to the many banks whose advertising is used to illustrate points made in the text, and especially to First United Financial Services, Inc., for Oak Park Trust & Savings Bank's Cash Station promotion; Jackson National Bank for its community relations program; and Bank One for its interstate banking advertising strategy. My thanks also to the following firms who provided input or examples: Paul D. Lucas, Jr., of Software Research Corporation; Bill Boulé of Maurice F. Blouin, Inc.; and Ann Clurman of Yankelovich Clancy Shulman.

My deepest gratitude goes to my husband and best friend, Joseph Pezzullo, who encouraged and supported me throughout this effort in hundreds of ways, great and small. I am also grateful to my parents for their encouragement and example and to the Spirit that has been at work through it all.

Mary Ann Pezzullo

HOW THIS BOOK IS ORGANIZED

Marketing for Bankers is presented in five parts. The first of these concerns itself with the concept of marketing. It explains what the word means, how the concept developed, what its goals are, and what tasks are performed under its rubric.

This introductory part provides the base for the rest of the book, which expands upon the definition of marketing and the marketing concept as they apply specifically to banking. The next several chapters (Part II) deal with the foundation of strategic marketing—the steps involved in initiating the process of marketing planning. Part III deals with techniques for identifying and understanding the target market, whose needs the marketer must meet. Part IV addresses strategies for applying each of the elements of the marketing mix: product, pricing, promotion, and distribution through both physical channels and through the personal selling of bank services.

The final section of the text addresses several remaining marketing issues. The first involves public relations and communications, the function generally responsible for assuring that bank marketing is carried out in a socially responsible manner. Next, this part concludes its treatment of the strategic marketing process by addressing the control aspect of marketing planning—the monitoring of the outcomes of the chosen strategies and any modifications that must be made as a result.

Then, since most of this text deals with retail bank marketing, there is a chapter that also addresses wholesale bank marketing. Finally, the last chapter examines some of the trends that may be part of the future of banking and their implications for bank marketers.

PART I   WHAT IS MARKETING?

This first of the five parts of *Marketing for Bankers* focuses on the term *marketing*: how it is defined, what it means conceptually, what its goal is, what tasks it entails, its history in this country, and its history in banking. This introduction to marketing forms the foundation for all that follows and establishes the overriding importance of "the customer."

After studying this chapter, the reader will see that marketing is a way of thinking and doing business—not just one of the many mundane tasks that a company or institution performs in its daily operations.

1 INTRODUCTION TO MARKETING AND KEY MARKETING CONCEPTS

OVERVIEW

Marketing surrounds us on a daily basis and influences our selection of nearly all products and services. But what exactly is marketing? And what role does it play in the banking industry? This chapter begins to answer these questions and illustrates why banks, like other businesses today, need to understand and practice effective marketing techniques.

The chapter begins, then, with a basic definition of marketing and a discussion of each of the elements relative to that definition. Next, it addresses a way of conducting business known as "**the marketing concept**," and when, why, and how marketing has evolved in the banking industry. Finally, this chapter focuses on why it is critically important for any organization to have a market definition of its business.

THE DEFINITION OF MARKETING

The American Marketing Association defines **marketing** as "the process of planning and executing the conception, pricing, promotion, and distribution of ideas, goods, and services to create exchanges that satisfy individual and organizational objectives."[1] This definition of marketing encompasses five key elements that will be expanded upon throughout this text:

1. Marketing involves the conception, pricing, promotion, and distribution of something.

2. Marketing's object can be a good, a service, or an idea.

3. Marketing seeks to meet the objectives of both individuals and organizations.

4. Marketing works through exchange processes.

5. Marketing is a planning process.

Let's look at each of these elements more closely.

Key Elements of the Definition

1. *Marketing involves the conception, pricing, promotion, and distribution of something.* The daily activities of people who are engaged in marketing revolve around the design, development, and enhancement of **products**. These people are also involved in setting the price for those products, communicating about them, and getting them into the hands of the target market. These activities constitute the four elements of what is known as the **marketing mix**. For ease in memorization, they are often referred to as "the four Ps" of marketing:

1. **product;**

2. **price;**

3. **promotion;** and

4. **place** (actually, distribution).

These are the four elements that the marketer works with in planning and executing marketing strategy and tactics, as shall be seen in subsequent chapters.

2. *Marketing's object can be a good, a service, or an idea.* Any good, service, or idea that satisfies a customer need or want is referred to as the product. The term *product* covers everything from cereal to certificates of deposit to the idea that drugs can damage your brain. While the product is one of the four ingredients in the marketing mix, it is the central element around which the other three rotate.

3. *Marketing seeks to satisfy the objectives of individuals and organizations.* The objective of the consumer (who may be an individual or an organization) is the satisfaction of certain needs and wants. The terms *needs* and *wants* tend to be used interchangeably, although most businesses today are really in the business of satisfying wants. People have a *need* for shelter, but they *want* a contemporary house on a third of an acre. They *need* clothing, but they *want* designer jeans. They *need* security, but they *want* the maximum rate of interest on their certificates of deposit.

The objective of the marketer, who may also be an individual or an organization, is to further a set of goals. These goals might involve attaining the leading share of the cereal market, maximizing return to shareholders, or reducing the number of drug abusers.

4. *Marketing works through exchange processes.* The existence of two parties with objectives that require satisfaction is essential to the marketing mix, but is not the sole condition necessary for marketing to occur. Marketing can occur when the party with the need for a certain product (the consumer) is capable of offering something of value that will also satisfy the marketer's objectives. In other words, an exchange of value occurs. Thus, the cereal manufacturer (the marketer) must be capable of exchanging its product for money or credit, and the consumer must be capable of exchanging money or credit for cereal. Similarly, a bank exchanges its checking, savings, and credit products for fees, service charges, and interest payments; and the drug abuse prevention organization exchanges the idea that it is okay to say no to drugs (that is, moral support) in return for public awareness that will help alleviate the drug problem. (See Exhibit 1-1.)

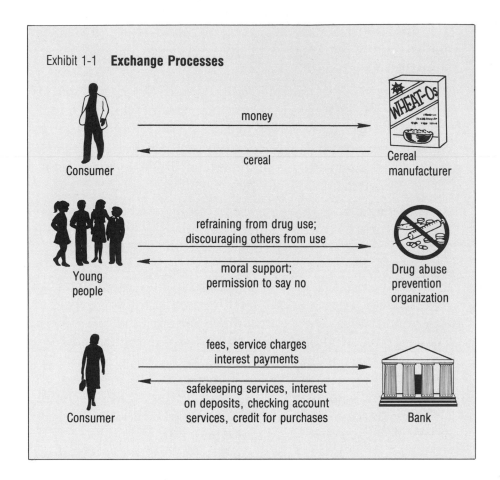

Exhibit 1-1 **Exchange Processes**

Consumer → money → Cereal manufacturer
Consumer ← cereal ← Cereal manufacturer

Young people → refraining from drug use; discouraging others from use → Drug abuse prevention organization
Young people ← moral support; permission to say no ← Drug abuse prevention organization

Consumer → fees, service charges interest payments → Bank
Consumer ← safekeeping services, interest on deposits, checking account services, credit for purchases ← Bank

To effect a successful exchange, the marketer must understand what the consumer wants, and consequently, what the marketer wants in return is an appropriate response, whether that be buying, voting, joining, or refraining.

Exchange processes have existed since the time of primitive man, when at some point, members of the earliest societies came to realize that barter or trade among people made it easier to satisfy human needs. Marketing as a science, however, did not develop until the twentieth century.

A discussion of exchange processes leads to the concept of the **market**. "A market consists of all the potential customers sharing a particular need or want who might be willing and able to engage in exchange to satisfy that need or want."[2] The term *able* is included because a member of a market does not necessarily have to have actual purchasing power, only access to it—that is, the ability to influence the buying decision. For example, a child who asks a parent to buy a specific brand of cereal is a customer, even though the cereal is bought with the parent's purchasing power. Keeping this definition in mind, the market for retail banking services consists of people with the capability, and the existing or potential inclination to use this capability, to satisfy their personal financial management needs.

Marketers use the term *market* to encompass various groups of potential customers. Bank marketers, for instance, talk about product markets ("the Individual Retirement Account [IRA] market"), demographic markets ("the seniors market"), geographic markets ("the bank's market area"), and **psychographic** (see Glossary) markets ("the sophisticated investor market").

5. *Marketing is a planning process.* As shall be explored in more detail later, marketing entails an ongoing process of planning, executing those plans, monitoring their results, and modifying them. In other words, marketing is a management process; the business of marketing must be organized and directed in order to be effective.

Just as there are many different management styles and management philosophies, there are a number of different philosophies to guide marketing management. Only one of them, however, leads to long-run marketing success.

THE MARKETING CONCEPT

The particular school of thought that has emerged over several decades as the guiding philosophy of the most successful marketing firms is known as the marketing concept. (See Exhibit 1-2.) It is a recognition that the objectives of the organization involve the

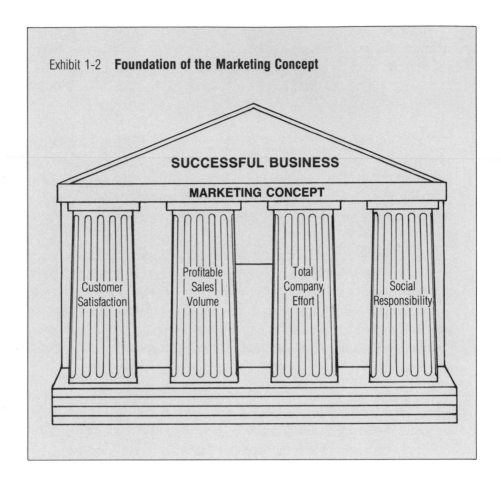

Exhibit 1-2 **Foundation of the Marketing Concept**

SUCCESSFUL BUSINESS

MARKETING CONCEPT

Customer Satisfaction

Profitable Sales Volume

Total Company Effort

Social Responsibility

achievement of ''customer satisfaction at a profitable volume in an integrated, efficient framework, carried out in a socially responsible mannerefficient framework, carried out in a socially responsible manner.''[3]

The marketing concept is a philosophy and a frame of mind; it is also a basis for decision making and a guide for effectively managing resources. Marketing, then, is not an activity that a business undertakes; instead, it is an organizational philosophy that influences and directs all the operations of a bank or other business.

The following section covers each element of the marketing concept in detail and shows how it applies to the business world.

Basic Elements of the Marketing Concept

Customer Satisfaction

The marketing concept recognizes that customer satisfaction is the business that all businesses are in. A truly marketing-oriented company believes that its own financial objectives will be best served by recognizing and responding to customer needs and wants. Marketing expert J.B. McKitterick has said that, under the marketing concept, it is not important to be skillful in making the customer do what suits the interest or convenience of the firm, but to be skillful in inducing the firm to do what suits the interest of the customer.[4] Clever advertising may lure a customer through the doors of a particular bank, but only a *satisfied* patron will remain a customer and refer additional business to that institution. This type of word-of-mouth advertising is an invaluable sales tool for *any* business.

Profitable Volume

The marketing concept does not imply that customer satisfaction is the only objective of an organization. It is not a philanthropic philosophy aimed at helping customers at the expense of the business institution. Rather, it recognizes that there must be a balance between customer satisfaction and profitability, and that a business must satisfy certain profit objectives. However, these objectives can best be met by providing customer satisfaction. (See Exhibit 1-3.)

The highly successful marketing organization finds ways to utilize its resources in the most efficient way possible consistent with customer wants and needs. Customer satisfaction in banking might be maximized by offering a checking account without fees, minimum balance requirements, or charges for stop payments or insufficient funds. However, a checking account is one of the most costly products offered by a bank, and it would be foolhardy to market such a product in that fashion. From a marketing perspective, the ideal

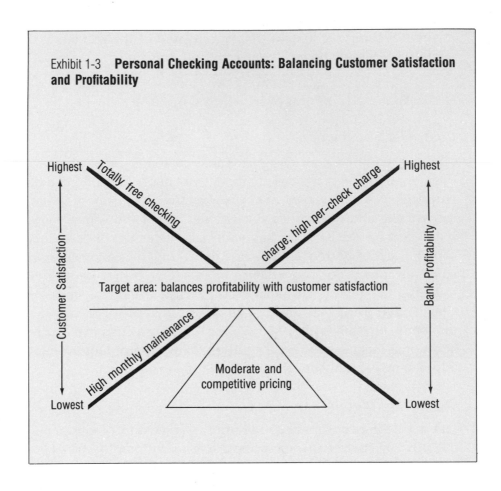

Exhibit 1-3 **Personal Checking Accounts: Balancing Customer Satisfaction and Profitability**

Highest

Totally free checking

charge; high per-check charge

Highest

Customer Satisfaction

Bank Profitability

Target area: balances profitability with customer satisfaction

High monthly maintenance

Moderate and competitive pricing

Lowest

Lowest

approach would be to find the service charge and minimum balance combination that best meets consumer demand while achieving product profitability.

Integrated, Efficient Framework

The marketing concept must become the philosophy of the entire organization, not just the marketing department. In banks, as in other organizations, the importance of effectively integrating and coordinating the activities of employees is based on a simple truth: Firms do not act upon and make decisions; people do. Marketing occurs every time the customer interacts with the bank. The teller practices marketing when greeting the customer. If the teller is rude, then as far as the customer is concerned, the bank is rude. The question is not whether the teller should engage in marketing, because marketing is inherent in the job. The question is whether the teller will market the bank's services effectively. Effective integration of the marketing concept throughout the bank's operations increases the likelihood that the teller's job will be carried out in a manner consistent with the marketing concept.

The marketing concept also ties together the various staff divisions in the bank: the customer contact personnel need the operations staff and the computer programmers. They, in turn, need the customer contact staff. In a marketing-oriented bank, there is the understanding that "if you aren't serving the customer yourself, you're serving someone who is."

Social Responsibility

Social responsibility is a crucial part of the marketing concept. It is quite possible for a company to satisfy its customers, yet be in conflict with the well-being of society as a whole. For example, a firm might market a product that satisfies a number of consumers but dangerously pollutes the environment. For years, a leading fast food chain used to package its products in styrofoam containers. Only after many years did the firm acknowledge the environmental impact of nonbiodegradable waste products and change its packaging.

Banks, like other firms that are respected institutions in the community, are expected to play an active, socially responsible role in civic affairs. It is not unusual for a bank to mandate that its officers be involved with local service organizations. Through their community relations programs, banks often support the arts, scholastic achievement, and amateur sporting events. Frequently, a bank will take the initiative in addressing a specific cause, such as neighborhood improvement or developing recreational opportunities for youth.

Unfortunately, not all firms conduct their business with a social conscience. Among the socially irresponsible acts they may perpetrate are environmental abuse, the dissemination of misleading advertising, discriminatory practices in hiring, and the manufacture of unsafe products. Sooner or later, companies that commit irresponsible acts are usually exposed by consumer advocates, ecologists, politicians, or community leaders. Often, this exposure leads to the passage of restrictions that are applied to all firms regardless of culpability. The passage of truth-in-saving legislation is an example of how all banks may be profoundly affected by the irresponsible actions of a few.

Indeed, the existence of the consumer movement itself may be proof that businesses have not genuinely integrated the marketing concept into their overall organizational philosophies. To quote author Peter Drucker: "That after twenty years of marketing rhetoric **consumerism** could become a powerful popular movement proves that not much marketing has been practiced. Consumerism is the 'shame of marketing.'"[5]

As noted above, the marketing concept has emerged over several decades, yet recognition of the importance of customer orientation does not yet pervade every business or industry.

Back in the 1970s, consumer service firms, including banks, insurance companies, and brokerage houses, started to display a heightened marketing awareness. Even Bell Telephone, which still had a monopoly at the time, conducted an aggressive marketing campaign to stimulate long-distance calling ("Reach out and touch someone").

At the onset of the 1980s, nonprofit organizations also became enlightened with respect to the need for effective marketing. Colleges instituted modern marketing techniques to help boost enrollments, hospitals used them to raise funds, and police departments did so to improve their public image.

Why has it taken many organizations so long to adopt the marketing concept, and what is it that prompts the realization of its importance among businesses?

EVOLUTION OF THE MARKETING CONCEPT

Firms usually discover—or rediscover—the marketing concept when they find that their profits are declining or stagnating because of one or more of the following situations:

- a decline in sales or market share;
- slow growth;
- a change in consumer buying patterns;
- increased competition; or
- increased marketing expenses.[6]

Key Factors in the Evolution

Declining Sales or Market Share

Diminishing sales or a reduced demand for a business' products or services is the most likely cause of heightened marketing awareness. Many small private colleges faced with declining enrollments turned to marketing research to help them understand how high school seniors made the decision to "buy" a college. The colleges then used this information to recruit the caliber of students they were seeking.

The commercial banking industry as a whole has been losing **market share** (see Glossary) for financial institution deposits since the late 1940s. (See Exhibit 1-4.) It has lost market share to thrift institutions and, more recently, to nonbank financial institutions. This loss has caused the industry to take a closer look at what those institutions are offering that commercial banks are not. It has become clear that the thrifts, which were by law permitted to pay higher rates of interest on deposits than commercial banks, were more effectively meeting customer demand for higher returns on savings. The nonbank financial institutions were offering a broader range of financial services to those individuals more willing to risk losing some principal. Thus, with a new awareness of the importance of marketing, the commercial banking industry started lobbying for deregulation of interest rates and expansion of banking powers.

Slow Growth

The demand for goods and services is not infinite, and sooner or later, markets become saturated. This condition leads marketers to become more attuned to other, related, consumer needs that can be met and, in the process, helps marketers increase sales. As the number of competitors in the fast food business multiplied,

Exhibit 1-4 The Precursors of Marketing Awareness in Commercial Banking

1. *Declining Market Share:* Since the end of World War II to the end of the 1970s, commercial banking's competition has come primarily from other deposit-taking financial institutions: savings and loans, savings banks, and credit unions ("thrift institutions"). Whereas commercial banks held about 80 percent of domestic deposits in 1949, in 30 years they lost 20 percent to the thrifts.

	Percentage of U.S. Deposits Held by	
	Commercial Banks	S&Ls, Savings Banks, & Credit Unions
1949	79.6	20.4
1964	63.0	37.0
1979	59.4	40.6
1984*	58.1	41.9

2. *Increasing Competition:* In the early 1980s, commercial banks continued to lose share to the thrifts, but the real competition was from nonbank financial institutions: money market funds, mutual funds, securities brokers and dealers, and others (insurance companies, pension funds, investment companies, finance companies, and real estate investment trusts). Since 1979, both commercial banks and thrifts have lost share to other financial institutions, whose share of the total market increased, while bank and thrift shares decreased.

	Percentage of Financial Assets Held by		
	Domestic Commercial Banks	S&Ls, Savings Banks, & Credit Unions	Other Financial Institutions
1970	37.3	20.6	42.1
1979	34.8	23.8	41.3
1984	31.5	22.7	45.8

3. *Slow Growth:* From 1979 to 1984, financial assets in commercial banks grew at a rate 16 percent slower than the total market, while nonbank assets grew 19 percent faster.

Five-Year Growth Rate of Financial Assets by Type of Institution	1979–1984 Growth Rate
Domestic Commercial Banks	57%
S&Ls, Savings Banks, and Credit Unions	65%
Nonbank Financial Institutions	92%

*1984 figures based on assets. If assets had been used for 1979 data, share figures would have been as shown, suggesting that shares for deposits and assets are comparable.

Source: *Statistical Abstract of the United States, 1986,* and George W. McKinney, Jr. and Robert W. Renner, Sr., "U.S. Banking's Dramatic Loss of Market Share," *ABA Banking Journal,* November 1980, pp. 66–67.

McDonald's launched a program to determine what type of additional foods and services customers wanted them to provide. As a result of this research, the giant franchiser started serving breakfast, leading to new business and increased sales.

Changing Buying Behavior

Customer wants and needs are not static, but constantly changing. One of the many reasons for this change is the increasing level of personal disposable income in this country. Another reason is the change in lifestyles brought about by growing incomes and changing values. For example, the amount of leisure time available to Americans has increased substantially, which has affected the marketing of recreational activities and related products such as casual clothing and sporting goods.

Advances in electronics and telecommunications have increased the interest in home entertainment products and, to some extent, have reduced the popularity of movies and live theater. Similarly, the growing number of working mothers has led to a swell in the demand for day-care centers for children, as well as for convenience foods and microwave cooking equipment.

Since customer needs are constantly changing, it is important that a bank monitor those changes in order to be able to adapt bank products and their distribution accordingly. For example, as banking customers have come to place a greater value on saving time than on bank loyalty, some banks have recognized the need for customers to be able to obtain loans with the utmost speed and convenience: instant loan approvals by telephone. A bank that offers the customer this service is in a position to charge a higher interest rate than one that requires customers to come into the bank to apply. Furthermore, since the convenience element is valued so highly by customers, those banks that were among the first in their areas to offer this service attracted a higher-than-normal share of the new loan market.

Buying patterns for consumer financial services have undergone dramatic changes in the past several years. The availability and success of mutual funds has drawn customers away from the safer, more secure, but lower yielding, banking products. Since deregulation, the blurring of the differences between commercial banks,

---

Exhibit 1-5   Some Nonbank Banks and the Companies That Own Them

A bank is defined as an institution that both takes demand deposits and makes commercial loans. Many organizations have entered the banking business and avoided coming under the jurisdiction of the Federal Reserve Board, which regulates bank holding companies, by establishing banks that either take deposits or make commercial loans, but not both. Some of these are:

Company	*Bank*
Avco Corp.	Avco National Bank
Beneficial Corp.	Beneficial National Bank
Dreyfus Corporation	Dreyfus Consumer Bank
Ford Motor Company	First Nationwide Savings
	First American Bank
E. C. Hutton Group Inc.	E.F. Hutton Bank
J. C. Penney Co., Inc.	JCPenney National Bank
Prudential Financial Services Corp.	Prudential Federal Savings and Loan Association
Sears, Roebuck & Co.	Greenwood Trust Company
American Express	Centurion Bank
Advanta Corporation	Colonial National Bank

---

savings institutions, savings and loan associations, and credit unions has provided customers with considerable alternatives in selecting financial institutions. With all this competition, bank marketers are finding it more difficult than ever to identify the financial and emotional needs of their **target audiences**.

Increased Competition

Many of the situations described above relate in one way or another to increased competition. There is probably nothing more effective for stirring up a complacent firm or a staid community bank than the sudden presence of a new competitor. When customers have just a few alternatives, the marketer has little motivation to meet their needs in the best possible way. As banks find themselves in increasingly competitive positions, the situation will become even more challenging. Nonbank financial institutions are not only powerful competitors, but many nonfinancial organizations such as Sears and J.C. Penney have entered the financial services market. (See Exhibit 1-5.)

Increased Marketing Expenses

Some organizations become more marketing conscious as a result of monetary concerns. An organization that sees that its marketing expenses are occupying a significant share of its operating budget might be motivated to look more closely at the marketing arm of the organization. One possible response by such a company might be a reorganization that better integrates marketing principles into the entire operation. However, this is probably the least common reason for a firm to become marketing conscious.

STAGES OF THE MARKETING CONCEPT

Regardless of why or how a company or an industry discovers the marketing concept, the process takes time and involves several stages. Author Philip Kotler identified five stages through which a firm passes on its way toward marketing enlightenment, and he dubbed them the "Law of Slow Learning." He used the banking industry to exemplify the stages:[7]

Stage 1: Marketing is advertising, sales promotion, and publicity. In the early 1950s, marketing had not yet dawned on the traditionally conservative banking community. (See Exhibit 1-6.) Banks operated in a seller's market. Customers needed the basic financial services that banks provided, so banks had no need to develop marketing savvy in order to sell their services. In line with their conservative image in the community, banks were built to look secure and imposing, and their interiors were often austere. Tellers rarely smiled.

Then, in the late 1950s, competition for savings accounts increased, and some banks took a cue from the consumer goods industries and started using advertising and sales promotion techniques. The competition soon followed suit, and the era of the "advertising and promotion concept" in bank marketing was born.

Stage 2: Marketing is a friendly atmosphere. In the growing battle for customers, banks learned that getting people to come to them was easy initially, but keeping them was not. So, marketing took on a new

Exhibit 1-6   The Emergence of Marketing in the Banking Industry

Year	Left events	Right events
1900	Brand names appear	
1910	Newspapers	Business and industry are primary bank customers
1920	Radio	
	Depression	
1930	Television invented	
1940	World War II / Pent-up consumer demand	Banks hold 80% of financial institution deposits
1950		Banks get into advertising/ public relations
1960	Marketing research / Consumer protection	Friendly, personal banking emerges / Bank premiums / Bank credit cards; innovation / Automated teller machines (ATMs)
1970		IRA; Keogh plans / Positioning
1980	Record inflation	NOW accounts; pricing / Money market accounts / Banks hold 58% of financial institution deposits; nonbank financial institution growth outstrips that of banks / Reg Q phaseout; interstate banking
1990		

dimension—that of trying to please the customer. Tellers began to smile, and the bars came off their windows. Bank interiors and exteriors were redesigned to create a warm and friendly atmosphere. Inevitably, friendliness became such an expected and common characteristic that it soon lost its distinctive edge and was no longer a primary consideration in a customer's choice of a bank.

Stage 3: Marketing is innovation. As all banks came to look alike, some recognized the need to find new ways of differentiating themselves from the competition. In the late 1960s, many banks responded by recognizing that their customers' changing financial needs called for new and improved services. At this stage, bank credit cards, overdraft credit lines, and other innovative marketing tools were developed.

Stage 4: Marketing is positioning. Inevitably, new banking services became widespread; so again, in the 1970s, there was a need for a competitive advantage. Banks began to think less in terms of being all things to all people, and more in terms of appealing to specific segments of the market. Some banks established their pricing and designed their services and advertising to appeal heavily to the very well-to-do segment of the population. Others aimed at the 25- to 45-year-old age group. Still others made a special effort to attract senior citizens.

Stage 5: Marketing is analysis, planning, and control. The fifth and last stage of Kotler's path to marketing enlightenment goes beyond cosmetic approaches to a deeper issue: whether the bank has installed effective systems for market analysis, planning, and control.[8] Kotler illustrates this issue by telling of a large bank whose commercial lending officers submitted their volume goals each year, usually projecting a 10 percent increase over the previous year's performance. No rationale or plans accompanied the budgets, and top management was satisfied with those officers who achieved their goals. Then, one loan officer retired and was replaced by another who proceeded to achieve a 50 percent volume growth over the previous year. The bank learned the painful lesson that it had failed to measure the potential of its various markets, to require systematic marketing plans, to set quotas, and to develop appropriate reward systems.[9]

Exhibit 1-7 Selling Benefits, Not Products

What business are you in?

Company	Production-oriented answer	Marketing-oriented answer	Advertising message
The Bell System	We run a telephone company.	We market interpersonal communications, sharing, and closeness.	"Reach out and touch someone."
General Electric	We make appliances.	We market convenience and the ability to do things well.	"We bring good things to life."
McDonald's	We sell hamburgers.	We market convenient, inexpensive meals in a family setting.	"We do it all for you."
AMF	We sell sports equipment.	We market exercise, recreation, and escape from work and tedium.	"We make weekends."
Sears	We sell retail merchandise.	We market products for a family's diverse needs.	"There's more for your life at Sears."
The U.S. Army	We defend the nation.	We provide young people with training, education, and experience—marketable skills.	"Be all you can be."
The *Wall Street Journal*	We publish a business newspaper.	We provide information that can help you advance your career and manage your personal finances.	"The daily diary of the American Dream."

Many of today's commercial banks are still in the third or fourth stage of marketing enlightenment; some are still in the first. Both individual banks and the banking industry as a whole must arrive at the fifth stage if they are to be successful in the rapidly changing and increasingly competitive era that lies ahead. Bank managers must develop a new way of thinking—a new philosophy—as leaders in other industries have done. This new way of thinking is the marketing concept.

THE IMPORTANCE OF A MARKET DEFINITION

When a firm adopts the marketing concept, it must reorient itself with respect to its identity. When an executive is asked, "What business are you in?" the answer tells a great deal about whether or not the firm has adopted the marketing concept. A marketing-oriented executive will answer in terms of what needs or wants the firm is satisfying. (See Exhibit 1-7.) While this might seem like an obvious answer, many businesses define themselves in other than market-oriented terms.

The Product Orientation

In 1960, a marketing and management scholar named Theodore Levitt wrote a seminal article related to this issue.[10] In "Marketing Myopia," he suggested that the decline of one-time growth industries (such as the railroad industry) is the result of management failure rather than market saturation. The principal failure of management, Levitt wrote, lies in defining a business in terms of current products instead of changing markets. In other words, because consumers' buying habits often change, firms should not define their businesses in terms of products currently being sold to fill consumer needs, but rather in terms of the broad range of customer needs.

For example, the railroads defined themselves as being in the railroad business, when the need they were actually serving was that of transport. Because they concentrated on railroads rather than branching into new business sectors such as air and highway transport, they lost their leading edge in the transportation business.

How does this idea apply to banking? In order to prosper in a rapidly changing market, banks must not see themselves simply as providers of traditional banking services, but also as being in the business of responding to the varied financial needs of individuals, businesses, and other organizations. Not only do banks have the normal hurdles to overcome on the path to marketing awareness, but they have also been hampered by the obstacle of regulation.

At a time when consumer financial behavior was undergoing more rapid change than it had in decades, banks found that they were incapable of responding because regulation limited their flexibility in terms of new product development and interest rates. A critical year in the history of banking was 1981, when money market mutual funds grew by $108 billion. (Growth in the previous 2 years had been about $30 billion a year.) That significant increase was a strong signal that financial needs were changing and that consumers were seeking and finding a way to take advantage of the record high interest rates of that time.

However, banks were not permitted to match the money market funds' product or rates. So, in response to considerable lobbying by the banking industry, the money market deposit account was authorized in December 1982. Although the money market funds lost $44 billion in deposits to the banking industry during 1983, the funds were established as a major competitor for consumer deposits, and they paved the way for the explosive growth of equity-based mutual funds.

Bankers should recognize that they are not just in the business of offering traditional banking products, but also of meeting the changing financial service needs of consumers. This recognition would benefit all marketing-oriented banks who strive for the passage of more liberal banking legislation.

The Selling Orientation

Some firms define themselves in terms of their sales efforts. This fact raises an important issue that warrants further discussion: the difference between selling and marketing. Many people confuse the two or think they are related. In fact, they are opposites. A sales-oriented business focuses on making a product or delivering a service, then attempts to sell it. In contrast, a marketing-oriented firm does research to find out what customers have a demand for, and then provides the product or service as a result. In the former case, the emphasis is on convincing consumers to do what the firm desires; in the latter, the intent is to get the firm to do what the consumer desires.

The Production Orientation

The production-oriented firm is more concerned with the method used in producing the product rather than with the product itself, the selling of it, or the needs of the consumer. This orientation channels the firm's energies into achieving greater efficiency. In a production-oriented bank, new products are developed by data processing or systems personnel and designed so that, first and foremost, they work for the bank rather than for the convenience of the customer.

If you refer to the example of monthly checking account statements (Exhibit 1-8), you will see that the production-oriented bank sees the statement as a required reporting record of the activity in the customer's account—deposits, checks cleared, transfers, automated teller transactions, and service charges. On the other hand, the marketing-oriented bank sees the statement from the customer's perspective, in that the statement can be reconciled easily with the customer's check register and can be read without confusion.

The marketing-oriented statement provides a listing of all checks cleared during the period, in numerical order, and it is designed in a simple and uncomplicated style. However, the production-oriented statement provides a listing of checks cleared by date only, and the individual transactions are difficult to interpret.

The Customer Orientation

The marketing concept is based on the orientation of an entire organization toward customer needs and wants. How customer-oriented is

Exhibit 1-8 Examples of a Production-Oriented and a Marketing-Oriented Statement

BANK A (PRODUCTION-ORIENTED)

ANN J. SMITH
JOHN SMITH
15 LARK DRIVE
ANYTOWN, USA 12345
For Period Ending 11/31/87

Type of Account	Account Number	Tax I.D. No.	Statement Date	Last Statement	Opening Balance
Checking	1-234-567-8	901-23-4567	11-31-87	10-31-87	2639.12

Check No.	Description	Amount	Date	Balance
0790	CHECK	1 500 00 −	11 02	1 139 12
0758	CHECK	25 00 −	11 04	1 114 12
DEPOSIT		1 160 12 +	11 06	2 274 24
CHECKBOOK CHG		12 43 −	11 13	2 261 81
0807	CHECK	25 00 −	11 18	2 236 81
0809	CHECK	80 22 −	11 18	2 156 59
0811	CHECK	10 00 −	11 18	2 146 59
0812	CHECK	350 00 −	11 19	1 796 59
DEPOSIT		1 160 12 +	11 20	2 956 71
0813	CHECK	10 00 −	11 25	2 946 71
0814	CHECK	125 31 −	11 27	2 821 40
0821	CHECK	15 04 −	11 27	2 806 36
0832	CHECK	220 00 −	11 27	606 36

the average bank? To answer that question, one need only examine some of the most basic wants that bank customers have expressed and then discern how well the industry is meeting them.

In many satisfaction surveys, when customers have been asked to voice their opinions on banking services, four wants invariably emerge:

1. *They want faster service at peak times.* Bank customers dislike waiting in long lines, but they have come to expect it because that is the way it

Exhibit 1-8 **continued**

BANK B (MARKETING-ORIENTED)

ANN J. SMITH
JOHN SMITH
15 LARK DRIVE
ANYTOWN, USA 12345

Account Number	Account Type	Previous Balance	Checks & Charges	Payments & Deposits	New Balance
1-234-567-8	Checking	2639.12	4353.00	2320.24	606.36

Checking Account Transactions and Balance Information Summary

Date	Transaction		Account Balance
10/30	PREVIOUS BALANCE		2639.12
11/02	CHECK 0790	− 1500.00	1139.12
11/04	CHECK 0758	− 25.00	1114.12
11/06	DEPOSIT	+ 1160.12	2274.24
11/13	NEW CHECKBOOK CHARGE	− 12.43	2261.81
11/18	CHECKS 0807, 0809, 0811	− 115.22	2146.59
11/19	CHECK 0812	− 350.00	1796.59
11/20	DEPOSIT	+ 1160.12	2956.71
11/25	CHECK 0813	− 10.00	2946.71
11/27	CHECKS 0814, 0821, 0832	− 2340.35	606.36

Checks Processed

Check No.	Date Paid	Amount	Check No.	Date Paid	Amount
0758	11/04	25.00	0812	11/19	350.00
0790	11/02	1500.00	0813	11/25	10.00
0807	11/18	25.00	0814	11/27	125.31
0809	11/18	80.22	0821	11/27	15.04
0811	11/18	10.00	0832	11/27	2200.00

has been for so long. Some banks use technology to monitor the length of time customers wait in line throughout the day. On the basis of these findings, they modify the manner in which they staff the teller line. One bank uses flex-time: half of the tellers report for work at 10 A.M., but they work through the lunch hour so that the maximum number of tellers can be on duty at that peak period. There are, however, many banks that place the desire of the tellers to eat lunch between 11 and 1 o'clock ahead of the customers' need to be served quickly during those same hours.

2. *They want to be treated as though they matter to the bank.* Customers often react with surprise and delight when the bank employee, whether a teller or a new accounts representative, somehow communicates that the bank is genuinely glad to be of service. Some bank employees treat customers in that fashion because it is their nature to do so. However, many bank employees are not cognizant of how their demeanor appears to customers, and their employers have obviously not required that they treat customers in a way that promotes positive customer/employee relations. Nor do many banks train their employees to do so. Instead, the emphasis seems to be on completing the transaction in the minimum amount of time rather than on satisfying the customer's emotional *and* financial needs.

3. *They want proper resolution of their problems.* It is interesting that bank customers do not expect a completely problem-free relationship with a bank. They do, however, expect that the error will be taken care of promptly and professionally. Unfortunately, very few banks have paid the attention to customer service that consumer goods firms have. Although many banks have a customer service department that the customer can call for account information and for problem resolution, employees are usually unequipped to handle dissatisfied customers with the appropriate degree of diplomacy. Furthermore, the prevailing attitude is that if there is a monetary dispute, the customer is wrong until the bank proves otherwise (except in the case of electronic funds transfers, which are governed by *Regulation E*, the Federal Reserve regulation that protects consumers using electronic funds transfer systems).

4. *They want to be able to do business when it is convenient for them.* In many cases, banks close before the end of the normal business day, so customers must bank on their lunch hours or on the one evening or weekend day that the bank may be open. As such, the hours that a bank keeps are often proof of its customer orientation. Although shopping centers are at their busiest on weekends because that is when retail customers are free to shop and take care of business, these are the days when most banks are closed. While customers may use automated tellers to make routine deposits or cash withdrawals, they cannot apply for a loan or open a certificate of deposit when the

bank is closed. As a result, some banks have recognized the need for bank branches within shopping malls, and certain banks are experimenting with Sunday hours.[11]

In conclusion, while some individual banks have demonstrated an unusual degree of orientation toward customer needs and wants (see Exhibit 1-9), the above observations suggest that the banking industry as a whole is only on the brink of delving into the most productive stages of marketing.

SUMMARY

Marketing involves the conception, pricing, promotion, and distribution of a product, a service, or an idea. The goal of marketing is to satisfy customer needs and wants and, in the process, to meet the marketer's objectives as well. Marketing works through exchange processes, in that each party involved in the transaction receives something of value from the other. A market encompasses all potential customers with a particular need or want who might be willing and able to engage in some form of exchange in order to satisfy that desire.

Marketing requires an ongoing process of planning, executing plans, monitoring their results, and modifying strategies. In other words, marketing is a management process, and the philosophy that can best assure long-term marketing success is known as the marketing concept. The marketing concept states that an organization's goals are best met by satisfying customers, at a profitable volume, through an integrated, efficient framework, and in a socially responsible manner.

Most industries and individual firms discover the truth of this philosophy and adopt it gradually. The stimulus for marketing enlightenment may come from any number of sources. The principal ones include a decline in sales or market share, slow growth, a change in consumer buying patterns, and increased competition and marketing expense. The evolution of the marketing concept in banking has been stimulated considerably by (1) the loss of market share

Exhibit 1-9   **A Customer-Oriented Bank: University National Bank & Trust Co., Palo Alto, California**

In 1980, Carl Schmitt, a former California banking commissioner, established a new bank to prove that a small, creative bank that emphasized customer service could be financially successful.

Schmitt used his 14 years of experience in banking and his understanding of marketing to create one of the most profitable small banks in California. He proved that the marketing concept works.

Note some of the marketing strategies that Schmitt utilizes:

- If more than three people are waiting in line, a bank employee will personally help move things along.

- If several people are waiting to enter the bank just prior to opening, the bank will open early for them.

- All monthly checking statements are mailed on the second business day of the month. A production-oriented bank would stagger the statement production and mailing throughout the month, but Schmitt believes that customers prefer to keep their records by calendar month. As a result, all 70 bank employees work late on the first night of the month in order to get the statements out on time.

- If customers need to buy stamps, need help balancing a checkbook, or have an emergency when the bank is closed, they get the help they need.

Is it working? The bank grew to $162 million in assets in just 7 years. Its return on assets, a measure of profitability, is greater than 1 percent (the national average is about 0.63 percent). Also, both customers and competitors alike speak highly of the bank and of the service it provides.

Source: Chris Oppenheimer, "Making a big splash," *Philadelphia Inquirer,* June 6, 1987, pp. 8-C ff.

to nonbank financial institutions, (2) slow growth, brought on by changes in consumer buying patterns which banks were unable to respond to due to regulation, and (3) increased competition from other banks and nonbank sources.

A firm that has adopted the marketing concept will define its business in terms of the need or want it is satisfying. In other words, it will have a customer orientation. Firms that have not yet reached that level of marketing sophistication may have a product orientation, a selling orientation, or a production orientation. In each of these cases, some objective, other than customer satisfaction, is the guiding force in determining how the business allocates its resources.

Banks have been, and continue to some extent to be, prevented from responding to changing consumer financial needs by regulation. However, the lack of response by certain banks to customer service needs suggests that the industry as a whole has not yet adopted the marketing concept. Certain individual banks demonstrate sensitivity to customer needs by providing customer service personnel, improving the efficiency of service, or providing more convenient hours. But as a whole, the industry appears to be just on the brink of fully entering the era of marketing enlightenment.

POINTS FOR REVIEW

1. Define or briefly explain the following key terms:
   - marketing
   - the market
   - the marketing concept
   - the product
   - customer orientation
   - the "Law of Slow Learning"
2. What five situations might cause a business to become more marketing conscious?
3. "Everyone in the bank is involved in marketing." How would you explain this statement to an employee in check processing, a teller, a secretary, a branch manager, and a loan officer?
4. Explain each of the four elements in the definition of the marketing concept.
5. Describe the difference between selling and marketing.
6. What is meant by "a market definition of the business"?
7. What would be a market definition of the business with respect to the following companies:

- Adidas
- United Air Lines
- *Better Homes & Gardens* magazine
- Neighborhood National Bank and Trust
- Revlon

8. What are some examples of nonbank competitors of commercial banks?

9. Explain how regulation is keeping commercial banks from responding to customer needs or wants.

10. Think of an example of a firm whose marketing strategies demonstrate a concern for carrying out the firm's business in a socially responsible way.

PART II STRATEGIC MARKETING

Everyone has remarked at one time or another, "Everything is changing so fast these days!" Due to advances in communications and the accelerating pace of scientific and technological discoveries, the environment in which we live goes through changes more quickly than ever. This reality dictates that the marketer be a strategic thinker. *Strategy* was once a term used primarily by the military in tactical planning. But today, as a result of the proliferation of new products and services, marketing has become a battleground where only the strategic survive.

The strategic marketer is a planner who looks at where the company is today, gives careful thought to where it wants to be at some time in the future, and then develops strategies and tactics for getting there. This part of the text presents the basics of marketing planning: why planning is needed and what it entails. It introduces the six-step marketing planning process: (1) situation analysis, (2) objective setting, (3) target market selection, (4) development of strategy and tactics, (5) implementation, and (6) evaluation. It then looks more closely at the early stages of that process: how to conduct a situation analysis; and on the basis of the information obtained in that process, how to establish strategic marketing objectives that accurately reflect management's projections for the future.

2 MARKETING PLANNING: THE BASICS

OVERVIEW

In any organization, marketing managers work with and within two broad sets of variables: those that relate to the marketing mix and those that make up the marketing environment. The marketing mix variables—product, pricing, promotion, and place (distribution)—are within the control and direction of the organization. The marketing manager selects from among alternative marketing mix strategies on the basis of what the target market needs and wants. (Part IV deals extensively with those marketing mix decisions.)

This strategizing does not take place in a vacuum. Rather, it occurs in a turbulent and ever-changing marketing environment, which, in turn, is affected by two broad groups of external forces over which the organization has little or no control. The first, and least controllable, group of forces encompass the **macroenvironmental** factors of demographics, economics, social and cultural factors, political and legal factors, and technology. On the other hand, the set of external environmental variables that the marketing organization has a modicum of control over are its markets, competitors, producers and suppliers, and marketing intermediaries. These are referred to as **microenvironmental** factors. While all marketers must deal with these macro- and microenvironmental realities, bank marketers, as shall be seen, are faced with some unique challenges that are not faced by manufacturers of tangible goods.

In light of the above, it should be apparent that marketing management means managing change—more specifically, adapting to change that is outside the company's control and initiating change that is within its control. Adapting to change in the macro- and microenvironments is the only viable option open to firms that hope to achieve greater economic success in a constantly changing world. The effective marketing manager uses the changing environment to make things happen; the mediocre manager lets things happen. The only way to market effectively under such changing circumstances is through a carefully thought-out process of planning.

In this chapter, we will review some of the major macro- and microenvironmental factors facing bank marketers and see how dealing with them requires strategic planning.

THE MARKETING ENVIRONMENT

There are numerous external forces that shape the market for any organization's goods and services. (See Exhibit 2-1.) Some of these forces are broadly based—even global—while others are closer to the firm and may be directly affected by it.

The Macroenvironment

The macroenvironmental forces that all marketers, including bank marketers, must cope with are the economic environment, the demographic environment, the social/cultural environment, the political/legal environment, and the technological environment.

Economic Environment

The level or lack of economic prosperity, the changing levels of disposable income, inflation, fluctuating interest rates, stock market performance, the rate of unemployment, shortages of raw materials—all of these influences have a far-reaching impact on the shape and nature of many markets.

The energy crisis of the 1970s, which arose from shortages of oil and, to a lesser extent, natural gas, provides a vivid example of this concept. The gasoline shortages and resulting high prices of fuel reduced the demand for large automobiles and houses and recreational vehicles, and placed a constraint on long-distance family vacations. These factors, in turn, led to a drop in consumer demand for hotels, motels, restaurants, and other travel-related services. Conversely, sales of many other goods and services got a sudden boost: wood-burning stoves, solar heating, warm clothing, passenger rail service, and smaller automobiles. Later, when the energy crisis abated, many of the affected markets did not return to their previous levels of consumer demand; buying patterns were permanently changed.

One of the economic variables that bank marketers must deal with on a daily basis is the interest rate environment and consumers' short- and long-term expectations concerning the level of interest rates. Banks compete for interest-bearing deposits with alternative investment possibilities, such as the stock and bond market. This combination of external environmental factors—interest rates and competition—creates marketing challenges.

For example, in 1987, interest rates were low and relatively stable, while the stock market (prior to the "crash") was enjoying unprecedented gains. Banking institutions experiencing heavy outflows from money market deposit accounts and maturing certificates of deposit rushed to design new savings products to compete with the higher-risk, higher-yield alternatives.

One New York bank developed a certificate whose interest rate was tied to the performance of the stock market. The investor was given the choice of getting an interest rate totally dependent upon the market's performance over the term of the certificate, or a low guaranteed rate plus a percentage of any gain in the index. Another institution sought to capitalize on the prevailing opinion that rates would stay flat or go down. It developed a 6-month certificate whose interest rate at maturity (if the funds were rolled over for another

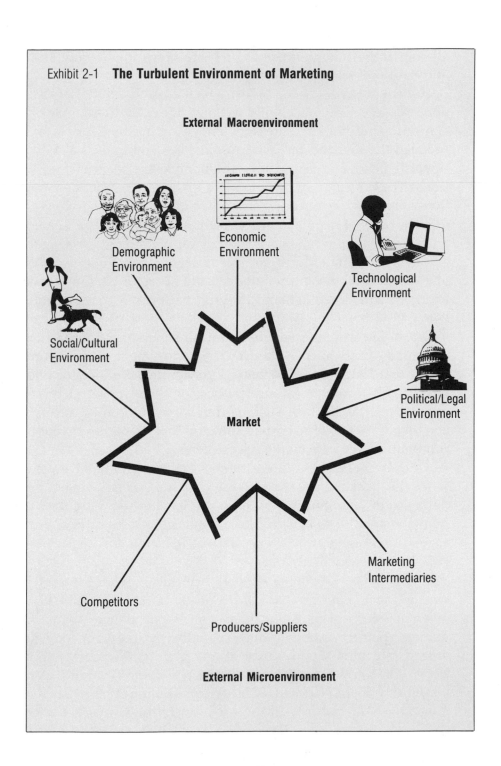

Exhibit 2-1   **The Turbulent Environment of Marketing**

External Macroenvironment

Demographic
Environment

Economic
Environment

Technological
Environment

Social/Cultural
Environment

Political/Legal
Environment

Market

Competitors

Producers/Suppliers

Marketing
Intermediaries

External Microenvironment

6-month term) would be at least the same as the original rate, but higher if prevailing rates went up by the time of renewal.

Another bank in the same market developed a 6-month certificate whose rate was guaranteed to increase a quarter of a percent every 6 months for up to 2 years. However, by the time this new product was developed and introduced, a new chairman had taken over at the Federal Reserve Board, and his first move was to raise interest rates. The effectiveness of this bank's well-planned promotion was hampered by an uncontrollable and unanticipated change in the economic macroenvironment.

Demographic Environment

Demographics is the science dealing with vital statistics of a population, and a population is a group of people who make up a market. Some of the major demographic changes taking place in the United States are the aging of the population; the declining birth rate; the changing makeup of the family; the different levels of education achieved; and the geographical shifting of population from colder, industrialized areas to the Sunbelt.

Another demographic factor that banks must deal with is the shift in population from the cities to the suburbs. When the customers of an urban bank move to the suburbs, the bank must adapt its distribution strategy in order to continue to serve its customers and retain its market share. This means establishing branches in the newly developing areas and providing other means of service distribution, such as automated teller machines (ATMs).

The increasing number of people with high school diplomas and college degrees has resulted in a more financially astute bank customer. As a result, banks are feeling the pressure to better train their customer service personnel so they can deal intelligently with this better-educated customer.

The fact that Americans are now living longer and having fewer children, combined with the aging of the post-war baby boom generation, is causing considerable growth in the number of adults aged 35 to 65. These people are at an age when they are either in their peak wage-earning years or when they have accumulated the maximum amount of their assets. Many banks have also packaged services to

In the 1970s, the crisis at the gas pump stunned Americans into becoming energy conscious.

Current trends in demographics argue against these children producing families as large as the one in which they grew up.

appeal to the over-65 market that may include travel discounts, senior citizen newsletters, and supplementary medical insurance to customers who maintain sizable savings or certificate balances on deposit.

Social/Cultural Environment

The social/cultural environment takes into account such factors as changing lifestyles and social values, as well as any other customs, beliefs, or practices that make one culture different from another. Some recent social/cultural developments include a return to the more traditional values that were challenged in the turbulent 1960s, a renewed focus on fitness and health, and the quality of life, and a heightened demand for convenience in every aspect of life from eating to shopping to banking.

In any one evening of television viewing, one can see the effect of social/cultural forces on the way consumer goods manufacturers advertise their products. Hardly an hour goes by without seeing an ad for a food product that is "high in fiber." Similarly, the automobile designed for the young urban market is presented within an upscale setting that the target market would aspire to, and then there is the easy-bake French bread cooking in the oven while the young, single woman dresses up for a dinner party where she wants to appear as both beautiful and a great cook.

Banks are very much aware of their customers' need for convenience. Some institutions have altered their hours of operation, and virtually all major banks provide ATMs. And, quite a few offer telephone banking so customers can be in touch with their accounts around the clock. Also, bank cards (both debit and credit) enable customers to purchase at will without having to use cash or write a check.

Political/Legal Environment

The political/legal or regulatory environment refers to the way in which public policy decisions affect the shape and nature of markets. The government exerts a certain amount of influence on business to protect consumers, natural resources, the economy, and other entities from various kinds of harm. For example, the Federal Trade

Commission (FTC), the Food and Drug Administration (FDA), the Civil Aeronautics Board (CAB), the Securities and Exchange Commission (SEC)—and, in the banking industry, the Federal Deposit Insurance Corporation (FDIC), the Federal Reserve Board, and the Comptroller of the Currency—regularly issue rules that organizations in the private sector must follow. These rules may limit, eliminate, or discourage certain product, pricing, promotion, or distribution alternatives.

The FDA's banning of cyclamates in 1969 is a good example of how the regulatory environment can affect the market. A sugar substitute used in low-calorie foods and drinks, cyclamates were banned after laboratory tests indicated that some test animals developed cancer after being fed large doses. Although the FDA intended to remove cyclamates from the market gradually, potential sales totaling an estimated $1 billion were affected virtually overnight. Although the ban was announced in the last quarter of 1969, sales of the diet soda Tab were down 33 percent from the previous year. Marketers responded quickly by substituting saccharin for cyclamates, enabling the soft drink industry to recapture its sales level by the early 1970s. This is a vivid example of how a market was altered as a result of regulation and how business responded in order to fulfill consumers' continuing demand for sugar-free food and beverages.

The political/legal environment exerts considerable impact on the banking market. Regulation and the slow pace of deregulation have limited banks' ability to compete in the changing market for financial services. Until the early 1980s, there was a ceiling on the interest rate that banks could pay on savings accounts, and banks had no discretion over the pricing or product design of their certificate of deposit offerings. This situation did eventually change, but not until banks had lost hundreds of millions of dollars of deposits to the unregulated money market mutual funds, whose rates were free to float with general market rates.

While **Regulation Q** limited bank product and pricing strategies, the **McFadden Act** has limited banks' distribution strategies by prohibiting branching across state lines. This sets an artificial limit to a bank's trade area, especially in markets where travel, commerce, and communication take place on a regional basis. For instance, residents of southern New Jersey who work in Philadelphia cannot enjoy the convenience of banking with the same bank both at home and near their work. While automated teller networks allow them to obtain cash in one location from a bank account in another, they cannot make deposits, apply for a loan, or open a certificate of deposit.

The Glass-Steagall Act of 1933, which resulted from the stock market crash and ensuing Depression, was passed to get banks out of the securities underwriting and brokerage businesses. In the 1980s, however, it serves to prevent banks from competing with mutual funds for investor deposits.

The regulatory limits on banking are gradually lessening, creating new challenges for bank marketers. Interstate banking through holding company ownership of banks across state lines is requiring marketers to adjust to broader and more diverse geographical markets. However, banks are still unable to provide consumers with a broad range of financial services, such as mutual funds, insurance, and full-service brokerage, except through third parties. As these barriers also fall, bank marketers will face the prospect of expanding their product lines and competing, with no prior experience, with organizations that have been in those businesses for many years. The changes due to deregulation are, indeed, the most important macroenvironmental issues that bank marketers will encounter in the years ahead.

Technological Environment

The technological environment is a product of the wealth of technical knowledge and advances in our society. Supersonic airplanes, laser beams, organ transplants, and computers are a few positive examples, but nerve gas, nuclear weapons, and harmful by-products such as air and water pollution are also part of the technological environment.[1] The fruits of technology, whether constructive or potentially destructive, have played a significant role in the development of our country. A high rate of personal consumption, a respect for higher education, the desire for excellence in all fields, and government support of basic research have all contributed to the rapidly changing technological environment in this country.

The technological environment creates new alternatives that give consumers a greater number of choices. The development of auto-

The stock market crash of 1929 had a dramatic effect on the economic and regulatory environment of commercial banks.

mated teller machines has directly affected the way that banking services are delivered. The proliferation of personal computers both in the home and in business has caused banks to react with new product and distribution strategies. Computers may be used to bring customers' account information into the home or office and to enable them to initiate transfers between accounts, to wire funds out of the bank, and to pay bills. Technological advances have enabled banks to automate the teller work station, facilitating customer service and eliminating the time-consuming practice of phoning for a balance and a hold before cashing a check. Platform automation in many banks is reducing the amount of paperwork involved in setting up a new account or changing addresses on existing accounts.

In addition, point-of-sale terminals in merchant locations allow consumers to pay for purchases and to get cash at supermarket checkout counters. Clearly, this is an example of how technology directly affects the distribution of bank products. However, technological advances in other industries can have a far-reaching impact on banking. For instance, the development of the birth-control pill resulted in smaller families, more working wives, greater family incomes, and larger expenditures on vacations, appliances, and many other goods.[2] All of these factors have, directly or indirectly, affected the market for deposits and consumer credit.

The Microenvironment

The microenvironment is external to the marketing organization but, nevertheless, related to its marketing efforts. The principal microenvironmental factors are the firm's markets, producers/suppliers, marketing intermediaries, and competitors.

The Market

The market in which an organization operates, or the set of all its actual and potential customers, is affected by all of the external macro- and microenvironmental factors, as well as being a changing microenvironmental entity in itself. The markets for a bank might include the consumer market, the business market, the government banking market, or the international market. Within these broad markets, bankers speak also of more specific-need markets: the savings market, the transaction account market, and the credit market. The market (as shown in Exhibit 2-1) is an entity with a shape that is constantly changing due to developments in the external environment as well as changes intrinsic to the market itself.

Producers/Suppliers

Most marketing organizations are dependent upon other producers or suppliers for their raw materials and for the services they need in order to produce and deliver their product. The cereal manufacturer depends on the grain farmer, the sugar processor, and the box and packaging manufacturer. It must also obtain a labor force, electricity, and other utilities, equipment, and elements of production.

Uncontrollable events that affect a firm's suppliers can have a serious impact on marketing management. For instance, shortages of raw materials can affect the producer's costs, which are then passed on to the consumer in the form of higher prices. Problems in labor/management relations can also affect production quality.

Many urban banks have recognized that there is a problem recruiting entry-level personnel. This resource shortage affects a bank's ability to deliver its products and to provide optimum customer service.

In most industries, marketing managers do not have to concern themselves much with the production and supply side of the business. Their efforts are focused on creating and meeting market demand for the product. This is one area in which banking is very different from other businesses. Bank marketers must be doubly marketing oriented. They must use marketing techniques both to acquire the raw material (deposits) and the users of the raw material (borrowers). The bank must implement an overall marketing strategy for each **source market** and each **use market.** This process is illustrated in Exhibit 2-2.

Marketing intermediaries

Marketing intermediaries are firms that assist in promoting, selling, and distributing the product to the consumer. The cereal manufac-

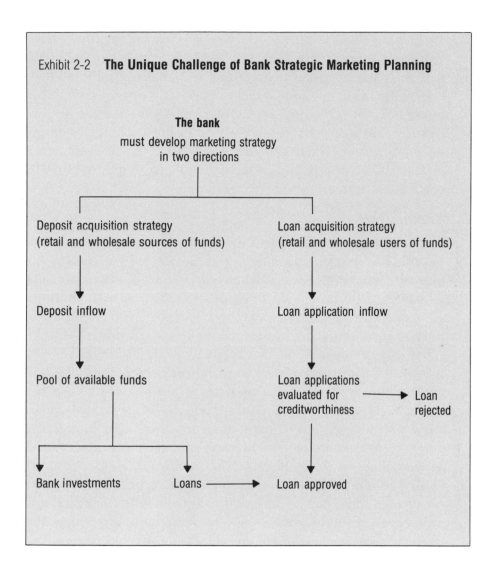

Exhibit 2-2 **The Unique Challenge of Bank Strategic Marketing Planning**

The bank
must develop marketing strategy
in two directions

Deposit acquisition strategy
(retail and wholesale sources of funds)

Loan acquisition strategy
(retail and wholesale users of funds)

Deposit inflow

Loan application inflow

Pool of available funds

Loan applications
evaluated for → Loan
creditworthiness   rejected

Bank investments   Loans ——→ Loan approved

turer, for instance, might use "middlemen" such as brokers, manufacturers' representatives, wholesalers, or retailers. Product
manufacturers also employ distribution firms such as warehouse and
transportation companies to distribute their product. Banking, how-

ever, is a service industry—its products are intangible. Therefore, bank marketers do not deal with traditional types of intermediaries. Rather, marketing intermediaries in the banking business are credit card companies, automated teller networks, suppliers of back-office operations for some high-technology products, and the automated clearing house system for the transfer of funds. In many cases, the use of marketing intermediaries enables the participating bank to offer a service or distribution technique through a third party that it could not afford to provide by itself.

Competitors

The marketing manager must always keep a wary eye on the **competitors** and formulate a strategy for responding to changes in the market. Competition occurs when two or more entities seek a similar end result. It occurs among students applying for a limited number of acceptances to medical school, political candidates seeking the same public office, or firms seeking a larger share of a given market.

Banks that understand that they are in the business of meeting financial service needs define the competition differently from those with a more myopic view. The latter might see the competition as including other commercial banks, savings and loans, savings banks, and credit unions. But many nonbanking firms also hold consumer deposits, extend credit, provide checking accounts, and offer other services that were once the exclusive province of banks. For example, insurance companies have chartered banks so they can issue savings certificates and credit cards, and brokerage firms offer check-writing privileges on funds earning money market interest rates. In fact, large national retailers attract more installment credit business than all the commercial banks in the country put together. With this kind of competitive pressure on banks, the need to adopt the marketing concept becomes all the more imperative. (Of course, banks must also have the regulatory freedom to compete.)

In an environment characterized by change and uncertainty, and with all of the changes taking place in the external macro- and microenvironments, the banking business is very different today than it was 10 years ago and than it will be in another 10 years. In order to survive in such an environment, banks must learn to adapt to considerable change. Planning is the process that will enable them to cope with this situation.

STAGES OF BANK PLANNING DEVELOPMENT

The focus of this text is on **strategic marketing planning.** But what is meant by this term, and how does strategic marketing planning differ from its alternatives?

Just as there are various stages of development of marketing awareness in the business world, there are also stages in the level of sophistication in the planning effort. For instance, a bank might prepare an annual budget that projects the bank's expectations for the upcoming calendar year for each category of deposits and loans as well as each type of income and expense. The overall budget is the composite of the detailed budgets of each of the operating divisions of the bank. This type of budget-oriented planning is usually based on past trends, and expectations about the level of interest rates in the upcoming year. But budgets do not qualify as plans in the sense used in this text. Banks whose planning is limited to budgeting are in an immature stage of development.

Many institutions have implemented an annual planning process in which broad goals are set by senior management or by the directors. The various departments then establish plans to help achieve those goals. Kotler has called this process "goals-down-plans-up" planning.[3] This process takes place in the late summer or early fall to allow time for the resulting budgets to be consolidated and adjusted as needed. Preliminary budgets are rarely accepted without modification since expenses reflect the strategies that department heads would ideally like to pursue. These budgets may need to be trimmed and priorities may have to be adjusted as part of the planning process.

Such annual planning is quite useful, but it addresses only short-range considerations. It also assumes continuation of the business along the same lines as those being currently pursued.

Many banks have graduated beyond the annual "goals-down-plans-up" stage and are engaged in strategic planning. Generally speaking, strategic planning has two unique characteristics:

1. *Emphasis on strategic goal setting.* The bank openly addresses the question, "What do we want to accomplish in the next 5 or more years?" While annual planning concentrates on the bank's business as it is, strategic planning looks at the business the bank is in and at other businesses in which it might operate. Then it considers which it should enter, grow, harvest, or exit. For example, a retail-oriented regional bank may decide, based upon analysis of several possible alternatives, that it wants to become the dominant corporate banking institution in its trade area. A money center bank may determine that its current market cannot grow at a sufficient rate to ensure long-run profitability in the credit card area. So, it might decide that in 5 years it wants to be generating 75 percent of its credit card business from residents of other states. Or, a regional bank might determine that the cost of being in the retail banking business does not provide a rate of return consistent with corporate objectives and decide to exit that area of its operation.

2. *Long-range planning or rolling plans.* Recognizing that the marketing environment is constantly changing, the bank develops a 5-year plan that is updated every year. In 1990, the 5-year plan that includes 1994 is updated to take 1995 into account, and so on. This process forces the bank to strategize on a consistent and continual basis.

STRATEGIC MARKETING PLANNING

Armed with the mission and objectives set forth in the long-range plan for the organization, the marketing manager applies the steps in the strategic planning process to a marketing plan that encompasses each of the bank's markets. While the corporate plan identifies those businesses that the bank wants to enter, grow, harvest, or exit the marketing plan sets forth the specific marketing strategies and tactics that will achieve those objectives. The stages in that process are discussed in the following chapter.

SUMMARY

Marketing managers deal with two broad sets of variables: those that relate to the marketing mix and those that relate to the marketing environment. The marketing mix variables are product, price, promotion, and place (distribution). The marketing environment has two components: the macroenvironment and the microenvironment, both of which pose numerous challenges to the marketing manager.

Macroenvironmental factors include demographics, economics, social/cultural factors, political/legal considerations, and technology—forces over which the marketing manager has no control. Microenvironmental factors, which are external to the marketing organization but which can be controlled to some degree, are producers/suppliers, marketing intermediaries, competitors, and the market itself.

These and other factors contribute to a turbulent marketing environment and to constantly changing markets. In order to survive and prosper in the face of this turbulence and change, the firm must implement strategic planning. Strategic planning differs from other approaches in that it takes a long-range, exploratory view, not only of where the organization is at present, but also where it wants to be several years hence. The marketing manager then assembles the tools needed for strategic marketing planning and aims them at the projected corporate objectives.

POINTS FOR REVIEW

1. Define or explain the following terms:
   - macroenvironment
   - microenvironment

2. Give an example of a current social factor that is affecting the banking market.

3. Describe a current economic factor that poses a challenge to bank marketers.

4. Think of a technological development that is currently affecting your bank.

5. What political/legal or regulatory factors are currently affecting the banks in your market area?

6. Give some examples of suppliers used by banks.

7. Give an example, preferably from your own bank, of a bank's use of an intermediary to deliver a service.

8. What element or elements make a bank's or firm's planning efforts "strategic"?

3 THE STRATEGIC MARKETING PROCESS

OVERVIEW

Strategic marketing is a management process that involves the development of marketing plans, their careful implementation, evaluation of their results, and then the adjustment and fine-tuning of the entire package. The process begins with the critically important task of marketing planning, a discipline that consists of four key steps. These steps answer three crucial questions: (1) Where are we now? (2) Where do we want to go? and (3) How are we going to get there? Evaluating the results of the plan's implementation poses the fourth question: (4) How will we know when we have arrived?

This chapter introduces the marketing management process and each of the steps that occur in the planning stages. Since planning is so important to the marketer, the chapter concludes with a discussion of the necessity of the planning process, the most common objections to planning, and the prerequisites for a successful planning process.

THE MARKETING MANAGEMENT PROCESS

Although all of a bank's employees are involved in marketing, the benefits that the organization will ultimately reap depend on how effectively the marketing management process is implemented.

Before discussing the marketing management process further, some key terms must be understood. It has been established that marketing is an activity directed at satisfying needs and wants through exchange processes. But what is management?

What is Management?

For the purposes of this text, **management** is "the process of planning, implementing, and evaluating the efforts of a group of people toward a common goal."[1] **Planning** is that part of the management process that attempts to control the organization's future condition. It includes all of the activities that lead to the definition of goals and the determination of the appropriate means to achieve them.

Most people have been involved in the process of managing at one time or another, whether it be organizing the family for a 2-week vacation, planning a surprise party for a friend, or overseeing the operation of a bank branch. The three fundamental steps of planning, implementing, and evaluating were most likely involved. If one completes the first two steps but does not evaluate the results, then the management job is incomplete. Basically, the evaluation step helps one learn from the management experience and can improve the performance of similar tasks in the future.

Exhibit 3-1 illustrates the management process. The circle represents the process of planning, implementing the plan, and evaluating the results. It applies to managers of all functions—financial, operations, sales—as well as to marketing managers.

The management process is shown as a circular flow because it reflects what should be dynamic and ongoing. Developing the marketing plan is not a one-time event, and the plan should not be cast in concrete once it is prepared. At any point during implementation and evaluation, unforeseen circumstances may require modification of the plan or the timetable for phasing it in. Specific marketing strategies may not function as originally intended. For example, there might be a major change in the market that, in turn, affects results. The flexibility to change, modify, adapt, and fine-tune must be built into the process.

What is Marketing Management?

Marketing management is simply "the marketing concept in action."[2] It involves planning, implementing, and evaluating activities aimed at meeting the objective of customer satisfaction at a profitable volume, carried out in an integrated framework, and in a socially responsible manner. Philip Kotler's formal definition of marketing management takes it a step further:

> Marketing management is the analysis, planning, implementation, and control of programs designed to create, build, and maintain mutually beneficial exchanges and relationships with target markets.[3]

The Task of Marketing Management

What task is marketing management attempting to accomplish? Essentially, it is the regulation of market demand. The term *regulate* is used instead of *increase* because the concept often goes beyond attempts to increase demand; a marketing department must sometimes decrease demand. This situation is referred to as **demarketing**. For example, utilities and oil companies use marketing strategies to convince people to consume less energy. Cruise lines use marketing strategies (especially pricing strategies) to shift demand to off-peak seasons. And, when the supply of money is limited, banks reduce the demand for loans by raising their interest rates.

At other times, marketing might be used to counteract demand. For example, the American Lung Association tries to persuade cigarette smokers to stop smoking, and the Partnership for a Drug-Free America attempts to keep people from experimenting with drugs.

Marketing management is, then, like all management, a planning/implementing/evaluating process. To expand on this concept,

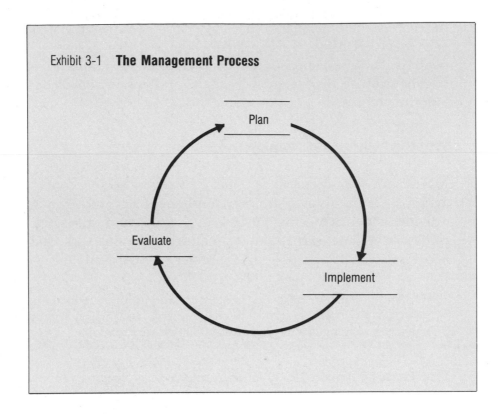

Exhibit 3-1   **The Management Process**

Plan

Evaluate

Implement

Exhibit 3-2 presents the model for the strategic marketing management process. As you can see, the planning stage is a detailed process in itself, consisting of four key steps:

- situation analysis;
- objective setting;
- target market selection; and
- strategy formulation.

The remainder of this chapter describes the elements of the marketing planning process, and then expands upon the implementation and evaluation stages involved in the strategic marketing management process.

THE MARKETING PLANNING PROCESS

As mentioned above, planning is that part of the management process that attempts to control the organization's future condition, by defining the appropriate goals and determining the most effective means to achieve them. It is critical for the marketing student to understand and recognize the importance of the planning process.

Planning versus the Plan

There is a very important distinction between marketing planning and a **marketing plan**. While the difference may seem quite subtle, it is, nevertheless, extremely important. Marketing planning, like management, is a process that is continual and, therefore, never completed. A marketing plan is the actual *output* of the planning process for a particular period of time—it is a document. Former president Dwight D. Eisenhower is reputed to have said, "Plans are nothing; planning is everything." In other words, without the planning process, the plans are irrelevant.

Why is marketing planning so important? As an old adage goes: "If you don't know where you want to go, any road will take you there." A great deal of energy is expended fulfilling the basic purpose of most organizations. Many people work 40 hours a week, or more. Resources are depleted and much expense is incurred carrying out routine activities of a particular firm. But without direction—an objective—the effort is likely to be less effective than it otherwise could be. At the same time, the effort a business exerts cannot be measured against some nebulous external standard, because the structure and needs of various firms are unique. For example, if a new loan officer were able to increase loan volume by 50 percent when 10 percent had been considered an acceptable objective by the bank's management, then, obviously, the bank has not developed a realistic marketing plan. Consequently, its loan volume prior to the arrival of the new loan officer was far lower than it could have been. There are three questions that the bank may have failed to answer:

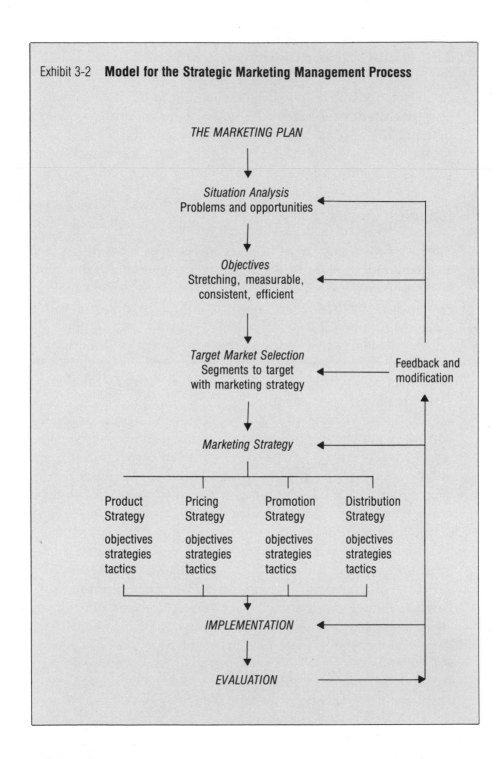

Exhibit 3-2 **Model for the Strategic Marketing Management Process**

THE MARKETING PLAN

Situation Analysis
Problems and opportunities

Objectives
Stretching, measurable,
consistent, efficient

Target Market Selection
Segments to target
with marketing strategy

Feedback and
modification

Marketing Strategy

Product Strategy	Pricing Strategy	Promotion Strategy	Distribution Strategy
objectives strategies tactics	objectives strategies tactics	objectives strategies tactics	objectives strategies tactics

IMPLEMENTATION

EVALUATION

(1) Where are we now? (2) Where do we want to go? and (3) How are we going to get there? The systematic answering of these three questions constitutes the process of planning.

Conducting the Situation Analysis

Before it is possible to set meaningful organizational and marketing objectives, a bank must go through a detailed self-examination in which data concerning the bank's past, present, and future performance are collected, summarized, and carefully evaluated. The **situation analysis** involves:

- gathering historical trend data on the bank and its competition;
- reviewing the markets and market segments in which the bank operates or would like to; and
- evaluating the external factors influencing markets (macroenvironmental factors—economic, demographic, social/cultural, political/legal, and technological—and microenvironmental factors, especially competition) in terms of their possible implication for the bank.

Not surprisingly, a situation analysis must be based on research. The information gathered about those forces affecting the market and the bank must be grounded in solid data. The means for collecting this type of information about the bank, its competition, the market, and the environmental forces affecting it is called **marketing research.**

The end product of the situation analysis is a summary of the bank's strengths and weaknesses. Armed with this type of information, the bank's management can make educated decisions that are in line with the bank's objectives.

Setting Marketing Objectives

Evaluating the situation analysis provides the basis for developing **marketing objectives**, which are specific written statements detailing what the organization would like to accomplish within a specific period of time. Such objectives should have the following characteristics:

The successful invasion of Europe in June 1944 earned Dwight D. Eisenhower a preeminent reputation as a master planner.

- They should help the bank stretch for excellence, yet be realistic.
- They should be measurable, regardless of whether the specific objective is **quantitative** (that is, to increase demand deposits by 15 percent) or **qualitative** (that is, to increase unaided bank awareness among the target audience from 30 percent to 60 percent).
- They should be consistent with one another.
- They should steer the bank toward an allocation of its resources that is most opportune in the long run.

A bank's marketing objectives must relate to the bank's strategic objectives. For instance, if a strategic objective is to achieve a 30 percent penetration of market area households, a marketing objective might be to add two new branches in growth areas. Or, the objective might be to increase awareness of the bank by some amount or to add to the number of personal transaction accounts by some percentage. Any one of the bank's overall objectives may translate into a number of marketing objectives.

Selecting the Target Market

Most firms, including banks, generally aim their marketing strategies at more than one target market at a time. To do so, they employ a variety of marketing mixes. For example, General Motors attempts to attract one sector of the automobile market with its Cadillac Coupe de Ville, another with its Chevrolet Corvette, and a third with its Pontiac Le Mans. Similarly, a bank might have different but simultaneous marketing programs to attract senior citizens and their savings deposits, college students seeking educational loans, newcomers to the community who need to open checking and savings accounts, and executives who require large lines of credit and highly personalized services.

In the situation analysis, the bank will analyze its customer base and how it compares with the market at large. While doing such an analysis, the bank might learn that its marketing strategies are attracting an older clientele rather than the desired share of young,

A striking photograph and a well-turned phrase are used here to discourage, rather than encourage, use of a product.

upwardly mobile professionals. Based on this information, the bank will identify specific segments within the market at large to which it will aim its strategies.

Designing the Marketing Strategy

Marketing strategy encompasses the elements of the marketing mix—product, price, promotion, and distribution—and seeks to attract the target audience. The target market selection process identifies potentially profitable market segments, each of which has relatively homogeneous needs that can be satisfied by using the same marketing mix. Which particular marketing mix is developed is determined by the distinctive needs of the targeted market segment.

Although each element of the marketing mix is important in itself, it is how well each element is blended and coordinated that ultimately determines whether a marketing strategy is successful.

Product Strategy

The product is the means to the end for the target market. More than just a physical object (toothpaste) or a service (extension of credit), it is a benefit provider—a way of directly satisfying existing or latent needs. The success of any one product is contingent on how well it solves the target market's needs or wants relative to the competition's product.

Firms that excel, as far as product strategy is concerned, develop and offer products designed specifically to solve the problems of their target markets. For example, much of IBM's earlier marketing success was due to its decision to provide their computer-buying customers with delivery, installation, operator training, warranty protection, preventive maintenance, and other services in addition to the computer itself.[4] Similarly, Maytag washing machines are designed for the target market that is willing to pay a premium for a product that is reliable and durable. And, in the 1970s, German and Japanese automobile manufacturers saw an unfulfilled need in the United States for small, fuel-efficient cars and successfully met that need, to the detriment of major American automakers.

Pricing Strategy

Selling a product at a price that the target market sees as commensurate with the product's perceived benefits is the key to success. Mercedes-Benz can sell its cars at a high price because of the workmanship and quality that go into the automobiles and the willingness of the target market to pay a commensurate amount of money for those selling points.

For years, banks were limited in their use of pricing strategies by regulation governing interest rates on deposits and loans. For example, only since the onset of deregulation have banks had the opportunity to select a deposit pricing strategy. Some banks choose to pay consistently high, but not top-of-market, rates. Some choose to be the market leader, and still others choose to price at the lower end of the market, perhaps believing that their target market is less responsive to interest rates and more responsive to factors such as superior service.

In addition to interest rates on loans and deposits, bank pricing consists of fees and charges levied for the performance of various services. Unlike many other industries, banking often finds that its pricing policies are under scrutiny by consumer groups. One example is the service charge levied for writing a check on insufficient funds. In some markets, the charge for this infraction may be as high as $30, and consumer groups are taking banks to court to challenge that type of pricing.

The pricing of a bank's retail, commercial, and trust products has a dramatic impact on the institution's bottom line. A bank's interest income from its retail and commercial loans plus its fee and service charge income might constitute 75 percent or more of its total income from all sources. The interest paid on deposits is a major expense for banks, but it is usually only about half of a bank's total expenses, which include salaries and other operating expenses. Due to the bottom-line implications, a decision made on the pricing of loans and deposits is usually a joint process that involves the bank's asset/liability management as well as the marketing management executive.

Promotion Strategy

This strategy focuses on communicating the availability of products or services to the target market. Advertising campaigns, point-of-purchase materials, sales promotion activities, direct marketing, and product publicity are the main elements of promotion. Personal selling is also considered to be a part of promotion strategy, but due to its importance in the providing and delivering of bank services, this function will be regarded (in this text) as part of distribution strategy.

The development and implementation of attention-getting, informative, and persuasive communication techniques is vital to market awareness of a bank's product. A product's positive attributes, its price, and its means of distribution are meaningless unless these benefits are clearly and forcefully communicated to prospective customers. In the banking industry, if personal selling techniques are underused, and if advertising messages come to mean more to bankers than to customers ("XYZ Bank is proud to announce its new RediChecks"), then the promotion strategy will need to be re-addressed.

Distribution Strategy

This strategy is mainly concerned with making the product available at the desired time and place. Even the "right" product for a market segment provides limited satisfaction—or none at all—if it is not available when and where the consumers want it.

For example, *TV Guide's* perceived value would be considerably diminished if each week's issue arrived 10 days late at the store. Similarly, a bank might have superior service and products, but if it is located in an area where potential customers must pass by several other financial institutions on the way, its ability to attract those customers will be greatly lessened. So, an important element of distribution strategy for banks is site location. Furthermore, the current social environment places a heavy emphasis on time as well as place convenience. As a result, many banks are responding by joining nationwide automated teller networks to maximize the number of locations where customers can access their accounts, or by providing telephone banking services that enable customers to perform transactions 24 hours a day, 7 days a week.

Since banking products and services are largely intangible, they are often difficult to separate from the people who distribute them. This is especially true at the time the customer initiates the relationship with a bank, but it also applies to the day-to-day servicing of accounts. Although the use of technology has reduced contact with tellers, there will always be a need for personal customer service, whether it be in person or by phone. Banks should recognize the importance of human relations and sales training as an element in distribution strategy.

IMPLEMENTING THE PLAN

Implementing a successful marketing plan requires the cooperation of both management and staff. For example, consider the implementation of a marketing plan for a new product—a home equity line of credit. (See *Case B*.) In order to develop the product and bring it to the market, the marketing manager needs the assistance and cooperation of the following divisions:

- *computer programming*—to modify the consumer loan system to manage this special type of account;
- *operations*—to process the checks, payments, and other paperwork related to servicing the accounts;
- *legal services*—to write the credit application and loan agreement within the appropriate regulations;
- *accounting*—to establish the accounts and reporting systems necessary for tracking this product's performance;
- *bank investments*—to assist in the pricing of this particular use of funds;
- *training*—to instruct the branch staff in the operational and sales aspects of the product; and
- *branch staff*—for the selling and ongoing servicing of the product.

Such cooperation will be more easily achieved if the planning process includes representatives from these areas. Many banks use the task force approach to the implementation of a marketing plan that entails the development of a new product. The product manager chairs the group, who develop the list of tasks to be accomplished in order to introduce the product. Each member of the task force has specific responsibilities and a timetable for completing them. The task force members are responsible for seeing that their individual departments complete the required tasks and for informing their managers of product development decisions.

When all the internal elements are in place, and it is time to execute the marketing strategy, the bank is ready to communicate with the target market in order to begin advertising and monitoring the results.

EVALUATING THE RESULTS

Prior to the implementation stage, the bank should determine how progress with respect to the attainment of the objectives is going to be measured, and who is responsible for that measurement. In other words, the plan itself should include the answer to the question: "How will we know when we have arrived?" It is essential to the marketing management process that the bank monitor the results of its marketing plan so that any needed adjustments to the plan may be made. Performance may be monitored through internal sources of information such as daily, weekly, and monthly computer-generated or manually prepared reports, which would show the number of applications received, accounts that are opened and closed, balance levels, and the source of new customers. The bank might also obtain external data to determine general awareness of the product by surveying customers as to how they learned of the new product and what their opinions of it are.

It is possible that the marketing strategy will not produce the precise results expected, or that some part of the marketing mix will not perform as intended. The causes may be internal, or the result of some activity on the part of a competitor or some change in the external macroenvironment. Whatever the cause, it is necessary to evaluate the source of the problem and adjust or fine-tune the marketing mix. This is why the model for the strategic marketing management process contains a feedback loop. The process does not stop at any one point—planning, implementing, or evaluating—but is an ongoing, cyclical process.

It is important to note, that while the concepts presented in this chapter might appear to be rational, logical, or even undeniably sensible, the approaches discussed are not necessarily accepted or practiced by all banks as a matter of course. In fact, many marketing managers who attempt to use this process, especially those working for smaller banks, might encounter resistance.

Why Plan? Some Specious Arguments

Bank marketers must be prepared to answer the question: "Why plan?" A bank's management may proffer many arguments to rationalize why planning is unnecessary. Several of the most common arguments follow, and they will help define and clarify the importance of marketing planning.[5]

"This bank has done fine for 150 years without planning." Recall the example cited in chapter 1: The bank thought it was doing well with its annual loan growth of 10 percent until a new loan officer increased volume by 50 percent in 1 year. The point is that there is always room for improvement, even when the bank is apparently doing well. More to the point, with the environment constantly changing as it is today, we cannot merely project the accomplishments of the past onto the future. There is no assurance that the growth rates of the past will continue under their own momentum.

"We are a hometown bank. We know this community, what it wants and needs, and how best to serve it." There is no doubt that local bankers get feedback from the people they meet and talk with, but there is a built-in bias with this type of information. What bankers hear is very much dependent on who they are and who they are talking to. To fully understand the market, bankers need to hear from a wide cross-section of people. They need unbiased, objective feedback from the

market, and this type of information can only be obtained through research.

"There are too many changes taking place. You cannot anticipate them, so planning is a wasted effort." Formal planning forces the bank to define its assumptions about the future, so it places the bank in a better position to recognize variations when they take place. Planning improves the chances of making the right decision in the face of unexpected events. Using a systematic process of analysis and reasoning puts the marketer in a better position to understand previously unexplained results. In fact, this process might lead to better decision making in the future.

"The sign of a good manager is the ability to respond to unanticipated events and react to change in a fast and efficient manner." This is true up to a point, but while one manager may be putting out brush fires, the competitor might be planning for the management of change. As chapter 2 pointed out, the effective marketing manager *is* a manager of change.

"Planning takes too much time." The time spent in planning should be seen as an investment in the future. Furthermore, planning is not a one-time activity, as has been shown. It is an ongoing process, and it is part of the entire management approach. Any manager who is not planning is not managing properly.

"Things change too fast in this business. It is more important to stay flexible. A plan is too rigid." Here again, it must be stressed that planning is a *process*. It requires constant review and adaptation. This means changing either the assumptions, or the objectives, or the strategies. Furthermore, planning improves the chances of recognizing and adapting to change before the competition does so.

"Planning means setting objectives and measuring results. My people are not used to being measured and they will not like it." On the contrary, employees will not mind being measured if they are given realistic goals, the tools to achieve them, and the compensation for doing so. Employees also like to feel as if they are part of an organized effort. Therefore, it is important that all personnel be included in the objective-setting process and understand their role in the overall plan.

"Why plan if you cannot measure your results?" This objection is directed at a major weakness in much of the informal, and even some of the formal, planning that banks do. Objectives are set, but the procedure for measuring the results is not defined. In the absence of such measurement, the effect of planning cannot really be understood, so the planning process is perceived as being worthless when actually, it is the objective-setting step at fault. The point is: Do not plan if you are not going to set measurable objectives.

In summary, there are a number of benefits derived from the planning process:

1. It motivates executives to set marketing objectives and evaluate the bank's current situation in an explicit manner, and it forces them to plan ahead in a systematic fashion.

2. It inspires the bank to consider new opportunities, which tend to stimulate growth and profits.

3. The process makes bank personnel more aware of their role and responsibility with respect to the overall marketing program of the bank, and it encourages cooperation and coordination of efforts.

4. Because the plan identifies specific targets, the bank's limited resources are used more efficiently.

5. The formal plan includes performance standards or control measurements that enable bank executives to evaluate and improve marketing efforts.

6. An analysis of the bank's current and anticipated market situation helps to distinguish among those factors that *are* within the bank's control and those that are not.

7. The planning process leads to a more efficient use of time. There will be fewer brush fires to contend with and more attention paid to achieving goals.

8. The planning process typically results in a state of better preparedness in light of unexpected developments. Since the changes that are taking place in banking are making it more difficult to maintain the growth rates of the past, formalized planning can help anticipate future problems, identify possible solutions, and develop strategies

for achieving desired performance levels in the face of such challenges.

Prerequisites for Planning

Before initiating the planning process, the marketer must be aware of several factors that will ensure a favorable atmosphere. When planning fails, the roots can be traced to one or more of these factors:

- *Senior management support and involvement.* Top management must convey the attitude that the planning process is important and that the firm is sincerely interested in the results. The chief executive officer must refer to the plan both in meetings and in correspondence and must communicate to the staff the bank's progress with respect to its goals.

- *Cooperation at all levels of the bank.* It is essential that each bank employee be educated with respect to the marketing importance of his or her position. When employees see themselves as part of an overall plan, the innate desire to be part of a winning team takes over, and cooperation results.

- *Willingness of management to conduct the required research.* The bank must continually gather information from the marketplace. It is necessary to study historical trends; the competition; market share; the local economy; and customer characteristics, attitudes, and behavior. This information forms the situation analysis—the foundation on which the plan is built. Some of it may be obtained from secondary sources, but certain crucial information will be obtained only through primary research. (See chapter 7.)

- *Designated responsibility for implementing the plan.* Setting measurable objectives and assigning their responsibility to specific individuals increases the likelihood of accomplishing a task. Delegating responsibility can be a motivating factor, especially if compensation is tied to performance. Each manager should develop measurable objectives, consistent with the bank's plan, for which he or she is accountable. In the ideal situation, each employee should also be given measurable objectives that relate to the plan. Within this framework, objectives are more likely to be accomplished. If they are not, the reasons will be more easily identified, and corrective measures can be taken.

- *Recognition that the plan will not be perfect and unchanging.* Since markets are in a constant state of flux, the successful marketer must be able to manage change. Planning must be an ongoing process, with periodic reviews to measure progress and to make adjustments.

SUMMARY

Strategic marketing is a management process that involves planning, the implementing of those plans, and the evaluation of results. It is a circular, ongoing process that recognizes that plans do not always turn out as they should, so the mechanism for adjusting them must be built into the process.

The marketing manager plans, implements, and evaluates marketing plans in order to pinpoint target market demand for the product in line with the organization's strategic marketing objectives. The elements of a plan include the situation analysis, the objectives, target market selection, and marketing strategy. The marketing strategy is the sum total of the marketing mix strategies. For each target market, the marketing manager develops product, pricing, promotion, and place (distribution) strategies that will meet the needs and wants of the target market in a way that is superior to the competition's offering.

In many instances, the implementation of a marketing plan requires the cooperation and assistance of many departments within a bank. This level of cooperation requires that those areas be included in the planning process.

The evaluation stage of the marketing management process is critical. The marketing manager must be able to report on the effectiveness of the marketing strategy and, therefore, must consider (in the plan) the various research techniques that will be used to measure results. On the basis of this information, the strategy can be changed or fine-tuned in order to attain the desired objectives.

Some executives do not believe in planning but instead, have a short-range view of the business. The marketing manager should be prepared to respond to the most common objections to planning and to pave the way for its success by seeing that its foundations are firmly in place. These foundations include senior management involvement, multilevel cooperation, willingness to do research and to assign responsibilities, and the recognition that the plan might need to be adjusted after implementation.

The next two chapters of this section will discuss the steps involved in conducting a situation analysis, the guidelines for the setting of objectives, and some general concepts and techniques for strategy formulation.

POINTS FOR REVIEW

1. Define or briefly explain the following:
   - the management process
   - the marketing management process
   - marketing strategy
   - demarketing

2. Why is the management process depicted as a circle?

3. Why do we say that the task of marketing management is to regulate market demand?

4. What are the four steps involved in the marketing planning process?

5. What is the end product of the situation analysis?

6. What are the characteristics of effective marketing objectives?

7. Select any magazine or television advertisement and describe the target market to which it appears to be directed.

8. Provide an example of a current consumer deposit or loan product strategy.

9. Think about your bank's most recent marketing program. How did its implementation affect your job?

10. Respond to the following statement made by a bank president: "We're growing at an acceptable annual rate that is in line with our major competitors. We don't need to plan."

4 THE DEVELOPMENT OF A SITUATION ANALYSIS

Previous chapters have discussed marketing planning and the four questions it addresses: (1) Where are we now? (2) Where do we want to go? (3) How are we going to get there? and (4) How will we know when we have arrived? The situation analysis answers the first of those questions.

The situation analysis is a formal, systematic procedure aimed at generating useful written information that will help management understand its current situation. Its purpose is to establish a clear understanding of the bank's strengths and weaknesses in order to set meaningful objectives. It should provide an accurate picture of the environment in which the bank is operating—not a still picture, but rather, a moving picture that reveals trends and that forecasts the condition of the environment throughout the planning process. The period covered by a plan may be as short as 3 months or as long as 5 years. Whatever the time frame, the situation analysis is a must in that it will perform one critical function: to help management understand what needs to be done.

WHY FORMALIZE THE SITUATION ANALYSIS?

Why is it necessary to formalize the situation analysis? There are three answers to that question. First, the start of the planning process is similar to the preparations involved before setting out on a trip to a distant place. Before mapping out a route, one must know the location from which to set out—that is, where to begin. Knowing the point of origin is essential to starting out on the right path toward a given destination.

Second, the critical planning steps of objective setting and the measurement and evaluation of results cannot be accomplished without the foundation of the formal situation analysis. The situation analysis generates a variety of statistics (such as share of market, number of services used per customer, level of consumer awareness of bank services, rate of growth of accounts, percent of noninterest income derived from fees, etc.). These statistics become the raw material for the objective-setting process. Worthwhile objectives might include increasing the share of market by 2 percent, raising the average number of services per customer from 1.5 to 1.8, or increasing consumer recall of the bank's advertising message from 10 to 25 percent. The measurement and evaluation of results may be seen as an updated situation analysis, one which concentrates on the specific areas that were targeted in the objective-setting process.

Third, the formalizing of the situation analysis has several distinct advantages. Every bank manager has an opinion or impression of what is going on in the market, how the bank is doing in comparison with the competition, and what the bank's strengths and weaknesses are. However, these opinions may not be based on facts. Being forced to record the situation analysis in black and white assures that the input to the goal-setting process will be factual and objective. Furthermore, putting the situation analysis down in writing can do wonders for internal public relations and motivation. There are many employees who are not personally involved in the development of marketing plans but whose cooperation will, nevertheless, be required for their execution. Sharing the written situation analysis with these employees will give them an understanding of the bank's current situation, the need for an integrated marketing plan, and the importance of their cooperation.

While the situation analysis is a critical first step in the planning process, it need not be a physical part of the document itself. A situation analysis generates a great deal of data as backup to the statement of strengths and weaknesses, problems and opportunities. If all of that data were placed at the front of a written plan, it could very well detract from the operational components of the plan—that is, the "to do's." The information should, of course, be referenced and available, but it is not an end in itself.

In the following pages, the steps involved in the process of developing a situation analysis—both on a bankwide scale and on a smaller, one-product scale, will be discussed. Throughout this chapter, the reader will be referred to *Cases B* and *F*. *Case F* is the overall marketing plan for a community bank; *Case B* is a marketing plan for a new product—specifically, a home equity credit line. These cases will demonstrate how the basic elements of a situation analysis are treated differently depending on the particular situation.

ELEMENTS OF A SITUATION ANALYSIS

There are four steps in the development of a situation analysis. Exhibit 4-1 outlines a situation analysis for a bank, presenting all the potential categories of information that might be included. However, not all of these categories will appear in every situation analysis. The scope of the particular marketing plan will dictate which of the many factors is relevant to the current situation. This will become clearer when studying *Cases B* and *F* while reading through the following pages.

Self-Analysis

The purpose of this part of the situation analysis is to learn as much as possible about a bank's performance and its current situation with respect to the particular marketing effort that is the subject of the

> **Exhibit 4-1   General Outline of a Situation Analysis for a Bank**
>
> (This list is not all-inclusive but rather, illustrative of the variety of information that might be gathered.)
>
> **I. SELF-ANALYSIS**
> A. Current marketing strategies and tactics; their effectiveness
> B. Market share and position
> C. Financial situation
>
> **II. ANALYSIS OF MACROENVIRONMENTAL FACTORS PERTINENT TO SITUATION**
> A. Economic Factors: effects of inflation, business cycle, employment trends, retail and commercial activity, construction activity
> B. Demographic Factors: effects of trends in size, age distribution, education, income, and geographic distribution of the population
> C. Social/Cultural Factors: changes in consumer values and lifestyles that affect target market purchase behavior
> D. Political/Legal Factors: effects of regulation and legislation
> E. Technological Factors: changes in technology affecting service offering and delivery
>
> **III. ANALYSIS OF MICROENVIRONMENTAL FACTORS PERTINENT TO SITUATION**
> A. Customers: profiles, needs, buying behavior, attitudes toward bank
> B. Markets
>   1. Size, growth, geographical distribution, and profitability (current and future)
>   2. Profiles of target market segments
> C. Competition: major competitors' strengths and weaknesses, sizes and trends in market share
> D. Marketing Intermediaries: comparison of alternatives; their cost, reliability, effectiveness, plans for enhancing their capabilities
>
> **IV. ANALYSIS OF PROBLEMS AND OPPORTUNITIES**
> Key problems to be overcome; key opportunities upon which to capitalize

plan. The self-analysis should include a review of the bank's current marketing mix strategies—that is, how its current product, pricing, promotion, and distribution strategies are working. It might include feedback from the bank's customers or prospects obtained through market research surveys. It would also include the bank's current market share and its position in the market.

Much of the information for the self-analysis of various products is available from internal secondary sources. For instance, internal data are available on trends in new and closed checking and savings accounts, new commercial and installment loans and mortgages, and demographic characteristics of new borrowers. The marketer's challenge is to locate this information within the bank, since it is collected for operational or credit rating reasons and is not generally compiled for or disseminated to the marketing department. For this reason, a useful first step in the self-analysis of a bank is to determine what information is available within the bank and to establish a system for its up-to-date dissemination to appropriate marketing personnel.

The bank should also look at its financial statements in comparison with the statements of competing banks and banks in its peer group—that is, banks that are of the same size but that are not necessarily competing in the same marketplace. By comparing various statistics and ratios, the bank can more easily identify its financial strengths and weaknesses. Some of the data that may be useful include: capital structure, return on assets, asset growth rate, loan portfolio mix, noninterest income as a percent of total income or assets, occupancy costs, and salaries and benefits as a percent of total expenses or assets. This information is available from annual reports and from Form 10-K, which is prepared by publicly held banks. Consumers National Bank (CNB), a fictitious name, did this analysis, but included it within the section on competition.

In addition to the aforementioned types of data, the bank's officers have a great deal of information stored in their minds that should be put down on paper. This information will encompass current competitive strategies and future expectations. For instance, the following questions might be answered:

- What are we doing to get new business? What kind of call program do we have? Have we identified our best prospects? What kind of call program does the competition have?

- What are we doing to cross-market our services to our present customers?

- What new services could negatively affect our market position?

- What will our customers' financial needs be in the future?

- How well do we train our employees in selling? In job performance?

The self-analysis in *Case B's* marketing plan for a new home equity line of credit lists several factors about the bank's current situation that provide an excellent foundation for offering the new product: prior experience with equity credit, a preponderance of fixed-rate credit in the portfolio, current penetration of the target market, a sales and operating staff that is accustomed to selling and servicing revolving credit products, efficiencies that enable the bank to price very competitively, and the fact that the competition is already offering such a product.

The self-analysis for Consumers National Bank, on the other hand, consists of only a brief overview, since the sections on customers and competitors look at the bank in more detail.

Analysis of Macroenvironmental Factors

This section of the situation analysis should address whichever of the macroenvironmental factors affect this particular marketing plan.

Economic Environment

The business of banking is very much affected by economic conditions in the bank's market area. The level of deposits reflects the cash position of individuals and businesses. New housing construction means more families with banking needs. When business is booming, manufacturers borrow to expand capacity or finance production. If people are confident of their future income, they will borrow to improve their homes or to make major purchases. This list could go on and on, but the point is, that in order to plan its marketing effort, the bank must have a handle on its trade area's economy. This means understanding the economic trends and, to some extent, making projections about the future of the economy.

The amount of economic information that might be gathered about a bank's marketplace is nearly endless. The objective is to gather enough useful information to be able to understand the basics of the environment and to make some future projections about the environment in which the bank will be operating.

Basically, for a total marketing plan, this analysis should at least include the following types of information:

1. Employment trends—growth by industry, composition of the area's industry, wage rates.

2. Evaluation of the retail sector of the economy.

3. Construction activity—business and residential.

Some long-range forecasts for the area should also be included in the above information.

Employment Trends

State departments of labor or employment, chambers of commerce, and public utility research departments may provide valuable sources of information about the labor market, including total work force, occupational distribution, industrial development, and labor market projections. Being aware of possible employment trends will enable the bank to project its own labor requirements. The accumulated information may reveal increased activity in a particular industry, which the bank might want to address by making one of its calling officers a specialist in that field.

Retail Activity

Information on retail establishments and sales is available from the *Census of Retail Trade*, published every 5 years (in years ending with 2 and 7) by the Bureau of the Census. This information shows if and how the retail business in the trade area is changing, and consumer buying trends with respect to goods and services.

Construction Activity

Information about residential and commercial construction gives the bank an indication of how much its own business may be expected to grow and alerts management to the need for new branch locations.

This discussion of the analysis of the bank's economic environment shows that it is possible to paint a picture of the bank's market with no out-of-pocket cost (except for that of state or government publications, many of which are available at the library). One can see a great deal about the composition of the market and its growth or decline trends. There is a wealth of available information that can be evaluated in order to get a broad indication of important changes in the market and to call attention to prospective problems and opportunities.

The extent of the information developed will vary with the scope of the plan. *Case F*, a total marketing plan for a community bank, goes to great lengths to review employment and unemployment rates and retail and construction activity. These issues help the bank understand the forces that are operating in its trade area, since they have implications for the bank's marketing strategy.

In contrast, *Case B* does not require extensive tabular data, but discusses the effect of earlier inflation on the buildup of home equity and of high interest rates on people's attitudes toward maintaining their current homes and taking on additional debt in the form of a secondary mortgage.

Demographic Environment

Demographic data is useful in that it gives the banker a picture of the population makeup in the bank's market area and how it is changing in terms of number, income, age, education, and occupation. The size and projected growth of the population are especially important since there is usually some relationship between the number of people in the market and the number of banking services that will be required. The two principal sources for demographic data are the census (conducted every 10 years) and each state's department of labor or employment.

Education and occupation are very much related to social class and income, and consumer buying and banking behavior varies between these social classes. The rate at which people adopt new products and services is related to age and social class. As a result, the marketer must have a good working knowledge and understanding of the characteristics of the area's population in order to develop marketing strategies that effectively reach the bank's customers and prospects.

In the exhibits in *Case F*, Consumers National Bank has collected some pertinent demographic information, citing the sources. These show population trends and projections, the aging of the population, and relevant population shifts, which have implications for branching policy (that is, distribution strategy).

In *Case B*, Marlton National Bank (MNB), a fictitious name, does not use tabular information, but alludes to the demographic foundations for the market for home equity credit lines—that is, the aging of the baby boom generation, increase in the divorce rate, and projected growth in the age group that constitutes the target market.

Social/Cultural Environment

As consumers' lifestyles and values change, their product and service needs and wants also change. The marketer must be tuned in to these factors. While Consumers National Bank's marketing plan does not refer to the social or cultural environment in its trade area, Marlton National Bank's plan mentions the social stigma once associated with second mortgages and notes that this bias is no longer prevalent in society—making the growth in home equity credit possible.

Political/Legal Environment

Regulatory and legislative factors are often operative in bank marketing situations. While they are not a factor in *Case F*, they are in *Case B*. The Tax Reform Act of 1986 affected the deductibility of some types of interest and increased demand for consumer credit secured by a second mortgage.

Technological Environment

Advances in technology are often material to the development of new service delivery techniques. For instance, the marketing plan for a new home banking service that utilizes a personal computer with a modem would include a discussion of the technology that permits that service as well as projections for increases in the number of households having personal computers. In neither of the two cases is a treatment of the technological environment relevant to the situation analysis.

Analysis of Microenvironmental Factors

The principal microenvironmental factors that bank marketers should consider are customers, markets, competitors, and marketing intermediaries.

Customers

The bank must understand its own customers—who they are demographically and how they compare with the market at large, how they differ from product line to product line within the bank, and how many services they have with the bank. It should also understand its customers' attitudes about the bank and their needs and preferences in banking matters. An organization that recognizes that it is in the business of meeting the needs of its customers will naturally attempt to find out as much as possible about their predilections and motivations.

By using survey techniques, the bank can learn a great deal about itself as well as its customers. Ideally, the bank should survey its checking, savings, and loan customers, but at the very least, a checking customer survey should be conducted, since customers consider checking to be their primary bank account. Such a survey may be done inexpensively by including it with the monthly checking statement or mailing it to a sample of checking account customers.

Consumers National Bank conducted such a survey as part of its planning process and also made use of the information amassed from its ongoing new account and closed (or inactive) account customer surveys. Exhibit 4-2 shows the questionnaire they used for the checking customer survey, which was mailed to 1 out of every 12 checking customers, selected at random by computer. (The numbers appearing next to the answers are codes for keypunching the respondent's answers.)

A new account survey might consist of ongoing or periodic monitoring of the profile of the bank's new customers. It can also be used to determine the source of new business by asking why the customer chose the bank and where the funds for the new account are coming from. (It should be noted that asking customers in this manner why they selected the bank provides only superficial, conscious responses. To understand the deeper, motivating forces behind consumer decisions requires more sophisticated research techniques.)

Exhibit 4-3 shows the form that is used by Consumers National Bank at the new accounts desk. When customers open a new account of any type, they are given this form to complete while the new accounts representative is doing the necessary paperwork.

It is wise for a bank to regularly monitor closed accounts in order to stay abreast of any unfavorable trends that may be developing. Indeed, some form of followup on closed accounts may be required by the bank's auditors as a way of ensuring that the accounts were actually closed by the customer and are not connected to any misbehavior on the part of bank personnel.

For the most part, customers close accounts because they are changing their residence or job, and the bank is no longer convenient. Other reasons most often cited for closing accounts are related to the quality of service received, or, when it comes to savings, the availability of a better rate of interest elsewhere. Exhibit 4-4 shows the closed account survey form used by Consumers National Bank.

In *Case F*, Consumers National Bank lists a number of important customer characteristics, attitudes, and behaviors that it collected as a result of its research efforts. On the other hand, in *Case B*, Marlton National Bank's knowledge of its customer base is reflected in the section describing the target market for the new product. It is clear that they sufficiently understand their current customer base to recognize that it closely parallels the demographics of the target market for the equity credit line.

Markets

This section of the situation analysis addresses the size, growth, geographic distribution, and current and future profitability of the relevant market or markets that might be targeted by the bank.

As a result of its economic, demographic, and customer analyses, Consumers National Bank has identified a need to target its marketing efforts toward higher income, professional and managerial workers, and newcomers to the area. Marlton National Bank, as already noted, has identified the target market and has addressed its growth in its situation analysis.

Competition

This section consists of data that compare relevant information about the bank with that of its principal competitors. The purpose of this

Exhibit 4-2   Sample Customer Survey Questionnaire

FOR OFFICE USE ONLY

1-
_____ 2-
3-

1. How long have you been a customer of this bank?

4-1 _____ 0–2 years		-4 _____ 10–15 years
-2 _____ 3–5 years		-5 _____ over 15 years
-3 _____ 6–9 years		

2. Which of our offices do you use most frequently?

5-1 _____ Bridgeboro	-5 _____ Milltown
-2 _____ No. Bridgeboro	-6 _____ Libby Plaza
-3 _____ New Hope	-7 _____ Walker Blvd.
-4 _____ Seabrook	-8 _____ Plattville

3. What factors led you to select our bank?

6-1 _____ convenient to home	-5 _____ recommended by friend/
-2 _____ convenient to work	relative
-3 _____ convenient to shopping	-6 _____ friendly, courteous staff
-4 _____ bank's reputation	-7 _____ had service I wanted

           (please name the service) _____ 7-

          -8 _____ other (please specify below)

_____ 8-
_____ 9-

4. How would you rate the bank on each of the following features? (Please circle the number that matches the rating you think applies.)

		Excellent	Good	Fair	Poor
Friendliness of tellers	10-	4	3	2	1
Teller service	11-	4	3	2	1
Helpfulness of platform staff	12-	4	3	2	1
Appearance of facilities	13-	4	3	2	1
Hours	14-	4	3	2	1
Parking facilities	15-	4	3	2	1
Drive-in facilities	16-	4	3	2	1
Locations	17-	4	3	2	1
Speed of service	18-	4	3	2	1
Variety of services offered	19-	4	3	2	1
Interest rates paid	20-	4	3	2	1

5. Please indicate which services you are currently using with our bank and with other banks or savings & loan associations. (Circle the number in the appropriate column.)

		CNB	Other Bank	Savings & Loan
Regular checking	21	-1	-2	-3
Interest checking	22	-1	-2	-3

Exhibit 4-2 **continued**

Cash reserve (no bounce or overdraft checking)	23	-1	-2	-3
Statement savings	24	-1	-2	-3
Christmas club	25	-1	-2	-3
Certificate of deposit	26	-1	-2	-3
IRA	27	-1	-2	-3
Auto loan	28	-1	-2	-3
Home equity loan	29	-1	-2	-3
Personal loan	30	-1	-2	-3
Mortgage	31	-1	-2	-3
Safe deposit box	32	-1	-2	-3

6. What are the names of the other banks or savings & loan associations with which you have accounts? _____ 33-
   _____
   _____
   _____

7. Have you opened any new bank accounts or loans within the past year?
   34-1 _____ No (go to question 8)   -2 _____ Yes (Please answer question 7a)

7a. What kind of account did you open? _____ 35-
    Where did you open it? _____ 36-
    _____
    _____
    Reason? _____ 37-
    _____

8. Have you closed any accounts in the past year?
   38-1 _____ No (go to question 9)   -2 _____ Yes (please answer question 8a)

8a. What kind of account did you close? _____ 39-
    What bank was it with? _____ 40-
    What was your reason for closing the account? _____ 41-
    _____
    _____
    _____

9. Which of the following cards do you have?
   42-1 _____ MasterCard
     -2 _____ Visa
     -3 _____ American Express
     -4 _____ Discover

10. Do you have any funds invested in a money market mutual fund (such as E.F. Hutton's Cash Reserve Management; Delaware Cash Reserve; Merrill Lynch Ready Asset Fund, etc.)?
    43-1 _____ Yes   -2 _____ No

11. Some other banks now have 24-hour banking machines. With these machines, you can withdraw cash from checking or statement savings, deposit to checking or statement

Exhibit 4-2 **continued**

savings, make transfers between your accounts, inquire about the balance in your accounts, and make payments on loans. How interested would you be in having this service at Consumers National?

	Very	Somewhat	Not very	Not at all
44-1 ____interested	-2 ____interested	-3 ____interested	-4 ____interested

12. Your bank is planning to offer a service in the fall called Pay-by-Phone. With this service you can pay all your recurring bills with a phone call (e.g., rent payments, mortgage payments, utilities, phone, credit card payments, department store charges). There would be no need to write a check, put it in an envelope, stamp and mail it. You would also be able to make transfers between your savings and checking accounts and make payments on your credit cards or loans with the bank.

For this service, you would pay the bank a basic monthly fee of $1.00 plus 15 cents for each bill paid (no charge for internal bank payments such as transfers between accounts or payments to bank loans).

How interested would you be in taking advantage of such a service?

	Very	Somewhat	Not very	Not at all
45-1 ____interested	-2 ____interested	-3 ____interested	-4 ____interested

Why do you say that? _____46-
_____

13. The following information is for statistical purposes only: (Please check the answers that apply to you.)

Age	Education	Family income	Marital status
47-1___under 25	48-1___some h.s.	49-1___under $10,000	50-1___single
-2___25–34	-2___h.s. grad	-2___$10,000–14,999	-2___married
-3___35–44	-3___some college	-3___$15,000–24,999	-3___divorced/
-4___45–54	-4___college grad	-4___$25,000–34,999	sep'd
-5___55–61	-5___some grad	-5___$35,000–49,999	-4___widowed
-6___62 or more	school	-6___$50,000 or	
	-6___grad degree	more	
	-7___trade school		

Occupation

clerical/sales	51-1	_____
equipment operator/driver	-2	_____
professional, technical	-3	_____
manager, officer, proprietor	-4	_____
crafts	-5	_____
service worker	-6	_____
laborer—farm	-7	_____
laborer—nonfarm	-8	_____
student	-9	_____
retired	-0	_____
at home	-X	_____

analysis is to evaluate the bank's performance in comparison with institutions that are operating in roughly the same economic, demographic, and competitive environment.

When thinking in terms of who the bank's competition is, the marketer should use a broad definition of the term. Competition includes other commercial banks, savings and loan associations, mutual savings banks, finance companies, credit unions, investment companies, brokerage firms, mutual funds, and money market funds that perform many of the same services as banks and are a competitive reality.

The type of information that should be gathered are various operating statistics, information on service offerings, comparison of advertising materials, physical plant, and quality of personnel. In other words, the objective is to compare the bank's performance with that of the competition and to compare the use of the two marketing mixes.

The three broad categories of information that should comprise the analysis of the bank's competitive environment are:

1. comparative operating statistics (this may be included in the self-analysis);

2. comparative market shares; and

3. comparison of marketing strategies (products, pricing, advertising and promotional activities, service delivery, and selling efforts).

Consumers National Bank's principal competitors are numerous because the bank is in a state that has long permitted statewide branching. The bank principally competes with five other commercial banks, two savings and loans, and a credit union. In addition, 4 other commercial banks each have a 2 percent or smaller market share.

While these institutions are the major financial institution competitors, Consumers National should be aware of other nonbank competition vying in the marketplace for specific services. For example, consumer finance companies compete for home equity loans and other personal loans; money market funds are competitors for both checking and savings funds. These competitors must be kept in mind

Exhibit 4-3　Sample New Account Survey Questionnaire

1–3

4-9　Date _____

What type of account are you opening today?

10-1 _____ Regular checking　　-4 _____ Statement savings　　-7 _____ Personal
　-2 _____ Cash reserve　　　　-5 _____ IRA　　　　　　　　　　loan
　-3 _____ Interest checking　　-6 _____ Certificate of deposit

Are you already a customer of this bank?

11-1 _____ Yes　If yes, please check which services you currently have with us

　　　　12-1 _____ Regular checking　　-6 _____ Certificate of deposit
　　　　　-2 _____ Cash reserve　　　 -7 _____ Loan
　　　　　-3 _____ Interest checking　 -8 _____ Trust services
　　　　　-4 _____ Statement savings
　　　　　-5 _____ IRA

11-2 _____ No　If no, why did you choose our bank? _____
　　　13- _____

How long have you lived at your present address?

14-1 _____ just moved in　　　　-4 _____ 6–10 years
　-2 _____ less than 1 year　　 -5 _____ over 10 years
　-3 _____ 1–5 years

Your answers to the following questions will be appreciated:

Education	Occupation	Sex
15-1 _____ some high school	16-1 _____ clerical/sales	17-1 _____ female
-2 _____ high school grad	-2 _____ trade or skilled laborer	-2 _____ male
-3 _____ some college	-3 _____ professional/	
-4 _____ college grad	managerial	
-5 _____ some graduate school	-4 _____ student	
-6 _____ graduate degree	-5 _____ retired	
-7 _____ trade school	-6 _____ other _____	

Age	Housing	1980 Gross family income
18-1 _____ Under 25	19-1 _____ own home	20-1 _____ Under $10,000
-2 _____ 25–34	-2 _____ rent	-2 _____ $10,000–14,999
-3 _____ 35–44		-3 _____ $15,000–24,999
-4 _____ 45–54		-4 _____ $25,000–34,999
-5 _____ 55–61		-5 _____ $35,000–49,999
-6 _____ 62 or more		-6 _____ over $50,000

For internal use

Type of account opened _____
Source of deposit _____
　transfer from _____

throughout the situation analysis, although the more banklike financial institutions will comprise the bulk of the data in the situation analysis in *Case F*.

Operating Statistics

Consumers National Bank compares its condition and income statements with those of its principal commercial banking competitors. The purpose of this analysis is to assess the bank's financial performance in comparison with them. Consumers National Bank operates in a county where only two of its competing commercial banks are headquartered. The rest of the competition have numerous offices out of the county in areas with considerably different economic and demographic characteristics. Therefore, to compare Consumers National Bank's financial statements with these banks', which generate so much of their business outside the trade area, would be meaningless. For this part of the situation analysis, Consumers National Bank compares itself with only the two other county-headquartered banks.

Exhibit F-8, found in *Case F*, shows selected operating statistics and ratios for Consumers and these two banks. This information may be obtained from Call Reports and Income Statements filed with the Federal Deposit Insurance Corporation. These reports are available upon request or they may be accessed by computer through a service bureau. Additionally, at least one firm compiles statistics for all the banks in a state under one cover.[1] Data are compiled as of year-end and are generally available in the middle of the following year.

Market Share

One of the better indicators of a bank's competitive strength is its market share. **Market share** is the proportion of all banking business accounted for by a particular bank or branch. Through analysis of data from various sources, it is possible to calculate a bank's share of deposits or loans in total or by type within a market area. In other words, one can determine the share of total demand deposits, savings and time deposits, public funds, personal loans, mortgages, and so on.

Exhibit 4-4 Sample Closed Account Survey Questionnaire

Dear Customer,

Our records indicate that you recently closed your savings account with our bank. It is important for us to know if you closed this account because of any dissatisfaction with our staff, our policies, or our service.

Please take a moment to complete this form. Then simply fold and staple or tape it closed and drop it in the mail. We look forward to hearing from you.

Jane Doe

Jane Doe
President

The savings account was closed for the following reason(s).

_____Transferred the funds to another account within the bank
_____Moved out of area
_____Needed the money for a specific purpose
_____Used the funds for investment purposes
_____Wanted to get more interest
_____Because of the service charge on balances under $100
_____Dissatisfied with service by bank staff
_____Other (please explain) _____
_____
_____

Comments

Please use this space for any other comments you would like to make.

_____
_____
_____

Thank you for your cooperation.

(fold, seal and mail)

Unfortunately, there are no secondary data available to measure share of personal or individual checking balances. This information is combined with deposits of partnerships and corporations. Information on share of personal demand deposits may be obtained through primary research or through information sharing. In some parts of the country, banks have an outside firm pool the selected data and provide to each member of the group the group's totals by category. In this way, confidential data about any specific bank are not made available to competitors.

In discussing the importance of market share, a warning is in order. Having the greatest market share is not in itself an ideal to be sought. A bank that offers totally free checking for individuals and businesses might very well experience greater-than-average increases in market share. Its earnings, however, are sure to suffer. Remember that the first part of the definition of marketing is "customer satisfaction *at a profitable volume.*" Being biggest is not necessarily best. The goal to strive for is increased share of profitable markets, but this is difficult to measure except by primary research.

The principal sources of market share data are reports filed with the financial regulators. Each year, as of June 30, all banks report deposit statistics by branch to the FDIC. Similar data are provided by savings and loans to their regulators. This information, along with information on credit union deposits, may be obtained in summary form from publishers who organize it by state, county, and municipality.[2] It may also be accessed directly through computer service bureaus on a time-sharing basis, or the tapes may be obtained from various regulators and manipulated on the bank's own computer. While the information is current to June 30, it is usually not available until spring of the following year. Despite this time lag, these are the only such data available and are therefore quite useful.

Information on share of loans can be obtained somewhat less easily from Call Reports filed with the regulators. These data are consolidated; that is, they are reported for the entire bank, not by branch. Therefore, in states that permit branching, loan information is not available by county or municipality. Because only two of CNB's principal competitors operate exclusively in the same trade area as

CNB, information on loans for Overland County, where CNB is located, is not available. This information could best be obtained through primary research in which individuals and businesses are surveyed about their current and recent borrowings. CNB's management felt that this expense was not warranted at this time and that their objectives with respect to loans could be formed based on existing data.

Marketing Strategies

While conducting the activities covered in the two previous sections, the marketer (or market researcher) has been sitting at the desk with a calculator or computer and reference material, poring over statistics to put them into meaningful order. Now it is time to look outward physically—to get up and see what the competition is doing. The focus is on the competition's use of the elements of the marketing mix—product, pricing, promotion, and place (distribution)—both physical and personal.

The competition includes not only existing financial institutions but also those that are making plans to enter the market. It is necessary to look at commercial banks, mutual savings banks, savings and loans, and credit unions. The focus should be on the following:

- *Products and Pricing*—What products are offered? What are the service or maintenance charges? What interest rates are paid or charged? What price changes have there been? What new services have been offered?

- *Promotional Activity*—What advertising and promotional techniques are the competitors using? What do their current strategies appear to be? What markets are they targeting? Are they being effective?

- *Physical Distribution*—What kind of facilities does the competition have? How do ours compare? How do our locations compare with theirs in terms of convenience and access? How do we compare for drive-up and automated teller service? How do we compare for hours of service?

- *Personal Selling*—How effective are their and our customer contact people? What sales training do we and our competitors provide?

How does the caliber and physical appearance of our staff compare with theirs? What changes have taken place in key personnel that might affect our market potential? What changes have taken place in policies, such as credit standards and rate changes, that might affect our ability to attract business?

There are two principal ways to obtain this kind of information: **observation** (including comparative service shopping) and **survey research**.

Service shopping is simply a matter of organizing information that is gained either from existing information or by having personnel actually go around and "shop" the competition, taking notes along the way. Much information can also be gained over the telephone by an employee posing as a prospective customer. Information gained in this way, however, should be verified by placing more than one call to different sources. Unfortunately, it is not unusual for bank employees to give incorrect information to callers. Placing such calls also reveals something about the level of sales awareness of the competition. Rarely will the person at the bank ask the caller for a name and address so that more detailed service information may be provided.

Much information about the relative strengths and weaknesses of the competition may be obtained from a survey of trade area residents. Through such research, a bank can learn a great deal about the profile of the customers of each bank, the relative image of each institution in the minds of customers and prospects, and the extent to which people are switching banks, as well as the reasons for it.

The results of competitive shopping done by Consumers National Bank appear in *Case F*. The exhibits present information only for the retail side of the business. Obviously, in conducting a situation analysis for a bank, information about services for businesses should also be developed. This part of the situation analysis might also contain information obtained by talking to one's own bank's officers. In Consumers National Bank's case, some of the information obtained in this way was quite useful.

In *Case B*, Marlton National Bank provides detailed information on its competitors' equity credit line product features and pricing. Because the scope of Consumers National Bank's plan is broader, it presents a comparison of basic products, hours, locations, and operating statistics, as well as competitive marketing strategies, to the extent that they are observable.

Marketing Intermediaries

As mentioned in chapter 2, marketing intermediaries in the banking business are firms or organizations that enable the bank to offer a service or distribute its products through a third party. The situation analysis in a marketing plan for a credit card or for a service such as automated balance reporting (where business customers might call in for balance information to a third party who collects and reports the information) would include a section addressing relevant factors concerning the intermediary. This is not the case for either Marlton National or Consumers National Bank.

Analysis of Problems and Opportunities

When all of the data have been gathered and analyzed, the final step of the situation analysis is to summarize the relevant information learned. Whether it is called a summary of the bank's strengths and weaknesses or problems and opportunities, it should simply be a set of factual statements, with no attempt to provide reasons for those facts or solutions to the problems. It should cover the main opportunities and problems facing the bank. This summary will become the foundation for the development of objectives, strategies, and tactics. The strengths can be used in developing strategies for the coming year (or other planning period). Identifying the weaknesses enables the bank to plan ways to correct them.

In *Case B*, Marlton National Bank has identified two problems or weaknesses that have a bearing on the introduction of an equity credit line: its late entry into the market and its preponderance of fixed rate assets in the loan portfolio, both of which will be resolved through the new product. On the other hand, it lists six opportunities or strengths on which it can capitalize with this new product. Consumers National Bank's summary of problems and opportunities lists 11 points, only 1 of which is positive. The bank clearly has a serious marketing challenge facing it.

Having answered the question, "Where are we now?" through the situation analysis, the next step is to answer the question, "Where do we want to go?" That question is answered through the objective-setting process and the selection of the target market(s). The next chapter treats objective setting and discusses the subsequent steps that will answer the question, "How are we going to get there?"

SUMMARY

There are four stages involved in developing a situation analysis, the first step in marketing planning. First, the bank must take a hard look at itself through the evaluation of internal secondary data and by amassing feedback from customers and noncustomers through primary research. The bank should evaluate its current marketing strategies—product, pricing, promotion, and place (distribution)—as well as its current market position and market share. This information may be obtained from internal primary and secondary sources, market research, financial statements, and from observation by the bank's staff.

The second part of the situation analysis is an analysis of the macroenvironmental factors that pertain to the topic covered by the marketing plan. The bank must understand the economic environment in which it has been and will continue working. Some of the data that should be part of the economic analysis are employment trends, retail trade activity, and construction activity. Some attempt should be made to forecast the environment over the period that the plan covers.

The bank should also study the relevant demographic environment because population size, shifts, age, education, and occupation all have a bearing on the selection of marketing strategies. Social and cultural factors affect values and attitudes, which in turn, affect consumer purchasing behavior. The political/legal environment is often a factor in bank marketing planning because banking regulation and legislation affect many bank product and distribution strategies. The technological environment most frequently affects the way banking products are serviced and delivered.

The third step in the situation analysis is an analysis of the micro-environmental factors that pertain to the topic of the plan. These factors include information on the bank's customers, much of which may be obtained from survey research. Actual and potential markets that the bank might target with its strategies should be identified and described in as much detail as possible. Information on the competitive environment should include operating statistics, market shares and trends, and a comparison of competitive strategies. Where marketing intermediaries will be used, these should also be treated in the situation analysis.

The final step in the situation analysis—the summary of the bank's problems and opportunities (or strengths and weaknesses)—concisely states what has been learned in the first three steps, without making any judgments or offering solutions. That is left for the objective-setting process.

The situation analysis is a necessary first step in any planning project, whether it be for an entire bank or for one particular product. Whatever the planning topic or period, the marketer must be able to answer the question, "Where are we now?" The situation analysis provides that answer.

POINTS FOR REVIEW

1. What are the four elements of a situation analysis?

2. How would you, as the marketing director, respond to the following statement by your bank's chief executive officer: "I know what our strengths and weaknesses are. We don't need to do all this situation analysis business. We can develop our objectives without it."?

3. What are at least three sources of information that might be used in a bank's self-analysis?

4. How might a lack of growth in retail sales in your bank's trade area affect your bank? Are there any other ways?

5. How have demographic factors affected the branching strategy of your bank?

6. List as many sources, internal and external, as you can think of for obtaining information about your bank's customers—their profile, service usage, and banking behavior.

7. What is the meaning of the term "market share"? Why is it of interest to bankers?

8. What characteristics should the statements of problems and opportunities have?

5 OBJECTIVE SETTING AND INTRODUCTION TO STRATEGY FORMULATION

OVERVIEW

Armed with the results of the situation analysis, the marketing planner is ready to answer the question, "Where do we want to go?" The objectives—or, to be more precise, the objectives and goals—answer that question. This chapter deals with objective setting and its importance to the planning process. It distinguishes between objectives and goals and defines the characteristics that goals should possess.

Once the objectives and goals have been decided upon, the planner is ready to select the market or markets that will be targeted and to design the marketing mix strategies that will attract them. This chapter introduces the concept of **market segmentation**, a way of subdividing markets into unique groups of consumers who will respond similarly to a particular marketing strategy. It also introduces the **product/market expansion matrix,** one of the tools that describes four strategies open to a marketer.

To relate this process to the real world, the chapter describes an eight-step procedure that a community bank might follow in developing a marketing plan. It then looks at two very different examples of marketing planning (*Cases B* and *F*): a product marketing plan and a total bank marketing plan. While the two are very different in scope, each contains the basic elements of a marketing plan: the situation analysis, objectives, target market identification, marketing strategies, and plans for evaluating results.

OBJECTIVE SETTING

Terminology

Before proceeding with a discussion of objective setting, a few terms need defining. Up to this point, the term *objective* has been used in a broad sense. As the details of the planning process are discussed in more detail, two levels of objectives will be dealt with. The first is called *objectives*, and the second is called *goals*.

Generally speaking, an **objective** is a broad statement of direction (such as: "to become the leading bank in the corporate market in our state"), while **goals** are statements of the specific, measurable results that are to be attained in the pursuit of that objective (such as: "to increase commercial loan volume by 15 percent"). While this is a useful distinction and one that will be used in this text, it is not universally accepted and, in fact, the two terms are often used interchangeably.

To further complicate the problem, both terms (which have to do with *results*) are often mistakenly used to describe *actions* taken in order to attain certain results. For example, the statement, "Each calling officer will make five new business calls per week," is an action, a tactic, not an objective or a goal.

This leads us to our next pair of terms: **strategy** and **tactics.** These, too, are frequently used interchangeably, although they have quite different meanings—as any military person will tell you. Strategy and tactics make up an action plan (as opposed to objectives and goals, which set the direction). Strategy describes the *route* the bank will take to get to its destination. Tactics define the specific *actions* to be taken and further define by whom they will be taken, when, and at what cost. Put another way, strategy defines *what* will be done; tactics concern *how* it will be done. To use a road trip example, the *objective* is to take a vacation; the *goal* is to reach Niagara Falls; the *strategy* is to map out a sequence of specific highways. The *tactics* define when we leave, which car we take, who will drive, and when we plan to get there. Exhibit 5-1 defines and compares these four terms.

Importance of Setting Objectives and Goals

Armed with the situation analysis, which tells management where the bank stands now and what the conditions in the marketing environment are, the bank must determine which problems and opportunities it wants to address and how it will go about doing that. This step is not necessarily easy, but it is critical. There are at least five good reasons for making the effort to establish objectives.

1. *They are a guide for planning strategies and tactics.* A destination must be defined before deciding how to get there. Likewise, in bank marketing planning, management must decide where the bank should go before it can set the marketing strategies and tactics to get it there. As mentioned earlier, "if you don't know where you want to go, any road will take you there."

2. *They form the basis for the budgeting process.* Once the strategies and tactics for accomplishing the bank's objectives are decided upon, their execution can be costed out. In the process of doing this, management will be able to compare the projected income and expenses related to the attainment of each objective. It is not unusual at this stage for management to find that the accomplishment of some objective is not justified by the anticipated results. At that point, it is necessary to either adjust to a less costly strategy or set of tactics, or to reorder the priorities.

3. *They form the basis for evaluating performance.* You cannot appraise how well something has been done if you do not know what was supposed to be accomplished. Bank marketing experts Joselyn and Humphries[1] use an excellent example of two football coaches, one with a 6-win/5-loss record and one with a 5-win/6-loss record. Which one did the better job? One cannot answer that question without being given additional information. In fact, the one with the 5–6 record was given a three-year contract while the other coach's contract was not renewed. The reason in each case has to do with

Exhibit 5-1	**The Terminology of Marketing Strategy**	
Term	*Meaning*	*Example*
Objective	Broad statement of mission or direction	"To become the leading cash management bank for the middle market in this region"
Goal	The specific measurable results to be attained in pursuit of the objective	"Achieve a 25 percent penetration of middle market companies using cash management services within 3 years"
Strategy	The specific method devised for achieving the goal	• Hire experienced product managers to improve products • Add to the sales force • Price well under the top of the market • Train lenders to refer cash management prospects • Establish a reward system
Tactic	The specific actions to be taken	• Add two product managers by July 1 • Begin product reviews with Account Reconciliation and Balance Reporting; plans due September 1 • Develop and implement cash management training program by September 1 • Prepare proposal for incentive program by August 15

performance relative to goals. The 6-5 team had been picked to win its conference, but it failed to reach its goal. The 5-6 team had not won at all the previous year, so winning 5 games represented a tremendous turnaround. Likewise, one cannot determine how well a bank has done if the goals have not been set in advance.

4. *They form the basis for determining corrective action when goals are exceeded or not met.* If objectives are being exceeded ahead of schedule or not being met, the bank has a basis for examining its situation analysis, strategies, tactics, and objectives in order to see where the weakness lies. Without the objectives, the bank would not know whether its strategies and tactics are working.

5. *They can help build team spirit.* By communicating the bank's broad objectives and then bringing the goal-setting process right down

through every level of the bank, each member of the staff sees his or her role in the bank's mission. Also, everyone recognizes that all the other employees are working toward the same objectives and that all are involved in a cooperative effort. By and large, employees like to see a purpose in what they are doing on the job every day. In fact, conscientious employees will frequently set their own unofficial objectives in the absence of clear direction from management. Since these goals may not be consistent with management's, it is far better to involve all personnel in the overall objective-setting process to ensure that everybody's efforts (that is, tactics) are being channeled in the right direction.

Categories of Objectives

In addition to the distinction between objectives and goals, there are three categories of objectives. They are the mission statement, the corporate objectives, and the marketing objectives. (See Exhibit 5-2.)

A **mission statement** is a set of broad objectives that every bank's board of directors should develop. Once completed, the statement changes very little over time. It might consist of objectives such as:

- Our bank is dedicated to meeting the financial needs of the people and businesses of Overland County.
- Our ultimate objective is to maximize shareholder value.

Corporate objectives are those set by the bank's executive management. They are broad statements of direction for the bank that are based primarily on input from the bank's financial statements. They tend to be long range in their focus. Some examples might be:

- to achieve a 1 percent return on average assets;
- to increase the ratio of interest-sensitive assets in the bank's portfolio; and
- to take a balanced position between the retail and commercial sectors of the business.

These corporate objectives should be communicated throughout the bank in order to establish a common purpose and to form the basis for setting marketing objectives.

Exhibit 5-2 **Categories of Objectives**

Category	Example
Mission statement	"To achieve a balanced position between the retail and commercial sectors of the business"
Corporate objective	"To increase revenue from cash management services"
Marketing objective	"To become the leading cash management bank for the middle market in this region"

Marketing objectives are also of a general nature, but they are set by senior and middle management and are based on the corporate objectives as well as upon input from the situation analysis. Their focus may be short term (one year or less) or longer. Some examples might be:

- to increase the proportion of variable rate credit in the consumer loan portfolio;
- to increase commercial loans relative to total loans;
- to create an image of being a strong hometown bank with a dedicated commitment to the local community; and
- to increase the use of bank services by existing customers.

All of these objectives will involve marketing efforts; that is, pricing, personal selling, promotion, and possibly product strategy and distribution strategy. Executing these objectives will involve many of the operating areas of the bank.

Characteristics of Goals

Goals are the very specific and measurable targets set by everyone from senior management all the way down through the organization. They take the marketing objectives a step further and add measurable results. Some examples might be:

- to achieve (within 6 months) a 40 percent recognition level in the marketplace that the bank is the only county bank represented in all 3 major cities;

- to increase the average number of services used per customer from 1.3 to 1.7 within one year;
- to increase commercial loans by 25 percent by year end; and
- to increase service charge income by 15 percent for the year.

Joselyn and Humphries[2] cite three characteristics of goals that should always be kept in mind when developing them:

1. *Goals must be developed in such a way as to accomplish the bank's corporate and marketing objectives.*

2. *Every individual should have a goal that is realistic within the context of his or her job.* Informing a teller that the bank's goal is to increase deposits by 20 percent is a waste of time. A more realistic goal might be to cross-sell at least three customers per week. The teller now has something to strive for that is within his or her capability.

3. *Goals must be flexible.* The bank must have an ongoing system for monitoring goal achievement. If a goal turns out to be unrealistic, the standards must be revised. If goals are realistic but not being met, corrective action can be taken.

To these, we add a fourth characteristic:

- *Goals should stretch the bank and each department in it to excellence.* That loan officer described in chapter 1 had consistently set as a goal, and met, a 10 percent increase in loan volume. His successor aimed much higher and achieved a 50 percent gain. The goal should relate to the market potential, and be realistic yet challenging.

INTRODUCTION TO STRATEGY FORMULATION

Once the bank's management has decided where it wants to go by setting objectives and goals, it is time to develop an action plan—a marketing strategy. This part of the planning process answers the question, "How are we going to get there?" A marketing strategy is simply the specific mix of product, price, promotion, and place (distribution) strategies aimed at meeting the needs of a target group of customers and/or prospects (that is, a market segment) in order to meet the bank's objectives and goals. Thus, the strategizing is a two-step process: first, the selection of the target market or markets, and then, the designing of the marketing mix strategies to attract them.

Segmentation and Target Market Selection

Market segmentation recognizes the wisdom of specializing to suit the needs of a segment of the market rather than trying to be "all things to all people." A company claiming that its product represents both the highest prestige and the lowest price has not identified its target market. It is probably being outstripped in the marketplace by other products promoted as being either prestigious or low-priced, but not both. The problem with trying to be all things to all people is that buyers in the market for the same product (for example, bank services, wristwatches, automobiles) are far from homogeneous with respect to how they want their needs and desires satisfied. Consequently, they differ in how they respond to specific marketing mixes. Market segmentation subdivides a market into more or less homogeneous subsets of customers, where any subset could be selected as a market target to be reached with a distinct marketing mix.[3]

There are many firms that have segmented their markets so successfully that they have dramatically influenced their industry. For instance, Timex is famous for having identified a market segment made up of people who desire an inexpensive, stylish, and durable watch. Timex proved that not everyone wants an expensive, elegantly styled watch with a high-prestige brand name.

In contrast, the manufacturer of Rolex watches targets an entirely different segment with its product and marketing mix strategies. The Rolex is priced in four figures, and its advertising is identified with success and prestige.

Since the object of market segmentation is to identify a specific user group and then pursue it with tailored product, pricing, promotion, and distribution strategies, market segments must have certain qualities that make it possible to specialize the marketing approach. They must be measurable, accessible, and substantial.[4] In other words, it must be possible to measure the size and purchasing power of the market segment. In addition, it must be feasible to reach members of that segment through advertising and distribution methods. And finally, the segment must be substantial or sizable enough to generate a profitable volume.

There are a number of different approaches to market segmentation. The approach a particular firm or bank chooses should enable the market to be segmented into target markets or groups of customers and prospects who differ considerably from one another in needs and wants. The various types of segmentation alternatives that a firm or bank might follow will be described in chapter 8.

Marketing Strategy and Tactics

Once the target market or markets have been identified, the process of determining which marketing mix strategies should be followed and which tactics should be used is a two-stage operation that requires considerable thought, much evaluation of alternatives, and plenty of imagination. The two stages are discussed below.

Marketing Strategy

The basic elements in the market mix are the bank's products and the specific groups of people to whom those products will be aimed. Once it is determined *what* will be sold *to whom*, the pricing, promotion, and distribution strategies will fall into place more easily.

Given any single objective or goal, there are any number of paths that can be followed for attaining it. One of the many tools that can help the marketing manager identify the alternative product and segmentation strategies that are possible is the *product/market expansion matrix*. (See Exhibit 5-3.) This matrix specifies the product and market mixes that the bank can use to establish its strategy for meeting its objectives and goals. Basically, it indicates that a firm can grow by selling more of its present products to present customers or to new customers, or by selling new products to present customers or to new customers.

As an example, let us assume that the personal credit product manager is seeking alternative ways to increase loan outstandings. The first task is to identify where on this matrix the bank is currently

Exhibit 5-3 **Product/Market Expansion Matrix**

Products Markets	Present	New
Present	**Market Penetration** Improve bank's position with present products in present markets	**Product Expansion** Develop new products for present markets
New	**Market Expansion** Find new markets to use bank's present products	**Diversification or Product/Market Expansion** Develop new products for new markets

concentrating the bulk of its energies. (This would have been defined as part of the situation analysis.)

Next, the matrix can be used to show that the product manager has four possible options: concentrate on one sector or move in all four directions simultaneously. The options, speaking very generally, are market penetration, market expansion, product expansion, and diversification.

Market Penetration (selling present products to present markets)

For example, one might choose to cross-sell personal lines of credit to present installment loan customers or sell new loans to present borrowers who have very few payments remaining. Many other examples of this type of strategy could and should be enumerated as part of the strategy-setting process.

Market Expansion (selling present products to new markets)

One way this might be done is through physical expansion, such as establishing a loan production office in a new territory. It might also involve finding new customers within the bank's present trade area. Some examples might include selling home equity loans through a direct mail solicitation to homeowners who meet certain income and property value criteria; running ads for a loan sale in the local media to attract a greater-than-average share of new auto and personal loans; or offering an incentive to encourage employees to bring in new loan customers.[5]

Product Expansion (developing and selling new products to present markets)

Product expansion might be accomplished by becoming a credit card-issuing bank or by designing a new installment loan product. An example would be the variable rate loan that enables the borrower to take advantage of anticipated reductions in general interest rates. In this way, the bank can offer new services to present customers and very likely attract new ones.

Diversification or Product/Market Expansion (developing and selling new products to new markets)

Following this strategy, the bank would develop new products intended to attract specific new markets. For instance, the installment loan product manager might decide to go after the high net worth market segment. Since these individuals borrow for investment and other purposes requiring larger-than-average sums of money, the product manager might propose the development of a $50,000 to $250,000 line of credit to be marketed to this group. *Case B* is an example of a product/market expansion strategy.

From these examples, we can see that there are several strategies that might be selected in pursuit of a specific objective, and that considerable time, thought, and imagination should be devoted to answering the question, "How are we going to get there?" It is all too easy for bankers and other professionals to fall into the routine of coming up with the same stale approaches year after year, without stretching their sights or their imaginations. The product/market expansion matrix can help stimulate this thought process.

Marketing Tactics

Tactics describe specific actions to be taken, by whom they will be taken, when, and at what cost. In order for the various elements of the marketing strategy to be implemented, a number of individuals will have to perform a variety of activities (in line with their job responsibilities) that are oriented toward the bank's objectives. (See *Case F*.) Ideally, every employee in the bank should have specific goals (which are really tactics) related to the accomplishment of the bank's strategy for achieving its objectives. If the objective is to increase the average number of services used per customer, the teller's goal/tactic might be to cross-sell a specific service three times per week, while the branch manager's goal/tactic might be to hold regular training sessions for the tellers to increase their understanding of the bank's products and services. The bank might choose to provide incentives to further motivate employees to reach or exceed their goals. (The use of incentives is a sales promotion strategy, as will be shown in chapter 13.)

STRATEGY FORMULATION IN ACTION

There are many variations in the way the planning process takes place from bank to bank, and the process varies depending upon a number of factors. The marketing planning process is affected by everything from the size of the institution, to the personality of the chief executive officer, to the status of marketing in the organization. Nevertheless, it is possible to talk about a model situation and to identify eight steps for establishing objectives, goals, strategies, and tactics within a bank.

The Eight-Step Process

The marketing director's role in these steps will vary from bank to bank. In some banks, he or she will organize and coordinate the entire process. In others, that role may be played by the planning director or another member of senior management.

The process should be started mid-year, after the presentation of the situation analysis. The reason for this early start is that the end result will be a written plan and a budget, and since bank budgets are generally finalized in October or November, the planning process must begin sufficiently before that time to allow for all the required steps to be completed thoroughly. The eight steps are as follows:

Step 1: The bank's corporate objectives should be reviewed by all managers. All banks have corporate objectives; however, it might be that they have not been clearly articulated and communicated. This must be done before going any further.

Step 2: Review both the corporate objectives and the situation analysis with all management personnel together. Ask each manager to prepare a set of recommended objectives for his or her area of responsibility. These will, at this stage, be general, but they will force individuals to review their own situations in light of the bank's overall situation and corporate objectives. Set a date for turning in these recommendations. If any revision in the situation analysis or corporate objectives is needed, it should be done at this point.

Step 3: Have each manager go back to his or her department and, working with the senior staff, develop broad objectives and general strategy for the department. These are to be submitted at the time specified at the meeting in step 2.

Step 4: Review each manager's recommended objectives individually to determine if they are consistent with the mission and corporate objectives and are realistic. For example, if population is declining, it may be unrealistic to set an objective calling for a 10 percent increase in retail deposits. Then, negotiate revisions and set a second date for meeting with all management to discuss specific objectives and goals, along with general strategies proposed to reach them. It is important at this point to have some idea as to the level of resources required to achieve recommended objectives.

Step 5: Meet with managers to finalize the objectives and related goals for each area of the bank. At this meeting, the managers will become aware of one another's objectives and goals and root out potential inconsistencies in the marketing plan. For instance, the consumer deposit product manager (or the head of retail banking) may want to increase the account base by promoting overdraft checking. The credit product manager, however, may be attempting to reduce credit losses by curtailing unsecured personal credit. At this meeting, top management can also allocate resources among alternative programs. By looking at the combined plans and the estimated resources required, it is possible to weigh potential gains in light of available resources.

Step 6: The managers should go back to their departments and work out specific strategies and tactics for accomplishing the goals. These are costed out, responsibility is assigned, and methods of measurement and control are determined.

Step 7: The managers will submit their budgets, which are then consolidated, to come up with a projected bottom line. In many cases, the results may not be acceptable to management the first time around. Therefore, budgets are reviewed with the various managers individually, and revisions are negotiated.

Step 8: Department heads and staff will develop the specific tactics and goals for each staff member in order to help execute the strategy. These may be put into a management-by-objectives format, so it will be clear what is required of each employee, as well as when the specific actions are to be completed and how performance will be measured. This will be discussed in more detail in the chapter on performance monitoring and evaluation.

Application to a Bank Marketing Plan

At this point, the reader should refer to *Case F* and the hypothetical Consumers National Bank to see how some of their objectives, goals, strategies, and tactics might look. This example is given for illustrative purposes only. It is not intended to be all-inclusive, and it focuses only on some of the retail deposit and commercial loan objectives of the bank. In Section II of *Case F,* four corporate objectives are presented. Although they are quite general, they clearly set the direction for the bank.

In addition, just 12 marketing objectives have been chosen. Notice that each of these objectives deals with a particular direction without saying what the specific destination is to be. They talk about "increasing" and "creating" without setting specific targets. That is left for the section in which goals for attaining those objectives are listed. Each of the objectives has been carried a step further, and a specific, measurable goal has been set. Furthermore, the dates by which the goals are to be achieved and the persons responsible for them have been identified and named.

Section III shows the beginning of an action plan for the achievement of these goals. A strategy is set, and then the tactics needed to implement it are spelled out. Again, the timing, the resource commitment, and the responsibility are clearly defined.

The next stages in the process—implementation and performance monitoring and evaluation—will be dealt with in chapter 15. However, a few words are in order at this point. The reader will recall that in chapter 1, it was stated that one can tell whether a bank (or any organization) has reached the ultimate phase of marketing enlightenment by determining whether it has installed systems for market analysis, planning, and *control*. In chapter 2, it was said that the marketing management process involves planning, implementation, and *evaluation of results*. At the risk of overemphasizing this point, it should be repeated again that measurement, evaluation, and control are necessary elements in the planning process because without it, the bank will not know when it has arrived at its destination. Without this step, the ongoing process of planning comes to a grinding halt.

It is to be anticipated that, in most marketing planning cases, the plan will not work as expected. Conditions change; people do not respond as expected; something does not work. By instituting an adequate program for monitoring the progress of the plan, the bank can identify problem areas and the reasons for them in order to make "in-flight" corrections to get the plan back on course. The plan must include a control mechanism—a monitoring system. Reports serve this purpose and are a necessary by-product of the planning process. Their frequency (weekly, monthly, quarterly) will depend upon the nature of the task involved. The more strategic the object of control or the more senior the person responsible, the less frequent the need for reports. Conversely, the more tactical the object of control and the more line-related the function, the more frequent the reports.

Application to a Product Marketing Plan

The planning process remains essentially the same regardless of the scope of the plan. This is demonstrated in *Case B,* which presents a marketing plan for a new home equity credit line for the hypothetical Marlton National Bank. All the elements of marketing strategy formulation are there in Sections II and III of the plan, which was prepared by the consumer credit product manager.

First, the corporate objectives that were agreed upon by the directors in approving the bank's 5-year retail plan specified their desire to increase the ratio of interest-sensitive assets in the bank's portfolio, and also to achieve a profit margin of at least 2 percent on consumer credit products.

The situation analysis had been conducted, and the summary of problems and opportunities was reviewed. As a result of this analysis, the product manager developed five marketing objectives and identified nine specific goals to be attained in working toward them. These objectives will require activity by product management, the advertising department, the marketing research department, the training department, accounting, and the consumer loan operations division. In other words, the accomplishment of the marketing objectives cuts across several areas within the bank.

The product manager, in this case, presents the detailed marketing strategy and tactics in Section III of the plan. The general marketing strategy being used is product and market expansion—the design of a new product to appeal to a specific new target market. While there are members of this target market within the bank's current customer base, the objective is to attract new customers to the bank who fit the description of high income heads of full-nest households.

The detailed marketing strategy spells out the product, pricing, promotion, and distribution strategies and tactics to be used in introducing the new home equity line of credit, as well as the areas responsible for them. For instance, the tactics to be used in executing the "niche" promotional strategy include specific plans for advertising, point-of-sale, direct mail, and telemarketing. Similarly, the distribution strategy specifies tactics for ensuring that the product is cross-sold by the bank staff who are in a position to do so.

Finally, the plan specifies the ways in which progress toward the nine goals will be measured and reported. It makes clear who is responsible for generating the reports and to whom they are to be provided.

When a plan such as this has been finalized, it is useful for the manager to prepare a chart such as the one in Exhibit 5-4. This chart shows, at a glance, the timetable for the various tactical elements and measurement of results. It might be posted in the marketing department where it would serve as a reminder both for management and all relevant staff members of the goals of the program and what should be happening at any time. In the ideal situation, the plan for the home equity credit line will be incorporated into the marketing plan for all retail installment loans, and these will become part of the total bank marketing plan.

In a bank that has not yet become planning oriented, such a one-product marketing plan can be completed for one department with great success. Managers who use this management process (which is what planning is) will distinguish themselves as the catalysts for getting planning initiated, and the process may ultimately spread to other departments throughout the bank.

SUMMARY

The objective-setting process answers the question, "Where are we going?" The term *objectives* encompasses both objectives and goals. Objectives are broad statements of direction, while goals are statements of the specific measurable results to be attained in pursuing an objective. Objectives and goals guide the planning of strategies and tactics; they form the basis for the budgeting process, for evaluating performance, and for determining corrective action; they also help build team spirit.

Mission statements are the broadest objectives, and they are generally set by the directors of an institution. Corporate objectives are long-range objectives that are also broad in scope but which tend to be financially oriented. Marketing objectives flow from the corporate objectives and may be long- or short-term in scope.

Exhibit 5-4 Home Equity Credit Line Marketing Strategy Overview (Case B)

Task	Jan 5	12	19	26	Feb 2	9	16	23	Mar 2	9	16	23	30	Apr 6	13	20	27	May 4	11	18	25	June 1	8	15	22	29	Responsibility
Advertising																											
Print									X	X		X		X			X			X							Advertising Mgr.
Distribute POS								X																			
Stuff inserts																											
Statement message																											
Direct mail																											Sales Promo. Mgr.
Telemarketing																											
Research																											
Ad tracking study report due																		X									Research Mgr.
Demographics tracking reports due																	X									X	
Product Management																											
Monthly report														X			X	X				X					Product Mgr.
Distribution Strategy																											
Product training materials						X																					Product Mgr.
Kickoff party						X																					Product Mgr.
Conduct training									X																		Training Mgr.
Pre- and post-test results																											Training Mgr.
Account officer mailing								X																			Product Mgr.
Reports due to Marketing																											
Volume & outstandings										X	X	X	X	X	X	X	X	X	X	X	X	X	X	X	X	X	Consumer loans
Approval ratio										X	X	X	X	X	X	X	X	X	X	X	X	X	X	X	X	X	Consumer loans

Goals are specific and measurable and should have certain characteristics: they should help the bank achieve its corporate and marketing objectives; they should extend to each individual and be realistic within the context of each individual's job; they should be flexible; and they should stretch the bank and everyone in it to excellence.

Through strategy formulation, the bank answers the question, "How are we going to get there?" Strategizing consists of two steps: target market selection and the designing of the marketing mix to reach the selected targets. Markets must first be studied so that they can be segmented into groups that are unique and that will react in the same way to a given marketing mix strategy. Once segmented, the bank can choose the segment or segments that will be targeted with its marketing strategies and tactics. There are many possible strategies open to the marketing planner, and one of the tools that can help the marketer think through the paths that might be followed is the product/market expansion matrix. This matrix encompasses four strategies known as market penetration, market expansion, product expansion, and diversification.

Marketing tactics are the specific actions that are to be taken when executing the marketing strategy. Their description should include the identification of who will undertake them and at what cost.

The planning process may vary from bank to bank and situation to situation, but the essential ingredients that should always be included in one way or another are the situation analysis, objectives and goals, target market identification, strategies and tactics, and the procedures for the measurement and evaluation of results.

POINTS FOR REVIEW

1. Define or briefly explain each of the following terms:
   - goal
   - market segmentation
   - mission statement
   - corporate objective
   - marketing objective

2. What are the four elements that constitute a marketing strategy?

3. What is the difference between a goal and a tactic?

4. For each of the following, indicate whether the statement is an objective, goal, strategy, or tactic:

   - to achieve a 1 percent return on assets
   - to be a consumer-oriented bank
   - to make three prospect calls per week
   - to develop a travel and entertainment card for professionals and business managers
   - to increase share of total deposits by 5 percent
   - to increase noninterest income by 25 percent
   - to impose service charges on low-balance, high-activity savings accounts

5. Indicate which type of strategy (that is, product expansion, market expansion, market penetration, or diversification) is represented by each of the following:

   - stock brokerage firms offering checking accounts
   - bank holding companies operating equipment leasing subsidiaries
   - direct mail marketing of bank credit cards across state lines
   - establishing a new branch outside the bank's trade area
   - using direct mail to promote the bank's equity credit line to trade area residents who are not customers

6. Suggest a useful way to segment the markets for each of the following:

   - cigarettes
   - shampoo
   - installment loans

PART III UNDERSTANDING THE MARKET

In part II, the strategic marketing process and the first two steps in the process—the situation analysis and the setting of objectives—were discussed in detail. Part III deals with the next step, a key element in the development of marketing strategy: selection of the market or markets that will be targeted in the pursuit of the organization's objectives.

As previously mentioned, the marketer must segment the market into groups that will respond in a similar way to a given marketing strategy. This task requires the marketer to have some understanding of what causes one group of people to react differently from other groups when exposed to the same strategy. In other words, the marketer must be a student of consumer behavior, whether the consumer is an individual or an organization.

This section of the text, then, deals with consumer and organizational buying behavior and the stages in the buying process. It also discusses **market research**—the tool used by the marketer to understand and measure potential target markets. It concludes with a discussion of a number of strategies for segmenting markets and for positioning the product offering in order to maximize appeal to the target audience.

6 CONSUMER AND ORGANIZATIONAL BUYING BEHAVIOR

How do individuals select a bank? When asked this question, people most frequently answered that they chose their bank because it was convenient for them. But in most cities and towns, there are a number of banks—sometimes as many as one on every corner of the main intersection. What motivates one person to choose the one on the northeast corner and another the one on the southeast corner? Clearly, there is more at work in the decision to "buy" a bank than whether it is convenient to the customer. Some of the other factors that enter into the decision-making process can be determined through skillful questioning of the customer. However, there are other factors at work that no amount of direct questioning will uncover because the customer is not even aware of them. Yet, these factors will move a person to act in a way that is different from that of one's next-door neighbor. The following sections deal with those factors that move or motivate people and organizations to behave as they do.

This chapter provides some background information culled from psychology and other behavioral sciences that will help the bank marketer gain a better understanding of why a consumer acts in a certain manner. Understanding why, what, and how people buy is the foundation for developing new bank products, advertising, distribution channels, personal selling, and related activities designed to meet customers' needs. Without some understanding of consumer behavior and the consumer buying process, bank marketers implementing a chosen marketing mix strategy are proceeding without direction.

MOTIVATION AND CONSUMER BEHAVIOR

A number of basic psychological concepts are fundamental to an understanding of consumer behavior. A good place to start is with the concept of **motivation**, which is defined as "all those inner striving conditions described as wishes and desires. It is an inner state that activates or moves."[1]

All behavior is motivated, and psychologists generally agree that people have reasons for doing the things they do. They contend that all human behavior is goal directed and revolves around the desire to satisfy needs.

The motivation process is illustrated in Exhibit 6-1. An unsatisfied need is the starting point in the process. It is the spark that initiates the chain of events leading to a certain behavior. A need that is unsatisfied (or not adequately satisfied) causes tension within the individual, as when the basic need for water is unmet. This desire causes the individual to engage in some kind of search behavior; that is, to seek a means to satisfy the need and thus reduce the tension. For example, a thirsty person *needs* water, and, motivated by a desire for the liquid, searches for a way to satisfy that need. Motivation, then, is a continual process, beginning with an unsatisfied need and ending with that need being met. Goal-directed search behavior is part of that process.

Different Needs as Motivators of Behavior

Many different kinds of needs are motivators of human behavior. One of the most widely adopted classification schemes is known as the **hierarchy of needs**, developed by psychologist A.H. Maslow.[2] His theory of motivation stresses two fundamental premises:

1. Man is a wanting animal whose needs depend on what he already has. This means that only needs not yet satisfied can influence behavior. A satisfied need is not a motivator.

2. Man's needs are arranged in a hierarchy of importance. In other words, once one need is satisfied, another, higher-level need emerges and demands satisfaction.

Maslow describes five classes of needs in order of importance:

1. physiological
2. security
3. belongingness
4. esteem
5. self-actualization

Exhibit 6-2 illustrates this hierarchy of needs.

Physiological

This category consists of the primary physical needs of the human body, such as food, water, and sex. When all other needs are unsatisfied, these needs will, nevertheless, dominate. In such cases, no higher-level need can serve as a basis for motivation. To cite an extreme case, people who are fighting starvation will not be motivated by a need to belong to a status group; they may even engage in behavior that lowers self-esteem because of the greater need for nourishment.

Security and Safety

This second most important level of needs consists of protection from things such as physical harm, ill health, economic disaster, and other unexpected crises. Many banking services address these needs, and bank advertisements often play up to them: "Going on vacation? Will your valuables be safe while you're away? For only pennies a day, you can rent a safe deposit box."

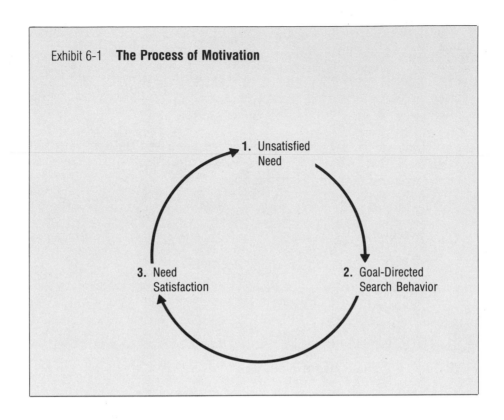

Exhibit 6-1   **The Process of Motivation**

1. Unsatisfied
   Need

2. Goal-Directed
   Search Behavior

3. Need
   Satisfaction

Belongingness and Love

These needs are related to the social nature of human beings and the need for companionship. This level and those above it are usually referred to as higher-level needs, and a failure to satisfy them may affect the mental health of an individual. When banks market credit cards through organizations such as major-league sports teams, university alumni associations, labor unions, and other affinity groups, they are appealing to the belongingness need of the target audience.

Esteem

This category encompasses both the awareness of one's own importance to others, or self-esteem, and the esteem demonstrated by others. Satisfaction of esteem needs leads to feelings of self-confidence and prestige. The practice of assigning a personal banker to each customer addresses esteem needs. Personal trust services appeal both to security and esteem needs because they contribute to the self-esteem derived from making provisions for one's heirs.

Self-Actualization

This refers to the need to fully realize one's potential talents and capabilities. Whether someone is a corporate executive, an athlete, a clerk, or a parent, the objective is to be effective and efficient in that particular role. This drive can be satisfied only after all other needs in the hierarchy have been achieved. In our society, where the standard of living is high (relative to that of most other nations), the majority of consumers act at this level. This may help to explain, in part, the tremendous growth in the use of credit cards and personal loans, as people acquire the tools that will help them attain fuller self-actualization. The Army addresses the need for self-actualization when it urges young people to "be all that you can be."

In real life, the need categories are not so disparate. Rather, individuals whose lower-level physiological and security needs are met are usually partially satisfied and dissatisfied in each of the higher-need categories. In other words, at any one time, they are being motivated by needs at several levels. Furthermore, for some individuals, the order of the hierarchy may differ. Esteem needs may take priority over social needs, for example. The value of the needs hierarchy is that it provides a framework for understanding individual behavior and motivation.

Behavior is motivated by unsatisfied needs, but why do people with the same needs go about satisfying them in very different ways? What shapes their behavior? The answer lies in their individual perceptions.

PERCEPTION AND CONSUMER BEHAVIOR

The following situation occurs several times a day at banking offices throughout the country: Three individuals approach the bank, which is located at the end of a mini-mall, all needing to deposit a paycheck

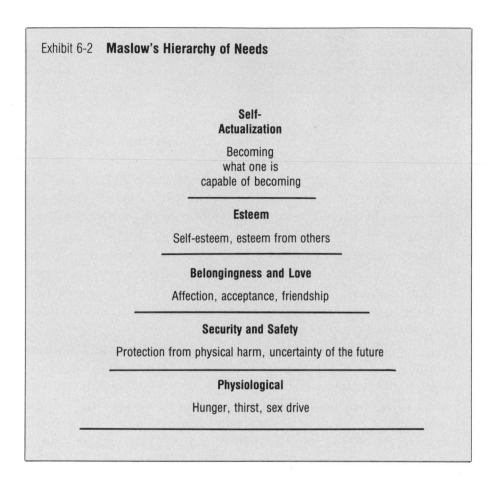

Exhibit 6-2   **Maslow's Hierarchy of Needs**

Self-Actualization

Becoming
what one is
capable of becoming

Esteem

Self-esteem, esteem from others

Belongingness and Love

Affection, acceptance, friendship

Security and Safety

Protection from physical harm, uncertainty of the future

Physiological

Hunger, thirst, sex drive

and obtain some cash. Two park their cars and walk through the front door, but one stops at the automated teller in the vestibule, where there is no one waiting in line. The other person enters the bank and waits in a short line in front of a teller station. The third customer pulls up to the drive-up window and waits behind four cars.

What motivates these varying modes of behavior? Why do people continue to buy one brand of soft drink, beer, or cigarettes when, while they are blindfolded, they cannot tell the difference between their regular brand and the competition's? The answer is that each individual brings a unique set of perceptions and attitudes to the process that influences behavior. **Perception** is the process by which people receive information (or stimuli) through the five senses, recognize it, and assign a meaning to it. How people perceive information depends on the nature of the information itself, on its context (that is, what surrounds it), and on conditions within themselves. Furthermore, there are three processes of **selectivity** going on within people at all times that limit perceptions. They are selective exposure, selective distortion, and selective retention.[3]

There are millions of stimuli in our surroundings every day, but people do not actually see most of them. Why is it that some are filtered out and others perceived? The answer is **selective exposure**, a process that explains the following:

- People are more likely to notice stimuli that relate to a current need. For example, people who are not in the market for a personal loan will not notice ads hyping low rates, but individuals who *are* shopping for a loan *will* notice these ads. Selective exposure explains the experience that most people have had at one time or another after buying something, such as a particular model car, and then noticing that seemingly half the cars seen on the road are of that same model.

- People are more likely to notice stimuli that they anticipate. This is especially important to bank marketers who are promoting non-traditional bank services, as people will not notice the discount brokerage desk or the insurance desk because they do not expect it to be there.

- People are more likely to notice stimuli that are large in relation to the normal size of the stimuli. For example, in a low-interest-rate environment, people are more likely to notice an ad showing a 10 percent rate than one showing a rate that is a half point above the norm.

Selective distortion, on the other hand, is the tendency people have to twist information to make it conform to their existing perceptions. In light of this inclination, marketers should understand the target audience's perception of the product or service being marketed and play into that perception, not contradict it. A bank should avoid saying something that is not consistent with the target's perception.

The second-tier bank that advertises, "We're the leading bank . . ." violates this precept. Since the message does not conform to what most people believe, the ad will probably not be noticed. For years, the largest thrift institution in a major metropolitan area paid the highest rates on savings. With the onset of deregulation, the institution started to pay rates that were comparable to the commercial banks. Yet, in research surveys, consumers continued to rate this bank as the institution with the highest interest rates. Despite the obvious facts, which could be verified by looking in the paper and comparing rates, the statistics could not alter consumers' long-developed perception that this bank was the best place to save.

Selective retention means that people retain only part of what is selectively received and that they are more likely to retain information that supports their existing attitudes and beliefs. Research has shown that consumers are much more likely to remember ads for their own bank than for those that they do not do business with because the ads support their choice of bank.

The job of the marketer—especially the advertiser—is to achieve selective exposure that falls within the perception range of the target market. This means selecting the appropriate media (for example, the right radio stations, newspapers, TV shows) and presenting a strong message that will be meaningful enough to be retained.

The factors that influence the way people perceive stimuli fall into four categories: the *social* factors and *cultural* factors (that influence us from the outside), and the *psychological* factors and *personal* factors (that affect us from within).

Social Factors

The way people see things and the way they behave is influenced quite extensively by the people to whom we relate (social factors). The major social factors influencing buyer behavior are *family, reference groups,* and *roles and status.*

Family Influence

Of all the groups that may have an influence on consumer behavior, the family is the most fundamental. Many of an individual's basic values are shaped by the family. Some examples of these values are attitudes toward material wealth, thrift, and human relations. In addition to being a basic shaper of values and attitudes, the family is also a strong reference group whose behavior is copied, especially by the young. In new customer surveys, when asked why they chose a certain bank, many respondents cited the fact that "my family has always banked here."

Reference Group Influence

A group that an individual seeks answers from when forming attitudes and opinions is described as a **reference group**. A person normally relies on several reference groups for information on various subjects or different decisions. For example, a person may use one reference group for purchasing food and another when seeking financial services or buying a car. The individual need not actually belong to these reference groups but may aspire to belong to them. Sports stars and other role models may constitute a reference group of one. When it comes to banking, people may look to opinion leaders and other professionals such as attorneys and accountants as guides in choosing a financial institution. Therefore, it is important that a bank's marketing strategy identify and reach those reference groups used by personal and corporate clients.

Roles and Status

Each individual belongs to many groups and has a specific position or role within each. Within a family, a person might function as a wife and mother; in a business organization, that same person may be a sales manager and a supervisor; and in the church, she might be a Sunday school teacher and a choir member. Each role can affect how the individual behaves when purchasing the tools related to that role.

Individuals in general are anxious to achieve greater status in a given role, and this desire also affects their buying behavior. Some products appeal directly to this desire for status. For instance, an ad might imply that good mothers keep a certain brand of children's aspirin handy at all times. Another ad might claim that carrying a certain credit card is a sign of success.

Cultural Factors

Human perceptions and behavior are also profoundly influenced by the particular culture in which people live. Cultural influences are felt from the culture at large, from a number of subcultures, and from social class.

Culture

Culture encompasses the concepts, habits, skills, art, institutions, and values of a given group of people at a particular place and time. People the world over have the same basic needs, but how they go about satisfying them varies greatly as a result of their diverse cultures. The United States is currently undergoing many cultural changes that affect consumer behavior including:

- the changing role of women and the impact on home and family life and on household income;
- the movement away from thrift and saving to spending freely and buying on credit;
- the increased emphasis on the quality of life; and
- the changing attitudes toward work and leisure.

An example of the influence of culture on banking behavior can be seen in the attitudes toward saving that different generations have held. People who emigrated to this country scrimped and saved to get here, and then saved even more to buy a house and to put down roots. As a result, their children were brought up with a savings ethic. Many first-generation Americans remember being taken to the bank when they could not even reach the teller counter in order to put their small savings into their own account. However, each succeeding generation is farther removed from the original culture and less likely to place as high a value on saving as the prior generation.

Subculture

Within the broader culture, there are smaller subcultures. These may be based on common regional, religious, ethnic, or racial characteristics. For example, a fried chicken franchise may find it necessary to use a different recipe in the North than in the South. Procter and Gamble has a special "western blend" of Folger's coffee because industry research has shown that people in the West drink a much higher percentage of black coffee than do people in other areas. The taste differences and other discernible variances among these sub-cultures often provide the basis for market segmentation.

Social Class

Most societies, including our own, exhibit some kind of stratification that we refer to as *class*. In some societies, the class system is based on religion, kinship, or landed wealth. In this country, education, occupation, and neighborhood of residence are more the determinants of social class than the degree of wealth or level of income.[4]

Different social classes tend to have varying attitudes and values that are reflected in the consumer behavior of their members. Researchers have identified a five-group class structure comprised of the *upper class, upper middle class, middle class, working class*, and *lower class*. The middle and working classes combined make up the **mass market** in this country. They account for about 70 percent of the total market, but while members of these two groups may have comparable incomes, their source and use patterns are quite different. Exhibit 6-3 shows some differences between these groups that have been identified by researchers. It should be noted that these attributions are generalizations and do not apply to each and every member of a certain class.

Psychological Factors

While social and cultural factors influence an individual's buying behavior externally, other factors operate from within—namely, psychological and personal factors. Motivation and perception are psychological factors that are at the foundation of all behavior. However, additional psychological factors that come into play in consumer behavior are the learning effect of past experiences, and beliefs and attitudes.

Exhibit 6-3 **Differences Between the Two Classes That Comprise the Mass Market**

Middle Class	Working Class
white collar workers and small business owners	blue collar workers and service workers
larger, well-cared-for houses in middle-income neighborhoods	smaller houses in lower-middle-income neighborhoods
imitate upper classes; spend increasing income on moving up	spend on larger cars, more kitchen appliances, bigger television; spend more on sports
future oriented; broader horizons	community oriented; support local teams; buy American; vacation nearby

Source: Adapted from Richard P. Coleman, ''The Continuing Significance of Social Class,'' *Journal of Consumer Research*, December 1983, pp. 270–272.

Learning

The learning associated with behavior is not comparable to the learning associated with studying something. As applied here, learning means changing one's behavior on the basis of past experiences. When a child gets burned by a stove, he or she learns not to touch it, and the child's mother capitalizes on this learning experience by saying ''hot'' or ''no'' when the child approaches an iron or an electrical outlet.

One popular theory holds that learning is the result of four influences: drive, cues, response, and reinforcement. This theory, as shall be seen, aligns with the steps in the buying process. Consider a consumer with a drive to improve the interest return on his or her savings. This drive needs to be satisfied, but cues help determine just when and where this will be done. A TV commercial for high-interest certificates, or a friend's recommendation to open a certificate, might be the cues that stimulate the consumer's response. Reinforcement occurs when the experience involved in making the transaction and the ongoing experience of dealing with the bank is rewarding in terms of interest earned as well as treatment by bank staff. If the response is indeed gratifying, a connection is made between the cue and the response, and a behavior pattern is learned.

Consumers form brand loyalties when they continually experience rewarding responses. If this action is not ultimately rewarding, the consumer will be open to cues from another bank or from other sources.

Beliefs and Attitudes

A *belief* is a specific, deeply held conviction. A person might believe that savings institutions pay a great deal more interest than commercial banks. This belief will probably influence the person's behavior; that is, he or she will bank at a savings institution. Bank marketers who are well attuned to consumer beliefs are more likely to see when such beliefs are erroneous and, therefore, act to correct them. However, as a result of selective distortion, the dissemination of messages that conflict with people's beliefs must be produced in a way that will reduce the likelihood of target audience dismissal.

An *attitude,* on the other hand, is a positive or negative evaluation, feeling, or tendency toward something. While beliefs are like accepted facts (right or wrong), attitudes are more like feelings (good or bad). People have attitudes toward just about everything, and changing them is quite difficult. Attitudes toward thrift ("You should always save a fixed portion of your income"), or toward the use of credit ("It should be used only for emergencies or major purchases"), greatly affect banking behavior.

Since attitudes are so hard to change, it is usually more advisable to design products and services to coincide with existing attitudes rather than to change them. People selectively retain information when it supports their beliefs and attitudes, and this is an important tenet to remember when producing advertising messages.

Personal Factors

Age, position in the **family life cycle**, personal economic circumstances, occupation, lifestyle, as well as personality and self-concept, are some of the personal factors that influence consumer behavior.

Exhibit 6-4 The Family Life Cycle and Banking Purchases

Stage	Financial Situation	Banking Needs
1. Bachelor stage: young single people	Few financial burdens; recreation oriented	Low-cost checking; auto loan; credit card
2. Young married couples with no children	Better off financially now than in near future	Joint checking; savings account; credit card
3. Full nest I: youngest child under six	Home purchasing peak; liquid assets low; some working wives	Mortgage; credit card; revolving credit line; bill consolidation loan
4. Full nest II: youngest child six or over	Financial position better; many working wives	Savings; certificates of deposit; saving for college; checking; credit card
5. Full nest III: older couples with dependent children	Financial position still better; many working wives	Home improvement loans; equity credit lines; certificates of deposit; money market deposit accounts; IRA
6. Empty nest I: older married couples, no children at home, head of family still working	Home ownership at peak; interested in travel, recreation, self-education	Mortgage on second home; savings; certificates of deposit; IRA
7. Empty nest II: older married couples, no children at home; head of family retired	Drastic cut in income	Rollover IRA; monthly income checks on certificates of deposit; estate planning; direct deposit of Social Security check
8. Solitary survivor in labor force	Income still good but likely to sell home	Savings; certificates of deposit
9. Solitary survivor, retired	Drastic cut in income	Free checking with direct deposit of Social Security check

Age and Life Cycle

From personal experience, marketers are aware that the nature of the goods and services people buy change over the course of their lifetime. Every family progresses through a number of stages that have a very important influence on the tastes and consumption patterns of the family unit.

The life cycle concept recognizes nine distinct stages that a typical middle class family undergoes.[5] It begins with a young, single, working person living independently, moves through the various stages of marriage and child-rearing, and ends with a solitary survivor of a marriage, retired and once again living alone. Obviously, these nine stages (see Exhibit 6-4) are based on broad generalizations. However, they are useful in marketing, as they help predict the buying patterns of potential target markets.

For example, couples with young children are usually interested in purchasing a home, and their liquid assets tend to be low. On the other end of the cycle, older couples, whose children have grown up and left home, tend to be more financially secure and are interested in taking more vacations, making home improvements, and enjoying other luxuries. Package accounts aimed at this segment might offer travel information and discounts in return for maintaining a high balance in savings.

Economic Circumstances

Personal economic factors such as income, savings, net worth, and ability to borrow, affect buying power for all types of goods and services, but they are especially relevant to the purchase of banking services. High-income individuals are targets for personal or executive banking services. Individuals with a substantial net worth are candidates for trust services. Lower-income individuals require banking services that meet their needs without charging much for such services. Basic checking accounts that allow a customer to write a limited number of checks for free or at a very low cost are aimed at this market.

Occupation

Employment patterns also affect the purchase of goods and services. Many jobs require specialized equipment or clothing. In addition, people buy goods and avail themselves of services that will give them greater status in the workplace. For example, unspoken dress codes may inspire an employee to buy a certain type of clothing due to the perception that the prestigious people in one's field are doing so.

Personality and Self-Concept

Personality can be defined as the aggregation of an individual's traits or characteristics that make him or her unique. Some people are outgoing; others are shy. Some are nonconformists; others are conventional. Some are risk-takers; others are conservative, and so on. One study found that more than 80 percent of a bank's customers who expressed preference for using drive-up and/or bank-by-mail services exhibited detached personalities;[6] that is, they were people who characteristically try to put emotional and physical distance between themselves and other persons.

Sometimes marketers look for specific personality traits in a target market audience and sell into it. A series of beer commercials in the late 1970s, for example, was based on findings that heavy beer drinkers were more rugged, gregarious, and aggressive than occasional beer drinkers. These commercials featured groups representative of such people and encouraged viewers to "go for the gusto." In recent years, there has been an emphasis on the importance of relationships among small groups of men and away from large-group membership, so many current beer commercials show men celebrating with and for one another (for example, "This Bud's for you").

Self-concept is closely related to personality; it refers to the way we see ourselves and think others see us. People select products, banks, and other services that coincide with their self-concept. If a bank promotes an image of catering to "old money," an individual who sees himself as an up-and-coming professional would be less likely to identify with and select that bank.

Psychographics

Many marketing researchers use a single term to refer to the combined effect of many personal and psychological factors that influence buying behavior. That term is **psychographics**. Through the use of psychographic principles, consumer markets can be segmented on the basis of lifestyle, personality traits, attitudes, and so on. Psychographics is being used in both bank and consumer product marketing today, so it is an important concept.

For example, the use of ATMs has been found to be related to psychographic variables. In one study, ATM users were found to be more self-reliant, impulsive, innovative, curious, and active than nonusers.[7] Put simply, they were considered to be on a faster track. In line with this theory, a television spot for an ATM network consists of fast-paced cuts from one scene to another, showing individuals in various situations that suggest impulsiveness, self-reliance, and a high level of activity.

THE CONSUMER BUYING PROCESS

The stages involved in the consumer buying process are illustrated in Exhibit 6-5. This exhibit is very similar to Exhibit 6-1, since the buying process is just a specific situation to which the motivation process can be applied. Exhibit 6-5 indicates that an unsatisfied need is the starting point in the buying process. The individual then searches for a way to satisfy the need and evaluates alternatives for doing so. This is referred to as prepurchase activity.

Finally, a decision is reached and a purchase is made. Then, postpurchase feelings arise, and the process begins again at the next unsatisfied need. Each step in the process shown in Exhibit 6-5 poses a significant challenge to the bank marketer, who must understand what happens at each point and develop a marketing program to capitalize on it. Customers move through each step to some degree, although they may not be conscious of it. The significance of this process will become more clear as each step is examined in detail.

Unsatisfied Needs

As mentioned previously, the starting point for any type of behavior, including consumer behavior, is an unsatisfied need. The buyer will not be motivated to buy unless there is a perceived need for the

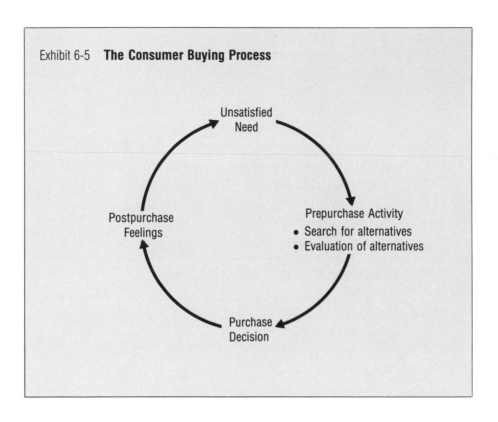

Exhibit 6-5   **The Consumer Buying Process**

Unsatisfied
Need

Prepurchase Activity
• Search for alternatives
• Evaluation of alternatives

Purchase
Decision

Postpurchase
Feelings

product. Thus, identifying customer needs is a prerequisite for successful marketing. If a bank product does not fill a need or is marketed to satisfy a need that customers do not perceive as such, the product will not be marketed successfully.

The bank marketer has the critical task of discovering the needs of the market and those that the bank's products serve. "What is the buyer really seeking when buying my product?" and "What need does my product satisfy?" are questions the marketer must constantly ask. Certain industries have answered these questions very successfully. Consider the cosmetic manufacturer who said: "In the factory we make cosmetics; in the drugstore we sell hope."

Bankers must also continually identify inadequately developed or insufficiently satisfied needs. Ford Motor Company successfully met those needs with its Mustang model. The cosmetics industry discovered that the need for sophisticated grooming products for men was a market that had not been sufficiently developed, and thus began marketing hair coloring, hair spray, cologne, and other cosmetics for male customers.

Insufficiently satisfied needs also might be the result of dissatisfaction with an existing product or service. In the case of banking, customer dissatisfaction with the level of service is the second most often cited reason why people change banks (the principal cause is related to the need for convenience).

The need for banking services is closely related to the satisfaction of needs at all levels; satisfying a need frequently involves making a purchase, which requires money. Checking accounts offer a convenient way of paying for food, clothing, and shelter while ensuring that money is kept in a safe place. Savings accounts are a form of security and a way to prepare for emergencies. Credit cards and loans enable customers to respond quickly to needs that arise unexpectedly.

A bank's customer service representative is in an excellent position to make customers more aware of unsatisfied needs. A customer buying a large amount of traveler's checks, for example, is probably going to be away from home for an extended period. This provides an opportunity for the bank employee to remind the customer about safe deposit boxes.

Bank versus Customer Needs

There has been an explosive growth in the development of new technology in banking, enabling banks to handle work more efficiently and to become less reliant on labor (which is becoming more expensive every year). As a result, many new bank services or service delivery mechanisms are introduced because they suit the banking industry's needs more than the consumer's. Sometimes, considerable time is needed to explain to bank customers how new services, which require a change in banking behavior, meet their needs.

An example is the direct deposit of Social Security checks. This service would seemingly appeal to senior citizens who fear the theft of their checks from the mailbox or the threat of being mugged on the way home from the bank. Yet, the majority of senior citizens have not taken advantage of this service. Part of the problem is that many older people do not trust what they cannot see; they fear that something could go wrong as a result of technology, the postal service, or simply human error, and that their money may not actually get into their account. Others view the trip to the bank on Social Security check day as a social event, a response to the need for belongingness. Furthermore, the service is aimed at a group of people who are not, by virtue of their age, innovators and who may be slow to adopt something new.

The point of this example is to show that when a banking service is targeted to a need that is not widely perceived, that requires a substantial change in behavior, or is aimed at a market that tends to be slow to respond, the bank should recognize that the service is likely to be adopted slowly and may require considerable effort in order to educate consumers.

Prepurchase Activity

People become sensitive to the cues around them that they believe will bring them closer to satisfying certain needs. A **cue** can be thought of as a piece of information that starts a thought process. In the marketing sense, cues might take the form of advertisements; conversations with friends, neighbors, and bank personnel; or contacts with business associates.

How long a person deliberates before purchasing will vary with the individual, the urgency and complexity of the need, and the extent of the consumer's knowledge about ways to satisfy that need. For example, with respect to purchasing automobiles and major appliances, there is usually considerable deliberation because the risk is high both financially and socially, whereas products such as toothpaste and soap usually are purchased out of habit, with little deliberation. The crucial point is that needs may incubate for a period of time while the individual engages in prepurchase search behavior and evaluates alternatives. During this period, the consumer is a prime target for communications from a bank; in fact, the buyer may be actively seeking such information. For this reason, it is important that literature explaining the bank's services is readily available and visible in bank lobbies. This is also why many banks regularly use inserts in periodic checking and savings statements to promote bank services. They are a relatively low-cost way of reaching a large number of customers, and while many people pay no attention to a particular stuffer, a certain proportion of customers will be in the prepurchase stage for the service and will be attuned to the message.

The purchase decision has some degree of risk attached to it. Much of the consumer's behavior in this stage will be directed toward reducing this risk. While consumers can turn to publications such as *Consumer Reports* as a source of information that will help minimize purchase risk, such research is not possible when shopping for banking services. This point underscores the importance of knowledgeable bank personnel and the availability of promotional literature within the banking office. The customer may also use other informational sources such as friends, other bank customers, or business associates. For this reason, as previously mentioned, it is important that banks establish strong ties with centers of influence in a community.

Purchase Decision

Most prepurchase activity culminates in a purchase. Actually, a purchase decision encompasses a myriad of decisions. It often involves a product type, model, size, color, price, means to pay, and dealer, among other factors. The same can be said concerning the selection of a bank and bank products. Once the consumer has decided to go to a particular bank for a new checking account, he must then choose between different types of checking accounts and select a style and color of checkbook and checks. The easier the bank and new accounts person makes these decisions, the more comfortable the customer will be with the purchase decision.

Postpurchase Feelings

The behavior leading up to the point of a "buy" decision and the purchase itself has been discussed. But what takes place and how the consumer feels after the purchase are also very important elements of the buying process and are, therefore, crucial to the marketer. Buyers often feel some anxiety after making a major purchase. This is understandable, since each of the alternatives from which the selection was made had both positive and negative features. The wise marketer helps make the buyer feel good about his or her choice. Some banks send a thank-you note to the new checking customer. While they may do this simply as a courtesy, or to check the address given by the customer, the gesture is grounded in behavioral psychology and helps to reduce postpurchase anxiety.

Providing the customer with excellent service to reduce postpurchase anxiety is especially important in the case of products that are bought infrequently, such as automobiles and banking services. If a new car owner's experience with the dealer's service department is unpleasant, the likelihood of repeat business or referrals to friends will be greatly diminished. Conversely, the bank customer who is treated with promptness, accuracy, and friendliness will feel that the decision to select that particular bank was justified.

Similarly, if customers who are satisfied with a particular bank's checking and savings services are more likely to use the bank's services when applying for a car loan. The more that reinforcement occurs, the more likely a habit of positive behavior will develop. In the marketing sense, habitual behavior leads to brand (or bank) loyalty. Such habits, once entrenched, are often extremely difficult for the competition to alter.

Again, the inference should not be that the consumer goes through a carefully executed set of stages each time a purchase is made. Instead, in many buying decisions, the stages occur simultaneously.

ORGANIZATIONAL BUYING BEHAVIOR

There are a number of differences, but many similarities, between the buying behavior of individual consumers and of organizations. The most obvious difference is that organizations generally purchase goods and services, not for consumption, but for application to the production process. In the case of banking services, for instance, manufacturers purchase money (that is, get loans) to finance production and expand capacity. A second major difference is that in an organization, more people are likely to be involved in making the purchase decision. Each of these individuals has a specific role to play in the process, and each is an individual subject to all the forces that influence consumer behavior—which makes the buying process much more complicated.

The Organizational Buying Process

As is the case for individuals, the buying process for organizations begins with recognition of a need and involves identifying and evaluating possible purchase alternatives. Organizational behavior experts Webster and Wind have developed a theory of organizational buying behavior that will be used throughout this section. They define *organizational buying behavior* as "the decision-making process by which formal organizations establish the need for purchased products and services, and identify, evaluate, and choose among alternative brands and suppliers."[8] This process is illustrated in Exhibit 6-6.

Need Identification

Need identification may arise from within an organization—for example, when it recognizes a need for working capital. Or, a bank might suggest a need to an organization through advertising ("We can put your overnight money to work for you"). Or, a need may be uncovered through skillful probing by a bank officer who has prepared well for the call on the company. The calling officer should have studied the firm's financial statements and become familiar with its current pattern of banking service use. Through that preparation, and by asking questions about how the firm manages its flow of cash through the working capital cycle, the officer may determine a way in which the bank can provide a service to the firm.

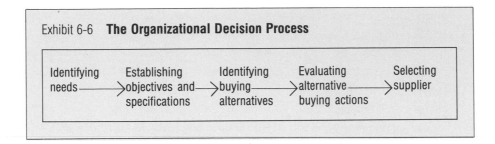

Exhibit 6-6 **The Organizational Decision Process**

Identifying needs → Establishing objectives and specifications → Identifying buying alternatives → Evaluating alternative buying actions → Selecting supplier

The need that is central to most corporate banking relationships is the need for credit, including the need for it to be delivered whenever and wherever without hassle. The need for credit services is the leading motivator for organizations when it comes to selecting a bank, and loan approval or rejection is the principal reason for firms establishing or ending a banking relationship.

Organizations also need noncredit services such as cash management to help them better manage their cash flow. Many banks see the unrecognized need for cash management services as a way to get a "foot in the door" of a company that is not actively seeking a credit provider.

Once the organization's need has been identified, the buyer defines the objectives and specifications that the product must fulfill; that is, what the product or service must be able to do. This step is more often related to the purchase of goods and noncredit banking services than to the purchase of credit services.

In the process of identifying the buying alternatives open to the business when it is buying banking services, the firm will generally consult the banks with which it is already doing business. In small- to medium-sized businesses, the firm's attorney or independent accountant may be asked to direct business to a specific bank. Since a great deal of bank business can be generated through these channels, it is very important that banks work to develop a good reputation among such centers of influence.

In the process of evaluating alternative buying decisions, the firm may study the services offered by several banks (for example, comparing lockbox facilities) and evaluate the differences between them in light of the firm's specific needs.

The process of selecting a supplier (or bank) generally involves several people and may reflect the relative power of various members of the purchasing group.

Factors Affecting Organizational Buying Decisions

Just as consumer behavior is shaped by psychological, personal, social, and cultural factors, four sets of factors also affect the buying behavior of organizations: environmental factors, interpersonal group factors, individual factors, and organizational or formal factors. Each of these influences can affect the buying decision directly or indirectly. In other words, they may affect the buying task itself or may influence variables that are separate from the buying task. This process is illustrated in Exhibit 6-7.

Since each of the participants in the buying process is an individual, the many factors that affect individual buying behavior also come into play in the organizational buying process.

The buying process in larger organizations usually involves several persons, each of whom plays a different role. Webster and Wind characterize these as *influencers, users, deciders, buyers,* and *gatekeepers.*

Deciders have the authority and responsibility for choosing a specific bank. Influencers can affect that decision but do not have the ultimate buying authority. Buyers are the individuals responsible for completing the decision. Users are those who will actually make use of the service but who may have little or no buying authority and varying amounts of influence. Gatekeepers are often secretaries or purchasing agents who screen the information flow to the influencer or user, and, thus, have an indirect influence on the process.

An example of these interrelationships can be found in a firm that is considering the purchase of direct deposit of payroll for its employees. The payroll department chief will be the user, and the firm's president may be the decider. However, the person with the power to affect the decision may be the treasurer. He may also be the buyer—the one who notifies the bank of the decision and handles the necessary paperwork. It is essential that corporate calling officers make a point to contact the gatekeepers and to identify the individuals who are the users, deciders, and influencers.

For the most part, since services vary little from one bank to another, individual and interpersonal factors take on great importance in the selling of banking services. Therefore, the caliber and performance of the calling officer is critical. Research has repeatedly shown that financial decision makers expect calling officers to have the ability to effect prompt decisions and action. Research has also shown that these deciders want attention; they like to feel that the bank knows them, wants their business, and cares about their needs. This can only be done through interpersonal contact, and it explains why the most successful corporate banking groups have substantial expense accounts.

The model described above is also applicable to the sale of goods and services to government agencies. The primary concern of government units, however, is to minimize cost to the taxpayer. For this reason, sales of products and services are more likely to be subject to open bidding, with the sale going to the bidder with the lowest price or the most favorable rate.[9]

SUMMARY

This chapter began with a study of the theories and techniques that form the basis for an understanding of markets. It is important to know why and how people buy in order to develop ways of meeting their needs with those products that are priced, distributed, and communicated effectively to the target market. Unmet or incompletely met needs motivate buyer behavior; the shape taken by that behavior is influenced by individuals' perceptions of the stimuli surrounding them.

Maslow's hierarchy is a useful framework for understanding the way various levels of needs motivate people. A multitude of factors influence buyer perceptions and their resulting behavior. These are external influences such as social and cultural factors and internal influences such as psychological and personal factors. The class structure in this country, for example, is a significant cultural factor that affects buyer behavior. Position in the life cycle is also a personal factor that greatly affects consumer needs and purchase behavior. Psychographics is a term used to refer to the combined effect of many personal and psychological factors.

The buying process is simply a specialized form of the general process of motivation. The four steps in the buying process are awareness of an unmet or incompletely satisfied need; engaging in the prepurchase activities (searching for alternative ways to meet the need and then evaluating the alternatives that have been identified); making the purchase decision; and experiencing postpurchase feelings. Marketing techniques can be applied to each step of the process, from making consumers' aware of the need, right through to providing them with evidence that they have made the right choices.

The buying behavior of organizations is, in some ways, similar to, and in other ways, quite different from that of individuals. There are five stages in the organizational buying process that closely parallel the four-stage consumer buying process. Furthermore, individuals involved in the organization's buying process can assume one of several roles. While the buying process of organizations involves more people and is more complex than that of the individual consumer, it is, nevertheless, true that unmet or incompletely satisfied needs are at the core of the process.

The next chapter looks at additional techniques that are helpful in gaining an understanding of the market, specifically marketing research techniques. Understanding consumers' needs, motivation, and perceptions is critical to marketers, and marketing research helps provide that understanding.

POINTS FOR REVIEW

1. Define or briefly explain the following terms:
   - motivation
   - hierarchy of needs
   - psychographics
   - reference group
   - life cycle
2. How does an understanding of consumer buying behavior help the bank marketer?
3. Which needs in Maslow's hierarchy might each of the following products or services satisfy?
   - Corvette sports car
   - Mercedes-Benz sedan
   - a smoke detector
   - ski equipment
   - personal trust services
4. What needs, if any, does a service such as home banking through one's personal computer satisfy?

5. Explain how a bank's use of lobby posters, brochures, statement stuffers, and handouts ties in with the consumer buying process.

6. Provide an example from current TV advertising of a product being marketed to a particular psychographic group (that is, a group with a particular set of values and attitudes toward life). In what way does the ad accomplish this?

7. How is the buying process of organizations similar to that of individuals? How is it different?

8. Centers of influence (for example, attorneys and accountants) were mentioned as important factors in the buying behavior of both individuals and organizations with respect to banking services. At which stage of each of the buying processes do these professionals come into play?

7 MARKETING INFORMATION AND RESEARCH

Research is a tool that is important at every stage in the marketing management process. When compiling the situation analysis, how does the marketer obtain information about the bank's internal and external macroenvironment? The answer is marketing research. How does the marketer establish objectives that are measurable when the goal has to do with such things as market penetration, increasing consumer awareness, or improving customer satisfaction? Again, the answer is marketing research. The statistics reported in research studies of customers and prospects become the benchmarks against which progress toward marketing objectives is measured.

Marketing research enables the marketer to identify and analyze the differences between various target markets. It provides information on how the members of various markets are motivated, how they perceive the world, and how they behave in response to various stimuli (for example, small differences in interest rates paid, or cash bonuses to attract deposits).

Marketing research is invaluable in the design of product mix strategies. New product ideas can come from market research; new product concepts can be tested in marketing research, and alternative pricing schemes can be tested among the target market. Research on the attitudes and behavior of the target market can provide input for the people who design the advertising. Then, research can be used to test the reactions to the advertising's creative strategy and the effectiveness of the ad copy.

Marketing research can identify the geographical areas into which the bank might expand its distribution network. It can be used to measure the sales effectiveness of the retail and commercial customer-contact staff. Completing the planning loop, research is an integral tool for evaluating and controlling the marketing management process. It can measure the success of the marketing strategy and track its effect over time. A repeat of the surveys used in benchmark setting provides the necessary feedback from the market on how the strategy is working.

This chapter provides an overview of the techniques used in marketing research and presents the seven-step process in conducting a research survey. It discusses the fine line of difference between *market research* and *marketing research* as well as the similarities and differences between *marketing research* and *marketing information systems*.

DEFINITION OF MARKETING RESEARCH

A formal definition of marketing research states that it is "the systematic gathering, recording, and analyzing of data relevant to the identification and solution of a marketing problem."[1]

Put another way, marketing research is the acquisition and use of information that can be beneficial to the marketing management process. How important is marketing research? If the goal of a business is to satisfy consumer needs and wants at a profit, and if research provides the information for management to make decisions toward that end, then research might well be seen as the most important function performed by a marketing department.

MARKETING RESEARCH IN BANKING

There is great variation among banks with respect to their use of marketing research. According to one industry analysis, banks spend from 1 to 4 percent of their total marketing budget on research.[2] (This represents out-of-pocket research expenditures and does not include the salaries of internal marketing research staff.)

Exhibit 7-1 shows the median marketing and research expenditures broken out by bank asset size. From that information, one can observe the following:

- Half of all banks with assets of $500 million or less spend less than $4,000 annually on marketing research. The other half, however, spend more.

- The larger the bank, the larger the share of the total marketing budget that is spent on research.

- Large banks (those with more than $5 billion in assets) spend hundreds of thousands of dollars on marketing research.

In short, the larger the bank, the greater the potential impact (both positive or negative) of alternative marketing decisions, and thus, the greater the need for information to help reduce the risk of making wrong decisions.

Banks also vary in the way they are staffed to conduct research. There are two opposing scenarios, with most banks falling somewhere in the middle. A bank may have an in-house staff of professionals who conduct research projects from start to finish. Or, a bank may contract with research suppliers and consultants to do each project. In reality, most banks use a combination of the two: some research is done entirely by the bank; other projects are done completely by consultants; and other projects are done partly in-house and partly by suppliers.

MARKETING OR MARKET RESEARCH?

There is a distinction between marketing research and market research.[3] A *market* is a geographical area in which a firm does business (such as a branch trade area), a group of customers (such as senior citizens), or an environment in which buyers and sellers make their decisions (such as a tight money market). The market, however, is only one of the elements marketing information is concerned with.

Exhibit 7-1   Bank Expenditures for Marketing and Marketing Research

Asset Size (millions)	Marketing Budget as a % of Assets	Median* Marketing Budget	Research as a % of Marketing Budget	Median* Research Expenditure
Less than $10	.137%	$ 5,800	3%	$ 3,500
$10–25	.107	13,500	4	3,400
$25–50	.085	27,400	1	2,000
$50–100	.082	54,300	1	1,000
$100–250	.080	124,500	2	3,000
$250–500	.070	228,600	2	4,300
$500–1,000	.089	551,800	3	14,200
$1,000–5,000	.040	1,323,000	3	27,000
More than $5,000	.045	4,683,200	4	201,700

*Half of the respondents in each asset category reported amounts greater, and half lesser. In other words, the figures represent the middle value of all those reported in that asset category.

Source: *Analysis of 1985 Bank Marketing Expenditures*, Bank Marketing Association, 1986. Based on information reported by 1,036 banks.

Marketing research not only helps to identify and analyze markets, it is also used for planning, problem solving, and control. Marketing research gathers information for the four elements of marketing mix strategy development: product, pricing, promotion, and distribution. In other words, marketing research has a broader scope than market research. (See Exhibit 7-2.)

Market Research

Information about the market is essential as a starting point in the planning process and as a foundation for building the marketing effort. Information that all banks, regardless of their size, should have readily available and up-to-date relates to:

- the bank's immediate geographical market;
- its customers;
- its competition; and
- its position in relation to the competition.

Types of Market Data

Collecting basic market information constitutes the situation analysis—the first step in the marketing planning process (see chapter 4). It should incorporate the development of three basic profiles: a customer profile, a market profile, and a competition profile.

Customer Profile

This information should answer such questions as "Who are the bank's customers?", "How do they differ from the customers of competing banks?", and "How do they differ from other residents of the trade area?" (For example, is the bank attracting a disproportionate share of younger or older customers?). In other words, customer profile information includes demographic information about age distribution, occupation, educational level, income, and ethnic composition. Such information may be obtained from internal data, surveys of customers, or records made at the new accounts desk.

The **customer profile** must include data about commercial as well as retail customers. Such data would include the number of customers by type of business, balance size, number and types of services used, length of banking relationship, and profitability.

Market Profile

The financial health of a bank is inexorably tied to the economics of the geographic area it serves. A market profile provides management with the information needed to identify potential problems and opportunities in both the retail and commercial markets. Much of the information is available from a wide range of existing sources, but keeping the information current requires special monitoring of economic trends.

A **market profile** defines the boundaries of the primary trade area (from which 75 percent of the bank's business is derived) and the secondary trade area (the broader area from which the balance of the business comes). It also includes the number and value of housing units, population data, and demographic information in those geographical areas. In commercial banking, the profile should include the number, types, and location of businesses in the trade area. Ideally, management should also have specific data about every firm

Exhibit 7-2	**Market Research and Marketing Research Contrasted**	
	Market Research	*Marketing Research*
Concerns	Information about the bank's market situation	Information for planning, problem solving, and control; information about the target market's behavior, attitudes, opinions, knowledge, motivation, and needs
Information Sources	External secondary data Internal secondary data	Primary data gathered from survey research Internal and external secondary data
Output	Customer profile Competitive profile Market profile	Textual interpretation of data obtained, supported by tables of data
Uses	Forms the foundation of the marketing plan Provides a benchmark for setting measurable objectives Tracks progress toward objectives	Helps to predict target market's reaction to alternative marketing strategies Helps select strategies for using the marketing mix (product, pricing, promotion, and distribution) Provides a benchmark for setting measurable objectives Tracks progress toward objectives

or merchant in the area, including information about the nature of the business, the approximate sales volume, the number of employees, and current banking affiliations. Such information forms the foundation of an effective officer-calling program.

Competition Profile

Marketing has taken on increased importance in banking because competition has become more of an issue than it was 30 years ago. Were it not for its competitors, banks would complacently sit back with their checking, savings, loan, and safekeeping services on the shelf, waiting for customers with a need for such services to come along. In today's market, however, competitors abound, and bank marketing decisions must take into account their operations (that is, pricing, hours, services, and so on) and possible reactions to market actions.

The questions to be answered by the competition profile are "Who are our competitors?", "What are their services and how are they priced?", "What is each institution's market share?", "Who is the market leader (if there is one)?", and "How do our services, facilities, hours, and staff compare with theirs?"

Profile information is neither difficult nor expensive to collect, and any bank that is operating without it is putting itself in a highly vulnerable situation. Consider the following scenario:

A bank in an old urban area hired a marketing research expert to work primarily on bank expansion. This person soon learned that the bank did not have the basic market information, so an immediate effort was made to gather the three kinds of profile data. The most alarming finding arose in the course of developing the customer profile. The bank's customers were substantially older than those of the other institutions in the city. The bank had a core of high-balance savings accounts, but its customer base was dying and not being replaced. Without corrective action, the bank would most likely be out of the retail business in about 10 years.

Obviously, failure to discern this type of information could be fatal to a banking institution.

Updating Market Data

Market information describes situations that are constantly changing. It would be naive to think that, once having gathered this basic information, banks could continue to rely on it over a period of years. Customer bases change as residents and businesses move in and out of trade areas. Also, the local economy of the trade area is affected by the state and national economies, both of which are dynamic. Furthermore, banks and other financial institutions make changes that affect the industry as a whole.

The point is that basic market information must be updated regularly so that management has a continual flow of information on the customer, the market, and the competition.

Market Data Sources

Some market profile information can be derived from information that exists either within the bank or from outside sources. This type of information is known as **secondary data**. Internal information can tell banks about their customers' behavior in relation to the bank. Through the central information file, banks can learn the proportion of customers having one, two, three, and more services with the bank. Banks can monitor the number of, and dollars in, checking, savings, and loan accounts opened and closed and thereby anticipate changing customer demand for services.

Information about the local market can be obtained from external sources such as the Bureau of the Census, local chambers of commerce, and municipal offices. Some information on competitors can be obtained from published reports put out by regulatory agencies. Information regarding their services and pricing can be obtained by calling or visiting other banks and posing as a prospective customer.

However, there is much information (especially regarding customer motivation and needs, opinions, knowledge, attitudes, and behavior) that cannot be obtained except by generating it. This kind of information is known as **primary data**. Such information usually is obtained by doing survey research.

Marketing Research: The Survey Research Process

This section discusses the seven steps involved in conducting a market research study, which encompass:

1. defining the problem;
2. selecting the sources of information;
3. preparing data collection materials;
4. designing the sample;
5. collecting the information;

6. analyzing the data; and

7. reporting the results.[4]

While this process is generally applicable to any research or problem-solving activity, it is especially relevant to survey research.

Step 1: Defining the problem. While the first step may seem obvious, it is, in fact, the most important stage in the research process. If the problem or question is not correctly identified and defined, the answer—however scientifically obtained and professionally presented—will be off the mark.

Sometimes management may not define the problem clearly. In such cases, exploratory research may be done to help bring the problem into focus.[5] Take the case of the State Bank of Wheatville, a small (under $50 million in assets) and relatively new (17 years old) bank in a two-bank town. The other bank, Western National Bank, had for many years been the only bank in town. State Bank was growing moderately, and its management was pleased, until a branch of a third bank, Warranty Bank, entered the market and began to grow rapidly. The management of State Bank had believed that the only issue hindering State Bank's ability to grow was loyalty to the old, established Western National Bank. However, these beliefs were shattered by the performance of the new market entrant, Warranty Bank.

The marketing research department was instructed to find out why the new bank was growing faster than State Bank. The answer could lie in any one or a combination of factors: services, hours, pricing, location, staff, image, or advertising. Fortunately, basic market research had already been done for the bank, and it was clear that State Bank was competitive with both of the other banks in town. Through exploratory interviews with State Bank's management and a few professionals working on the town's main thoroughfare, the researchers formulated the hypothesis that the bank did not have as much contact with the centers of influence in the community as did its older and newer competitors. Further research confirmed this hypothesis, and as a result, staffing changes were made and a formal call program was initiated.

In this case, the real problem had nothing to do with the new competitor. The ability to narrow down the question from "Why are we not doing as well as our new competitor?" to "Does our bank have as good a reputation with the town's centers of influence as our competitors?" simplified the research effort by focusing on the relevant market (community opinion leaders, influential business owners, and professionals).

Step 2: Selecting the sources of information. After the problem to be studied has been identified, the next step is to find out where the required information can be obtained. Information can be collected either from secondary data sources or through primary research.

Secondary data sources may be internal or external to the bank. Examples of internal secondary data are reports from other departments (for example, accounting and branch administration) and information gathered at the point of sale (signature cards and new account information forms). A large volume of external secondary data is available from regulatory agencies, the American Bankers Association library and Information Services Division, trade associations, the federal government, state and local governments, and the media.

A thorough search of existing data should always be made before conducting primary research, since the answers to management's questions can often be found in the information that is readily available. As a precautionary note, however, it should be recognized that secondary data may be out of date, and past experience is not necessarily a reliable predictor of the future. Nevertheless, secondary data should be examined before conducting one's own primary research. Exhibit 7-3 lists a number of secondary sources useful to bankers.

Primary data are obtained from original sources in order to answer the question at hand. The collection of primary data can range from simply observing customer behavior at the point of sale, to using a complex multistage study starting with small group discussions and followed with numerous personal interviews. A marketing research survey that is administered among several hundred respondents produces **quantitative** primary data; that is, it generates percentages, frequency distributions, and other statistical information that identifies similarities and differences among various groups of respondents. However, there are times when the researcher needs more **qualitative** data about how people think, feel, and talk about a need or a product. This type of information can be obtained by conducting a small number of individual in-depth interviews or by holding focused discussions with small groups of people who are representative of the target audience.

For example, when a toiletries manufacturer wanted to develop and promote a shampoo aimed specifically at teenage girls, the firm held focused group sessions at which 10 or 12 teens were guided through a conversation about shampooing and hair care products. Through this research, the firm discovered that the target market associated hair cleanliness with the "squeaky" sound that occurs after rinsing. As a result, the firm developed a shampoo whose chemical composition produced a squeak and then promoted it by making significant use of the expression "squeaky clean."

Step 3: Preparing data collection materials. The next step in the research process is determining how to collect the information and how to design the questionnaire or survey form.

Survey Method

The principal method for collecting primary information is the **survey**. The three primary survey tools are the personal interview, the telephone interview, and the self-administered questionnaire. Each of these methods has strengths and weaknesses. For instance, respondents are likely to be more receptive to a personal, face-to-face interview than a telephone interview, so the personal interview questionnaire can be longer, thus generating more information. However, it is also more expensive to conduct and more subject to interviewer bias and cheating (for example, filling out a questionnaire without conducting the interview).

The self-administered questionnaire is the least expensive and the device least subject to interviewer bias, but it is also the least likely to be completed and offers the least amount of control over the composition of the sample. For example, if a bank mailed a survey to 20

Exhibit 7-3　**Selected Secondary Sources Useful to Bankers**

I. Information on the Competitive Environment

A. Individual Bank Data

   1. Bank quarterly and annual reports; 10-K reports

   2. Report of condition and report of income and dividends (available for individual banks from the FDIC)

B. Banking Data

   1. The 12 regional Federal Reserve banks publish a great deal of banking data. Availability varies by region. In addition, the Federal Reserve Board publishes a great deal of useful information. Some examples are:

    • Functional cost analysis (annually)

    • Assets and liabilities of insured domestically chartered and foreign-related banking institutions (weekly)

    • Weekly consolidated condition report of large commercial banks and domestic subsidiaries

    • Commercial and industrial loan commitments at selected large commercial banks (monthly)

    • Consumer installment credit (monthly)

    • Debits and deposit turnover at commercial banks (monthly)

    • Loans and securities at all commercial banks (monthly)

    • Flow of funds: seasonally adjusted and unadjusted (quarterly)

   2. Federal Deposit Insurance Corporation

    • Bank operating statistics (annually)

    • Summary of deposits (by branch, annually)

   3. Federal Home Loan Banks

    • Monthly report on deposits at savings and loan associations (by major city)

II. Information on the Economic Environment

A. Population

   1. U.S. Department of Commerce, Bureau of Census

    • Census of population (every decade)

    • Current population reports (irregularly)

    • Statistical Abstract of the United States (annually)

    • County and city data book (irregularly)

   2. State departments of economic research

B. Regional Income and Employment

   1. Survey of buying power (published annually by *Sales Management Magazine*)

   2. State departments of labor or employment agencies

C. Construction Activity

   1. *Construction News* (monthly), F.W. Dodge, a division of McGraw-Hill Information Systems Co.

   2. State departments of economic research

percent of all checking account customers, the response might be greater from customers who have been with the bank the longest, who are most favorably disposed toward the bank, or who have the most free time. Telephoning customers, however, eliminates this selection problem.

Exhibit 7-4 ranks each type of interview on a scale of one to three with respect to nine variables that should be considered when designing a survey.[6] In the exhibit, a ranking of one means that the particular interview category is the best method to use with respect to each variable. For example, the most information can be obtained by conducting a personal interview, and the least is usually obtained through a telephone interview. Similarly, a self-administered questionnaire is the best method to use if interviewer bias or cheating is a concern.

The exhibit also shows that all three interview techniques have very close (total) scores. This indicates that no one technique is the

Exhibit 7-4	Comparison of Survey Techniques		
Variables	Personal Interview	Telephone Interview	Self-administered Questionnaire
Amount of information	1	3	2
Types of information	1	2	3
Complexity	1	3	2
Completion rate	1	2	3
Interviewer bias or cheating	3	2	1
Respondent bias	3	2	1
Sample composition	2	1	3
Cost	3	2	1
Speed	2	1	3
Total Score	17	18	19

most effective in all cases. Therefore, the choice must be made on a case-by-case basis, choosing the method that best suits the particular situation. In testing alternative advertising strategies, only personal interviews can be used, since the respondent must see the advertising. When testing customer awareness and comprehension of services, any of the three methods may be used, so the decision must be based on other factors such as the complexity of the information presented, cost, or the time frame within which answers must be obtained.

Questionnaire Design

After determining which survey technique to use, the researcher must develop the questionnaire. This data collection device must fulfill three objectives:[7]

1. It must encourage cooperation and honest responses. A questionnaire that annoys or embarrasses respondents will result in unanswered questions or incomplete interviews. An example is asking respondents their income at the start of a questionnaire. Many people

refuse to answer such a question. This reduces the amount of the other information collected, increases cost (more contacts must be made), and raises the possibility of error in the results.

2. It must obtain responses that are valid. One of the difficulties that must be overcome in designing a questionnaire is the tendency that people "will answer questions on any topic, and they will answer whether or not they know anything about that topic."[8] For example, in 1981 the United States government was deliberating about selling sophisticated radar planes to Saudi Arabia. A poll was conducted to measure the public's opinion on the subject. Virtually everyone stated an opinion on whether the sale should be made, yet fewer than half could name the country to which the planes would be sold.

Grouping all respondents together regardless of their level of knowledge of an issue could mask the reality that those who are knowledgeable hold one opinion and those who are not tend to hold the opposite opinion.

3. It must obtain responses that are comparable. For example, if a term or a word suggests different meanings to different respondents, the survey results will be meaningless or misleading. For example, in corporate banking research, there is always much concern over the relationship between a firm and a lead bank. However, the term *lead bank* can mean:

- the bank used most often for borrowing;
- the bank where the principal transaction account is held; or
- the bank used by the head office or parent company as the concentration bank.

Therefore, asking a firm to name its lead bank without defining that term will elicit responses that are not truly comparable.

Another difficulty in the design of questionnaires is the matter of respondent consciousness. Most survey research assumes that people understand the meaning and implications of their answers.[9] Yet there is often a wide gap between what people say they will do (for example, in response to a new service offered by a bank) and what they actually do. This is perhaps the least recognized and most frequently encountered pitfall in bank marketing research—especially in research conducted to aid pricing decisions. A bank marketing researcher might ask individuals if they would move their checking account if charged a one dollar per month increase in the service charge. However, the researcher would be seriously wrong in projecting that just because 25 percent said they would be very likely to move their accounts, 25 percent would actually do so. The researcher should use these responses only to analyze the variation in responses across different groups of people as a way to predict which groups will be most and least price sensitive. (See *Case A*.)

The way questions are worded is also critical. Poorly worded questions can be loaded with unintended meaning, can be emotionally colored, or ambiguous; as such, they influence the respondent's answers and thus invalidate them. "How likely would you be to switch banks if another bank were more convenient and had better hours?" If the respondent answers this question by saying "very likely," there is no way of knowing whether the opinion is based on the respondent's concern about the hours or the location.

Questionnaire design calls upon a number of disciplines, including psychology and statistics, and there are many potential pitfalls facing the inexperienced. Therefore, the design of questionnaires should be left to professionals, or at the very least, a professional should be called on to assist in this task.

Step 4: Designing the sample. In marketing research, as in most aspects of daily life, conclusions are drawn about something by sampling a small part of it. The temperature of bath water is judged by sticking in one toe; a bunch of grapes is judged by eating one; a book is assessed by reading a few pages.

Likewise, in survey research, having determined the group of people marketers want to know more about (for example, all checking account customers, persons 60 and older, businesses in the $20 million to $125 million sales category), a representative sample of that group to whom the questionnaire will be administered must be selected.

To project what is learned about the sample group to the entire group (or "universe"), the sample size and the method of selection must be done scientifically. If information about checking account customers is to be acquired, stopping 25 customers during the day at 4 of 50 branches and interviewing them will provide some information, but such a sample would not be representative of all of the bank's checking customers. There will be errors in the information to the extent that (1) the individuals who use these 4 branches are different economically, socially, or attitudinally from the people who use the other 46 branches; and (2) the people who come into the branch differ from people who use the automated teller, drive-in, who bank by mail, and who may do their banking only on evenings or Saturdays. Because of the many factors that influence consumer behavior, it is likely that there will be significant differences between these groups of people.

Sample design requires a knowledge of the theory of statistics. While it is not possible to go into considerable detail on the subject here, most libraries have a basic statistics text for the interested student.

Step 5: Collecting the information. The next step in the survey process is administering the questionnaire to the sample group that has been selected (also known as fielding the study). As with questionnaire and sample design, there are a number of potential pitfalls in this step of the research process that can introduce bias or error into the results.

In the case of the personal or telephone interview, interviewers must be carefully selected and trained, since the interviewer can be a source of bias. If the interviewer fails to state the questions exactly the same way in each interview, tends to put more emphasis on one of the possible responses, or simply introduces a subtle variation in the tone of voice, the respondent's answer could be influenced.

Whether the interview is face-to-face, by telephone, or self-administered, the respondent may be a source of bias to the extent that he or she does not answer accurately (either deliberately or because of a lack of correct information), lacks knowledge or understanding, or guesses. Another source of bias is nonresponse error, which was alluded to in an earlier discussion of the self-administered questionnaire. If those who refuse to answer (or could not be reached) differ in some way from those who did participate, these differences will be understated.

Step 6: Analyzing the data. When the completed questionnaires are returned, the challenge of analyzing the collected information begins. Responses to open-ended questions (that is, in which the respondent uses his or her own words to answer, as opposed to being given an answer from which to choose) must be categorized or coded. By reading through a substantial proportion of the answers to a question, it soon becomes clear that many respondents communicate the same thought but simply say it differently. Identifying these principal thoughts is the function of coding.

Next, the number of persons who responded to each particular answer must be tabulated. Survey results can be tabulated by hand, but a computer is faster and much more flexible in that it allows the responses to be cross-tabulated. For example, responses to each question can be broken out by age of respondent, sex, income, job classification, and behavior or psychographic variables. (See Exhibits A-3 to A-6 in *Case A* for examples of cross-tabulation.) Clearly, these various classifications should be determined during the questionnaire design phase so that the appropriate classification questions will be asked of respondents.

Step 7: Reporting the results. After the survey results are analyzed, they must be presented in a way that will maximize their usefulness to management. Remember that the purpose of research is to aid management in decision making. Research results that sit on a shelf unread or not acted upon are not only a waste of money, but they also damage the credibility of research in general and of the department that generated it. The goal of the report is to get the results read and used. Therefore, results should be summarized briefly at the beginning of the report, with supporting data following.

There are two philosophies of research report writing. One is to present results only; the other is to present both results and recommendations for action. The former is usually an impractical exercise. If the research process is carefully followed, there should be helpful conclusions and recommendations emanating from the study. While management may choose not to act upon the recommendations or to take some alternative action, it is the responsibility of marketing management to generate information that will be acted upon.

Researchers should always be prepared to answer the question, "What should we do, or do differently, as a result of this research?"

Why Results Are Not Used

Whether or not the results of marketing research are used in making bank decisions depends on several factors. One of the jobs of the researcher is to avoid those errors that result in research not being used.

When research is not used, the problem is generally the result of one or more fundamental problems: (1) the client's or end-user's lack of receptivity; (2) the researcher's preoccupation with methodology; (3) the absence of interpretive material; and (4) the unreliability of results.

Client's or end-user's lack of receptivity. Sometimes the end-user has already made up his or her mind about the answer to the problem being researched. It may be that the president, division head, or other authority in the organization has a strong bias and will ignore or undermine results that conflict with this bias. Advertising professionals frequently encounter this problem when a client decides that he or she does not like an advertising campaign even though research results demonstrate its effectiveness.

Researcher's preoccupation with methodology. Sometimes researchers get carried away with the methodology and lose sight of the stated objectives of the research. Perhaps they concentrate on their sophisticated processes for analyzing the data or become preoccupied with digging out countless pieces of information that are not relevant to the problem at hand. The researcher may find details of the research approach fascinating, but this is usually not of interest to the firm's management, which is seeking concise information on which to base a marketing decision.

Absence of interpretive material. Some research reports contain page after page of tables, but leave it to the user to figure out what it all means. The research report should always answer the question, "What can we do, or do differently, now that we have this information?"

Unreliability of results. Sometimes results cannot be projected to the market at large. In some cases, the methodology is not sufficiently scientific. If the sample of people questioned is too small, if the interviewers were biased, if the questions were loaded—all these flaws will render the results unreliable and, therefore, not usable.

Why Results Are Used

As might be expected, the reasons why research *does* get used are the inverse of the reasons why it does not. Research results are likely to be used when:

- the end-user or client is aware of the problem being studied and receptive to information that will enable him or her to understand how to deal with it;
- the researcher has correctly identified the purpose of the study and keeps it in view when writing the results;
- the research makes clear to the end-user how the findings can be interpreted and used; and
- the end-user is confident that the results are reliable and applicable to the market at large.

MARKETING INFORMATION SYSTEMS

Since this chapter covers the research methodology and tools that can help the marketer understand the market, the discussion would be incomplete without mention of **marketing information systems (MISs).**

There is no doubt that business is experiencing an information explosion. Managers are faced with more information than they could possibly read or absorb. However, computer science can be put to use to reduce information to manageable and usable proportions, thus making it more effective.

One way this can be achieved is to store, update, and manipulate data from both secondary and primary sources in a computer data base. Such a data base may be used to develop models that describe market behavior on the basis of past experience. These models may then be used to test alternative marketing strategies by asking "What if" types of questions.

For example, a bank might store trend data on the prime rate, the bank's and its competitors' money market deposit interests rates, daily deposit inflows and outflows, its advertising schedule, and the amount of advertising expenditures. Using a model based on experiences of the past, the marketer might predict the deposit inflows that can be expected with various levels of advertising and determine whether incremental amounts of advertising expenditure can be justified on the basis of increased deposits, assuming interest rates hold constant. Or, the marketer might use the model to predict what might happen if the bank's money market deposit interest rate is increased to above the market level.

Clearly, this kind of information can improve the quality of the decisions made and reduce the risks associated with them. A marketing information system can be an invaluable tool in the marketing planning process. In fact, it is a requirement for serious strategic planning.

MIS AND MARKETING RESEARCH

A marketing information system can be defined as:

> a structured, interacting complex of persons, machines, and procedures designed to generate an orderly flow of pertinent information, collected from both intra- and extra-firm sources, for use as the basis for decision making in specified responsibility areas of marketing management.[10]

Comparing this definition with that of marketing research, it is obvious that the objective of the two are essentially the same: to provide information for marketing decision making. One difference, however, is that an MIS provides a system for managing marketing information. It helps make effective use of many kinds of available information; it can handle internal and external secondary data as well as primary data; and it can store subjective estimates when facts are not available.

Exhibit 7-5 **Contrasting Characteristics of Marketing Research and a Marketing Information System**

Marketing Research	Marketing Information System
1. Emphasis is on handling external information	1. Handles both internal and external data
2. Concerned with solving problems	2. Concerned with preventing as well as solving problems
3. Operates in a fragmented, intermittent fashion—on a project-to-project basis	3. Operates continuously—is a system
4. Tends to focus on past information	4. Tends to be future oriented
5. Not necessarily a computer-based process	5. A computer-based process
6. One source of information input into a marketing information system	6. Includes other subsystems besides marketing research

Source: William J. Stanton and Charles Futrell, *Fundamentals of Marketing* (New York: McGraw-Hill, Inc., 1987), p. 64.

A second major difference is that an MIS provides an environment in which learning can take place. It provides the ability to store and process information in a way that makes it easy to recall and evaluate past experiences, thus allowing lessons to be learned and remembered.[11] Therefore, the marketing information system is broader and more flexible than marketing research.

Another difference between marketing research and an MIS is that the former tends to be done on a project-to-project basis, while the latter is ongoing. In a marketing research department, there might typically be four or five different problems being researched at one time to address several questions involving advertising, product development, pricing, or distribution. The MIS, on the other hand, is a continuous system rather than a one-time study. Nevertheless, the two can work together. The results of the marketing research project can be an important source of input to the MIS. The chart in Exhibit 7-5 summarizes the contrasting characteristics of marketing research and an MIS.

Banking's use of marketing information systems is sure to grow and spread because of the dramatic expansion of data that confronts managers, the increasing frequency and speed of changes in market conditions within which banks operate, and the recognition by banking executives that the old methods of evaluating this information are no longer adequate.

SUMMARY

This chapter defined marketing research as the major source of information to aid management in making decisions about marketing. Market research was described as but one aspect of marketing research. The chapter outlined the basic market information that the management of every bank should have at its disposal and then described each of the seven steps in the research process, emphasizing the importance of defining the problem precisely. It stressed the fact that research results must be capable of being acted on, and it looked at factors that reduce research effectiveness. Because various errors can be introduced into research results, the value of using professional researchers (internal or external to the bank), was underscored. Finally, the concept of a marketing information system was discussed, including the differences and similarities between marketing research and marketing information systems.

Having studied the many factors that shape consumer behavior and the research tools that help the marketer identify and understand potential target markets, the discussion will now turn to the process of selecting the markets that will be targeted with the marketing strategy, and positioning the product offering to maximize appeal to the target market.

POINTS FOR REVIEW

1. Define or briefly explain the following terms:
   - marketing research
   - market research
   - marketing information system

- primary data
- secondary data
- sample
- qualitative data
- quantitative data
- research process

2. Why might marketing research be seen as the most important function performed by the marketing department?

3. Describe the basic market information that every bank should have available to its management.

4. Obtain the following information for the most recent year using secondary data sources:

   - total deposits in commercial banks in your bank's home state
   - your bank's share of the above
   - number of commercial banking offices in your state
   - number of savings banks and savings and loan offices
   - number of households in your state as of the most recently available census or state data
   - number of households per financial institution office

5. Describe the relative merits of personal, phone, and self-administered surveys on the basis of speed, cost, accuracy, and amount of information obtained.

6. Find out if your bank has conducted any primary research in the past year and report the following information:

   - problem being addressed
   - size of sample selected
   - survey method used
   - who was responsible for interviewing, coding, tabulating, and reporting results
   - the general results
   - how the results were used
   - reasons that the research results were or were not used

7. Does your bank maintain a profile of its commercial banking customers? What form is it in (cards, files, on computer), and what information is maintained?

8. What are the differences between marketing research and a marketing information system?

8 TARGET MARKET SELECTION AND POSITIONING STRATEGIES

OVERVIEW

As discussed in previous chapters, there are many variables that can affect the behavior of consumers as they select the particular way in which they will satisfy their needs and wants. There has also been a discussion of marketing research, which may be used to help the marketer identify, measure, and understand market segments. This chapter deals with the many choices facing the marketer, who must segment the market and select those segments that will be targeted with marketing mix strategies.

First, five approaches to market segmentation will be covered: geographic, demographic, psychographic, volume, and benefit segmentation. The segmentation strategies used in addressing the corporate banking market will also be reviewed. Next, guidelines for selecting target markets, and three alternative approaches to segment selection, will be discussed: **undifferentiated marketing**, **differentiated marketing**, and **concentrated marketing**. In conclusion, the concept of **positioning**, or creating a unique place in the target's mind for the institution or the product, will be addressed.

A wide range of wrist watch styles points to the existence of many market segments for a single item.

SEGMENTING THE MARKET

Market segmentation, as an element of marketing strategy, recognizes the wisdom of specializing to suit the needs of a segment of the market rather than trying to be "all things to all people." The problem with the latter approach is that buyers in the market for the same product (whether it be checking services or automobiles) are far from homogeneous with respect to how they want their needs and wants satisfied. Consequently, they differ in how they respond to a particular marketing mix strategy. Market segmentation subdivides a market into more or less homogeneous subsets of customers, where any subset could be selected as a market target to be reached with a distinct marketing mix.

There are many firms that have done such a good job of segmenting and selecting a target market that they have dramatically influenced their industry. For example, consider the wristwatch market. For years, the major watch companies made prestigious, expensive watches and sold them through jewelry stores. The U.S. Time Company recognized a market segment whose wants were not being met. The company developed a durable, low-cost watch that it marketed through mass merchandisers, and the Timex watch made U.S. Time one of the world's largest watch manufacturers.[1]

The object of market segmentation is to identify a specific user group and then pursue it with a tailored product, supported by appropriate pricing, promotion, and distribution strategies. This identification requires that market segments have certain qualities that make it possible to specialize the marketing approach. To be viable as segments, they must be *measurable, accessible*, and *sizable*.[2] In other words, it must be possible to measure the size and purchasing power of the market segment; it must be feasible to reach the segment through advertising and through the distribution system; and there must be enough members in the segment to generate a profitable volume.

Segmentation Strategies

There are a number of different approaches to market segmentation. The approach a particular firm or bank chooses should subdivide the

Exhibit 8-1 Benefit Segmentation and the Savings Market*

Types of Customers

	The Sophisticated Investor Segment	The Cautious Segment	The Time-Conscious Segment	The Rainy Day Segment
Principal Benefit Sought	Best return per dollar invested	Assurance of the safety of their money	Convenience	Building a nest egg for the future
Demographic Characteristics	Educated, professional, executive-level occupation, higher income	Less educated, older age groups, lower income	Children at home, two-income households	Less educated; blue collar workers
Socio-Psychological Characteristics	Higher social classes, upwardly mobile	Lower social classes	Middle classes	Lower social classes
Special Behavioral Characteristics	Intent on expressing financial acumen to others, beating inflation	Intent on conserving what they have, defer trying new products, comfortable with the familiar	Always busy, club joiners, active in community affairs	Behaviorally conservative, careful planner, budgeter
Preferred Investment Alternatives	Stocks, bonds, real estate, mutual funds, precious metals, coins	Banks, savings and loans, credit unions, Treasury Bills and Notes	Money market funds, mutual funds, banks, savings and loans	Banks, savings and loans, credit unions, mutual funds

Source: Adapted from Leonard L. Berry, ''Marketing: The Time is Now,'' *Savings and Loan News*, April 1969, p. 61.
*Content is hypothetical and for illustrative purpose only.

market into groups that differ considerably from one another with respect to their preferences. Some principal segmentation alternatives are:

- geographic segmentation;
- demographic segmentation;
- psychographic segmentation;
- volume segmentation; and
- benefit segmentation.

Geographic segmentation divides the market according to geographic units. A decision is made that the firm will market different products in different areas, or that it will market only in selected areas and not in others. For example, the range of cornmeal products marketed by the Quaker Oats Company in the Northeast is limited to yellow and white cornmeal, while in the South, the consumer will find not only two types of cornmeal but also corn flour and a variety of cornmeal baking mixes, as Southerners cook with corn products more than Northerners do. A bank practices geographic segmentation when it decides on the location of a new branch. The bank cannot have locations everywhere, so it must use its limited resources to obtain the best return. It does that by locating its branch office(s) in the most promising geographic market area.

Demographic segmentation refers to categorizing the market in terms of population characteristics such as age, sex, income, occupation, and position in the life cycle. For example, the bank that establishes an executive banking group specifically for attorneys, accountants, and doctors has targeted an occupational segment. When the bank develops an equity credit line aimed at homeowners with incomes in excess of $35,000, it is targeting a specific demographic segment.

Psychographic segmentation means classifying the market in behavioral terms according to lifestyle, social class, or personality profile. For example, a bank might identify the young professional on the fast track as a prime credit card market segment. Marlboro (cigarettes) has targeted just one psychographic segment for many years: the independent, free-spirited smoker, personified by the lone cowboy out on the trail.

"I LIKE MILLER LITE IN A BOTTLE BECAUSE I STILL HATE PITCHERS."

Lite BEER

GREG "THE BULL" LUZINSKI
EX-SLUGGER

Beer advertising frequently appeals exclusively to sports fans.

The beer that batted .800

8 out of 10 young beer drinkers who recently tried this beer in unmarked bottles liked it. They said it was good tasting and smooth.

And when we tried it on more beer drinkers, they were surprised to find out it was Schaefer Beer.

They said things like, "I didn't think I'd like Schaefer, but I really do." And, "Next time I go to the mountains, this is coming with me."

Today's Schaefer is being brewed by the Stroh family, who have devoted their 200 years of brewing experience to making Schaefer better than ever.

Try today's Schaefer. It will make a Schaefer drinker out of you.

© 1982, Schaefer Brewing Company, Lehigh Valley, PA

Volume segmentation refers to the marketer's attempt to distinguish heavy, medium, and light users of a product. In many businesses, a small proportion of the users accounts for a large proportion of sales. This is as true for savings accounts as it is for beer. Banks generally find that 20 percent of their savings customers generate 80 percent of their savings deposits. A reasonable marketing strategy is to determine the characteristics that those 20 percent have in common and then to direct the marketing effort toward attracting more people like them. Schaefer targeted the heavy beer drinker when it advertised, "Schaefer is the one beer to have when you're having more than one."

Benefit segmentation is the process of categorizing the market in terms of the main product-related benefits sought by different groups. The various approaches used in marketing toothpaste illustrates this type of segmentation. Some people wish to avoid decay and plaque; others are primarily concerned with having whiter, brighter teeth; and still others want a fresh taste. Each of these groups has been found to have certain demographic and psychographic characteristics.[3] For example, those whose primary concern is to avoid decay tended to have large families, be conservative, and be heavy users of toothpaste. Crest has successfully aimed its marketing strategies at this segment for many years, showing children coming home from their dental checkups with no cavities. Those seeking cosmetic benefits tend to be teens, young adults, smokers, and socially active people. Macleans and UltraBrite aim their strategy at this segment.

Exhibit 8-1 illustrates this approach as it applies to the market for savings. It portrays the market as made up of four major segments: the "sophisticated investor" segment, the "caution-first" segment, the "time-conscious" segment, and the "rainy-day" segment. Each of these groups seeks a different principal benefit when saving. A bank using benefit segmentation would build its strategy around the delivery of a specific benefit. For example, a bank targeting the "time-conscious" segment might develop a marketing strategy built around extended banking hours, providing a large number of automated tellers for around-the-clock banking, offering drive-up windows,

Exhibit 8-2

All roads lead to X-Press 24.

You don't have to look too far to find an X-Press 24®, whatever roads you travel in Massachusetts and New Hampshire. With over 700 conveniently located X-Press 24 automated tellers, there's bound to be one down the street, around the corner, or up the block from you. And, you'll find X-Press 24 automated tellers open around the clock, 365 days a year.

In fact, if you take a look at the bottom of this page, you'll find a list of the BayBanks X-Press 24 locations nearby.

The BayBank Card offers you the fastest, most convenient banking in the area. Plus, when you're traveling in Massachusetts and New Hampshire, you'll find an X-Press 24 just about everywhere you turn.

With your BayBank Card, *all* roads lead to X-Press 24, so, if you don't have a BayBank Card yet, simply go to your nearest BayBank today. After you get one, you'll never be lost for cash!

BayBank®

IT JUST KEEPS GETTING BETTER.™

Needham—40 First Avenue (at Needham Industrial Center), 1055 Great Plain Avenue, Needham Heights (968 Highland Avenue), 399 Chestnut Street (next to Roche Bros.); **Wellesley**—197 Linden Street, Wellesley Hills (342 Washington Street), Wellesley Lower Falls (29 Washington Street), Wellesley Square (15 Central Street), *Wellesley College (Schneider Student Center). *Available during regular business/University hours only.
For more X-Press 24 locations, please call the X-Press 24 Hotline at 1-800-342-8888.

Member FDIC

adjusting teller staffing to reduce waiting time on peak volume days, and advertising heavily to communicate these time-saving conveniences.

Banks vary greatly in the way they use segmentation strategy. Most banks segment the markets for individual bank products. For instance, in any one geographic market at any one time, all commercial banks are offering installment loans. One bank might target the rate-sensitive loan customer and prominently feature the bank's current interest rate, inviting consumers to compare it with the rates of other loan providers. Another bank might target the segment that seeks the benefits of speed and convenience. This bank would promote its telephone loan service, promising same-day approval; there might be no mention of the interest rate in the advertising. In fact, the rate might be 50 or 100 basis points higher than the rate advertised by the competition. A third bank might aim at the segment that is planning to borrow in order to realize some aspiration or ambition. Its advertising would feature people talking about the wonderful things they would do with the proceeds of a loan.

Most banks' checking product line reflects a demographic segmentation strategy. The bank that has a "no-frills" type of checking account for people who maintain low balances and write few checks, a regular checking account for the mass market, and an interest-bearing checking account with a high minimum balance requirement, is segmenting along the income demographic.

Some banks select a target market that the entire institution and all its product marketing efforts will be directed toward. BayBanks, which is headquartered in Boston, targeted the psychographic segment that values speed and accessibility and that enjoys the convenience of automated banking. (See Exhibit 8-2.)

Segmenting the Commercial Banking Market

Segmentation strategy can be applied to the commercial banking market as well as to the consumer market. The three segmentation strategies most likely to be used by banks in their approach to the commercial banking market are *geographic segmentation*, *sales volume segmentation*, and *industry segmentation*.

A bank might use all three strategies simultaneously. For example, if a bank were to segment the commercial market by sales volume, it might have a small business department that addresses the needs of firms with sales of $2 million or less. Another department might target firms with sales of between $2 million and $20 million; a third might handle customers with sales from $20 million to $120 million; and a fourth department might concentrate on the few very large firms with sales over $120 million. Within any one of these target markets, the bank might also practice some geographic segmentation.

For instance, since the number of firms in the segment with sales of $2 million to $20 million is large, the bank might establish regional loan centers in the downtown area and in the northern, southern, eastern, and western suburbs. The bank might also target a distant geographical market—one that is not within the area served by its existing branches. At that distant regional office, the commercial banking officers might work to develop business among firms of all sizes, from $2 million on up.

The same bank might also practice industrial segmentation. It would identify specific industries that have enough members located within the bank's trade area to be a sizable and potentially profitable target. Furthermore, the segment should ideally have unique financing needs. Some examples would be the health care industry (hospitals, nursing homes); higher education (colleges and universities); insurance companies; commercial real estate developers; and government entities (states, cities, municipalities). Whichever approach the bank chooses to take, the segments targeted must meet the criteria of being measurable and accessible and must have enough members to be a potentially profitable target.

Once an organization has identified the market segments that it might address, the next step is to select the target market or markets.

TARGET MARKET SELECTION

There are some general guidelines that should be followed by the bank or firm when selecting target markets.[4]

1. *The target should be consistent, or at least compatible, with the bank's goals and image.* For instance, a bank that is known as a leading wholesale bank cannot suddenly target the market for retail installment loans with much success. Recall the importance of perceptions and the need to present a message that will support, rather than contradict, the target market's perceptions.

2. *The firm should seek markets that are consistent with its resources.* If a particular market segment can be reached only through mass media advertising, and the firm cannot afford the level of expenditure necessary to carry out a media campaign, the project is doomed. Similarly, if the target market is one that requires a high level of knowledge and sales skill at the point of sale, but the bank has not taken steps to provide that level of service, it should not aim at that market. The new, small bank in the heart of a large metropolitan area may experience considerable success by carefully targeting the executive with the six-figure salary who requires a high level of personal service. Trying to take on the major metropolitan banks in the mass market would be extremely expensive and thus impossible to justify.

3. *The firm should seek markets that will not only generate sufficient volume but also profitable volume.* The bank that targets the cost-conscious checking customer by offering totally free checking might find itself doing a land-office business but losing money on 80 percent of its accounts. It should always be kept in mind that the marketing concept calls for customer satisfaction at a *profitable* volume.

4. *The firm should seek a target market for which the number and size of competitors is small.* Aiming at a market that is already saturated with competitors requires taking customers away from the competition. It is much harder to shift customers away from a need-satisfying situation than it is to fill an unmet, or incompletely met, need.

There are three strategies that a bank or firm might use in selecting a target market or markets: undifferentiated marketing, differentiated marketing, and concentrated marketing. (See Exhibit 8-3.)

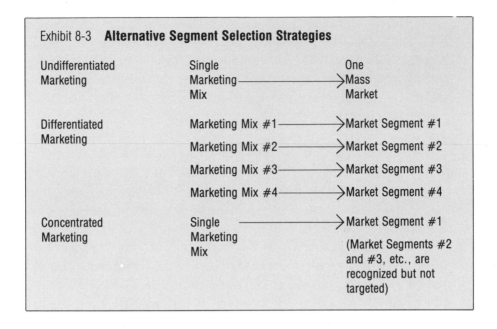

Exhibit 8-3   **Alternative Segment Selection Strategies**

Undifferentiated Marketing	Single Marketing Mix ──────────→	One Mass Market
Differentiated Marketing	Marketing Mix #1 ──────────→	Market Segment #1
	Marketing Mix #2 ──────────→	Market Segment #2
	Marketing Mix #3 ──────────→	Market Segment #3
	Marketing Mix #4 ──────────→	Market Segment #4
Concentrated Marketing	Single Marketing Mix ──────────→	Market Segment #1 (Market Segments #2 and #3, etc., are recognized but not targeted)

Undifferentiated Marketing

This strategy, which is also known as market aggregation, avoids segmentation altogether and targets the mass market with a single offer. The firm designs one product, pricing structure, distribution system, and promotional program to appeal to the largest number of people. This type of strategy is most often found in industries where there is little real difference between competing products. In such cases, the firm seeks to gain a competitive edge by differentiating itself from its competitors on image dimensions. For example, table salt is a product that does not admit to any real variation and is not aimed at any specific segment. But Morton's distinguishes itself from the competition with its slogan, "When it rains, it pours."[5] In many respects, banking is an industry where there is little product differentiation between institutions. As a result, many banks engage in undifferentiated marketing with their mass media image-building campaigns that are designed to set the bank apart from the competition in the minds of customers.

Differentiated Marketing

Differentiated marketing is also referred to as multiple segmentation. With differentiated marketing, the firm selects two or more different segments as its target markets and develops separate offers for each segment. There are two ways in which this might be done: the firm might offer different products to each of the different segments, or it might offer the same product, but vary the offer through the promotional strategy.

Some examples of differentiated marketing using different products for each segment are major automobile manufacturers such as General Motors, Ford, and Chrysler, which manufacture a variety of models aimed at different market segments. Banks that offer different varieties of checking accounts for different demographic segments are also practicing this type of differentiated marketing segmentation strategy.

An example of a firm marketing the same product to different segments using different promotional strategies for each segment is Johnson & Johnson. They market their baby shampoo to adults who seek the specific benefit of gentleness, as well as to mothers who need a "no more tears" shampoo for their small children. Banks practice this strategy when they develop different ads for one product. For example, when promoting an equity credit line, a bank might target different benefit segments. One ad might be aimed at parents of college-bound students who need additional financing, and another ad at households who seek a home improvement loan.

Differentiated marketing is likely to result in greater sales volume than undifferentiated marketing because it can lead to greater penetration of smaller markets. This contrasts with undifferentiated marketing, which leads to low penetration of the total market. However, it also tends to be a higher cost strategy than undifferentiated marketing due to the cost involved in producing and delivering different products and in executing a variety of promotional strategies. Most

Students, families, senior citizens, and executives may have vastly different expectations from their banks.

banks use differentiated marketing as their approach to market segmentation.

Concentrated Marketing

Concentrated marketing is sometimes referred to as single-segment marketing.[6] When using this strategy, the marketer selects one target market and develops only one marketing mix strategy to address it.

This strategy enables a firm to make good use of limited resources as a result of the economies that can be realized by having specialized product, distribution, and promotional strategies. It also enables the firm to penetrate one market deeply and to develop a reputation as an expert or specialist in that market. However, on the down side, the risks associated with this strategy are great. If the firm is highly successful, other firms may be attracted to the market, thus increasing competition and possibly reducing sales volume and increasing promotional expenses. Second, the danger in pursuing only one target market is that if the market's purchasing behavior changes for any reason, the firm could be out of business.

Some firms that have followed a concentrated segmentation strategy are Volkswagen, which entered the United States market by targeting the small-car market; and Rolls Royce, which targets the upper end of a high-income market. Irving Trust is an example of a bank that has targeted an upscale market with its personal banking approach.

POSITIONING

Having identified and selected the target market or markets, the firm must carve out a position for itself and its product in the minds of the members of the target market. The concept of positioning came to prominence in 1972 when Jack Trout and Al Ries wrote a series of articles entitled "The Positioning Era" for the trade publication *Advertising Age*. Since that time, they have written a book called *Positioning:*

The Battle for Your Mind, in which they use a number of familiar cases to demonstrate positioning successes and failures.

Trout and Ries define positioning as "not what you do to a product," but rather "what you do to the mind of the prospect. . . . You position the product in the mind of the prospect."[7]

There are several possible positioning strategies, some of which are:

- *Positioning in relation to a competitor*. A classic example is the strategy used by Avis, which positioned itself against the rental car industry leader, Hertz, by saying, "We're No. 2; we try harder." *Case E* describes "The Fast-Moving Bank" strategy developed by Trout and Ries to position United Jersey Banks against its big-name competitors.

- *Positioning in relation to a product class*. When Tylenol initiated the marketing campaign that led to its position as the leading analgesic, it positioned itself against aspirin, pointing out that aspirin was upsetting to the stomach, triggered allergic reactions, caused some internal bleeding, and more. Then, it offered itself as the alternative. In a similar vein, 7-Up has positioned itself as the alternative to cola drinks by calling itself "the uncola."

- *Positioning along price or quality dimensions*. Piaget positions itself as "the most expensive watch in the world," while Maytag positions itself as the highest quality washing machine manufacturer.

While this list of positioning strategies is not exhaustive,[8] it demonstrates that positioning is a strategy that addresses the way the target market thinks, and then either finds an opening that can be filled or creates one.

This chapter concludes the discussion of the critically important planning task of selecting the target market. The theories and the research tools for understanding markets, and the alternative strategies for target market selection have been addressed. Finally, the concept of positioning, or making a place for the product or the institution in the mind of the target, has been introduced.

The following section deals with the next step in the planning process: designing the marketing mix strategies to appeal to, and communicate with, the target market.

SUMMARY

Market segmentation recognizes the wisdom of specializing in order to suit the needs of a segment of the market rather than trying to be all things to all people. The object of segmentation is to identify a specific user group and then pursue it with a tailored product that is supported by appropriate pricing, promotion, and distribution strategies.

The market segments selected should be measurable, accessible, and sizable. Marketers can segment along a variety of lines: geography, demographics, psychographics, usage volume, and benefits sought. Banks generally segment the market for consumer products using a combination of segmentation strategies. The corporate banking market is usually segmented geographically, by sales size, or by industrial classification.

Some guidelines for selecting a target market are that it should be consistent with the organization's goals, image, and resources; it should be capable of generating profitable volume; and it should be one that is not already being targeted by a large number of competitors. The three target market selection strategies are undifferentiated marketing, which is basically the absence of targeting; differentiated marketing, in which the marketer selects two or more targets; and concentrated marketing, in which the marketer selects only one target. Having selected a target market, the marketer can use positioning strategy in order to create a special place for the product or the institution in the minds of the targeted segment.

POINTS FOR REVIEW

1. Define or briefly explain the following:
   - market segmentation
   - differentiated marketing
   - undifferentiated marketing
   - concentrated marketing

- benefit segmentation
- positioning

2. Select any magazine or newspaper advertisement that appears to be clearly aimed at a particular market segment.

   - Define the segment that is being targeted.
   - Explain which segmentation strategy is being used (benefit, geographic, demographic, etc.).
   - Describe the way in which the advertiser has appealed to the target.

3. Describe one way in which your bank segments the market for any one of its products, and explain how that segmentation strategy is reflected in its product design, service distribution methods, or promotional strategy.

4. How does your bank use segmentation strategy in its approach to the corporate banking market?

5. Provide an example from current advertising of a bank or consumer product that is using a strong positioning strategy.

PART IV MARKETING MIX STRATEGIES

Part III was concerned with techniques for understanding how and why consumers behave as they do and how to measure potential markets. These tools are indispensable in selecting target markets and in designing strategies that will appeal to them. Part IV addresses the next step in marketing planning: the design of product, pricing, place (distribution), and promotion strategies—in other words, the development of marketing mix strategies that will reach the target markets and achieve the plan's objectives.

Chapter 9 deals with the concept of the product and with alternative product strategies. It also addresses the new product development process and discusses the concept of product management. Chapter 10 deals with pricing strategy, and chapter 11 takes a look at distribution strategy. Since the distribution, and especially the sale, of banking services is difficult to separate from the people who are delivering those services, personal selling is considered to be part of distribution strategy. (General marketing texts treat selling as part of promotion strategy.) Chapter 12 deals with the important role of personal selling in banking.

Once the marketer has put together the offer consisting of a product or service aimed at a target market, priced to maximize appeal while providing a profit for the firm, and has put into place a system for distributing it, the marketer is then ready to communicate that offer to the target market. The final chapter in this part of the text, therefore, addresses promotion strategy. Here, the marketer brings to bear all that is known about the target market's needs, perceptions, motivations, and behavior to develop an appealing, creatively executed message designed to inspire members of the target market to select this one particular product or service over all the others.

9 PRODUCT STRATEGY AND NEW PRODUCT DEVELOPMENT

OVERVIEW

This chapter takes a look at the fourth key element in the planning process: the formulation of a detailed marketing mix strategy. Strategy formulation involves determining how the marketing mix will be used. This chapter on product strategy begins with the meaning of the term *product* and the similarities and differences between products and services. It presents some alternative product strategies and introduces the concepts of the product life cycle and product adopter categories. It also describes the new product development process as it applies specifically to banking products. The chapter also discusses the product management concept and delves into some of the reasons why some products fail.

IMPORTANCE OF THE PRODUCT

The product is the key element in the marketing mix. There are two fundamental reasons for this:

1. *The product (or service) is the firm's reason for being.* All firms are in the business of satisfying customer needs, and they do this through their product. A firm that does not deliver a need-satisfying product should not be in existence. In fact, competition usually drives such a company out of the market.

2. *All the other elements of the marketing mix revolve around the product.* This does not imply that the other elements of the mix are not vital. Rather, they typically play the role of facilitating market acceptance of the product. This is illustrated by Exhibit 9-1, which shows the elements of the marketing mix as a three-legged stool. The three legs (pricing, distribution, and promotion) would serve no useful purpose without the seat (the product). Likewise, the seat is not very useful without the legs. *Distribution strategy* is concerned with making the product available when and where the market wants it. *Pricing strategy* is concerned with making the product available at a price that is both attractive to the market and helpful to the realization of the organization's sales and profit objectives. *Promotion strategy* is concerned with communicating the potential benefits available to the market as the result of the product, distribution, and the price attributes.

What is a Product?

Speaking very generally, a product is a source of potential satisfaction or solutions to prospective customers. Kotler gives a more detailed definition: "A *product* is anything that can be offered to a market for attention, acquisition, use, or consumption. It includes physical objects, services, persons, places, organizations, and ideas."[1] Within this context, banking services (savings accounts and certificates of deposit, check processing, safekeeping services, lockbox operations, cash management services, loans, and so on) are "products." So are candidates for public office, the Bahamas, the Army, and the idea that smoking may be harmful to your health.

In order to better comprehend the concept of "product" from a marketing point of view, one should understand that there are three aspects of "product":[2]

1. the core product;

2. the tangible product; and

3. the augmented product.

Core Product

The core product is the essential benefit the buyer expects to receive from the product. As Charles Revson of Revlon has said, "In the factory we make cosmetics, and in the drugstore we sell hope." When a woman buys "blusher," she is not buying a set of chemical components to color her face; she is buying beauty. When customers open a checking account, they are not buying a checkbook and a monthly statement; they are buying bill-paying convenience. The marketer's job (and the new accounts person's job) is to sell the customer the benefit—the core product.

Tangible Product

The tangible product is the thing that the target market recognizes as the object being sold. Makeup, checking accounts, political candidates, and so forth, are all tangible products.

Tangible products may have a number of characteristics: a certain level of *quality*, various *features*, certain *styling*, a *brand* name, and *packaging*. A customer shopping for a razor is confronted with a shelf full of different products that are, fundamentally, all razors. Each one bears a brand name, is associated with a certain quality level in the customer's mind, has a different color and shape of package, various features (disposability, plastic construction, metal construction) and styling (shaped to fit the hand, usable with a certain type of blade).

Although services, such as those offered in the banking industry, may not be literally tangible, they may have some or all of these

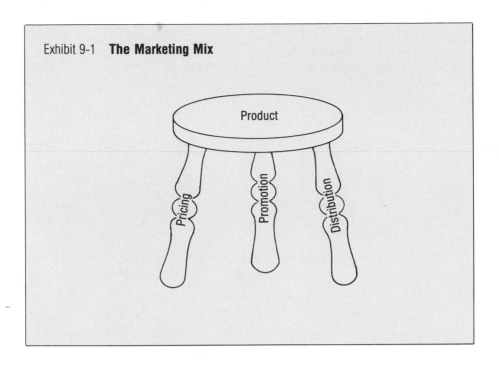

Exhibit 9-1 **The Marketing Mix**

characteristics. For example, the materials handed out to the new checking account customer are part of the ''packaging'' of the account, as is the treatment the customer receives, and the environment in which the transaction takes place. The quality of the checking account may be considered ''high'' by the customer because of the reputation of the bank (that is, the name identification). The account might have a special name, such as ''Custom Checking,'' and may have features such as overdraft protection and a monthly statement that lists checks sequentially.

Augmented Product

The augmented product is the tangible product accompanied by a host of related tangible or intangible offerings. For instance, when a person buys a circular saw from Sears, he is not only buying the saw (the tangible product), but a whole range of accompanying services, including a satisfaction guarantee, a warranty, and maintenance and repair service.

IBM has excelled in the computer field because it recognizes that the customer wants not just a computer but instruction, software, programming services, maintenance, repairs, guarantees, and flexibility to keep up with the latest technology. These exemplify the concept of **systems selling**—the strategy of marketing coordinated solutions to the totality of the customer's problem. Later in this chapter, this concept will be applied to the packaging of banking services.

Exhibit 9-2 looks at Marlton National Bank's new Home Equity Credit Line from the perspective of the three aspects of "product."

Related Product Concepts

In addition to the definition and various conceptualizations of the term *product*, there are three related concepts that the marketing student should be familiar with: the product item, the product line, and the product mix.

A **product item** is a specific version of a product, such as a 6-month certificate of deposit. A **product line** is a group of product items that are closely related, such as the full line of savings services (money market savings, passbook and statement savings, short- and long-term savings certificates, savings clubs, and so on). The **product mix** is the full list of products offered for sale by the bank or firm. For example, it is not unusual for a large bank to offer over 100 different services. All of these make up the product mix.

Any given tangible or augmented product is also a product item, which is part of a product line, which is very likely part of a product mix. Exhibit 9-3 provides examples of a retail and commercial product item, line, and mix.

Services versus Products

Before proceeding with the discussion of product strategy, it will be useful to look at the differences between products and services since

Exhibit 9-2 The Three Aspects of "Product"

Aspect	Components
Core Product	The benefit to the customer
	Example Write yourself a loan No need to reapply each time you want to borrow
Tangible Product	The product's features, style, packaging, brand, quality
	Example Marlton National Bank's home equity line of credit, priced at prime + 1.75%, adjusted quarterly; accessible by check or automated teller; 120-month repayment period; amounts up to 70% of the appraised value of the house, with a minimum of $10,000 and maximum of $100,000
Augmented Product	Tangible and intangible accompaniments such as service, warranty, installation, free delivery
	Example The way the customer is treated during the application and approval process A legible and understandable monthly statement Prompt response to customer service questions
Equals	Equals

THE PRODUCT FROM THE MARKETER'S POINT OF VIEW

this text deals with marketing in a service industry. While there are many similarities between the marketing of tangible products and services, there are also many differences that the bank marketing student must understand.

The term *product* was defined to include services under that general category. Nevertheless, there are a number of differences between products and services that deserve some attention.

First, it is necessary to define the term: "**Services** are those separately identifiable, essentially intangible activities that provide want satisfaction and that are not necessarily tied to the sale of a product or another service."[3] Health care, private education, transportation, communication, and professional services are examples of service industries.

Services have certain characteristics that create special challenges for marketers. As a result of these characteristics, the marketing techniques used by banks and other service industries are often very different from those found in product marketing. These characteristics are as follows:[4]

- intangibility;
- inseparability;
- heterogeneity; and
- perishability and fluctuating demand.

Intangibility

Since services cannot be seen, felt, tasted, touched, or otherwise experienced by the senses, it is all the more imperative that the marketing effort stress benefits provided by the service. Advertising, promotional material, and personal selling must concentrate on emphasizing the benefits the service offers rather than its features or the way it works. Just as the telephone company tells business professionals how they can save money by calling long distance rather than making personal visits, so banks tell consumers how using automated tellers will enable them to avoid waiting in long lines and to bank whenever they want.

Inseparability

Frequently, services cannot be separated from the person who is the seller. A vivid example is the service provided by a dentist. In many cases, the direct sale or personal contact is an important channel of the distribution. You can open a checking account, in most cases, only by going to an employee of a bank.

Likewise, because of inseparability, the bank's services are largely sold only in markets where there is an office. Innovative banks have found ways around this limitation and solicit new business (especially credit business) through the mail. Nevertheless, more

Exhibit 9-3 **Banking Examples of Product Mix, Product Line, and Product Items**

	Retail Market	Commercial Market
Product Mix	All products and services offered to the retail market	All products and services offered to the commercial market
Product Line	Retail checking products	Collection and concentration products
Product Items	• Basic checking • Regular checking • Money market checking	• Lockbox • Zero balance accounts • Depository transfer checks

individualized banking services, such as financial counseling, require personal contact.

Heterogeneity

Although many service outlets (such as branches of a particular bank) may be selling and delivering the same services, the augmented products they are dispensing are not homogeneous (that is, uniform) from branch to branch. It is not possible to have precisely the same standard of service in every office at every moment. It is much easier for mass-produced products to be standardized so that everyone buying a package of a specific brand of aspirin gets the exact same product.

But the way the checking account customer is serviced and the quality of the service he or she receives cannot easily be standardized. Thus, it is all the more important for the bank or other service company to pay particular attention to sales and product knowledge training and to the standardizing of the operational end of the service with the goal of ensuring a consistently high quality of performance.

Perishability and Fluctuating Demand

The reader no doubt thinks of lettuce as being perishable, but not banking services. Yet, services are highly perishable since they cannot be stored. For example, empty seats from one football game cannot be carried over to provide more seating at the next. Similarly, hours when tellers are idle cannot be used to expand service at noon on Friday when long lines are forming.

Furthermore, the market for many services fluctuates considerably by season, day of the week, and by hour of the day. Consider the telephone service, public transportation, and restaurants as examples of this fact; it is also true of banking. The day before a holiday weekend, most Mondays and Fridays, lunch hours, and the third of each month (Social Security check day) are heavier-than-normal banking times.

The combination of perishability and fluctuating demand presents challenges for marketers in the product planning, pricing, promotion, and distribution areas. Telephone companies try to spread out the demand for their services by pricing off-peak hours to make them more attractive to callers. Some banks price their check-cashing service to encourage the use of automated tellers and to reduce lobby traffic. Through advertising, banks can highlight the convenience of banking day and night rather than just when the bank is open.

Related to this characteristic of fluctuating demand is the fact that the decision to buy a banking service (that is, an individual's demand for banking services) is made infrequently. Banking does not involve a repeat purchase as is true for most consumer products. If customers do not buy one brand of toothpaste this month, maybe they will next month. In banking, there are not as many chances to capture the customer. All of these factors present special challenges for the marketer of banking services.

PRODUCT STRATEGIES

There are any number of product strategies that a bank or business may select, and for the most part they fall into two broad categories: strategies relating to the product mix, and strategies relating to the product life cycle.

Exhibit 9-4   **Depth and Breadth and the Product Mix**

Breadth (number of product lines) →

	Checking	Savings	CDs	Personal Credit
Depth (items within a line) ↓	Basic checking	Passbook savings	3 mos.	Installment loan—fixed rate
	Regular checking	Statement savings	6 mos.	Installment loan—variable rate
	Money market checking	Money market savings	12 mos.	Unsecured revolving credit line
		Holiday club	30 mos.	Equity credit line
		Vacation club	60 mos.	Credit card
				Gold credit card

Product Mix Strategies

The most common product mix strategies are:[5]

- product expansion;
- product contraction;
- product modification;
- product repositioning; and
- trading up or trading down.

Product Expansion

A company engages in product expansion by adding new product lines to an existing product mix or by adding new products to an existing product line. When adding new lines, the company is broadening the product mix; when adding items to a product line, it is deepening the line. (See Exhibit 9-4.) For example, when Coca-Cola introduced Tab and Diet Coke, it was expanding or deepening the product line of cola drinks. However, when it started marketing sportswear bearing the Coca-Cola logo, it was broadening its product mix. When a bank adds a basic checking account to its line of checking products, it is deepening the product line. When that bank enters the discount brokerage business, it is broadening its product mix.

Exhibit 9-4 illustrates the depth and breadth of a consumer banking product line, and Exhibit 9-5 provides an example of product expansion strategies.

Product Contraction

Sometimes firms thin out their product lines by eliminating products, or entire product lines, that may be contributing little to profits. They do this in order to concentrate their resources on a narrow product mix that will generate more profits. At one point, General Electric dropped a number of products from its mix (blenders, vacuum cleaners, fans, heaters, and humidifiers). When Bankers Trust sold its retail branches in order to concentrate on wholesale banking, it was eliminating the retail product mix, an extreme example of product contraction.

A less drastic example of this strategy is seen in the case of banks that aim their marketing efforts at a particular market segment—such as individuals with high incomes and/or high net worth. Their pricing and promotion strategies are geared to this select market and result in the loss of many less profitable accounts. In a very real sense, these banks have contracted their product mix.

A word of caution is in order on this subject. While upscale customers may be more profitable than most and may represent an important target market, banks have a responsibility to meet the banking needs of individuals of all kinds. Banks are granted their charters and branch approvals by regulators based on their proven ability to meet the convenience and needs of the banking public. This includes the low-and moderate-income public as well as the high net worth public. The consumer pressure placed on banks to offer low-cost checking accounts illustrates the fact that many banks have lost sight of this fact. There will be further discussion on this subject in chapter 15, which addresses public relations and social responsibility.

Product Modification

A firm can improve its product, or redesign or repackage it—perhaps even give it a new name—in the hope of increasing sales. General

Mills did just this with their Bisquick product when it was 35 years old. Sales had been declining, so they changed some of the ingredients, switched from milk to buttermilk solids, and now "Bisquick Buttermilk Baking Mix" is more than 50 years old.[6]

Banks are continually modifying and enhancing existing products. For example, a bank might add new features and benefits to its credit card product by allowing customers to write checks against the credit line, offering a credit card registration service, or making the credit line available through the bank's automated tellers.

Product Repositioning

As was mentioned in chapter 8, positioning is not something that is done to the product as much as it is something that is done to the collective minds of the target market. It sets the product apart from the competition. The makers of the Snickers candy bar repositioned their product as a wholesome, between-meal snack, setting it apart from its competitors. Orange growers repositioned orange juice when they advertised: "It isn't just for breakfast anymore."

Many banks have repositioned themselves as a result of mergers and acquisitions. When several banks in eastern Pennsylvania merged, they formed a banking organization that was several times the size of any one of them individually. They changed the name of the bank and engaged in a massive media campaign that effectively obliterated the image of the individual banks and created a new organization in the minds of the residents of the market area. This situation has repeated itself in many parts of the country as regional and interstate banking has spread.

Trading Up or Trading Down

This strategy is a particular type of product expansion strategy that is very much related to the appeal of prestige. By adding a higher priced or prestige item to its product line, a manufacturer may hope to attract customers for its lower priced items as well. Trading down involves adding a lower priced item to a prestige line in the hope that people who are attracted to, but cannot afford, the original will buy the lower priced item. Mercedes did this when it introduced the "190 Series" of smaller, lower priced, sporty cars. K-Mart, on the other hand, engages in trading up by offering higher priced, name brand items in the hope of attracting both the value shopper and the discount shopper.

Banks that offer totally free checking as a means of selling the customer additional services might be said to be trading down.

Product Life Cycle Strategies

Products come and go—some going sooner than others. By looking at the sales histories of many different types of products, the concept of the **product life cycle** has been developed. The typical life cycle, showing the pattern of sales and profits at each stage in the cycle, is shown in Exhibit 9-6. This chart is a useful, simplified model, but it is not meant to imply that all products go through precisely this type of experience. Some products enter the market, take off quickly, and die off just as fast. Others enter into the decline phase and are revived, their life cycle looking more like a double-humped camel. Nevertheless, for these purposes, the life cycle shown in Exhibit 9-6 is a useful tool for understanding product strategy and the importance of new products to businesses.

Exhibit 9-6 depicts the life cycle of a product class (such as the personal checking account or videocassette recorders) rather than a particular firm's product (First National Bank's checking account or Sony's VCR). The vertical axis represents dollar value of sales and profits, and the horizontal axis represents time. There are four stages through which the product passes: *introduction, growth, maturity,* and *decline*. (Some products also pass through a fifth stage: *abandonment*.) For reasons that will soon become apparent, the total market sales curve for the product is quite different from its total market profit curve.

Introduction

The introduction stage is characterized by a slow growth in sales as the product is introduced into the market. The profit curve shows a negative profit during this phase due to the heavy expenses incurred in introducing the product. In addition to the substantial advertising expense required to make the market aware of the new product, there are research and development costs and the cost of getting the distribution system in place to deliver the new product to the market. In banking, there are substantial costs involved in developing the computer systems required to deliver a new product. This up-front cost makes it impractical to test market bank products, except for the purpose of testing the system prior to large-scale product introduction.

Home banking by personal computer is in the introduction stage of its life cycle in the late 1980s. Because it involves changing customer banking and bill-paying behavior, the growth in numbers of customers using the service is slow. Advertising strategy concentrates on educating the public about the benefits of the service. The promotional emphasis is on customer education and getting people to try it.

Growth

The growth stage is characterized by an acceleration in sales of the new product as more people become aware of the product, are attracted to it, and buy it. The increased sales alert those firms that are not yet in the market that they should get into it. However, until they do get into the market, the innovative firm has the edge in an increasing market—which is an ideal position to be in. As a result of limited competition and accelerating sales, the nonprofitability turns to profitability and then profits increase, leveling off as the next phase approaches.

Maturity

The profitability of the growth stage attracts intense competition as the maturity stage approaches. Maturity is characterized by a slowed rate of sales growth, as most of the prospects for the product are using it. This stage is also characterized by aggressive advertising, which contributes to the increased cost and, thus, reduced profitability of the product.

Many traditional banking services are in the maturity stage. In this stage, it is likely that prices will be cut as more competitors try to increase sales of their specific product. Checking accounts provide an example of such a product. In the mid-1970s, many banks moved to totally free checking in an effort to increase their market share for this product. The strategy backfired when many banks followed suit, thus reducing revenues for all involved and cutting seriously into profits. One researcher, studying the situation in the city of Pittsburgh, estimated that the 12-month gross loss to that city's banks was

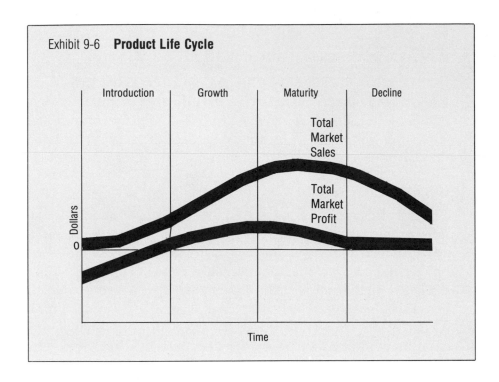

Exhibit 9-6 **Product Life Cycle**

$4–$4.5 million.[7] Since that time, banks have become more rational and, responding to pressures on earnings, have restored service charges on checking. This has shifted up the profit curve while checking account sales remain at or near a peak level.

Another strategy, besides price cutting, that characterizes the maturity stage is product modification and improvement. There was an earlier reference to General Mills' product, Bisquick, which experienced a declining sales curve after 35 years. The company changed some of the components, and thus gave new life to the product—causing the sales and profit curves to turn up.

Another appealing product strategy for many industries (including banking) when products are in the mature stage, is that of systems selling. But before discussing systems selling, it would be useful to cover the last stage in the product life cycle—the decline stage.

Decline

When total market sales begin to downturn markedly, the decline stage has been reached. Regular savings accounts are in this stage of the life cycle.

The decline stage may be due to any number of forces including new products that come along to replace the product. For example, money market funds had much to do with the gradual demise of regular savings accounts. Technological innovation may also be responsible, such as the development of color television, causing sales of black and white TVs to decline.

Actions of Congress or the federal regulatory agencies may also be responsible for pushing a product into decline. For instance, in the late 1960s, the ban on cyclamates as sugar substitutes plunged many products into decline. Through innovation and the discovery of another sugar substitute, however, there was a resurgence for some of these products. The money market deposit account, which was a much-needed creation of the monetary authorities, also contributed to the decline of regular savings accounts at banks.

Finally, social change may be responsible for a product's decline. The fact that men no longer wear dress hats or that fewer people drive large, fuel-inefficient cars can be traced to social and environmental factors.

The decline phase is characterized by fewer firms offering the product, by reduced promotion, and by a restricted variety of product offerings. Although it is possible for one or more firms to continue to profit from the product, total market profit drops substantially during the decline stage.

Product Adopter Categories

Closely related to the product life cycle is the pattern in which consumers accept and adopt new products. Consumers vary from one another in the rate of their response to a new product offering. Some people tend to try something new soon after it is introduced; others wait a long time, and still others may never adopt the product.

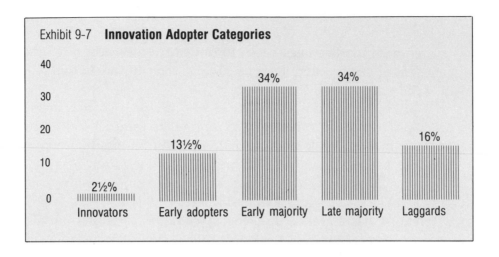

Exhibit 9-7 **Innovation Adopter Categories**

Five product adoption categories have been identified by researchers. They are **innovators, early adopters,** the **early** and **late majority,** and **laggards**. (Those who never adopt the product are not included.) Exhibit 9-7 shows the relative proportion of these adopter categories in the total adopter population. The category into which a consumer falls is generally related to demographics, social status, and information sources. Innovators are risk-takers and, along with the early adopters and early majority, tend to be younger, better educated, and have higher incomes and social standing than late adopters. In addition, their sources of information tend to be multimedia-based and, thus, more varied. In contrast, the late majority and laggards tend to have limited information sources and often rely on their reference groups to form their opinions.

The amount of elapsed time between adoption by innovators and by the early and late majority depends upon a number of factors. The greater the perceived advantage of the innovation, the shorter that time period will be. On the other hand, the more complex the innovation, the longer it will be. Telephone bill payment is a product that has been on the market for a number of years in some markets, but consumer adoption has been slow. Only the innovators and very early adopters are users, probably due to the complexity of the product and the inability of consumers to sample or try out the service.

Systems Selling

Earlier, it was mentioned that many bank products are in the maturity stage, and that one possible strategy for this phase of the life cycle is systems selling. **Systems selling** involves *the marketing of coordinated solutions to the totality of the customer's problem*. This strategy is based on the recognition by marketing-oriented executives that customers buy solutions to problems or need satisfaction, not products.

The careful observer will find systems selling in operation in many industries today. IBM is a good example, with their full range of products, servicing, related equipment, and so on. Other examples of systems selling include companies that market total home protection systems—not just locks—and companies that market total interiors—not just furniture or floor coverings.

With reference to bank marketing, systems selling takes the form of **service packaging**. Generally speaking, there are two basic alternatives for implementing systems selling in banks:

1. predetermined packages of bank services; and

2. individualized packages of bank services.

Predetermined Packages of Bank Services

One alternative in the use of systems selling is the marketing of predetermined packages or systems of banking services to specific segments of the market. This is precisely what Wells Fargo Bank did in the early 1970s with the "Wells Fargo Gold Account." This program, which was the forerunner of a number of similar programs across the country, at one time attracted 7,000 new accounts during one month—3 times the normal new account rate at that bank.

In its original form, the Gold Account customer received, for $3 dollars per month, a total banking relationship, including unlimited check writing, credit card, safe deposit box, overdraft protection, cashier's checks, money orders, special rates on installment loans, and special savings plans, among other services.

Packages or systems of financial services, such as the Gold Account, make sense for customers because they conveniently provide a total solution to the financial problems facing them. They make sense for the bank, because built into the concept is an automatic vehicle for increasing the number of bank services used per bank customer. This is highly desirable because statistics show that the more relationships customers have with the bank, the less likely they are to switch banks.

The concept of predetermined packages of bank services can be worked in a number of ways, depending upon a bank's capabilities, imagination, and market characteristics. For instance, a bank in a college town might develop one package for college-age consumers, another for young-adult households, a third for middle-aged adults, and a fourth for business accounts. There can be one price for the total package or several prices, depending upon the number of services the customer wishes to obtain. But a cautionary note is due: having too great a spread between the sum of individual service prices and package prices, or failure to allow purchase of certain services unless they are packaged, may violate federal or state antitrust laws.

Individualized Packages of Bank Services

An alternative to predetermined packages of bank services is the marketing of custom packages of bank services. This may be done through a **personal banker** program whereby participating bank customers are assigned their own liaison person within the bank. Ideally, the personal banker (1) consults on the customer's financial situation; (2) sells the services needed; (3) makes the arrangements for the services to be provided; (4) solves any problems that may arise; and (5) stays in continuing contact with the customer.

The personal banker is, in effect, the customer's contact point within the bank for virtually all matters with the exception of routine transactions such as cashing a check or making a deposit. However, in serving the very high net worth or high-income segment, the personal banker may even conduct these routine transactions for the customer.

The personal banker approach lends itself nicely to systems selling. In the role of financial consultant, the personal banker is in a position to develop a package derived from the bank's available services that can be tailored to the specific financial service needs of the client. Staff members put into this type of position must have adequate knowledge and expertise to be able to function effectively and to win the confidence of the more knowledgeable and sophisticated customers. Moreover, the personal banker can help both the bank and its clients by truly educating customers regarding the various services available in the bank.

In addition, the personal banker represents an accountable contact point in the bank for the customer. One of the conditions underlying the consumer movement is the frustration consumers feel when they take a grievance to a representative of a company only to be told, "I don't make the rules, I just work here;" or "Sorry, that's not my area of responsibility."

Finally, the personal banker can be a source of important marketing information for the bank. By dealing with the problems, needs, satisfactions, frustrations, fears, levels of awareness, and behavior of clients on a continual basis, the personal banker can impart valuable marketing information to management.

In short, the personal banker concept, if conceived and marketed properly, results in one expert person serving as a systems salesman, consultant, educator, contact point, and data source. In addition, the personal banker concept is a vehicle for truly personalizing the bank, a task that is more difficult as banks grow larger and become more automated.

NEW PRODUCT DEVELOPMENT

The realities of the product life cycle underscore the importance of new products to a firm. Since products tend to be most profitable in the growth stage, the firm should ideally have a solid proportion of its product mix in this stage at all times. Conversely, a firm that is not interested in **new product development** can eventually expect to become totally dependent on the later (and theoretically less profitable) stages of its various products' life cycles. This is true for banking as well as for other industries, especially since banking faces increasing competition from nonbank providers of financial products. Finding ways to offer new products is especially challenging in banking due to the limitations of regulation. For example, product managers are challenged to develop products to compete with stock-based mutual funds while being limited in the ways the bank can use those funds to generate a return (that is, without being able to invest the deposits in the stock market).

The way a bank approaches product development depends upon its size and structure. More than any other area of bank marketing, product development has a considerable operational component. In some banks, the product development department reports to the director of marketing. In others, the responsibility for product development lies within each of the line functions of the bank (retail, commercial, trust). In others, a team approach is used, with representatives from systems and programming, operations, and the relevant line department, coordinated and headed by the product manager or marketing head.[8] Wherever the responsibility lies, the business of getting a product developed and marketed in a bank, or in any other organization, involves coordinating the efforts of a number of different departments.

Progressive-Rejection System

Regardless of how a firm is organized for product development, the foremost question is how the firm can maximize new product development potential and avoid mistakes. Although there is no magic formula, a firm can go a long way toward generating new ideas and reducing risk by establishing a formal procedure for new product development. It is imperative that the market point of view be built into such a system from the start. One example of a new product development system is the eight-stage progressive-rejection system (see Exhibit 9-8), in which a new product idea must survive each phase of evaluation before proceeding to the subsequent phase.[9]

Exploration and Idea Generation

This is the formal search in the market for new product ideas. In a bank, new product ideas might come from ongoing research to help identify consumer banking needs that are not being met. Or, they might come from management and employees. Some firms offer cash incentives to employees for generating new product ideas. Ideas might also come from customers, banks in other parts of the country, or from the competition. Also, new products occasionally come from banking regulators. The money market deposit account arose from this source.

Screening

This stage entails screening new product ideas against product objectives, product policy, and company resources. Not every new product idea can or should be pursued. A preliminary judgment must be made as to whether each idea deserves further study. In an aggressive and imaginative bank, an unusual idea that at first appears to be unworkable and not within present regulatory constraints should not be screened out until it has been evaluated in more detail.

Business Analysis

This stage involves development of a written business case and recommendation based on the results of market analysis, production feasibility analysis, marketing strategy development, and cost and revenue projections. In short, a situation analysis must be developed for the new product, along with preliminary objectives, target market selection, and strategy. If the recommendation is approved by management, the product development coordinator will pull together the group necessary for developing the product. *Case B* presents just such a business plan for a new home equity credit line.

Development

The development stage involves production of prototypes or samples of the new product. In banking, the development phase for a new

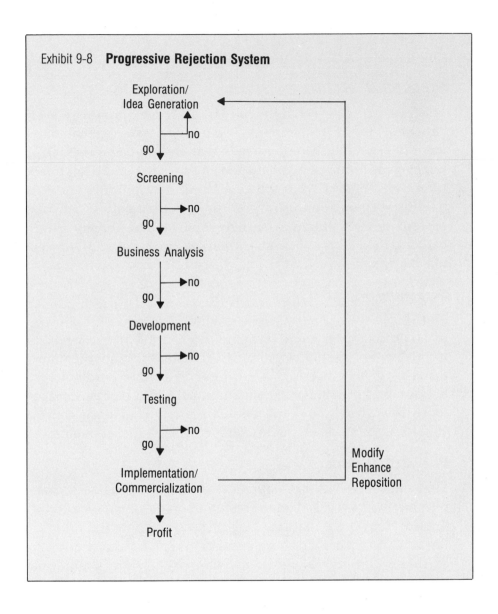

Exhibit 9-8 **Progressive Rejection System**

Exploration/
Idea Generation
no
go

Screening
no
go

Business Analysis
no
go

Development
no
go

Testing
no
go

Implementation/
Commercialization

Modify
Enhance
Reposition

Profit

savings product would involve modification of the savings computer system by the programming staff, the design of forms and documents that will be used to set up the accounts, and the writing of procedures for the branch staff to follow in completing the forms and processing them.

Testing

This is a crucial phase in new product development. Production testing, in-use consumer testing, concept testing, and test marketing are all elements of the testing stage. Some or all of them may be used in banking.

Concept Testing

This is done through consumer research. In developing a new banking (or other) product, there is little value to asking a large number of consumers what they think of a new product idea. This type of questioning fails to reach the underlying attitudes, beliefs, and concerns that consumers might have about a new product, nor does it gain insight into how they might behave if the product were available. There would be no frozen foods today if the industry had been guided by preliminary consumer reaction to the concept. It is best to first assemble small **focus groups** to explore reaction to a new product concept. This type of research, as indicated in chapter 7, draws out information about feelings and motivation with regard to the new product. It can also provide insight into how the product might be positioned or promoted.

On the basis of insight gained through such qualitative research, it is possible to design a meaningful questionnaire for quantitative research among members of the market. This method will generate data that is scientifically sound with respect to the probable market response to the product. This type of survey research can also help identify those particular market segments to whom the product is most attractive.

Consumer goods manufacturers (and occasionally, banks) test market new products. It is not unusual for a company to try out a new product in one or two geographic markets, perhaps using a different promotional approach in each to test their relative effectiveness. It is said that in the packaged goods business, only about half of the products rolled out for **test marketing** ever make it to the commercialization stage. This type of testing is less prevalent in banking, although at least one institution set up a "laboratory branch" where new services and products were tested before being distributed to the branch network.[10] Such testing enabled the bank to test customer response as well as to familiarize employees with the planned new products.

Implementation or Commercialization

This is the stage at which a company commits its resources to full-scale introduction. Introducing a new banking product entails heavy involvement by the marketing department. Ideally, the training director undertakes programs to be sure each customer-contact employee understands the service and how to sell it (that is, its *benefits* as opposed to its features). It is not unusual to tie the launching of a new product to an employee incentive campaign to boost initial sales. Sales promotion techniques might include offering a premium to the customer for purchasing the new product.

One of the problems that banks face in the introduction of many new deposit services is the resulting drain on deposits in existing products. For instance, when the money market deposit account was introduced, dollars were drained out of lower-cost regular savings and checking accounts, increasing the cost of these funds to the bank. Because of this effect, it is especially important that banks attempt to enter the market early with new product innovations. This serves to offset the cannibalizing of their existing deposits by attracting new customers and deposits from outside the bank. Naturally, the first bank(s) into the market with a good new product stand to gain. But it does not usually take long for the market followers to offer the same product, thus diluting the competitive advantage and placing the total market for the product on that part of the life cycle where profits start to flatten out.

Evaluation

The final stage in new product development involves the use of primary and secondary research to monitor the new product's progress toward its goals. An important point to reiterate is that the marketing planning process, which is what a new product development plan is, must include a system for monitoring the results of the plan. This enables the bank to take corrective action where needed, as well as to glean from each experience some knowledge that will facilitate the introduction of the next new product. In other words, the purpose of the evaluation stage is to learn from experience.

PRODUCT MANAGEMENT

Once a product has been launched and is part of the bank's overall service offering, what happens to it? Increasingly, there is an emergence in banking of the **product management** concept; that is, assigning to one person the responsibility for a specific product or group of products.

The product management concept began at Procter & Gamble in 1927. Sales of the firm's new Camay soap were not doing well, so one person was assigned the task of developing and promoting the product. This concept has been copied by other firms and is now found in banking as well.

The amount of responsibility and authority held by **product managers** varies greatly from firm to firm and from bank to bank. The general responsibilities of the product manager are to *develop annual product marketing plans, create strategies, see that they are put into action, monitor the results, and take corrective action as needed.*[11] In many cases, however, the product manager is a staff person with no profit responsibility for a product. This puts the manager in a position of having to manage by persuasion and having to negotiate the cooperation of individuals who have the ability to make or break the product.

In other situations, however, product management is a line function,[12] with the manager assuming profit and loss responsibility for the product. For example, a manager from the institutional banking department would manage those products that are used primarily by financial institutions, while the retail credit department would assign a manager to oversee all types of personal credit. In this type of organization, the product manager not only has responsibility for product marketing plans, but is accountable for their success, and has the authority to get them executed.

As profit margins continue to be squeezed by the increasing cost of funds and the rising cost of doing business, the product management concept is becoming more popular in banking circles as a way of maximizing the performance of every item in the product line.

PRODUCT FAILURES

There are many statistics cited about the high failure rate for new products of all types. These statistics vary widely, but the underlying truth is that many new products never make it beyond the introduction phase. New product failure is a common occurrence in industry, and banking is no exception.

Besides reasons that relate to a weakness in one or more of the elements of the marketing mix—such as pricing, promotion, or sales strategy—there are four underlying reasons for product failure directly related to the product itself. They are:

1. failure to look at the new product from the market point of view;

2. failure to research the needs of the market segments creatively;

3. failure to consider the degree of behavioral change required for the prospective customer; and

4. failure to communicate a new product's benefits clearly.

Each of these reasons will be discussed individually.

Failure: The Market Point of View

One common error that contributes to new product failure in smaller institutions is the temptation for bankers to depend on their intuition as a basis for new product development. The problem is that the intuitive process tends to be disproportionately biased in favor of one's own experiences, values, and needs. As a result, benefits that the banker sees as real and important may be viewed as unimportant or nonexistent by members of the market. The new product marketer must do everything feasible to view the new product idea from the buyer's viewpoint. This means conducting valid research.

For example, in the mid-1980s, one such banker felt that there was an untapped market for money market deposit accounts among older and more conservative people who liked having a passbook and who distrusted rates that fluctuated. She conceived the idea of a passbook money market account with a rate that would be guaranteed for 30 days at a time (the maximum length of time for which a rate could be fixed under the prevailing regulations). When selling the product, the implication to the customer would be that the rate would have to be reset every 30 days but that the bank would keep the rate constant as long as possible, given the changing cost of funds. The product was introduced and had moderate success, but it did not achieve the projected level of consumer acceptance. While it was a good idea, it was a new concept that needed to be explained, and because of its size, the bank could not afford the level of advertising needed to educate the market. Research would probably have uncovered the fact that the product would require considerable consumer education. Then, the bank would have been faced with the decision of whether to introduce the product given the higher-than-normal level of promotional advertising that would have been required.

This example points out the importance of assessing a new product from the market point of view before committing resources to it.

Failure: Market Research

Once bank executives decide to base the product development process on research findings about consumer needs (instead of depending on intuition), they still face a complex problem: creative research must now be conducted to delve deeper into the specific needs of various market segments.

Conducting extensive interviews and asking respondents to indicate what new products they want from a bank are useless because consumers do not know what services are possible (they lack knowledge), and, in many cases, they are not truly in touch with their unmet needs (they lack consciousness). A better route would be to hold periodic, informal dialogue sessions with small groups of respondents who can be asked to discuss issues such as what they like and dislike about dealing with a bank; what they would do if they were running the bank; and how, when, and why they use certain banking products. These sessions are a type of focus group research. For best results, they should be composed of compatible types of people—such as all college students, all newcomers, all local executives, and so forth.

The purpose of such sessions is not to ask the participants to design a new bank product, but rather to get them to focus on their own financial management so that important and yet unfulfilled needs might surface. While members of the market may not be able to articulate precisely what they need from a bank, given the proper atmosphere, their comments may enable the creative and innovative banker to see new product opportunities for the bank.

Failure: Behavioral Change

One factor that sometimes contributes to poor marketing results is the introduction of a new product that requires a change in the banking behavior of the customer. The marketing effort must recognize this and be aimed at minimizing the customer's psychological discomfort.

An example is the direct deposit of Social Security checks. Although this service has been offered for many years, a substantial proportion of senior citizens does not take advantage of it. Despite the safety and convenience of direct deposit, using it requires older people to alter established patterns of banking and to rely on automation. For a generation that matured before the proliferation of computers and automation, entrusting one's regular income to such a system is threatening. Advertising by the government has attempted to overcome these fears by using familiar, trusted spokespersons to communicate the safety of the service. Nevertheless, the penetration among the target market is relatively low.

Failure: Benefits Communication

Another factor that sometimes contributes to a new product's demise is failure to make it clear what the benefit is to the customer. Ultimately, the customer wants to know, "What's in it for me?"

One of the reasons behind this problem is that bankers have a tendency to talk banker language instead of customer language when communicating with the market. Consider the difference between "overdraft checking" and "no-bounce checking," or "Super NOW account" and "interest checking," as examples. Another reason for a communication problem comes about when banks try to find a clever name for a promotion. One bank chose to promote installment loans by offering a discount and calling the program a "Green Sale." Customer interviews revealed that 55 percent of respondents had no idea what a green sale was, and when they guessed, 68 percent tied it to a sale of lawn and garden supplies. The following year, the bank had more success with their "Loan Sale."

PRODUCT ELIMINATION

The various stages of the product life cycle and some of the strategies associated with each have been discussed, but the subject has not yet reached its natural conclusion. What happens when a product dies? What does one do with a product when it declines steadily and cannot be revived? The answer is that the product should be eliminated. While this may seem obvious, the fact is that few banks or firms have a system for product elimination.

Most companies, including banks, do not have a well-planned procedure for handling their declining products. American industry has traditionally paid less attention to establishing formalized product elimination procedures than it has to establishing formalized new product development procedures.

Benefits of Product Elimination

Perhaps the most obvious benefit derived from formalized product elimination procedures is the potential effect on profitability. As Drucker[13] and others have shown, it is quite common for a large percentage of a firm's product mix to account for a small percentage of its total sales and profits. Most likely, at least some of these products are actually unprofitable or have a return on investment lower than the figure deemed acceptable by management. For example, one firm with annual sales of $40 million eliminated 16 products that accounted for only 8 percent of its sales volume. Within 3 years, its profits increased 20-fold: the product abandonment step was considered by management to be the prime reason.[14]

Moreover, since weak products may be consuming important company resources, their elimination can spur overall company sales by freeing resources for more promising uses. Marginal products tie up sales personnel, warehouse space, advertising budgets, equipment, raw materials, and other resources just as strong products do.[15] Also, weak products tend to attract a disproportionate amount of management time.[16]

In addition, a formalized product elimination procedure more or less "forces management to analyze why certain products need to be dropped. As a result, chances are better that past mistakes will be identified and practices instituted to lower the probability of their recurrence."[17]

Also, by not being dropped at the proper time, weak products may well delay an aggressive search for replacement products. In other words, weak products may not only depress present sales and profitability; they may also jeopardize future profitability by delaying the search for replacement products.[18]

Due to the regulatory changes that have been implemented, banks have had to face the issue of product elimination in the retail deposit product lines. At one time, banks could offer only noninterest-bearing checking, and most banks had two such accounts: one for the writer of few checks (with a low monthly maintenance charge and an item charge) and one for the heavier volume customer (generally with no charge above a certain balance level). Then, 5.25 percent interest-bearing NOW accounts were allowed, and several years later, money market-rate Super NOW accounts were allowed. Banks found themselves with four or more types of interest- and noninterest-bearing retail demand accounts.

In 1986, with the elimination of all rate ceilings, many banks restructured their product line by reducing the number of transaction accounts to only two, one with and one without interest. A similar pattern developed in the certificate of deposit product line as the number of allowable maturities increased over the years. Having too many product offerings is difficult and time-consuming for the account-opening staff as well as confusing to the customer. The elimination of rate ceilings facilitated a much-needed exercise of product elimination, and refinement of the retail deposit product lines for banks.

Industry Resistance to Product Elimination

In a classic article, R.S. Alexander has written of the role of sentiment in lack of attention to product elimination:

> . . . putting products to death—or letting them die—is a drab business, and often engenders much of the sadness of a final parting with old and tired friends. "The portable six-sided pretzel polisher was the first product The Company ever made. Our line will no longer be our line without it."[19]

Aside from sentimentality, firms tend to resist product abandonment for other reasons:

- Dropping a product may be disruptive to the organization since personnel may have to be shifted or laid off.

- It may be thought that dropping a product will alienate certain key customers dependent upon it, adversely affecting other business with them.

- Due to the need to "save face," there is a tendency to take less drastic action (such as changing the advertising or modifying the pricing), even when eliminating the product is clearly warranted.

There is no evidence suggesting that banks are any more adroit at product elimination than industry in general. Nor is there any evidence suggesting that the need for formalized product abandonment procedures is any less pressing for banks than for other industries. With the increasing competition and pressure on profit margins faced by banks, the necessity for periodic and rigorous review of the product mix seems particularly important. Perhaps banks should look at that proud list of the "over 100 services" they offer and determine which ones they might do just as well, or better, without.

SUMMARY

This chapter initiated a detailed study of marketing strategy. It started with product strategy because the product is the organization's reason for being, and it is the pivotal element in the marketing mix. *Product* was defined in such a way as to make it clear that the term, in marketers' parlance, means much more than the tangible or intangible thing being sold. The thing itself (the tangible product) is only part of the product. In addition, there is the core product, which is the benefit sold; and the augmented product, which is the sum total of all the related features that go along with it.

It has been shown that there are characteristics that differentiate services from products—specifically intangibility, inseparability, heterogeneity, perishability, and fluctuating demand. Each of these poses specific challenges for the service marketer—challenges that are not faced by the tangible goods marketer.

There are various strategies that relate to the product mix and to the product life cycle. Product mix strategies include product expansion and contraction, product modification, repositioning, and trading up or trading down. There is also a variety of product strategies for a product's introduction, growth, maturity, and decline stages. One strategy for the maturity stage is systems selling, which deals with the marketing of coordinated solutions to the totality of the customer's need. Predetermined and individualized packaging of bank services is a prime example of this concept.

New product development is important for the health of a bank, so the bank should have a system for introducing new products while minimizing the chance of product failure. Product management originated in consumer goods firms and is widespread in banks today as individuals within the bank are given varying degrees of responsibility and authority over specific products or product lines.

There are four major reasons why some bank products fail—all relating to a lack of understanding of customers and their needs. When products have served their purpose and constitute a drain on company resources, they should be eliminated. But, there is generally great reluctance within a bank or other firm to actually remove a product from the market.

As a product is developed and introduced, and as it progresses through its life cycle, decisions must be made about the pricing of the product. As a result of the close link between the product and its price, pricing strategy will be the subject of the next chapter.

POINTS FOR REVIEW

1. Define or briefly explain the following key terms and concepts:
   - product
   - services
   - product manager
   - systems selling
   - product item
   - product line
   - product mix
   - product life cycle
   - core product
   - tangible product
   - augmented product

2. Cite two reasons why the product and the product strategy are the primary elements in the marketing mix.

3. How does the fact that services are intangible and inseparable affect:
   - the promotion of services
   - the physical distribution of services
   - the personal selling of services

4. Explain why some new banking products fail.

5. From current magazines and newspapers, select three ads that stress product benefits and three that stress product features.

6. What are the advantages of product elimination?

7. Name three products currently in the market that are in each stage of the product life cycle.

8. Why is it important for a firm to have a good proportion of its products in the growth stage of the life cycle?

9. What are some current product strategies being practiced by your own bank or by banks in your market area?

10. Explain the seven stages in the new product development system.

10 PRICING STRATEGY

OVERVIEW

One of the principal objectives of a firm is customer satisfaction at a profitable volume. In chapter 9, the product was pinpointed as the instrument for attaining customer satisfaction. In this chapter, the way the product is priced will be seen as a key factor in the attainment of profitable volume.

Making the product conveniently available (distribution) and communicating its need-satisfying capacities (promotion) facilitate the product's acceptance. Conversely, an unacceptable price impedes product acceptance. Therefore, pricing strategy is an extremely important element in the marketing mix and, when handled unwisely, can produce product failure.

The element that marketers call *price* has many names:[1] fares, fees, charges, tuition, rent, assessment, and price. In banking, prices are interest rates, monthly maintenance charges, transaction or item charges, compensating balance requirements, commissions, and service fees. With the exception of interest paid on deposits, which is an expense to the bank, those prices show up on the bank's financial statements as income: interest income and noninterest (or operating) income. Pricing is the only element in the marketing mix that generates income. All the others—producing, selling, delivering, and promoting the product—are costs. While all the elements of the marketing mix affect the volume of sales, only price directly generates profit.[2]

Generally speaking, the pricing of a product affects how much of it will be sold. The person who said, "There ain't no brand loyalty that two-cents-off can't overcome," must have been selling products for which sales volume was primarily related to price. In the pricing of bank services, the relationship between pricing and sales volume is not that simple a matter, as this chapter will demonstrate.

PRICING AND THE BANK'S PROFITABILITY

The pricing of bank services has a direct impact on the profitability of the bank because (1) prices paid by customers generate income, and (2) price affects the volume of sales (to a greater or lesser extent). Therefore, in this section there will be a discussion of how a bank generates a profit—that is, how it derives a net income—and a look at the relationship between the price of a product and the demand for it.

The Way a Bank Earns a Profit

Reduced to the simplest terms, a bank makes money (earns a profit) by taking in deposits and putting them out as loans or investments (after setting aside a portion of the deposits for reserves). In this process, it incurs expense in the interest it pays on those deposits, and it earns income from the interest charged or earned on the loans and investments it makes. The difference between interest income and interest expense is called **spread**, and the object is that the spread should be a positive number. In other words, interest income should exceed interest expense by some margin.

When conducting these operations, the bank incurs many other expenses, such as salaries, benefits, occupancy, taxes, advertising, and other operating expenses. It also has other sources of income: service charges, maintenance charges, trust department income, fees, commissions, and so on. The object is to have income from all sources (interest and operating income) exceed expenses from all sources (interest and operating expenses). The difference is net operating income. When this is adjusted for income taxes, dividends on preferred stock, and extraordinary items, it becomes net income or profit. All businesses try to maximize that number. The four basic elements in the equation provide management with four areas on which to concentrate in order to maximize profit:

$$
\begin{array}{l}
+ \text{ interest income} \\
- \text{ interest expense} \\
\hline
= \text{ net interest income (spread)}
\end{array}
$$

$$
\begin{array}{l}
+ \text{ noninterest income} \\
- \text{ noninterest expense} \\
\hline
= \text{ income before taxes, preferred stock dividends, and extraordinary}
\end{array}
$$
items (income *after* these items is net income or profit)

Since deregulation, the interest that banks pay on deposits is largely dictated by market conditions, so interest expense is one type of expense that is difficult to manage. Operating expenses are more easily controlled. Banks can hold the line on salary increases and watch carefully over highly controllable expenses, such as travel, entertainment, and advertising. In other words, expenses can, to some extent, be manipulated to improve earnings. However, the greatest potential for improving earnings is to increase income.

On the income side of the equation, the interest a bank earns or can charge is heavily influenced by market conditions and by regulation. A bank can concentrate its efforts on generating more of the kind of loan business that provides the greatest potential return (such as variable rate commercial loans, which are tied to the prime rate). But the greatest opportunity in most banks for increasing income is in the category of other operating income: fees and service charges.

Attention to the pricing of bank services can have a major impact on earnings, and the results can be realized almost immediately. According to one pricing consultant, "With proper pricing procedures, a financial institution can increase its profits within one year from a minimum of 20 percent to a maximum of 73 percent. Such an increase calls for sound, intelligent pricing methods."[3]

How Pricing Affects Demand

While pricing can have a positive and immediate impact on profit, it does not take place in a vacuum. The major challenge to the marketer who is trying to determine the pricing strategy for a particular product is the uncertainty about how the market will react in response to the price change. The theory of elasticity of demand addresses this question.

Demand Elasticity

Generally speaking, as the price of any product increases, the demand for it diminishes. But demand might diminish very quickly or very slowly in response to the increase. When the response is quick, demand is said to be **elastic**; and when the response is slow, demand is said to be **inelastic**. Exhibit 10-1 illustrates this concept.

All other things being equal, then, a firm trying to maximize total revenue would increase the price of inelastic products and reduce the price of elastic ones. Of course, both of these examples are highly oversimplified. There is more to consider in making pricing decisions than total revenue. In the case of a price cut, the cost of providing the extra products or services may more than offset the increase in revenues. For instance, offering totally free checking may bring in many new accounts, but they may be low in balances and high in activity and, thus, very costly to the bank.

In the case of a price increase, the firm might find that its cost of operating does not decline as the number of products made and sold declines, so while total revenue increases, profit may not increase proportionately.

Factors Affecting Elasticity

Why is the demand for some products very sensitive to price and the demand for others relatively insensitive? There are a number of factors that affect **price sensitivity**:[4]

- existence of close substitutes;
- awareness of price differences;
- length of time of a price difference;

- range of use;
- significance and frequency of purchase; and
- nonprice benefits.

Existence of Close Substitutes

If there is a less expensive alternative of similar quality available, customers will tend to respond more quickly to price changes. This underscores the importance of positioning bank services and finding ways to differentiate the bank's services from the competition so that close substitutes are not readily perceived by the customer. The packaging of bank services—tying a group of services together as one offering—is a good way of differentiating a bank's product and reducing customer price elasticity.

As an example of the effect of a lower-cost close substitute, consider the pricing of commercial bank checking accounts. Because most thrift institutions offer totally free checking, there is a limit to the charges that can be imposed by commercial banks.

Awareness of Price Differences

Buyers must be able to perceive meaningful differences in price before they will make the effort to switch suppliers. Bankers are often surprised to find out how unaware their customers are of the prices at other banks. This is especially true for those unadvertised prices in the form of service fees, late charges, returned item charges, check cashing fees, and so on.

Length of Time of a Price Difference

The longer a price differential exists between suppliers, the greater the chance that customers will switch. If the customers of a bank that has recently raised its prices expect that all banks will eventually raise their prices too, they may not make the effort to get the better price in the short run.

Range of Use

Products that have a wide range of use tend to be more elastic. If something can be used in more than one way, lower prices may

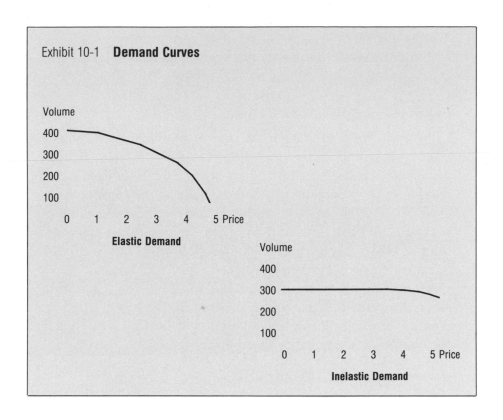

Exhibit 10-1 **Demand Curves**

Elastic Demand

Inelastic Demand

encourage heavier use for secondary purposes. For example, totally free checking encourages people to write checks for small items that would normally be paid for in cash.

Significance and Frequency of Purchase

If the cost of the product is small relative to one's income or expenditures, price responsiveness is not likely to be great. This is also true if the product is purchased infrequently. Banking services do not involve repeat purchases. On the contrary, people change banks on the average of only once every 5 years. While they may add an individual service more frequently than this, the decision to buy a banking service is clearly made infrequently. Therefore, price responsiveness is generally less of an issue in banking than in some other industries.

Nonprice Benefits

Banks differ in terms of community standing, convenience, reputation, and caliber of staff. These side benefits are not measurable, but they do have a value to the customer and can hinder price elasticity or, in other words, help maintain customer loyalty.

Market versus Bank Elasticity of Demand

When discussing elasticity, it is important to distinguish between market elasticity of demand and bank or company elasticity of demand. **Market elasticity** tells how total market demand for a product reacts to a change in the price of all competitors; **bank elasticity** indicates the willingness of customers to shift banks on the basis of price.

If the total market demand for a product is elastic, a price reduction will increase the total number of products sold. This assumes that there are many potential customers who are being kept out of the market because of price considerations. If market demand is inelastic, on the other hand, it means that no matter how much price is cut, total sales volume will not be affected because everyone who wants the product is satisfied with the present quantity. In such a situation, one bank might cut price and experience a short-term increase in demand; but if all banks follow suit, total revenue to all banks declines while total services sold remain the same as before the price cut. That bank's demand curve is elastic, while the market demand curve is inelastic.

Since so many banking services are in the mature stage of the product life cycle, the market demand for them is inelastic. If 92 percent of the households in the United States possess a checking account, no amount of price adjustment is going to expand that market. In a particular geographic market, however, it may be possible for one bank to lower its price on checking accounts and acquire additional customers. However, banks have a tendency to respond

A focus group reacts to various suggestions concerning the introduction of a new product.

rather quickly to significant price changes that appear to be affecting volume. These two factors combine to produce a phenomenon all too often seen in banking; namely, that one bank lowers its price, the others follow suit, and everyone ends up with the same market share as before the price change, but with lower income.

While the elasticity theory helps explain the relationship between price and demand for a product, in reality the relationship is not so easily defined. In the following section, the problem of trying to estimate customer response to price changes will be dealt with.

Estimating Customer Response to Price Changes

One of the challenges inherent in formulating pricing strategy is that marketers do not generally have precise information about the shape of the demand curve for a product, so they cannot precisely predict the outcome of a proposed price change. This absence of information can be overcome to some degree through the acquisition of primary and secondary data—that is, through research.

Primary Data and Pricing

Using primary research as a way of making pricing decisions must be done very carefully and professionally. Asking people outright how they will react to a price change, or what price they would be willing to pay, is practically useless. On the one hand, consumers are unwilling to reveal their sensitivity to price because they do not want to appear to be "cheap." On the other hand, they cannot be expected to identify and isolate the influence that pricing has on their decision to make a purchase or obtain a service. Remembering the concept of the extended product (chapter 9), one can understand that there are many features and characteristics that contribute to a customer's value judgment where a particular product or service is concerned.

Furthermore, research on banking services has repeatedly shown that "free" (in terms of price or service charge) and "more" (in terms of interest received) are always better in the mind of the customer. Questions about price increases are always met with unfavorable response, although in practice, behavior in response to price increases is not always negative.

Quantitative primary research (for example, surveys) can be useful in measuring the relative appeal of alternative pricing schemes to various market segments. An example of this can be found in *Case A*, in which several possible methods of pricing a basic checking account are measured. Respondents were asked to indicate a preference among five pairs of pricing schemes ranging from a flat monthly fee, to a combination of fee and item charge, to an item charge alone. Exhibit A-6 shows the results of this trade-off analysis broken down by various demographics.

Qualitative research in the form of focus groups can be very useful in helping to identify the value that customers attach to banking services, their general willingness to pay, their willingness to shift to competitors, and their preferences for different methods of charging.[5]

Due to the limitations of primary research in providing pricing information, it is best to get as much information as possible from secondary data sources regarding elasticity of demand for banking services.

Secondary Data and Pricing

There are three sources of secondary data regarding customer reaction that should be tapped for input to the price decision-making process. They are *the bank's own records, the experience of other banks and other markets,* and *the pricing of the competition.*

Records of the reaction to a bank's price changes over time can be quite useful in helping to estimate the response to a proposed price change. The more banks review and revise their pricing, the better their information will be for each subsequent decision.

Frequently, certain regions of the country adopt new pricing policies ahead of the rest of the nation. Where this is the case, it is often possible to get information about the reaction to pricing in other markets. While it is dangerous to assume that the reaction experienced in the Rockies will be precisely the same as that in the Northeast, such information can be useful in evaluating alternative pricing strategies or in comparing the results of primary research with actual experience. For instance, if 20 percent of customers interviewed indicated that they would switch banks in response to a price increase, but only 5 percent actually did so, that ratio of proposed to actual switchers might hold true in other market areas as well.

Finally, before making any pricing decisions, the bank should develop a chart showing the prices of all its major competitors. This information should not, however, be used as an indicator of what the prices should be. Relatively few banks have done a thorough job of evaluating their costs and pricing, and many prefer to be price followers—changing only after a price leader does so.

For example, a large mid-Atlantic bank observed that a substantial proportion of its statement savings accounts had balances under $100. A cost analysis indicated that the spread (that is, the difference between interest earned and interest paid) on these accounts was not sufficient to cover the cost of servicing them. A competitive survey indicated that no banks in the area were imposing a service charge on savings accounts. The bank imposed a quarterly charge of $2 on any account whose average quarterly balance was under $100. Within 3 months, the two leading competitors followed suit—one with a higher service charge. The result of the price increase was the addition of thousands of dollars to the bank's income, a reduction in the number of low-balance savings accounts, and no measurable change in savings deposit balances.

PRICING DECISIONS

Having studied the effect of price on the volume of sales and profits, the process of pricing in a banking environment will now be discussed.

When Pricing Decisions are Made

Pricing decisions are made in connection with pricing new products or changing prices of existing products. A bank must *consider* changing the price of an established product when (1) there is a sudden change in the firm's costs; (2) competition initiates a price change; and (3) as a result of a change in regulation, the establishment of a new price is permissible. The emphasis is placed on the word *consider* because all of these situations demand that the bank take a fresh look at its pricing. It may well be that no price change will be made as a result of that consideration.

Pricing New Products

When pricing a new product (whether it is new to the firm, new to the market, or both) the management will have at least three general objectives in mind: (1) getting the product accepted; (2) maintaining strength in the market in the face of competition; and (3) creating profits.[6]

Two of the most important strategies for pricing new products are skimming pricing and penetration pricing. A third, which is much discussed by bank marketers, is value pricing.

Skimming pricing is a strategy that involves setting a high initial price for the product so as to just "skim the cream" of demand for the product. It is especially suitable for new products for several reasons:

- The amount of the product that can be sold is less likely to be affected by price when the product is new, than later, when competition has more of an influence.

- A skimming price strategy allows the marketer to attract less price-sensitive members of the market before attempting to attract those that are more price-sensitive by lowering prices. As Benson Shapiro has written: "As the price is lowered, many consumers will consider the new price a bargain because it is below the old price. . . ."[7]

- A high initial price may help the new product gain an image of quality and prestige. This was apparently part of the strategy of Wells Fargo Bank marketers in the early 1970s when they introduced their Gold Account. Although some observers thought the package was not worth its initial price of $3 per month, Wells' intention was to attract VIP customers.

- A skimming price can be a means for testing the demand for a product. Frequently, it is easier to begin with a high price and then reduce it as the realities of the market's demand emerge, rather than to begin with a low price and then raise it to cover unforeseen costs or to capitalize fully on the popularity of the product.

- A high initial price will often produce more revenue in the early stages of market development than will a low initial price. If this is the case, skimming pricing helps provide the funds for financing expansion into the larger volume sector of the market.

Penetration pricing is the opposite of skimming pricing. It uses a low initial price as a means of capturing a large share of the market as early as possible. This strategy warrants serious consideration when one or more of the following conditions exist:

- the quantity of product sold is highly sensitive to price, even in the introductory stage of the product life cycle;

- substantial economies in production and/or distribution costs can be achieved with a large volume of sales;

- the product will be faced with the threat of strong competition soon after introduction; or

- there is probably not an elite market—that is, a group of prospects willing to pay a premium price to obtain the product early.

A large-scale adoption of the penetration pricing strategy was seen in the early 1980s when financial institutions across the country were first allowed to offer NOW (interest-bearing checking) accounts. Savings banks and savings and loan associations, which had not previously been able to offer checking accounts, priced the accounts low, either by requiring very low or no minimum balances in order to receive interest on checking. In general, commercial banks, which already had the power to offer checking, priced the service high—requiring as much as $2,000 or more in order to avoid service charges.

The thrift institutions expected that the market would be price sensitive. Second, they had put in place the operating capability to handle checking accounts and therefore wanted to build volume. Additionally, all checking deposits would be new money to them, and at a regulated rate of 5¼ percent, this was, at the time, a very inexpensive source of funds.

Commercial banks, on the other hand, perceived that the bulk of their NOW accounts would be transfers from noninterest-bearing checking accounts—thus raising the cost of those existing funds by 5¼ percent without providing any additional earning power. They chose to skim. It would seem that the strategy of each group of institutions was appropriate to its market situation.

Value pricing is a pricing strategy that does not ask, "What does it cost us to deliver this product?" but rather, "What is the perceived value of this product to the customer?" The more tangible and intangible features (including such things as prestige) that are added to a product, the higher the value perceived by the customer will be and consequently, the higher the price that can be charged. In effect, the organization seeking to use value pricing must reduce the customer's price sensitivity or demand elasticity by differentiating the product, tying other products to it, or adding nonprice benefits.

This reality of consumer behavior helps justify a bank's expenditure for developing an image or position in the market and for making the investment necessary to provide a high quality of customer service. Fee income has become a more important source of revenue for a bank since the deregulation of interest rates on consumer deposits. The bank with a reputation for quality products and a high level of service, and whose overall awareness and image among the target market is highly favorable, will be able to exact slightly higher fees and charges for its products than its competitors.

Changing the Price of Existing Products

Determining the price of a new product is not the only occasion for determining pricing strategy. Banks change the price of existing products either on their own initiative or to respond to a competitive or regulated price change.

Initiating Price Changes

Firms initiate price changes for many reasons. For example, a price might be reduced to increase the demand for a product, or a price might be increased to pass along increased costs. See Exhibit 10-2 for a list of various pricing difficulties that may cause banks to change the prices of existing products.[8]

There are many factors that must be considered as part of the pricing strategy. For instance, management must determine the timing of the price change—when it should be announced and when it should take effect. It is also necessary to consider the number of price changes—whether to reprice a broad spectrum of products or just one or two. Management must also consider the effect on other products. If a bank has two or three personal checking services and changes the pricing of only one, customers will shift to the account with the most favorable pricing. It is very important that the prices for related bank services be consistent with one another in order to avoid the situation described in item 5, Exhibit 10-2. Additionally, price changes can be combined with other marketing actions, such as a packaging or advertising change, or an upgrading in product quality.

Finally, prices might be changed in some markets but not in others. This strategy is less often observed in banks than in the consumer goods market.

Changing the price of a product is a more complex problem than first meets the eye. Whatever the decision, it will affect customers, employees, prospects, and competitors. The eventual success of the price change relates directly to the response of those who are affected. The difficulty involved in anticipating these responses simply adds to the complexity of effective pricing strategy.

However, despite the complexity and challenge involved, properly timed, well-conceived price changes can produce results well worth the effort and risk. For example, bank marketing expert Neil Ford[9] reports on the case of a bank attempting to service students from a major metropolitan university as well as their customers permanently residing in the community. The bank found that the students were requesting a variety of services, some of which were being provided unprofitably, such as check cashing. The bank experienced a sizable volume of checks that were being cashed on other banks and considerable bad check loss. Also, supervisors' time devoted to the cashing of these checks was significant.

In response to these conditions, the bank initiated a $.50 to $2 per check service charge for cashing out-of-town checks or checks on other banks when cashed by noncustomers. Long distance calls to confirm account balance information were charged at cost. As a result of the bank's pricing policy, there were some complaints, and a few customers closed their accounts. However, the addition of the service charge was projected to increase revenue by $25,000 at year-end. Moreover, many students opened accounts at the bank in order to have the convenience of check cashing.

Reacting to Competitive Price Changes

Sometimes firms are forced to consider price changes because of price changes by competitors. In circumstances where there is little difference among competing products, there tends to be acute pressure for responding to a competitor's price cut. Gasoline price wars are an example of this.

However, when competing products are not essentially alike (for example, automobiles), a firm has more flexibility in responding to a competitor's price cut because buyers tend to select sellers on the basis of multiple considerations, not just price. When there are differences among these other considerations (such as service, quality, convenience), a competitor's price drop may cause only a slight shift in buying patterns. In other words, how a firm reacts to a competitive price change depends upon the expected elasticity of demand for the product in question.

Whether and to what extent a firm chooses to meet a competitor's price cut (or counter it by modifying other elements of its marketing mix), should depend upon considerations such as the following:[10]

- Why did the competitor change the price?

- Will the price change be temporary or permanent?

- What will happen to the firm's market share and profits if it ignores the price drop?

- How will other firms in the industry respond?
- What is the competitor's (and other firms') likely response to each possible reaction?

Similar questions can be asked when a competitor raises, rather than lowers, its price.

Responding to Regulations Affecting Pricing

Another situation in which banks frequently find themselves confronting a pricing decision is when a regulated price is deregulated or revised. For example, Regulation Q ceilings on interest rates payable on savings deposits were phased out between 1980 and 1986, causing banks to address the matter of pricing savings and other interest-bearing accounts and to rethink the savings and checking product lines.

How Pricing Decisions are Made

Up to this point, the discussion has concentrated on *when* pricing decisions are made. This section will deal with *how* pricing decisions are made. The fundamental element upon which pricing decisions are based will be examined: the cost of producing and delivering the product.

Costs

Unless a firm makes the intentional decision to sell a product at a loss for reasons it considers appropriate, the cost to the firm for providing the product must serve as the floor under which the price must not go. Fundamentally, there are two categories of cost: variable or incremental costs, and fixed costs. **Variable costs** are those that vary with the volume of sales (or accounts). These include postage, supplies, materials, part-time help, and the like.

   Fixed costs, on the other hand, are incurred regardless of volume. In banking, fixed costs are generally broken down into two categories: direct costs and general and administrative expenses (G & A). Direct costs are the principal resources the bank has in place to provide its services, including such things as buildings, land, equipment, full-time staff, and data processing expenses. As a rule, they do not vary with volume over short periods of time. They *can* vary with volume over a longer period of time, however. If the volume of business at a branch grows to the point where the office requires expansion, this would be an example of a fixed cost varying over time.

G & A costs are costs that are incurred to support and administer the organization. Examples of these are advertising, interest on debt, administrative salaries and expenses, insurance, and so on.

Ideally, a product's price should cover its fair share of fixed costs, its variable costs, and a reasonable margin of profit. However, as one might expect, pricing based on a determination of costs is not that simple a matter.[11] There is considerable disagreement over which costs should be taken into consideration when determining the pricing of bank services. Basically, the argument revolves around two approaches: (1) pricing based on incremental cost only, and (2) pricing based on fully allocated cost.

Incremental versus Fully Allocated Cost

Incremental cost is the change in total cost—both variable and fixed—due to a change in volume or a new service being added.[12] **Fully allocated cost** includes not only the incremental costs of each service but also that service's "fair share" of indirect expense and other fixed costs. Pricing systems based on fully allocated costs will recover a fair share of fixed costs only if the bank is operating at or above its normal capacity. The problem is that fixed costs remain even when volume drops. Therefore, if the bank prices high to cover these costs, and if the market demand is elastic, volume will decline and the bank might find itself in an uncomfortable position—that is, not covering its direct costs.

For example, if the capacity of the installment loan area is 5,000 loans per year and fixed costs are $150,000, each loan must cover $30 of fixed cost plus its variable costs. However, if the bank increases prices to reflect these costs, and loan volume drops to 4,000 loans per year, that $30 per loan will cover only $120,000 of the fixed costs. Now the allocated fixed cost should be $37.50. One could imagine a situation in which a bank keeps adjusting its price upward in response to these "increased costs" until it has no loans at all, but still has its $150,000 fixed cost. While this is an exaggeration, it serves to illustrate the point that it is dangerous in some situations to price products and services based on fully allocated cost.

The argument in favor of pricing on the basis of incremental costs is that they more accurately reflect future, as distinct from present, cost levels.[13] In pricing, the concern is to estimate the *changes* in total revenue and total cost, so that only incremental costs are relevant. This does not mean that the bank should not assign a share of fixed costs to each service. Rather, it means that for pricing purposes, care should be taken before allocating these costs to each service on a per unit basis. Incremental costs should include both variable costs and "semivariable" costs that may change due to higher volume levels.

Choosing between fully allocated and incremental costing is not a simple matter. Generally speaking, incremental costing is preferable when pricing a new service (that is, a *really* new service, not one which will simply cannibalize an existing service). When setting prices on basic services and on services for which volumes are reasonably predictable, a bank is more likely to use fully allocated costing. However, it is important to regularly update costs to reflect current levels when using this approach.

Who Makes Pricing Decisions?

Because pricing is critical to the profitability of the bank, executive management should establish the pricing policy that directs the bank's pricing strategies. The policy, which should be (but in most community banks is not[14]) in writing, might indicate that:

- the bank will be a price leader;
- the bank will consistently rank in the upper third of its competitors; or
- the bank will consistently rank in the middle of its competitors.

The way a bank organizes to establish pricing strategies will depend upon its size and structure. Many banks have adopted the pricing committee or task force approach. For example, one bank reports having two pricing committees,[15] one for retail and one for business pricing. They meet regularly and, on a quarterly basis, make recommendations to management for pricing revisions. Both committees have representatives from marketing, operations, the branch system, managerial accounting, planning, and data processing. The retail pricing group has a representative from installment lending, and the business pricing group has representatives from national accounts, international accounts, and corporate lending.

As banks continue to become more price conscious, this type of formal organization for price decision making is likely to become more popular. Of course, the smaller the institution, the fewer the individuals involved—but the work and planning required remain the same.

OTHER PRICING STRATEGIES

The strategies of skimming, penetration, and value pricing with respect to the introduction of a new product have been discussed. There are two other pricing strategies that may be used by banks when repricing existing products or when pricing new ones. They are **relationship pricing** and **behavior modification pricing**.

Relationship pricing stems from the recognition that there are benefits for the bank in encouraging customers to have multiple accounts and services with the bank. This encouragement is provided in the form of lower fees, higher savings interest rates, or lower loan interest rates for customers with multiple accounts. Some examples are:

- allowing balances in savings to offset balance requirements for no-charge checking;

- charging less on personal loans to a checking customer who has the monthly payment automatically deducted from checking;

- charging a lower annual fee, or lower interest rate, to credit card customers with checking or savings accounts; and

- paying a higher interest rate on larger savings or certificate balances.

A prerequisite to this type of pricing is either an integrated system that enables the various computer applications for checking, savings, and loans to communicate with one another, or the presence of a monthly updated central information file linking all relationships for a given individual or household.

The benefits of the relationship pricing strategy to the bank are largely threefold: The first is an economic one. It is less labor- and paper-intensive to service one customer with five accounts than five customers with one account each. (This assumes that the accounts can be consolidated on one statement for customer reporting purposes.) The second is the benefit of customer retention. As mentioned earlier, the more services a customer uses, the more likely a bank is to retain the customer's business. The third benefit is, or should be, increased profitability for the customer. When packaging products, a bank must take care that the total profitability of the package of products is at least as great as the profitability of those products if sold separately.[16]

Behavior modification pricing is the technique of using pricing to get your customers to take a certain action because it would result in lower costs for the bank. A simple example of this type of pricing is to charge customers for using tellers to cash checks, while allowing unlimited free automated teller transactions. This strategy will work only to the extent that demand for use of a teller is elastic. That elasticity can be enhanced by the existence of a close substitute (that is, an equally convenient automated teller) and by making customers aware of the price difference through effective communication.

A more complex example of behavior modification pricing strategy is the case of Philadelphia's Girard Bank (now Mellon Bank). The bank's objectives were to reduce the flow of paper and encourage the use of automated tellers and bill payment by phone. The bank had used the product strategy of contraction of the product mix in the pursuit of its objective. It eliminated some product lines that were heavily paper based, such as holiday and vacation clubs.

In the area of pricing strategy, the bank gave an earnings credit on transaction account balances and, at the same time, charged a fee for every check written and every transaction conducted. The credits earned were used to offset the charges. To encourage the use of automated tellers, funds deposited through them earned an even higher earnings credit, as did funds deposited electronically through direct payroll deposit. To encourage use of the telephone payment system, the transaction charge for phone payments was lower than the cost of writing a check. Before the bank was acquired and the pricing changed completely, they had made significant progress in changing the way their customers banked.

Finally, a pricing strategy that was at one time used frequently in banking is the offering of premiums and giveaways. When the maximum allowable rate of interest on deposits was fixed by law, the offering of a gift was a way to provide added value to the customer and, thus, a higher implicit rate of return on deposited funds. While premiums are generally considered a promotional strategy, the fact that they now are used so seldom by banks, when interest rates are no longer regulated, demonstrates that they were being used as a pricing strategy. Now that there is no ceiling on the rates that banks may pay on deposits, they are competing more on the basis of interest rate alone and are relying less on premiums to add value.

REACTIONS TO PRICING

When making pricing decisions, the bank marketer must keep in mind the range of reactions possible from various sources, and a well-thought-out pricing strategy will include plans for dealing with these reactions. The three groups whose reactions are of most concern are customers, employees, and the competition.

Customers' Reaction

Earlier in this chapter, customer reaction in terms of demand elasticity was discussed. Generally speaking, the demand curve for traditional banking services is somewhat inelastic, which means that customers do not switch banks in large numbers or very quickly, in response to price increases. However, switching banks is not the only reaction that a bank should be concerned with. As Jack Whittle has written:

> . . . bank customers are not bothered by price increase. At first glance, that statement would seem to jar against fundamental economic principles. But our research and experience indicate that customers are much more concerned with how they learn about a price increase rather than with the increase itself. (Therefore) proper delivery of the message is far more important than the actual increase.[17]

In most cases, banking regulation sets down minimum standards for the timing and form required to notify retail customers of a change in price. These standards may range from simple posting of a notice in a conspicuous place in the bank to a 30-day written notice. A bank that tries to change a price (for instance, imposing or raising the fee for a returned item) by simply posting notice in the branches is asking for negative customer reaction. In some locations, half of the bank's customers never set foot inside the branch. In this case, to notify customers of the change in writing would be an expensive and extreme measure. However, the bank might prepare a fee schedule and insert it in all statements the month before the change goes into effect.

When increasing interest rates on revolving credit, increasing minimum balance requirements on checking, or imposing a service charge on savings accounts, a statement stuffer or letter is definitely in order. The wording used to communicate the message is critically important. Customers prefer that the bank be straightforward rather than make excuses or couch the increase in a sales pitch. It is simply not credible for a bank to tell its customers that a price increase is required "in order to help us serve you better."

While the bank must take care in how it communicates a price increase to customers, there is another group whose reaction to a price increase must also be anticipated.

Employees' Reaction

Employees, not customers, present the greatest challenge when making price changes. The smaller the bank, the more difficult the problem because employees are likely to feel more personally involved with their customers. It is imperative that a price change be explained fully and clearly to employees so that they are aligned on the side of the bank's management through the transition phase.

In many banks, management adopts a somewhat paternalistic attitude toward employees in the sense of concealing financial information from them. In many cases, customer-contact employees do not really understand how the bank makes money, and they are not kept informed about how the bank is performing with respect to earnings. A bank that does not keep its staff aware of the realities of costs and the squeeze on profit margins will have an especially difficult time selling its employees on its revised pricing strategies.

Competition's Reaction

Generally speaking, if a bank reduces its price on a product for which demand is elastic, the competition will follow suit. In that beneficial situation in which both market and bank demand are elastic, the total revenue of all banks increases and everyone is better off. But this is rarely the case in banking. Bank demand is elastic but market demand is inelastic, so all competitors suffer reduced profits when they cut price to hold market share. The free checking wars of the 1970s proved this.

Competing firms will respond to a price increase if they believe that their demand curve is inelastic. In that case, there is no point in maintaining a lower price if the affected customers are not expected to switch banks. If, on the other hand, they believe that demand is elastic, they might advertise and promote the fact that their prices are still lower than the price raiser's. For instance, when New York banks were first permitted to impose a fee on credit cardholders, a few smaller banks chose not to impose the fee and to promote that fact heavily. One reported that it acquired not only a large volume of new credit card customers, but related deposit business as well. This was a case of taking advantage of an elastic bank demand curve.

LEGISLATION AND THE PRICING OF BANK SERVICES

All businesses are subject to some regulation of their conduct when it comes to pricing, and banking has been more regulated in this respect than most industries. Banking is under the same edict as other industries with regard to practices that might reduce or eliminate competition between businesses. For example, it is against the law for competing banks to get together to set prices. Such collusion in price setting is considered to be a "conspiracy in restraint of trade."

While it is highly unlikely that competing banks would meet to discuss their plans for pricing a new product, it has not been unusual for one or two price leaders to announce their proposed pricing well in advance of the date of the introduction of a newly legislated service. When NOW (interest-paying checking) accounts first became legal in New York, Chemical Bank announced its pricing early. When they were about to be introduced nationwide, Bank of America announced its pricing. In these cases, one can assume that the intention was to set the tone for the pricing and to communicate to other banks that they were going to price this product high so as to minimize losses. This kind of price signaling is within the law because it does not involve any explicit or implicit agreement between competitors regarding price.

Banks have, in the past, been limited by the FDIC as to the price they pay on deposits. Now, the rates banks pay are determined by market forces and business decisions rather than by edict. Interest rates that can be charged for loans are still governed largely by state usury ceilings. As ceilings were lifted from the price banks pay for deposits, it has been necessary to liberalize loan rates, allowing them to reflect the new market conditions. There are some states, however, in which banks are paying market rates for retail deposits, but are not permitted to charge market rates for loans. The effect is to reduce the supply of funds available for personal loans and mortgages as bankers seek better-yielding commercial loans and investments in order to produce an acceptable spread.

Bank service and maintenance fees are also subject to scrutiny, if not to explicit regulation. In some cases, class action suits have been filed against banks for their pricing practices. It is important that banks understand the true costs of providing services in order to be able to justify changes in these prices.

SUMMARY

Pricing is the only element of the marketing mix that directly generates income. Price affects the volume of goods and services sold to a greater or lesser degree, depending upon the elasticity of demand for the product. Through intelligent pricing of services, banks can have substantial impact on their earnings because, for most banking services, demand is relatively inelastic. For many traditional, mature banking services, market demand is inelastic, but individual bank demand may be elastic. This opens the door to price cutting and diminished earnings for all competitors.

Banks can use both primary and secondary research to gain information for pricing decisions. Qualitative research may prove more useful than quantitative research because of the difficulty involved in asking people to isolate the potential effect of price on their decision to buy or switch banks.

Pricing decisions are made when introducing a new product or repricing existing products. The latter situation arises when costs increase, competition changes a price, or when regulation allows or requires a price change. Two of the most important new product pricing strategies are skimming and penetration pricing. Other pricing strategies are relationship pricing, value pricing, and behavior modification pricing. Pricing decisions must be based on a number of factors, but the costs of providing a service set the floor below which a price should not be set. There is considerable discussion over whether price should be based on incremental cost or on fully allocated costs, or on some combination of the two.

It is critical that price changes be carefully communicated to customers. They must also be carefully communicated and explained to employees so that they will be supportive of the bank's objectives.

Finally, in all their pricing decisions, banks must be cognizant of regulatory restrictions and of the possibility of drawing adverse reaction from consumer groups or regulators.

Now that the product and its pricing have been discussed, that element of the marketing mix that has to do with getting the product to the customer—distribution strategy—will be studied. First, there will be a look at the physical distribution of banking services and second, the personal sales and service aspect of the distribution of bank services.

POINTS FOR REVIEW

1. Define or briefly explain the following key terms or concepts:
   - price
   - elasticity of demand
   - skimming pricing
   - penetration pricing
   - incremental costs
   - fixed costs
   - market elasticity
   - bank elasticity
   - relationship pricing
   - value pricing
   - behavior modification pricing

2. Give some examples of consumer goods that have elastic demand curves and inelastic demand curves.

3. For each of the following new products, which pricing strategy would you have recommended to the manufacturer—skimming or penetration pricing:
   - light beer
   - yogurt with fresh fruit
   - electric automobile

4. Name at least four ways a bank can increase its profits.

5. What are some things a bank can do to make its customers less responsive to competitors' reductions in pricing?

6. Explain how pricing a product on a fully allocated cost basis could have a negative effect on a bank.

7. Name three groups about whose reactions banks must be concerned when making a pricing decision.

8. When and how would you tell your bank's employees that a major change in the service charge on personal checking accounts is about to be made?

11 DISTRIBUTION STRATEGY: PHYSICAL DISTRIBUTION

OVERVIEW

In the last two chapters, the decisions involved in formulating the marketing mix with regard to having the right product at the right price aimed at the right market were discussed. But having these elements is not sufficient to assure marketing success. It is necessary that the product be available at the right place and time and that the offering be communicated effectively to the target audience. This chapter and the next deal with distribution strategy—making the product available in the right place at the right time.

While there are many similarities between the marketing of goods and the marketing of services, there are also many differences.[1] This is perhaps most clearly seen in the area of distribution strategy. The unique characteristics of services described in chapter 9 impose severe restrictions on their delivery. Because of the intangible and inseparable characteristics of services, it is rarely possible for service industries to use middlemen in the delivery process. Generally speaking, direct sale and direct personal contact are the leading methods of distributing most services.

While banks are finding ways around this limitation, the element of personal sales and service are still very much a part of the way banks distribute their services. For this reason, in this text personal selling has been included as part of distribution strategy. In most marketing texts, personal selling is considered one aspect of promoting products, not distributing them, so it is generally included in the treatment of promotion strategy. When dealing with the marketing of physical products, that is where personal selling fits in. However, when dealing with services, personal involvement is critical in the distribution phase because the product is not a tangible thing. This should become increasingly obvious as the reader progresses through these two chapters.

Before getting into the personal sales aspect of distributing bank services (or with people as a channel of distribution), this chapter will deal with the physical channels of distribution: the bank's physical location, and techniques and devices that make the bank's services more convenient and accessible to the user.

CHANNELS OF DISTRIBUTION

In order to understand the concept of distribution in banking, it is important to look at the concept of a channel of distribution as applied to any industry. A **channel of distribution** is the sequence of firms involved in moving the goods from the producer to the consumer.[2]

The concept is easier to comprehend if one thinks in terms of physical products. For example, some typical channels of distribution for consumer products are illustrated in Exhibit 11-1. As shown, some manufacturers (although very few) may use a *direct* channel, selling directly to the ultimate consumer. W. Atlee Burpee mail-order seed company is an example of this type of distribution system. More typically, a manufacturer will sell directly to retailers or indirectly through wholesalers to retailers. For example, a cold remedy manufacturer will sell to drug wholesalers who, in turn, sell a vast array of drug products to various retail outlets. Small manufacturers, on the other hand, may use agents since they may not have sufficient capital to support their own sales force. In all but the first case, the manufacturer depends upon middlemen to get the product to the ultimate user.

Distribution in a Service Industry

Distribution is the *means* through which a seller makes the product available to the buyer. This applies to both goods and services; the process is just more difficult for the service marketer because of the unique characteristics of services (such as intangibility, inseparability, heterogeneity, and perishability and fluctuating demand, as discussed in chapter 9). As shown in Exhibit 11-1, making a product available is usually achieved through the use of various middlemen. This is not generally possible, however, in a service industry. Banks sometimes use auto, mobile home, and boat dealers as middlemen for the indirect distribution of some loans, but the use of middlemen is not typical in a service industry. Therefore, we must think of a channel of distribution in a somewhat different manner. A *distribution channel* is any means of increasing the availability and/or convenience of a service that also increases its use or the revenues from its use. The channel may help to maintain existing users, increase use among existing users, or attract new users.

An Example from the Communications Industry

American Telephone and Telegraph Company provides an excellent example of an organization that continually finds ways to increase the availability and convenience of its service, namely telephone communications. As early as the 1950s, AT&T found that 85 percent of the population of the United States had telephone service. The possibility of increasing revenues from increased penetration of households was, therefore, quite limited. They decided that they could best expand by increasing the availability, convenience, and attractiveness of the service they had to offer. They began doing this in the 1950s and have continued to find ways to make their service delivery system more attractive, convenient, and available. Some of the ways this has been done follow.

- *Packaged services for the home.* The firm developed new phones for various rooms of the house and, in effect, offered the customer a package of telephones. In more recent years, it has multiplied the variety of styles of telephones from the simple countertop or wall-mounted touch-tone phone, to a phone in the shape of Mickey

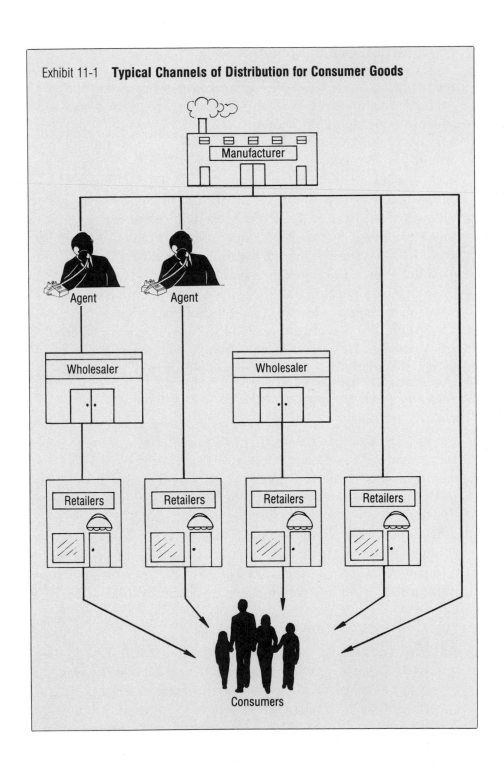

Exhibit 11-1 **Typical Channels of Distribution for Consumer Goods**

Mouse. In addition, the company has developed the technology to make installing a phone as simple as plugging it into a wall so that phones can be changed without the need of a service person. All of this makes having phones—several of them—a simple matter. The flexibility of design makes using them more fun and more appealing.

- *Walk-up phones.* The company began expanding its service outside the home by placing public coin-operated telephones at roadsides, thus putting the service within convenient reach of the traveler. This service has been enhanced by the elimination of the need for a coin in order to make an operator-assisted call. More recently, the company has installed special phones with no coin capacity at all for people wishing to make credit card or other operator-assisted calls. Making a call is as simple as lifting the receiver and dialing.

As mentioned earlier, the primary product of the telephone company is telephone communication. Any new method that increases the availability and/or convenience of that service is a new channel of distribution for that product. The walk-up phone was an innovation in the distribution of telephone communication since it enabled the phone company to sell more of its product through increased availability and convenience. The same is true for providing additional and more attractive phones within the home, and cellular mobile phones for use in vehicles.

This kind of strategy is clearly different from such methods as charging lower rates for long-distance calls during time periods when there is much idle telephone capacity (late nights and weekends). That strategy is designed to help manage line loads more efficiently, increase the use of otherwise idle capacity, and promote a service that is already available (telephone service for homes). In contrast, walk-up and mobile phones are primarily a distribution innovation.

Challenges to the Distribution of Bank Services

The objective of bank distribution decisions is the same as in the consumer goods or communications sectors—that is, to select channels that will maximize the firm's profit position over the long run. For the bank, this involves providing optimum service and coverage at a minimum cost.

However, services provided by a bank possess several unique characteristics. As a result, the traditional concept of channels of distribution (as described for goods marketing) is of very little value when facing the problem of banking services distribution. These characteristics are explained in chapter 9. In order to appreciate the unique and complex problems surrounding the distribution of bank services, it is necessary to look at these characteristics again within the distribution context. One more characteristic not mentioned earlier will be added, and that is the client relationship aspect of banking. Some of the characteristics mentioned below are of positive value to the bank marketer, while others serve to complicate the distribution of bank services.

Intangibility

Most of the problems as well as many of the opportunities encountered in the distribution of bank services are due to their intangible nature. Because many bank services (such as deposit accounts) are simply pieces of information stored in a computer, advances in electronics and telecommunications have helped extend their availability. This will be discussed in more detail later in this chapter. However, the fact that bank services cannot appeal to the senses places a burden on the bank's marketing organization. Since the bank is usually selling an idea, not a physical product, it must tell the buyer what the service will do for him or her. It must communicate the benefit of the service because it is usually unable to demonstrate or display the service in use. For example, what is a home equity loan? How can you show one to a prospective customer? The fact is that you cannot, but you can tell the prospect how it will benefit him or her.

Therefore, the promotional efforts and the personal sales efforts must concentrate on telling the customer what the loan can do for him or her—for example, add a room, take a vacation, send a child to college. In initiating or selling the service, its intangibility heightens the need for a direct channel of distribution because of the importance of personal contact between the buyer and the seller. It is for this reason that the second half of the treatment of distribution strategy in banking deals with personal selling.

Inseparability

In many cases, bank services cannot be separated from the person of the seller or deliverer. The services are often created and marketed simultaneously. A customer simply cannot get a home equity loan without, at some point, interfacing with a person at the bank. It may be done over the phone or through the mail, but a customer cannot simply pick up a home equity loan without the involvement of bank staff. Thus, inseparability often means that direct sale is the only feasible channel of distribution.

Again, however, due to the computer-based nature of many services, banks have been able to work around the characteristic of inseparability and partially overcome its limitations. The credit card is an example. It enables the customer to obtain credit repeatedly without interfacing with the bank. Of course, in order to first obtain the credit card, one must somehow communicate with the credit department of the bank.

Heterogeneity

Consumer goods are stamped out on the production line, one after the other, and are all the same. They are homogeneous within product items. For example, Pink Pearl erasers are all the same size, shape, and color, have the same composition, and work the same way. In contrast, all personal checking accounts within the same bank, although they may be the same operationally, are all different in terms of the way customers experience them. The ambience of the specific branch used by the customer, the personality of the specific teller who takes the deposit, the length of time the customer has to wait in line to get to the teller—all these and more contribute to the heterogeneity of bank services and add to the difficulty of standardizing the level and quality of service delivered in a bank. These are problems associated with the personal distribution of bank services. An advantage of electronic channels of distribution, such as automated tellers, is that the distribution of the service is homogeneous and standardized. The machine may occasionally be "down," but when it is working, it provides the same service in the same way to each customer.

Perishability and Fluctuating Demand

Bank services are not tangible and, therefore, cannot be inventoried, so they are perishable. Unlike goods manufacturers, bankers need not be concerned with storage, transportation, and inventory control. Since bank services cannot be inventoried, there can be no middlemen such as those illustrated in Exhibit 11-1.

This inability to inventory means that there is a limited capacity for business, and this can cause difficulties in times of excessively high demand. For example, there is an upper limit on the number of items that a lockbox operation can process in a day. During a very busy day in a peak period, some of the work may not get processed within the usual time schedule. This inability to inventory severely limits the alternatives available to the bank marketer and necessitates the use of direct channels. However, banks have shown some innovation in finding alternatives for the traditional middleman, as shall be seen later in this chapter.

Client Relationship

In many bank transactions, a client rather than a customer relationship exists between the buyer and seller. This is especially true in the case of many corporate, private banking, and trust accounts. In these transactions, buyers place themselves in the hands of sellers and abide by their suggestions or advice. Obviously, such a relationship will dictate the type of channel of distribution for the service. Where a close, personal, professional client relationship must exist, direct channels are the only feasible choice.

PHYSICAL CHANNELS OF DISTRIBUTION FOR BANK SERVICES

As stated in the previous section, a channel of distribution for a service should be thought of as any means used to increase the availability and/or convenience of the service that also helps maintain existing users or increases use by existing or new users. In banking there are *physical* channels of distribution and *personal* channels of distribution. The physical channels are of four broad types. The first and most obvious physical channel of distribution for bank services is the *banking office*. The others are the array of techniques and systems that extend the delivery of banking services beyond the "brick and mortar" locations of the bank. They may be grouped according to the three means of access used by the customer: *the telephone, the personal computer,* and *the plastic card*. In this section, the decisions involved in selecting a banking site will be looked at as well as some examples of these three channels for distributing bank services.

The Branch Network

Due to the characteristic of inseparability, the creation of time and place convenience is vital in banking. Therefore, the factor of location—where to put the bank's offices—is a primary part of the channel selection decisions of bank marketers. The technical aspects of location analysis will not be delved into in detail here. However, the basic decisions that must be made and the types of data necessary in doing a feasibility study will be examined.[3]

Consumer goods manufacturers find that the more willing an individual is to shop around for a particular product, the less effort the manufacturer needs to exert in finding convenient outlets. For this reason, cigarettes are available at numerous locations, but a high-priced line of designer clothes may be available at only a handful of outlets. People are more likely to shop carefully and discriminatingly for a designer garment than for a pack of cigarettes.

There are important parallels in banking. Banking is fundamentally a convenience business. People are not likely to shop around for banking services, but rather, they select the most convenient location. If there are several convenient alternatives, they might very well shop around among them, but generally speaking, if there is a branch of a bank within a half mile of home and another 4 miles away, the choice will be the closer bank. Therefore, location decisions are extremely important to the success of the marketing mix for most banks.

New Site Location Decisions

The laws of each state govern the ability of a local or out-of-state commercial bank or bank holding company to expand its service delivery system through branching or acquiring banks. In some states, banks are limited to one office (unit-banking states). In others, banks may branch within certain regions of the state, such as the home office county and contiguous counties. Other states allow statewide branching. Still others promote regional and interstate banking through reciprocal banking agreements.

Regardless of the branching and banking laws, when a bank seeks a new location, there are important matters that must be decided.[4] The comments pertaining to the establishment of branches are also applicable to the establishment of a new bank or branch by a bank or holding company.

When expanding, the bank faces two major classes of location decisions. First, decisions must be made about expansion within the bank's present trading area; then, decisions must be made regarding expansion to new trading areas.

As a city grows and expands, it may be necessary for the bank to expand in order to maintain its existing customers, as well as to attract new customers. This may be caused by population shifts within the city, as well as by new residents moving into the city. If a city is growing, other banks will be attracted to it, so establishing additional branches becomes necessary as a defensive move. If the competitor's location is more convenient to a segment of the trade area population, the bank stands to lose many of its customers from that area.

On the other hand, the move may be an offensive one, designed to forestall the entry of new competitors, or to attract new customers from the competition or from a newly developing part of the city. In either event, the bank will have to decide not only where, but what type of branch, to open—a full-service office, a drive-in auxiliary, a minibranch, a limited service branch, or a fully automated branch—depending upon the bank's objectives and the needs of the local market.

If a bank is legally and financially able to locate branches within a state or region, it is faced with a decision as to which new trade area to enter. Once the new area is identified, the decision must be made to either enter the market by acquiring an existing bank or by adding a new branch (often referred to as *de novo* expansion). If the decision is to open a new branch, then the bank must select the specific trade area and also a specific site within that trade area.

Factors in Location Selection

There are two levels of decisions that must be made when deciding on potential locations for delivering the bank's services: (1) selecting the general location or area, and (2) selecting the specific site within the most favorable area. (See Exhibit 11-2.)

- *General area analysis.* The general area may be either an entire community or a section of that community. In a large city, it may be less than one city block, or it may be simply one building. In an industrial area, it may be a single industrial park. For each of these general locations, basic information regarding the area's resident and/or daytime working population, business, industry, and banking situation must be obtained and evaluated.

Much of this information is readily available from published sources.[5] It must be obtained through on-site investigation and questioning of various individuals who may be sources of information. Many larger banks have developed computerized models for evaluating sites to determine their feasibility, and they make this service available to smaller institutions. Also, there are private consultants who may be called upon to perform this task. A bank that has had limited or no experience in branching would be well advised to obtain objective, outside assistance.

The information required for area analysis generally includes the following:

1. *Population characteristics.* Such information as the current and projected residential population, median household income, the distribution of household income, size and income of the daytime working population, and employment characteristics of the resident population is needed. Area employment data by occupation category and by location should be collected, as well as information on residential housing, present and planned. Some of the housing infor-

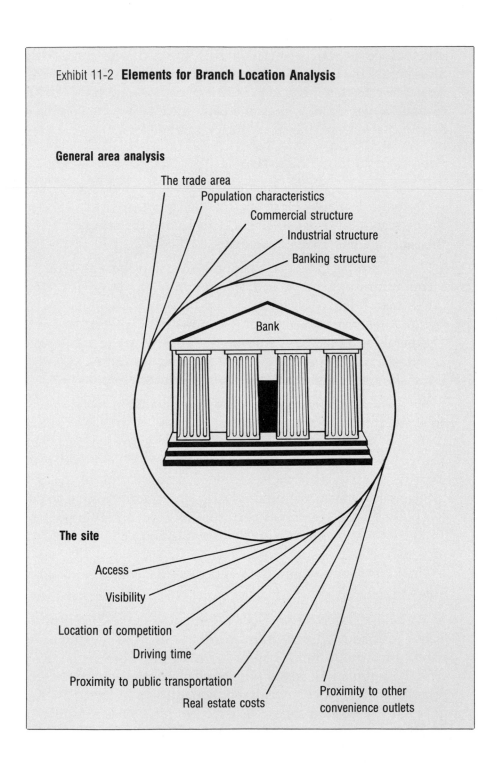

Exhibit 11-2 **Elements for Branch Location Analysis**

General area analysis

The trade area
Population characteristics
Commercial structure
Industrial structure
Banking structure

Bank

The site

Access
Visibility
Location of competition
Driving time
Proximity to public transportation
Real estate costs
Proximity to other convenience outlets

mation includes condition and value of residences, proportion of owner- versus renter-occupied units, and occupant turnover. All this information is needed in order to arrive at some estimate of retail or personal deposit and loan potential for the area.

2. *Commercial structure.* This includes the number of commercial establishments by classification, retail establishments, service establishments, and wholesalers. Also included are estimates of the annual sales volume of these classifications, as well as location of major shopping areas.

3. *Industrial structure.* This should include the number of major industrial firms and annual sales volume, the working population by industrial categories, and working hours. This information, along with the information in item 2, is needed to arrive at an estimate of commercial and industrial deposit and loan potential.

4. *Banking structure.* This includes the number, location, and deposits of all the offices of existing financial institutions (commercial banks, savings banks, and savings and loan associations) within and immediately adjacent to the trade area. It should also include data on credit unions, finance companies, and other organizations competing for banking services. Information regarding banking hours, services offered, size and type of offices, parking facilities, and drive-in, walk-up, or automated banking facilities is also needed.

This is by no means an exhaustive list of the data needed for a trade area analysis, but it provides the reader with a general idea of the kinds of information needed for this decision-making process. After analyzing the data, it is necessary to estimate the level of deposits that a branch in the area might obtain in its first few years of operation. This information is required as part of the branch application. Earnings on these deposits, along with the costs of operation, determine the profitability of the branch.

The problem of estimating deposit potential for a trade area has been greatly simplified by the annual publication of deposit information for every branch of every bank, savings and loan association, and credit union.[6] By compiling this data and looking at trends in deposits in the area's financial institution offices, it is possible to see

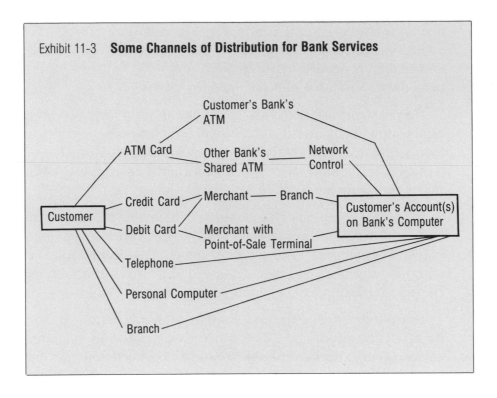

Exhibit 11-3   **Some Channels of Distribution for Bank Services**

whether and to what extent area deposit potential has been increasing. Although it cannot be assumed that all the deposits of the residents, businesses, and workers in the trade area are maintained in local offices, these data are a good indicator of the volume of deposits available in the area the bank seeks to penetrate.

- *Specific site analysis.* After all the above information has been gathered and evaluated and the general area has been selected, several possible sites within that area might be available for consideration. In selecting the specific site, such factors as the following should be considered:

1. *Access.* Is it convenient to enter and leave the site? Will traffic in front of the site make it difficult to enter and leave quickly and safely?

Is there room for stacking cars in a drive-up? Is it on the right side of the street to fit into the predominant traffic pattern of the area? Is there room to provide adequate parking, or is there an adjacent business with whom some parking spaces may be shared?

2. *Visibility.* Will the office and its signs be visible to passing foot and vehicular traffic? Are there any obstacles present or planned that would obscure visibility?

3. *Location of competition.* Where are the nearest competitors? The existence of a branch of another bank within several hundred feet of a potential location should not necessarily be thought of as a deterrent. It makes more sense to locate next door to the competition if a site is very convenient to the bulk of trade area residents than to locate in a less convenient location away from the competition. It is no accident that in many towns the major intersection has a bank on each of the four corners.

4. *Driving time.* Is the bank within a reasonable distance of residential concentrations, business districts, or industrial plants?

5. *Proximity to public transportation.* Locating a branch at an end-point of a travel pattern is generally a good strategy. Locating a branch at an interchange point is generally not a good strategy. While there may be a great deal of traffic at the site, it is traffic-in-transit and may result in no banking activity but, as one bank reports, plenty of litter.

6. *Real estate costs.* Financial considerations might weigh heavily in the decision. However, the bank must be careful that, in being economical, it is not being "penny-wise and pound foolish." A more costly site may, in the long run, generate a greater return on the investment than a less expensive but less convenient or accessible alternative. This is a situation in which obtaining outside professional advice can be valuable. One bank, on such advice, bought a branch site in a developing community when the site looked more like a pasture than a commercial location. The bank held onto the site, although it could have doubled its money by selling it after 3 years. Now the branch sits right in the center of the new development, and it became profitable in its first year of operation.

7. *Proximity to other convenience outlets.* Since banking is a "convenience good," it is advantageous to locate near food and other convenience-type stores.

These seven factors (and any others relevant to the particular situation) should be examined as to their influence on the future deposit potential of the proposed site. The site that offers the most advantages and fewest drawbacks should be chosen as the location for the facility.

The bank must then make application to its regulatory agencies for permission to establish the bank or branch. Generally speaking, two agencies are involved. State banks that are not members of the Federal Reserve System apply to the state Department of Banking and the FDIC. State banks that are members apply to the Federal Reserve rather than to the FDIC. National banks apply to the Comptroller of the Currency and the Federal Reserve. While each of these agencies has slightly different requirements, they are all concerned that the proposed location meets three criteria: (1) that the office has a reasonable promise of successful operation; (2) that the convenience and needs of the banking public be served; and (3) that no harm will occur to existing offices of financial institutions.

The length of time required to obtain approval for an office also varies from state to state and regulator to regulator. Generally speaking, unless the application is contested by a competitor so that written and oral arguments must be conducted, the approval process takes from 3 to 6 months.

The Decision to Close a Branch

For any number of reasons, a bank's management may be faced with the decision to eliminate a branch. This is never an easy decision as it has social as well as economic implications. Managers face this decision when a branch is losing money—that is, not earning enough to cover its costs. This generally happens in one of two ways. An older branch may be located in an area that was once economically vital and healthy but has undergone deterioration. A newer branch may have been projected to break even in its second or third year of operation, but is still losing money after 5 years or more. In these kinds of situations, the bank must be concerned about its public image, but the negative consequences of the branch closing can be minimized if there is another office of the bank nearby to which customers may be referred.

BEYOND BRICK AND MORTAR

As alluded to earlier, bankers are increasingly finding ways to overcome the limitations imposed by the unique characteristics of banking services—especially inseparability. They are finding ways of using middlemen, if not in the strict sense of the word, at least in a broad sense.

In this section, attention shall be devoted to some of these electronic and telecommunication-based distribution channels. (See Exhibit 11-3.) Since they are tools that are performing a facilitating role in making bank services available to users, they may clearly be thought of as distribution channels.

The Telephone

The telephone is increasingly being used by banks as a way to extend transaction capability and account information to any location where a customer can reach a phone. This is done through *telephone banking* and *telephone bill payment*. With telephone banking, the customer may access account information such as a current balance or whether a specific check has cleared, as well as make transfers between accounts. With telephone bill payment, the customer can instruct the bank to pay specific bills either in response to the called-in instruction or on a prearranged basis. Both of these services are usually available 24 hours a day, 7 days a week, allowing the phone in the home, office, car, or anywhere else, to bring the bank to the customer.

The Personal Computer

The increased use of personal computers in the home and the office has opened up another service delivery opportunity to banks. Since bank products are simply bits of information stored in the bank's computer, and since computers can communicate with one another (over phone lines), personal and business customers can access their accounts and conduct transactions at their own PCs. Individual customers can obtain balance and transaction information, pay bills, and move funds between accounts. Business customers can do all that and more. Many banks offer firms the capability to initiate wire transfers and letters of credit, invest excess balances, and pay down loans.

Plastic Cards

Bank **credit** and **debit cards** are also innovations in the distribution of a bank's credit and deposit services. Their purpose is similar to that of the walk-up telephone of AT&T: they are designed to increase the use of the bank's capacity to provide credit and deposit services by increasing the number of locations where those services can be used.

While inseparability limits the geographical area that the bank can reach, the credit card has helped to overcome this problem for credit services. It can be applied for, and received, through the mail, so it has enabled many banks to maintain credit customers far outside their immediate trading area.

Additionally, the credit card has enabled bankers to utilize the retail merchant as a middleman in the distribution of credit. In the marketing of credit cards, heavy reliance is placed on the retail merchant to assist banks by encouraging their customers to apply for the cards. Thus, when retail merchants become part of a bank's credit card plan, they are, in effect, becoming middlemen in the channel of distribution for this particular bank service.

The debit card may be either a national label (Visa or MasterCard) or private label card (the bank's own card). A debit card looks like a credit card and is accepted in payment of purchases wherever that name is accepted. The difference is that the amount of the purchase is deducted directly from the customer's checking account rather than being billed. The effect is the same as if a check had been written, but the transaction is much simpler. The service makes the funds in that deposit account more available, since the card is acceptable to more merchants than a personal check would be.

At the point of sale, the plastic card (debit or credit) may be used to initiate a paper-based transaction, or it may become the "key" that activates a terminal-based transaction. Typically, the merchant uses the customer's card to prepare a sales voucher, which is deposited with a bank much as a customer's check would be deposited. Many merchants have point-of-sale terminals linked with the bank's computers into which the card is inserted, along with information about the transaction. The entire transaction—that is, the debit to the customer's demand account and the credit to the merchant's account, takes place instantaneously.

Automated teller access cards provide customers with an entry to a bank's automated teller network. ATMs are another way in which a bank makes its services more accessible and convenient for customers. Because they are generally available around the clock, customers can bank on their own schedule.

Nationwide ATM networks have further increased the geographic availability of a customer's bank accounts. By participating in such networks as Cirrus and PLUS, banks make their customers' funds available to them in any city or town where there is an ATM that is part of the network.

SUMMARY

In a consumer goods industry, channels of distribution are the middlemen that move the product from the producer to the ultimate user. Because services are intangible, their distribution cannot be handled in this way. Channels of distribution in a service industry are any means of increasing the availability and/or convenience of the service that also increases its use or the revenues from its use.

The fact that banking services are inseparable from the person of the seller means that the sales force—the customer-contact people—are a primary channel of distribution. The way banking services are delivered can vary greatly from customer to customer and location to location, so it is difficult for the bank to standardize its products and deliver a homogeneous service that is the same at all times and all places. Since services are perishable (not capable of being stored), middlemen in the traditional sense cannot be used to distribute them. However, banks have been innovative in finding ways to increase the availability of their services.

The most obvious channel of distribution for a bank's services is the bank location. Site location involves research to identify feasible areas that hold promise for the bank and to identify specific sites for the banking location. Considerable information must be gathered about the economic and demographic characteristics of the area, not only for the bank's use, but to present to the relevant banking regulatory agencies in defense of the branch or bank application. Bank locations may range from full-service branches to self-contained automated tellers.

Among the less obvious ways a bank delivers its services are through the telephone, personal computer, and plastic card. These methods have helped banks overcome some of the limitations of inseparability.

Regardless of these innovations, there will always be some need for personal contact (for sales and service) in the delivery of banking services. In the next chapter, the personal selling aspect of delivering bank services will be discussed.

POINTS FOR REVIEW

1. Define or briefly explain the following terms and concepts:
   - channel of distribution in a consumer goods industry
   - channel of distribution in a service industry
   - direct channel
   - middleman

2. Give an example of a banking service that is highly inseparable—that is, that cannot be separated from the person selling or delivering it.

3. The safekeeping of savings funds is an intangible service performed by banks. How does this feature affect the distribution of this service?

4. How does the heterogeneity of banking services affect the way in which they are distributed?

5. Which banking services are more heavily dependent upon direct channels (or person-to-person dealings)?

6. The more willing an individual is to shop around for a product, the less effort the manufacturer needs to exert in making the product conveniently available. Provide an example of this kind of a consumer goods marketing situation (other than the one in the text).

7. Why is physical location so important in banking?

8. What services does your bank provide to retail or commercial customers over the telephone or by means of personal computer?

9. What type of information would you gather to determine the feasibility of establishing a branch in an office and industrial park?

10. Select a bank location with which you are familiar and rate it on the basis of the factors given in this chapter for specific site analysis.

12 DISTRIBUTION STRATEGY: PERSONAL SELLING

Personal selling will be found in most, if not all, marketing texts within the broader topic of promotional strategy, not distribution strategy. Selling is generally considered part of the promotional effort, along with advertising. Advertising is a form of mass communication. Selling, too, involves communication, although on a one-to-one basis. Therefore, there is some logic to the thinking that puts the selling effort into the same element of the marketing mix as advertising.

However, this is not a general marketing text. Most marketing texts deal almost exclusively with consumer goods industries. This text deals almost exclusively with a service industry—specifically, the banking industry. While much of marketing theory is applicable to both consumer goods and services, there are some very real differences. Some have already been encountered in the discussion of product strategy, pricing strategy, and physical distribution strategy. When it comes to the role of personal selling, the differences between consumer goods and banking services become even greater.

Generally speaking, direct sale and direct personal contact are the leading methods of distributing most services. Because the service is an intangible product, there is a need for personal contact in getting it from the producer (the bank) to the user (the customer). And since the product cannot be seen or touched, that person must be adept at communicating how the service will benefit the customer.

283

As mentioned in chapter 11, bank services are difficult to separate from the person of the seller. While banks are increasingly finding ways of getting around this limitation, there will always be a need for personal selling or some degree of personal service at some point in each customer's relationship with a bank, even if it only takes the form of a well-written letter or a responsive customer service phone call.

It is for these reasons that personal selling is considered part of distribution strategy in this text. Because of their unique characteristics, bank services require *ongoing sales efforts*. This is intrinsic to the job of getting bank services to the consumer. Promotional strategy does not generally result in a constant level of effort, and advertising is often done in waves. It would be erroneous to categorize personal selling, which must be an ongoing effort in banking, with the promotional effort.

In this chapter, our emphasis will be on direct sales, primarily in the retail banking area. (Chapter 16 deals with selling in the wholesale banking area.) However, it should be understood that everyone in the bank sells in an indirect way. How a phone is answered, how a teller handles a complaint, how a letter is typed when the payment is processed—all of these factors and more are part of the ongoing selling activities of the bank. It is important that one does not lose sight of the fact that it is not only the people who sell directly, but those who are involved in the continuing process of delivering bank services, who are part of the distribution system.

PERSONAL SELLING AND BANKING

Before delving more deeply into the subject, there are three misconceptions about selling in general and selling in banking, in particular, that must be addressed. The first is that selling and marketing are the same thing; the second is that very few people in the bank have the opportunity to sell; and the third is that selling is not something bankers really need to be concerned with, except perhaps in the commercial calling area.

Difference Between Selling and Marketing

For some reason, many people think that selling is marketing or that marketing is selling. By now, the reader should understand that marketing is a very broad area and that selling is only one part of it. Professor Theodore Levitt made this point clear in one short sentence: "Selling is finding customers for what you have; marketing is making sure you have what customers want."[1] A marketing organization or a market-driven bank will have products that fit the needs of the target markets. The sales force—whether it be the commercial calling officers or the customer service representatives or the branch managers—works at getting new customers for those products.

Who Sells in a Bank?

In a marketing-oriented bank, everyone might see his or her job as somehow involved in selling the bank and its services. To understand this concept, look at two definitions of selling given by Webster's Dictionary. The first is "to persuade or influence to a course of action or to the acceptance of something." This definition clearly describes the activities of people who are actively involved in direct selling. They are helping to influence a course of action by the customer or prospect. Examples of this type of selling situation in a bank are:

- bank officer call programs directed at businesses and correspondent banks;
- calls on consumers by bank personnel or branch bank neighborhood representatives;
- deliberate selling efforts by members of advisory committees and boards of directors; and
- employee efforts to sell financial services other than the one presently being used. This is referred to as **cross-selling**.

The second definition states that to sell is "to develop a belief in the truth, value, or desirability of something." You will recall that the final step in the consumer buying process (see chapter 6) is the experiencing of post-purchase feelings. In the section on consumer behavior theory, it was mentioned that for a service industry, the giving of good service on an ongoing basis helps reduce post-purchase anxiety and reinforce the customer's decision. Everyone with whom the customer comes into contact can help that customer confirm his or her belief that dealing with this bank is a good thing to do. This is indirect selling and is done by everyone with whom the customer comes into contact, be it ever so casually—receptionists, tellers, telephone operators, safe deposit attendants, and maintenance people. Back office staff are equally important because their work, regardless of what it is, in some way supports the activities involved in selling and servicing the customer. Every job in a bank can be traced ultimately to some point of contact with the customer.

Importance of Selling in Banking

Personal selling is more important for some products than for others. Some products are "presold." Examples of these products are national brand convenience goods, such as grocery products and cosmetics. These are purchased by the consumer with little assistance from store personnel.

Other products (such as industrial goods, automobiles, bank services), however, are seldom presold, and personal selling must play an important role in finalizing the sale. In the case of many banking products, consumers have limited knowledge concerning competitive offerings with which to make comparisons. Personal selling becomes an important factor in such a situation.

The basic purpose of any particular business is customer satisfaction at a profitable volume. Selling directly affects the attainment of that profitable volume. It affects the income of the bank through customer acquisition and retention and, less directly, by helping to improve staff productivity and by maximizing the return on the bank's advertising expenditures.

Customer Acquisition

Assuming that the bank's services are priced correctly, each new account contributes to the income of the bank. New accounts are generally the result of a selling process. The extent of the selling effort will vary with respect to what is being sold. Two distinct levels of selling are usually identified: low-level selling and high-level selling.

1. *Low-level selling.* This involves consummating a sale with a customer who already has a clear notion of what he or she wants. Basically, the salesperson performs a service function and is often actually sought out by the buyer. This is frequently the case in retail bank services. In most cases, the type of selling involved in opening personal savings or checking accounts would probably fall into this category. The process of selling in a low-level selling situation should not, however, lead to a situation in which the bank employee is simply taking orders from customers. As competition from nonbank financial sources increases and banking consumers become more knowledgeable about their various savings and investment alternatives, branch sales staff must also become more knowledgeable.

2. *High-level selling.* Often called creative salesmanship, high-level selling involves arousing demand for new products or influencing change in patronage from one seller to another. In such cases, neutral or negative attitudes are converted into positive wants or demands, since the prospect often does not recognize his or her own need for the product. Cross-selling by bank customer contact personnel falls into this category, and much of the selling activity of loan officers would, in most cases, be considered high-level selling.

While some individuals in the bank have a direct responsibility to bring in new business, everyone in the bank can do this to some extent. Many banks have had great success with employee incentive programs in which all employees are encouraged to bring in new customers or new accounts. It is amazing how many friends, neighbors, and relations can be found and convinced to do business with the bank by personnel in all types of positions within the bank.

Customer Retention

One of the most significant ways that selling (or more specifically, cross-selling) can affect the bank's profitability is through retention of present customers. The process of opening and closing accounts is expensive in terms of staff time and processing costs. A bank that is able to hold on to its customers will operate more efficiently and more profitably than the one with high customer turnover.

Exhibit 12-1	**Cross-Selling and Customer Retention**	
If a customer has . . .	*The odds against losing that customer are . . .*
Checking only	1-1
Savings only	2-1
Checking and savings	10-1
Checking, savings, and installment loan	18-1
Checking, savings, installment loan, and safe deposit box	100-1

Selling additional services to new or present customers is referred to as cross-selling. It is an established fact that the more bank services a customer uses, the less likely that customer will be to switch banks. Exhibit 12-1 shows that the bank has a 50-50 chance of losing a customer who has only a checking account. (The odds are a little more favorable if the only account the customer has is savings.) That customer is vulnerable to the sales efforts of the competition or to other factors that might cause him or her to think of closing the account. For instance, an unpleasant experience with the bank, such as the bank bouncing a check in error and not repairing the damage done to the customer's reputation with the payee, might make a customer angry enough to close an account, especially if that is the only account with the bank.

If the checking customer has a savings account as well, he or she is 10 times less likely to leave the bank than if checking were the only service held. The combination of checking, savings, loan, and safe deposit box virtually assures that the customer will be retained.

The best time to sell a customer an additional service is at the time the first account relationship is being opened. In this situation, the customer has come to the bank with an unfulfilled need and is ready to buy. What happens in those first few minutes of contact with the bank is critical. In *Case C* there are dialogues (see dialogues 1 and 2) of two different ways such a situation might be handled by the new accounts person—one resulting in the sale of a money market checking account, savings account with bimonthly automatic transfers, and automated teller access cards to a man who came into the bank to open only a checking account, and one resulting in no account being opened by a person looking for a checking account. The key in both cases is the way the customer is handled during those few precious minutes. Taking advantage of this time to cross-sell is extremely important since as many as half of a bank's customers do not physically enter the branch once they become customers. They bank at the drive-in, or walk-up, or automated teller, or by mail, so the personal sales contact is lost.

Improved Productivity

Increasing the average number of services held by the customer also increases the productivity of the bank's staff. It should be easy to understand that it is less expensive and more efficient for a bank to service 1,000 customers who have two accounts each than to service 2,000 customers who have one account each. The volume of time and paperwork increases with the number of different individuals served more than with the number of accounts opened.

Surveys show that most people deal with more than one bank or financial institution, and some do business with several. Therefore, there is great potential for the bank with a good sales orientation to cross-sell additional services to its new customers as well as its existing ones.

Maximized Return on Advertising Expenditures

The fourth way in which a bank's profitability can be affected by a sales orientation is by maximizing the return on the dollars spent on advertising. Banks spend hundreds of millions of dollars on advertising every year. This represents a substantial expense item that may account for 5 percent of the bank's total noninterest expenses. (To put this in perspective, salaries and benefits make up half or more of a bank's total noninterest expenses.) These dollars can be rendered useless by the failure to train employees to sell.

The purpose of a bank's retail advertising is to bring customers through the doors. What happens next will result either in a sale, a multiple sale, or loss of a potential customer. (See *Case C* for examples.) If the sale is lost, the advertising dollars were wasted. If the employee acts only as an order-taker and opens just the account the customer came looking for, the advertising dollars are not as fruitful as if the customer had been cross-sold an additional service.

Similarly, the purpose of advertising directed at the corporate banking market is to create an image and to predispose the prospective customer to receive and listen to the calling officer. (See Exhibit 12-2.) If the calling officer is calling simply to fill a quota of calls made and does not have the objective of making a sale, or if he or she is not equipped to sell, the advertising spent on the corporate banking advertising program is also wasted. An example of such a situation would be a branch manager going out to call on a merchant who is clearly a good prospect for a credit card depository relationship without bringing the forms necessary for the prospect to sign up for the service on the spot.

You might ask if this is really a problem for most banks. According to published statistics,[2] approximately 50 to 75 percent of the marketing budget of banks is spent on media advertising (as distinguished from point-of-sale displays, premiums, public relations, marketing research, and so on). In contrast, only 1 to 4 percent is spent on sales and customer relations training. While some sales training expenses might appear in the budgets of personnel departments rather than marketing departments, many banks have not yet fully grasped the importance of selling in helping to make their marketing efforts effective. Personal selling is just not considered a marketing tool in these banks, although there are some indications that this is changing. In the next section, some of the reasons for this phenomenon will be discussed.

Why Selling Has Come Late to Banking

The banking industry in this country is centuries old. For most of that time, banking services were not something that needed to be sold; the banker performed a necessary service. There were relatively few banks, so when there was a need, the customer came to the bank. The nature of the business attracted employees of a certain personality or orientation. Such personalities were well suited to getting the work of the bank done, but they were not necessarily the characteristics found in good salespeople.

With the tremendous increase in competition for bank customers (not just from banks but from nonfinancial organizations as well), banks have become more marketing oriented. For the same reason, they are also beginning to recognize the need for increased emphasis on selling. Because banks were not organized for selling in the past, many changes are necessary today to turn this situation around. Job descriptions have to be rewritten to include sales responsibilities, and employee recruitment efforts have to be reoriented toward finding the type of personality that is attuned to selling. Selling objectives have to be set, and a system has to be developed for rewarding sales performance.

All of this means changing the banking environment, and this kind of change does not come quickly or easily. It requires a change in the way many bankers see their jobs, since many do not see selling as part of the job. Even in such areas as commercial lending, calling officers may only consider some low-level selling as part of their jobs. For example, this might involve appraising the creditworthiness of a customer and providing financial advice and recommendations, but only after the customer first seeks out the banker. Beyond this low-level selling, it appears that some bankers mistakenly see their judgmental role of lending officer or credit analyst as a selling role.[3]

Another reason why selling has come late to banking is that many bankers see selling as the role of advertising.

> They [bankers] seem unaware that while advertising may do the better job in creating awareness and arousing interest in potential customers, it may not be nearly as effective as personal selling in creating preferences, closing sales, and so on. Simply stated, a great number of bankers view advertising and personal selling as substitutes and, viewed as such, they prefer advertising.[4]

As mentioned earlier, the nature of most bank services is such that they require personal selling. In the case of service marketing, advertising and personal selling are not substitutes, but rather, they are complements. Each must be an element in the marketing strategy for most bank services.

As a case in point, one particular bank had initiated an aggressive corporate banking advertising campaign with the goal of creating an image for the bank and its staff. Research indicated that the campaign was having the desired effect on what people thought about the

Exhibit 12-2

"*I don't know who you are.*
I don't know your company.
I don't know your company's product.
I don't know what your company stands for.
I don't know your company's customers.
I don't know your company's record.
I don't know your company's reputation.
Now—what was it you wanted to sell me?"

MORAL: Sales start **before** your salesman calls—with **business** publication advertising.

McGRAW-HILL MAGAZINES
BUSINESS • PROFESSIONAL • TECHNICAL

bank. The senior commercial bank officer, however, wanted to cancel the campaign because it did not "bring in customers." In other words, the bank could not directly trace any business to the advertising campaign. The advertising director reminded the bank officer that bringing in new customers had not been the objective of this particular campaign, and the officer replied, "If advertising doesn't sell, what good is it?"

While some advertising for corporate banking services might actually cause customers to contact the bank, that should not be its purpose. Advertising, as shall be seen in the next chapter, is paid mass communication. Its goal is to have an effect on a vast number of people. Selling, on the other hand—especially the selling of corporate banking services—is a one-on-one communication effort.

Another reason why selling and sales training are not implemented in some banks is due to a confusion about where it belongs. In other words, management is unsure as to whether the responsibility should lie with marketing or with personnel. In one large institution, it took over 3 years for the marketing director to get approval to put sales training dollars into the budget because the chief executive could not decide whether it belonged in marketing or personnel. Since most other training functions are part of the personnel department's responsibilities, sales training is often handled by that department.

Wherever it resides, there must be considerable involvement and interaction with the marketing staff. They are in the best position to understand the product from the consumer's viewpoint and will already have developed the strategy for selling each product as part of the total marketing effort. Sales training and product knowledge training are, after all, part of the marketing mix.

THE CHARACTERISTICS OF THE SUCCESSFUL SALESPERSON

Banking does not traditionally attract people with the type of characteristics that make good salespeople. In this section, some of those necessary characteristics will be identified.

There is an old saying that "salesmen are born, not made." But what is it that makes a successful salesperson? There is no absolute answer to that question, but it is true that a salesperson's performance is influenced heavily by two things: (1) personal attributes, and (2) selling skills.

Personal Attributes

While many attributes might be listed as desirable qualities for a salesperson, there is general agreement that an effective one will possess more of certain attributes than an ineffective salesperson.[5] Exhibit 12-3 lists some of these traits. Singling out certain traits, however, is misleading and somewhat shortsighted because it seems to assume that if an individual is ambitious, confident, and persuasive, he or she will automatically be a good salesperson. These characteristics are clearly not sufficient by themselves to assure success, and, furthermore, this theory ignores the role and needs of the customer.

Two researchers have developed a shorter list of traits common to superior salespersons.[6] Based on 7 years of work, they concluded that good salespersons possess two basic qualities:

1. *Empathy*—the ability to feel as the customer feels.

2. *Ego drive*—an intense need to complete the sale—not merely for the monetary gain.

Having established these two traits, the researchers were able to make fairly accurate predictions about the subsequent sales performance of applicants for sales positions in three different industries.

It may be true that certain personal attributes or traits will help make an individual a good salesperson in any type of business. If a firm can select an individual with these qualities, the chances of success are increased but not ensured, because these traits are usually not enough in themselves. Each selling job is characterized by a unique set of duties and challenges. Each has different customers with different personalities, educational levels, needs, and expectations. One need only consider the selling task facing a computer salesperson, automobile salesperson, loan officer, and teller to appreciate these differences. What this means is that personal attributes are a necessary but not a sufficient condition for success as a salesperson. The effective salesperson also needs superior selling skills.

Selling Skills

Most experts believe that, given appropriate training, the majority of individuals can be made into salespersons and that both the few "born" salespersons and the "made" ones can improve with continued training. Most sales executives recognize that formally planned and executed sales training programs contribute significantly to the improvement of selling performance. For instance, IBM expects its sales representatives to spend 15 percent of their time every year in additional training.[7] Because it is such an important issue, sales training in the banking environment will be discussed in more detail later in this chapter.

THE SELLING PROCESS

The actual process of selling is extremely complex because it involves so many variables that are difficult to measure and control. Also, the process varies depending on whether low-level or high-level selling is being done. There are many "how-to" formulas for selling, but they usually describe only what a salesperson does or should do without explaining the "why" of the salesperson's behavior. Nevertheless, one formula is presented here that lists the steps that lead to a successful sale and a satisfied customer.

This approach to personal selling involves a formula, or step-by-step procedure, known as the **AIDAS** formula:

1. Gain the prospect's *Attention*.

2. Arouse his or her *Interest*.

3. Stimulate *Desire* for the product.

Exhibit 12-3 **Personal Attributes of Effective Salespersons**

1. Self-confidence

2. Planning ability

3. Industriousness

4. Persuasiveness

5. Intelligence

6. Technical knowledge

7. Job interest

8. Ambition

9. Health

10. Social development

4. Get buying *Action*.

5. Build *Satisfaction* into the transaction.

This approach to selling implies two things: first, that the prospect or potential buyer actually goes through these five stages; and second, that the salesperson can, to a large extent, control the behavior of the prospect if this process is managed skillfully. Unfortunately, neither of the two assumptions has ever been proven true. Yet the formula is useful; it gives the salesperson something to strive toward. Also, it might be more applicable in some situations than others. For example, a bank officer calling on a corporate account would probably find this approach more useful than a teller attempting to cross-sell a personal checking account customer.

But the major limitation to the AIDAS approach is that it emphasizes the "how to" and ignores the "why." More modern approaches to selling are strongly based in the behavioral sciences, and they view selling in terms of interpersonal interactions. For example, two behavioral scientists have defined personal selling as follows:

> Interpersonal, face-to-face interaction for the purpose of creating, modifying, exploiting, or maintaining a communicative relationship between . . . seller and . . . buyer.[8]

This behavioral view recognizes personal selling not in terms of mechanistic formulas, such as AIDAS, but as a social situation involving two people. Note that, in the mechanistic view, the buyer plays a very limited, passive role in the sales transaction; in the behavioral view, however, the buyer has an expanded, active role. In fact, it is believed that the salesperson's characteristics and actions combine with the buyer's characteristics and actions to determine the outcome. The interaction of the two people, in turn, depends upon the economic, social, physical, and personality characteristics of the seller and the buyer. A successful sale is situationally determined by these factors and involves social behavior as much as individual behavior.[9]

The implications of this expanded view of personal selling are important. The behavioral view suggests more emphasis on training in selling techniques and less emphasis on selecting individuals with certain personality characteristics for developing effective sales personnel. Specifically, training would be needed in three areas:[10]

1. The effective salesperson would need training in *listening skills* in order to comprehend the prospect's description of problems and his or her answers to questions that were designed to reveal the prospect's personal and social needs.

2. The salesperson would need to develop *interaction skills* as an aid in sensing the prospect's predispositions and, most important, how the prospect expects the salesperson to behave. This would enable the salesperson to judge the impact of his or her comments on the prospect and to alter them based on the feedback from the prospect's reactions.

3. The salesperson would need some basic *communication skills* and an understanding of interpersonal interaction. This would involve knowledge of how the characteristics of receivers, messages, and communicators interact to determine selling effectiveness.

Examples 1 and 3 in *Case C* demonstrate the application of these skills, while example 2 shows a situation in which they were clearly absent.

The Need for Sales Training

If certain individuals in a bank (tellers, loan officers, new accounts personnel, calling officers, branch managers) have a responsibility and the opportunity to do some direct selling, then these individuals need training in how to sell. Obviously, the complexity of the selling task will also dictate the amount and kind of training needed. For example, an officer calling on corporate accounts needs different training than does a safe deposit attendant. However, most sales trainers agree that any good salesperson should be familiar with the following:[11]

- *the customer*—his or her specific needs, particular problems, and activities;
- *the bank*—especially its position, growth, marketing policies, and goals;
- *the product*—complete knowledge of the various bank products offered—advantages, disadvantages, features, and benefits;

- *the competition*—competitors' product offerings and their strengths and weaknesses compared with one's own; and
- *selling methods*—presenting sales messages, principles of communication, listening, handling objections, behavioral skills, and self-development.

Considering this list of requirements, it is apparent that most employees of a bank need some kind of sales training, however basic. Even bank officers who are thoroughly familiar with the bank, its product mix, and their corporate accounts may still need training in selling methods. People in other positions, such as tellers, should have complete product knowledge and an understanding of their marketing role, with less emphasis on selling methods, perhaps. The important point is that if someone has a selling element in his or her job, then that person should receive some type of sales training. Another way of looking at the issue is to ask the question, "What is the cost of *not* training your sales force?" One bank training director answers as follows:[12]

- the *cost* of employee turnover;
- the *cost* of employee ineffectiveness;
- the *cost* of poor customer service; and
- the *cost* of business lost to competitors.

MANAGING THE SELLING PROCESS

There are four primary elements involved in the management of a bank's personal selling strategy. They involve training in areas of product knowledge and sales methods, monitoring sales efforts, and rewarding the results of sales efforts.

Product Knowledge Training

The first element, and the foundation of a successful selling program, is *product knowledge*. Those individuals involved in direct selling should have a thorough understanding of all the products and services they will be called upon to sell. The information must encompass not only what the service is and how it works from an operational viewpoint, but also its customer benefits and comparative advantages and disadvantages.

The second element is *how it benefits the customer*. For example, "You can earn monthly income from this certificate, and to save you time, we can put it directly into your checking or money market account for you" is a benefit statement. In contrast, a features statement would tell only how the service works without involving the prospective customer: "This certificate comes with automatic crediting of monthly interest."

The third element takes into account the *advantages compared with other services of the bank and its competitors*. For example, "Our Money Market Checking Account pays interest on checking balances for those who can afford to keep the required balances, but many people who write few checks and prefer to keep a small balance in checking prefer our regular checking account."

The fourth element has to do with *disadvantages compared with competitors' offerings*. For example, "Yes, it's true that they require a lower minimum balance on money market checking accounts, but if you have $1,000 in a regular savings account, those balances can count toward your minimum balance requirement and give you the benefit of a money market checking account with no service charge. Furthermore, with our account you can also pay your bills by phone or have them automatically paid every month, so you don't have to worry about forgetting to make your loan or mortgage payment."

Many banks develop a product manual or guide in which all the bank's services are listed. This is usually done in looseleaf format so that, as changes are made, the manual can be easily updated. For example, for each service it might contain such information as:

1. a brief description of the product;

2. a listing of the product features and their related benefits to the customer;

3. the audience for whom this product is intended;

4. the special requirements for purchase or use of this product, such as minimum deposit, line of credit, officer approval, and so on;

5. other products and services that are natural complements to this product for cross-selling purposes;

6. who or what area handles the product; and

7. location and telephone extension.

This is not to imply that the new accounts person should have expert knowledge of, for instance, trust services. That person should, however, have a basic understanding of the variety of trust services available, be able to recognize a prospect, and know whom to refer that person to.

Before undertaking a product knowledge and sales training program, it is useful to conduct a survey of customer contact staff to assess the present level of product knowledge and to identify specific areas of weakness. Having this information also provides a benchmark against which to measure results after the program has been completed. It is also possible through this research to gain a better understanding of employees' attitudes toward various services and toward selling itself. It would not be surprising to find, for example, that many people who are in a position to cross-sell personal loans or a personal line of credit to customers believe that borrowing is something that should be done only in an emergency. The more information of this kind that is available, the more finely tuned the bank's training program can be.

Sales Training Programs

The success of a sales training program depends upon the organization, the trainee, the training program, and the desired end results—that is, improved selling performance. These factors are illustrated in Exhibit 12-4. This diagram indicates that for learning to occur, the bank employee must feel the need for it. The employee's motivation to learn about selling will be influenced by the trainee's perception of management's views on selling and marketing in general. If the

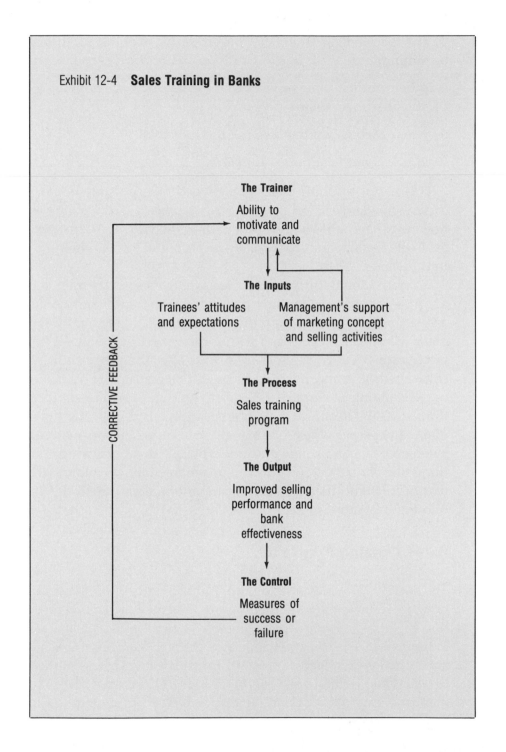

Exhibit 12-4   **Sales Training in Banks**

The Trainer

Ability to
motivate and
communicate

The Inputs

Trainees' attitudes
and expectations

Management's support
of marketing concept
and selling activities

The Process

Sales training
program

The Output

Improved selling
performance and
bank
effectiveness

The Control

Measures of
success or
failure

CORRECTIVE FEEDBACK

trainee believes that management is ambivalent, then little learning is likely to occur. So, the commitment of management is vital.

Exhibit 12-4 also indicates that the end results of a sales training program are influenced not only by the content of the program itself, but also by the attitudes and expectations of the trainees, which in turn are strongly influenced by their perceptions of management's philosophy. There are six elements that are essential for achieving sales training objectives:

1. definition of training aims;

2. determination of sales skills needed for a job;

3. identification of the target group;

4. determination of the content of the training program;

5. determination of training methods; and

6. execution of the sales training program.

1. *Definition of training aims.* This involves deciding what the sales training program should accomplish in specific terms. Although increasing productivity through improved sales performance is the general aim, it must be translated into more specific aims stated in operational terms. This requires a clear understanding of what knowledge, skills, or attitudes the trainee is supposed to acquire during the training period and how these fit into the demands of the particular job or the needs of the bank in general.

The best way to begin is to conduct a shopper study to develop statistics about the current level of the selling effort. This is done by having individuals who are trained for this kind of research go to a representative sample of the branches (or all of them) several times in order to open accounts or ask for information. The interviewer then records the entire experience, including not only how the staff handled the situation, but also impressions about the overall appearance of the office and the staff, and other observations (tone of the office, noise level, general atmosphere, and so on).

From this type of research, the bank might find, for instance, that one-third of its new accounts staff actively cross-sells services and one-third tries to sell, but is not effective. The other third might be classified as "order takers"—you get only what you ask for. This type of study might also reveal a general lack of courtesy or a below standard appearance on the part of many employees. All of these methods might be used to set measurable goals for the program, with follow-up research to be conducted again at the end of the training period.

2. *Determination of sales skills needed for a job.* A key factor that must be considered is the specific sales skill involved in each job. This will determine, to a great extent, the content of the training programs for each level of employee. Obviously, these needs will vary depending upon the position of the employee being trained. This will also help determine if continuing training is necessary, and if so, what the continuing training needs are.

For example, if bank calling officers are being trained, the products they sell should be specified, and the requirements of selling the products should be identified. Some questions to be answered are: How much time is expended on selling? Which products sell themselves and which do not? Which selling approaches or philosophies will be stressed? Answers to these and related questions help formulate the knowledge and selling skills an individual position requires. This approach should be taken for each position in the bank that has an element of selling to it.

3. *Identification of the target group.* It is necessary to identify the specific group in the bank that will receive the training. As mentioned earlier, every position with a selling element should receive some kind of sales training. Since every group cannot be trained simultaneously, some priorities must be established. Usually, the positions that present the most selling opportunities have the greatest need for training and, therefore, should receive training first. Ideally, though, training should begin at the top levels of the bank since the initial target group that sets the crucial precedent for training encompasses the top level of executives.

4. *Determination of the content of the training program.* For both initial and continuing training programs, the content should be derived from the definition of training aims and needs. Course material on

some mix of the five factors previously cited—the customer, the bank, the product, the competition, and selling methods—is usually included. The actual content within each of those categories, and whether greater emphasis is given to one over the others, will depend again on the needs of the trainees. For example, a teller needs less training in actual selling techniques than a calling officer. The calling officer would need knowledge of sales techniques that would aid in overcoming objections and closing a sale. Thus, the content of the training program would differ for each group.

5. *Determination of training methods.* After determining the training aims and content for each group, the appropriate instructional methods must be selected. There are many available. The problem is to select those that will most effectively and economically achieve the aims of the program. Two convenient categories are group instructional methods and individual training. The former includes lectures, seminars, role playing, simulation of banking situations, or games. The latter would include on-the-job training, personal conferences, correspondence courses, and programmed instruction manuals.[13] Each has been widely used in sales training programs, and the approach chosen will depend upon numerous factors, such as the needs of the trainees, the training task, and the number of people to be trained.

6. *Execution of the sales training program.* When implementing the training program, decisions must be made with respect to selection of the trainees and the instructional facilities location, the development of instructional materials and training aids, and the all-important question of who will do the training. It is no small administrative problem to schedule training sessions for platform personnel, for instance, because most banking offices are not overstaffed, and the absence of even one platform person for a couple of days may have severe repercussions. Training might be done on bank premises, if the space is available, or conducted at an off-premise site. In either case, the trainees must be free from distractions and be physically comfortable in the training situation.

Sales training programs are available in numerous forms. There are canned programs that can be bought from training firms or consultants, or consultants can tailor a program to fit the particular needs of the bank. On the other hand, the training department in the bank may want to design the program. Similarly, the actual training might be conducted by a consultant, or by an in-bank trainer, or by some combination of the two. There are some excellent "train the trainer" programs that can be used to good advantage by the bank that wishes to develop its own training staff.

Monitoring the Results of the Sales Training Program

Not only is monitoring results essential in an overall marketing strategy, it is an important step in the sales training program as well. As with marketing planning, the bank must know where it wants to go (set the training goals) and be able to determine when it gets there (monitor results). This step, unfortunately, is often avoided. The reasons are twofold: a lack of definition of the training aims, and the difficulty of measuring training effectiveness. However, measuring techniques are available. For example, a shopper study may be used to identify sales training needs and set goals before the training program and be used again at the conclusion of the program to measure the difference in behavior. Likewise, employee surveys may be used to test product knowledge before and after training.

It is also possible to set up or purchase from a vendor a system for keeping track of cross-sales activity. With this kind of system, the new accounts personnel maintain records on every customer who comes in to open an account and record the products that the employee unsuccessfully attempted to sell, as well as those which were successfully sold. This data is then computer analyzed, and reports are generated by branch and by employee. Some banks have incorporated this type of tracking system into a single account opening form that makes it easy for the new accounts representative to open up several accounts at once and keep track of each employee's sales record. This matter of simplicity in account opening procedures is an important one: if there is a substantial amount of paperwork involved in opening multiple accounts, that factor will have a tendency to inhibit sales attempts by the new accounts representative.

One bank that keeps track of its cross-sales statistics reports that before the institution of a sales training and motivation system, the number of accounts opened per new account customer was 1.07. That is, for every 100 customers opening a new account, only 7 were sold a second service. One year after the start of the program, the cross-sales ratio was 2.84; the average new account customer was being sold nearly three services—and in many cases, five and six services were being cross-sold. It is clear that the bank's management will want to know whether the expenditures for sales training have been justified by results. Without this, or some comparable kind of information, that question cannot be answered, and the future of the sales training effort will be in jeopardy.

Rewarding Results of the Sales Effort

A sales training program will have lasting results if those who have been trained are somehow rewarded for putting what they have learned into practice. There are three ways in which this can be done.

First, if the bank has recognized the need for a sales orientation, job descriptions should be written to include the responsibility for selling. The employee's objectives will include selling goals, and the annual performance evaluation will be structured so that the employee is rated on his or her sales effectiveness, as well as on the other elements of the job (this, of course, requires that some tracking or measuring system is in place). Salary increases will be related to how well that part of the job has been accomplished.

A second way to reward results is through an incentive or commission program. This may be a one-time program or an ongoing one. With an incentive program, the employee is awarded points on the basis of sales made or business brought into the bank and directly attributable to the specific employee. These points accumulate and may be redeemed either for cash or merchandise. The commission or sales percentage of approach has not yet been widely applied in banking. Some areas, such as trust, lend themselves especially well to commissions due to the difficulty of the sale and the substantial income that can result from the sale. Chief executives who approve commission systems might well find that some of their superior salespeople will earn more money than they do. If these people are indeed bringing in the type of business that the bank wants and which will contribute significantly to profit, then it is only right that such a situation might exist. However, it requires very enlightened and altruistic chief executives to make such a decision.

A third way to reward results is through recognition. The bank mentioned above established a structured program for recognizing individuals who were performing well in the cross-sales program. The form in which the recognition was given ranged from having one's name and/or picture in the monthly program newsletter, to notes from the president, a "winner's cup" mug, wall-mounted plaques, and attendance at a semiannual awards banquet. While there was a small fee paid for each account cross-sold, the program manager felt that the peer and management recognition was more of a driving force than the commission, which averaged out to only about $40 per employee per year.[14]

SUMMARY

Personal selling is one element of the overall marketing effort, but due to the unique characteristics of banking services, it is a very important element. Because of the intangible and inseparable characteristics of bank services, personal selling is often the only means for selling and delivering them.

Effective selling helps the bank's profit picture by attracting new and profitable relationships and retaining existing ones. It also helps increase productivity and helps maximize the return on the dollars spent on advertising, which is geared to bring customers to the bank or make them aware of the bank and its people and its services.

Selling is still in its infancy in banking but is becoming more recognized as banks face increased competition from all sides. Since banking has not historically been a sales-oriented industry, many changes to old and existing ways of doing things will have to occur. Among these are the ways jobs are defined, evaluated, and remunerated. This type of structural change does not come easily to an organization.

Two important characteristics that help make a successful salesperson are empathy and ego drive. These, coupled with selling skills, help the salesperson to "close the deal" while demonstrating sincere interest in meeting customer needs.

Sales training must encompass knowledge of the customer, the bank, the products, and the competition, as well as selling methods. Sales training programs should be based on research that helps identify the program's aims, target the trainees, structure the content, and determine the methods to be used. It is imperative that results be measured and rewarded.

In the next chapter, the last, and possibly most exciting, element of the marketing mix will be discussed. Armed with competitive, need-satisfying services that are profitably priced, professionally sold, and conveniently delivered, the bank must communicate to the target market what it has to offer. This is the objective of promotional strategy.

POINTS FOR REVIEW

1. What is meant by the term *cross-selling*?
2. Explain why, in a treatment of bank marketing, personal selling should be considered part of distribution strategy rather than promotion strategy.
3. How would you answer someone who says that they know all about marketing because they have taken a course in salesmanship?
4. How would you respond to the following statement made by a teller and by a bookkeeper: "In my job, I don't have an opportunity to sell."
5. Describe the four ways in which selling can directly or indirectly affect the bank's profitability.
6. When McDonald's runs a heavy advertising campaign to promote its breakfast service, they expect to see the sales of Egg

McMuffins, etc., increase. Can bankers expect the same results from heavy advertising of checking and savings services? Why do you say that?

7. Recall your most recent experience making a purchase with the assistance of a salesperson. Did that person follow the steps in the AIDAS formula? Did he or she listen to you, react to your comments, and really communicate with you? Was that person instrumental in your buying the product?

8. What is the difference between a product benefit and a product feature?

9. The next time you visit a bank office, pretend that you are a "mystery shopper." How would you rate the staff in terms of attentiveness, appearance, courtesy, and sales ability?

10. If you were the first person to be named to the position of sales training director for a small bank, what would your initial plan of action be?

13 PROMOTION STRATEGY: ADVERTISING AND SALES PROMOTION

OVERVIEW

This chapter deals with the last, and arguably, the most interesting, element of the marketing mix. It is certainly the most visible element and one to which consumers are exposed every time they pick up a newspaper or magazine, turn on the television or radio, drive along a highway, or enter a store or bank. Advertising is a critical element of the marketing mix, but as explained in chapter 9, there is no single most important element in the marketing mix.

Once a bank has developed its product, priced it competitively, and arranged for its distribution to prospective customers, it must inform the target market about its product offering. It must communicate the need-satisfying benefits in order to generate sales and profits. That communication is done through the use of advertising, sales promotion, publicity, and personal selling—four elements that comprise the **promotion mix**. This chapter deals largely with advertising and sales promotion. This text treats personal selling as an element in distribution strategy; however, since it is a form of communication—specifically, one-on-one communication—personal selling is also part of the promotion mix.

THE COMMUNICATION PROCESS

Since communication is the foundation of promotion, it is important to first define communication and look at what takes place during the process of communication before moving on to each of the elements of the promotion mix.

The word *communication* is derived from a Latin word that means *to share*, and more fundamentally from the root word *communis*, which means *common*. Webster's Dictionary defines communication as the art of "imparting, conferring, or delivering knowledge, opinions, or facts." When one communicates, one attempts to deliver a specific message to a target audience. Effective communication results when there is a common understanding between the communicator and the audience.

Exhibit 13-1 illustrates the general process of communication. It consists of five elements: the communicator, the message, the medium, the audience, and feedback. This may be summarized simply as: who . . . says what . . . in what way . . . to whom . . . with what effect.[1]

Exhibit 13-2 illustrates the way communication works. The banker must first encode the message or the idea or fact that he or she hopes to communicate effectively to the target audience. The message must be translated into a systematic set of symbols—pictures, words, or numbers—that express it. The encoded message is sent via some path or medium to the receiving audience. Each member of the audience then decodes the message or interprets it in light of his or her own experience and frame of reference.

During the process of communication, any number of things might go wrong. Communication experts agree that the factor that most commonly breaks down the understanding between the communicator and the audience is the variation that takes place between encoding and decoding. When the encoding and decoding processes are homogeneous, communication is most effective. When they are not, communication breaks down. This problem is depicted in Exhibit 13-2 by the overlapping fields of experience of communicator and audience. If the circles share a large area in common, communication is facilitated. If the circles do not share any area in common—if there has been no common experience—then communication becomes impossible or highly distorted.

For example, recall the bank that had promoted a "Green Sale." To the bank, this meant a loan sale, but to the audience it meant something to do with lawns. The bank in that case failed to encode its message in terms that were clear to the audience, and the audience interpreted it on the basis of its own frame of reference. There was no common area of understanding with respect to the phrase "Green Sale."

The framework of the marketing communication process can be applied to banking as follows:

- The *communicator* is the bank.
- The *message* may be an idea, a fact, or an image that the bank wants to communicate.
- The *medium* may be advertising in the newspaper, radio, TV, etc.; or it may be a seminar, a brochure, or some other promotion mix element.
- The *audience* is the target market with which the bank wants to communicate (senior citizens, young people, high-income people, corporate treasurers, etc.).
- The *feedback* is the response made by the audience; it may take the form of a change in attitude, an increased level of awareness, the mailing in of a coupon, or the opening of an account. Research can help measure feedback.

In the following sections, messages, media, and some ways of measuring feedback will be discussed.

THE PROMOTION MIX

In this section, each of the elements in the promotion mix will be looked at, as well as some of the factors that affect the relative use or mixing of those elements, and the concept of the promotional campaign.

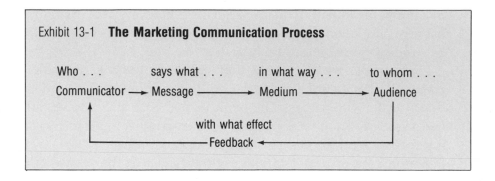

Exhibit 13-1 **The Marketing Communication Process**

Who . . . says what . . . in what way . . . to whom . . .

Communicator → Message ———→ Medium ———→ Audience

with what effect

——————Feedback ◄——

Elements of the Promotion Mix

There are four elements that are part of the promotion mix: advertising, sales promotion, publicity, and personal selling. **Advertising** is "mass, paid communication, the ultimate purpose of which is to impart information, develop attitude, and induce action beneficial to the advertiser."[2] The word *paid* differentiates advertising from other forms of mass communication, particularly from publicity, which is obtained free of charge. This paid mass communication takes place through a variety of media: print media (magazines and newspapers, for example), broadcast media (radio, television), outdoor and transit advertising, and direct mail.

Sales promotion refers to selling activities that cannot be classified in any of the other promotion categories. The American Marketing Association has defined it as:

> Those marketing activities other than personal selling, advertising and publicity, that stimulate consumer purchasing and dealer effectiveness, such as displays, shows, and exhibitions, demonstrations, and various nonrecurring selling efforts not in the ordinary routine.[3]

Some examples of sales promotion in banking are point-of-purchase displays, posters, statement stuffers, literature racks, premium promotions, employee incentive programs, and seminars.

Publicity refers to the stimulation of demand for a product by placing news about it in a publication or by obtaining favorable commentary about it on radio, television, or some other medium not paid for by the sponsor. In other words, it is free space in the press, and it is achieved by packaging the message in a way that is newsworthy so that the media will pick it up. This kind of promotion has a relatively high degree of credibility because it is not paid for by the bank.

Personal selling is a form of communication that takes place one-on-one. The sales force's efforts must be coordinated with the rest of the bank's communications—its advertising, sales promotion, and publicity.

Relative Use of the Promotion Mix Elements

The elements of the promotion mix are, to some extent, interchangeable with one another, and each promotion tool has advantages in certain situations. One of the questions that bank marketers face (especially at budgeting time) is, "Would we increase profits by concentrating more of our efforts and dollars on personal selling and less on advertising . . . or more on internal promotion efforts . . . or more on publicity?" There is no hard and fast answer to this question, but when attempting to answer it, there are at least four factors that the marketing manager should consider: the communication goal, the type of product or service, the nature of the market, and the product's life cycle stage.

The Communication Goal

The combined efforts of all the bank's communications should be geared toward moving customers through the buying process by creating in them a state of mind conducive to making a purchase. When making a buying decision, the customer passes through successive levels of "the communications spectrum."[4] The lowest level of this spectrum is a state of *unawareness* of the bank or the specific product being sold. The next stage is *awareness*. There is an axiom about the importance of awareness: "Share of mind precedes share of market." In other words, before you can expect to make a sale, the customer must, at the very least, be aware of what you are offering.

This stage is followed by *comprehension*, when the customer understands to some extent who the bank is or what the product does. The

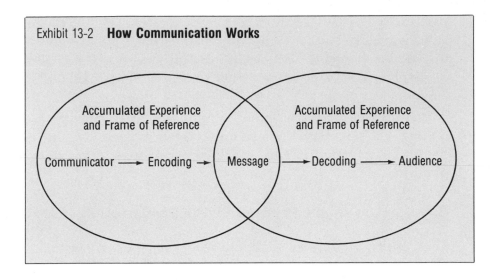

Exhibit 13-2   **How Communication Works**

Accumulated Experience
and Frame of Reference

Accumulated Experience
and Frame of Reference

Communicator ⟶ Encoding → Message →Decoding ⟶ Audience

next stage is *conviction*, when the customer thinks, "The next time I switch banks, I'm going there," or "That service would help me save money on a regular basis, and I need that." The final stage is *action*, when the customer actually visits or contacts the bank with the intention of making a purchase. Exhibit 13-3 compares the stages in the buying process and the stages in the communications spectrum and provides an example of an appropriate promotion message for each of these stages.

Speaking very generally, personal selling becomes more effective and advertising becomes less effective as the consumer passes through the spectrum from awareness to action. Looking specifically at the market for retail banking services, the relative importance of the different promotion elements might appear the way it does in Exhibit 13-4. Personal selling increases in importance and advertising diminishes in importance as the customer approaches the buy decision. Publicity is more effective at the time of new product introduction when awareness is the communication goal. Sales promotion has a relatively constant level of importance. Here, the reference is specifically to point-of-sale merchandising, statement stuffers, premium offerings, and other customer educational tools.

Type of Product or Service

Some bank services require a different promotion mix than others due to their specific characteristics. For example, because they are tailored to the needs of the individual customer, trust services call for a greater personal selling effort than some other banking services. The promotion mix for a campaign offering a special high interest rate on a certificate of deposit might consist more of media advertising and in-branch sales promotion, and less on publicity and personal selling.

Nature of the Market

Most banks operate in several distinct markets—such as the corporate banking market, the retail banking market, the government banking market, and the small business market. Each of these markets requires a somewhat different promotion mix. For example, larger corporate customers usually require more personal selling than small businesses or retail customers.

However, even among retail customers, the level of personal selling will vary depending upon the customer and the product being sold (for example, a personal trust versus a personal checking account). When new retail products are introduced, customers generally go to their own bank first to see if the product is being offered. Therefore, internal sales promotion techniques that make it clear to customers that the bank is offering the service are very important in capturing and retaining this market.

Life Cycle Stage

The effectiveness of the various promotional tools varies also by the position of the product in its life cycle. Advertising, sales promotion, and publicity are especially important in the introduction stage when the principal communication task is to build awareness and comprehension. During the growth stage when sales are increasing, advertising and sales promotion are used to help differentiate the bank's product from its competitors in an effort to attract a greater-than-average share of the market.

Exhibit 13-3 Bank Advertising Objectives and Stages in the Buying Process

Stage in Buying Process	General Advertising Objective	Examples
1. Unsatisfied need	Awareness	1. "We have car loans." 2. "We're now open 24 hours." 3. "We have a banking plan specifically for you if you're over 60."
2. Prepurchase behavior	Comprehension	1. "Here's how you can earn 15 percent more interest." 2. "This is how we compute interest on your account."
3. Purchase decision	Conviction/ Action	1. "Our loan rate is the lowest in town." 2. "You pay interest only on the money you borrow for the precise time you borrow it." 3. "Come in and talk to our savings counselor."
4. Postpurchase feelings	Reassurance	1. "We're the bank for your money." 2. "You're our first concern."

When a product reaches the maturity stage and sales have leveled off, advertising is generally increased; this approach adds to the already declining profits at this stage. In retail banking, however, advertising generally stops, and sales promotion and personal selling take over the promotion task for a mature product. For example, very few banks promote regular personal checking, although it is imperative that information on this service be available at the point of sale and that the customer contact staff attempt to cross-sell the service to new loan and savings customers.

In the decline stage, promotional efforts should be diverted to new growth products or to enhancements in the old product that might help to stimulate sales. Holiday and vacation clubs are in the decline stage, and there is little point in spending promotional dollars to attempt to generate sales of this noncompetitive product in the face of higher-yielding savings alternatives.

ADVERTISING

Billions of dollars are spent on advertising every year in this country, yet there is a nagging question that often lurks in the minds of business executives: "What am I really getting for all those dollars?" Retailer John Wanamaker expressed this concern when he said, "I know that about half of my advertising is wasted, but I don't know which half."

As a result of this deep-seated doubt, advertising is usually the first to suffer when expenses must be curtailed. Yet, studies conducted over six recession and post-recession periods have shown that companies that maintained or increased their advertising budgets during recession years increased their profits significantly more in the post-recessionary periods than did those that had cut their advertising budgets.[5]

Some people praise advertising for being a major contributor to the high standard of living in this country. Others criticize it, saying that it creates false aspirations and stimulates demand for products and services that are not truly necessary. Whatever its role, advertising is unquestionably the most widely used promotion tool in the banking industry and the largest part of a bank's marketing budget. Therefore, this discussion of advertising will start from the budget perspective.

The Size of the Marketing Budget

The marketing budget for a bank generally consists of expenditures for five activities:

1. advertising;

2. sales promotion;

3. marketing research;

4. sales/customer service training; and

5. public relations.

"How much should a bank spend on marketing?" is a recurring question among both marketers and senior management of a bank,

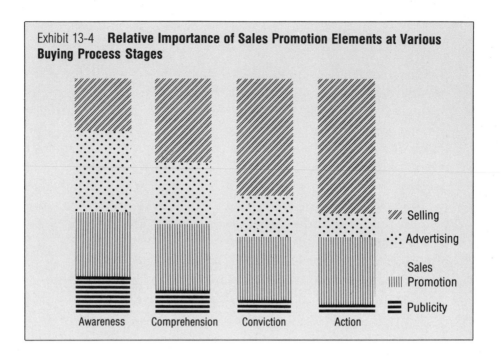

Exhibit 13-4 **Relative Importance of Sales Promotion Elements at Various Buying Process Stages**

especially at budgeting time. There are no easy rules of thumb, but there are some data that indicate that banks actually spend from about 1/20th of 1 percent of total assets, for larger banks, to 1/10th of 1 percent for smaller banks.[6] These figures are averages, however, and as such, they are subject to all the problems associated with averages. They should not be used to determine what a bank should spend in carrying out its marketing objectives. That amount will vary by geographic region, degree of competition, and the aggressiveness of the bank's marketing objectives.

Advertising's Share of the Bank's Marketing Budget

The proportion of a bank's total marketing budget that is spent on various marketing activities is very much a function of bank size. As Exhibit 13-5 shows, the largest banks spend considerably more of their total marketing dollars on advertising (70 percent) than the smallest banks (54 percent). This does not imply that larger banks are less concerned with nonadvertising activities such as sales promotion, public relations, or sales training. Rather, it is due to the economies of scale that the larger banks enjoy in those nonadvertising areas. If a very small community bank allocated only 13 percent of its marketing budget to public relations (as the largest banks do), it would probably not have sufficient funds to support its community relations activities as it should. In contrast, if a major money center bank spent 25 percent of its marketing budget on public relations, that might be considered inordinate. That level of expenditure is not necessary in order to enable the bank to meet its community and public relations goals.

Clearly, however, advertising is the largest component of a bank's marketing budget. Public relations runs a distant second, and sales promotion ranks third. The proportion of the budget spent on sales training seems relatively small, considering the importance of personal selling as a promotion and distribution tool in banking. However, to the extent that sales training expenses are borne by personnel departments, they would not be included in these figures.

It is interesting to note that larger banks spend a larger proportion of their marketing budgets on marketing research than smaller banks. Because of their size and the costs that can be involved in making a marketing error, large banks do considerable research among their various markets (retail, commercial, trust, etc.) to measure the results of their efforts and to help them maintain their leadership in the ongoing process of new product development.

How Advertising Dollars Are Spent

The major forms of media that carry bank advertising messages are newspapers, radio, television, magazines, direct marketing, and outdoor and transit advertising. Exhibit 13-6 shows the relative merits and disadvantages of each.

The relative use of these various advertising media varies by bank size and geographical market. Exhibit 13-7 shows the way advertising dollars are allocated among the media by banks of various sizes.

Exhibit 13-5 How Banks of Various Sizes Allocate Total Marketing Expenditures

Asset size in millions

	$25–50	$100–250		$1,000–5,000
Advertising	54%	67%		70%
Public Relations	24	17		13
Sales Promotion	15	9		10
Sales/Customer Service Training	3	1		1
Marketing Research	1	2		3
All Other	1	4		2
	98%*	100%		99%*

*due to rounding

Source: Analysis of 1985 Bank Marketing Expenditures (Chicago: Bank Marketing Association, 1986).

Within the advertising budget, the largest expense for most banks is newspaper advertising, with radio advertising following. Large banks spend proportionately more on television, the most expensive medium. Radio is a much less expensive medium than television, and the cost of producing radio commercials is also significantly less than that of producing television spots. Indeed, there is no production cost at all when a radio spot is simply read by an announcer. This may not be the most effective way to communicate the specific message, however.

Magazines are also used more by larger banks than smaller ones because of their wide-reaching circulation. Since each magazine has a specific type of audience, this medium can be used to target desired market segments. It is possible to buy space in a group of national magazines on a regional basis, enabling banks to confine their advertising to their trade areas.

Direct response marketing is used more heavily by the largest banks because it is a very efficient way to reach specific target markets. Direct response consists primarily of **direct mail** and

telemarketing. It is possible for a bank to purchase or develop lists of residents in targeted income areas, persons who are likely to have the same economic and demographic characteristics as the target market for a specific product, persons who have automobiles or houses more than 2 years old, and so on. The bank may also obtain from its own records lists of borrowers with only a few payments remaining on a loan, or customers with only one account who might be prospects for other bank services. Through direct mail and telephone contact, used either in conjunction with one another or separately, banks can market to such prospects and even extend beyond their geographic trade area to market services that do not require physical proximity to the bank. For example, many banks have utilized direct mail advertising to expand their credit card business beyond state lines.

Outdoor advertising can be an effective medium, especially when used in support of advertising in other media. Due to the speed at which people pass the billboards and the confined space available, the message must be brief and clear. (See Exhibit 13-8.) A rule of thumb is that an outdoor message should contain no more than 11 words, including the name of the bank.

Another very important element of the advertising budget that is not shown here is the structure of fees and commissions paid in connection with the design and development of advertising. These expenses account for about 13 percent of the smaller bank's budget to 20 percent of the larger bank's. They include fees paid to advertising agencies, artists, photographers, typesetters, talent, sound mixers, film and tape editors, production staff, and others involved in the process of producing print, radio, television, and other advertising.

Advertising's Objectives

It is imperative that specific objectives be set for advertising, especially when considerable dollars are to be spent, and that these objectives be distinct from the overall marketing objectives of the bank.[7] What is an appropriate objective for advertising? Altogether too many bankers would be quick to answer, "Sales—the purpose of advertising is to sell our bank, our products." Many of those same executives are not so quick to give the credit to advertising when, in

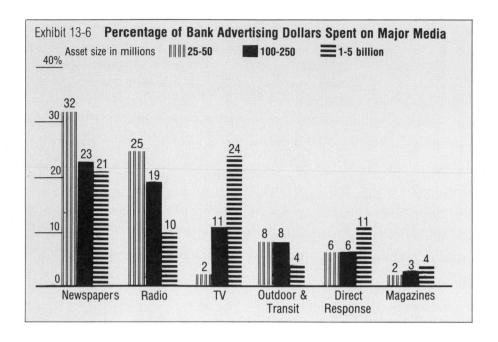

Exhibit 13-6 **Percentage of Bank Advertising Dollars Spent on Major Media**

Asset size in millions: 25-50, 100-250, 1-5 billion

	Newspapers	Radio	TV	Outdoor & Transit	Direct Response	Magazines
25-50	32	25	2	8	6	2
100-250	23	19	11	8	6	3
1-5 billion	21	10	24	4	11	4

fact, there is an unusual upturn in sales revenue or the number of new accounts takes an upswing during a promotion.

However, sales should *not* be the objective of advertising because *there is no direct causal relationship between advertising and sales.* The number of customers opening accounts of various types is very much affected by other elements of both the marketing mix and the promotion mix. The product itself, the pricing, the distribution system, the personal selling effort, the publicity, the sales promotion devices, and the advertising—all these blend to result in a sale.

If the objective of advertising is not sales, what then? The answer is that advertising's objectives should relate to factors that are affected only by advertising. A marketing objective might be to achieve an increase in commercial loan volume of 15 percent. A related advertising goal would be a specific communication objective—for example, to increase awareness of the bank among corporate financial executives within the bank's trade area. *Case E* addresses this point.

Advertising goals should relate to one or more of the stages in the communication spectrum. They should be set in terms of increasing the proportion of the target market:

- who are *aware* of the bank, its product, or the idea the bank seeks to communicate;

- who understand (that is, *comprehend*) the message or the benefit to them of using the bank or the service;

- who say they would consider (that is, have formed a *conviction* about) using the bank or the service; or

- who have already taken some *action* to do so (for example, submitted to a demonstration of an automated teller; come into the bank for a free piece of informative literature; sent back a coupon from an ad).

Since bank advertising is most effective in the awareness and comprehension stages, most bank ads fall into those two categories. For instance, when First Union National Bank of North Carolina entered the Florida banking market, they used Hollywood-style special effects on television to make residents throughout Florida aware that "there's a new source of power in town" (Exhibit 13-9). Centerre Bank's print ad (Exhibit 13-10) promotes its zero coupon certificates by getting parents of small children to consider how much money they are going to need to send those children to college—that is, by making them aware of the need to start saving now.

On the other hand, People's Bank's credit card ad (Exhibit 13-11) was designed to foster the conviction that their credit card interest rate is significantly lower than their major competitors'. In contrast, other advertisements for bank products stimulate action by including an application within the body of the ad. This is an example of direct response advertising.

In order to set communication objectives, it is necessary to establish a benchmark—a reference point or starting position—and this is done through research. The benchmark identifies the point from which the advertising is to move people. During and after the advertising, follow-up research should be conducted to measure the change that takes place within the target audience.

Exhibit 13-7 **Some Relative Merits of Major Advertising Media**

Newspapers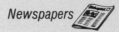

Advantages
1. Flexible and timely
2. Intense coverage of local markets
3. Broad acceptance and use
4. High believability of printed word

Disadvantages
1. Short life
2. Read hastily
3. Small "pass-along" audience

Television

Advantages
1. Combination of sight, sound, and motion
2. Appeals to senses
3. Mass audience coverage

Disadvantages
1. Limited selectivity of audience
2. Fleeting impressions
3. Short life (30 seconds)
4. Expensive

Radio

Advantages
1. Mass usage
2. Audience selectivity via station format
3. Low cost
4. Geographic flexibility

Disadvantages
1. Audio presentation only
2. Less attention than TV
3. Chaotic buying (nonstandardized rate structures)
4. Short life (60 seconds)

Magazines

Advantages
1. Highly selective audience
2. Read at a leisurely pace
3. Quality of reproduction
4. Pass-along readership

Disadvantages
1. Long closing periods (6 to 8 weeks prior to publication)
2. Some waste circulation
3. No guarantee of position (unless premium is paid)

Outdoor

Advantages
1. Flexible
2. Relative absence of competing advertisements
3. Repeat exposure
4. Relatively inexpensive
5. Supports other media

Disadvantages
1. Creative limitations
2. Many distractions for viewer
3. Public attack (ecological implications)
4. No selectivity of audience

Direct Response

Advantages
1. Audience selectivity; little waste
2. Flexible
3. No competition from competing advertisements
4. Personalized

Disadvantages
1. Relatively high cost
2. Consumers often pay little attention since they are subject to a great deal of direct mail and telemarketing

Executing the Advertising Message

There is an infinite variety of ways to creatively execute any one advertising message.[8] The task of an advertising agency's creative staff is to develop the style, tone, wording, and format for maximum effect. However the ad is created, the benefit provided by the product or service should be clear to the audience.

Style

There are at least nine styles for communicating a message:

1. *Slice-of-life.* This approach shows people enjoying the benefits of the service in a normal setting. For example, the equity credit line ad of Norstar Bank, now Fleet Bank of Maine, (Exhibit 13-12) shows a family posing in front of a new refrigerator as part of their kitchen home improvement.

2. *Lifestyle.* This style illustrates how the service fits in with a particular lifestyle. For example, a jogger in his mid-30s making a quick stop at his bank's automated teller relates to a particular lifestyle.

3. *Fantasy.* This style creates a fantasy about what might happen in connection with the use of the bank or respective service. Atlantic Financial does this through the consistent use of a sailing yacht in all its print and television advertising. (See Exhibit 13-13.) The fantasy created by these ads is that banking with Atlantic can somehow help you enjoy the lifestyle depicted in the ads.

4. *Mood or image.* This style builds an evocative mood or image around the product or the bank—happiness, security, tradition, leadership, acceptance. Much institutional (that is, nonproduct) advertising by banks is done in this style. Norwest Banks does this in a series of ads (Exhibit 13-14) in which the bank calls attention to its long history of strength, stability, and security by tying in nineteenth century photographs with the bank and the reader.

5. *Musical.* This style is used in radio or television advertising and involves one or more persons singing a jingle about the bank. Some consumer products use television commercials that are full-scale song-and-dance productions.

Exhibit 13-8

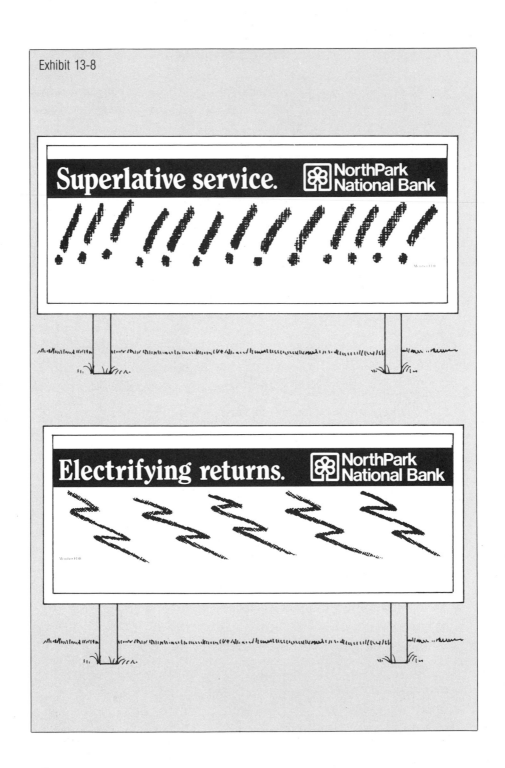

6. *Personality symbol.* This style creates a character that represents or personifies the bank. For example, the Harris Lion is the mascot for Harris Trust, and Elbert the Bighorn is the mascot for First National Bank of Denver.

7. *Technical expertise.* This style features the care that the bank exercises and the experience of its personnel. For example, showing the bank's president and international banking officer getting off a plane in the Orient, or highlighting a member of the bank's staff as an example of the kind of people who serve the bank's customers, are aimed at creating an impression of expertise.

8. *Scientific evidence.* This style presents survey or scientific evidence that the bank or its services perform better than the competition. An example would be showing how the bank's earnings on its trust assets outperformed the Dow Jones Industrial Average and/or other financial institutions over a period of years.

9. *Testimonial evidence.* This style features a highly credible or likeable source endorsing the bank or the service. Examples are the use of a sports or entertainment star as the spokesperson for the bank, or the use of a locally recognized businessperson stating how the bank has helped his or her firm.

Tone

The tone of the ad must also contribute to the effective communication of the message. Humor can be very effective. For instance, Sovran Bank (Exhibit 13-15) used a humorous approach to communicate the message about its many locations throughout Virginia, Maryland, and Washington. It is possible for humor, especially on radio and television, to be so effective in itself that it detracts from the main message. Some banks use a consistently positive, upbeat tone; some use a defiant tone; some are very conservative; others are almost playful and funloving. Some banks have taken on a helpful tone with a consumer-oriented approach.

Wording

The wording (copy) must be attention-getting and memorable, and this is especially important in the development of headlines that will

Exhibit 13-9

FIRST UNION NATIONAL BANK OF FLORIDA

"ANNOUNCEMENT" :90, :60, :30

There's a new source of power in town . . .

More service than any bank in Florida, anywhere.

A new power in banking . . .

First Union National Bank.

More lending power . . .

Let the power be with you."

compel the reader to read further. The benefit to the customer should be clear in the headline. Altogether too many bank ads leave the reader with the feeling, "So what?" An example of this is "Bank XYZ announces Flexifund." Where is the benefit in that statement? What appeal is there for the reader to pause and read further?

There are seven basic types of headlines:

1. *News.* "The cost of managing your money is about to go up." "Now your money can work even longer hours than you do." "Introducing First Interstate Bank."

2. *Question.* "Need a home improvement loan?" "What would you say if somebody asked how your bank performs?" "Are you living on a gold mine?" "Is your bank holding you up?"

3. *Narrative.* "Back in 1952, my biggest savings problem was keeping my piggy bank hidden from my brother." "I may never need it. But I sleep better knowing I have a line of credit."

4. *Command.* "If you have a certificate maturing, read this message." "Keep your money where it belongs."

5. *1-2-3 Ways.* "Two ways to earn the highest yield in town on short-term certificates." "135 ways to pay your bills without leaving home."

6. *How-What-Where-When-Why.* "How to start a car" (automobile loan ad). "Where to go when you run out of cash before you run out of holiday." "Why Morgan is a good bank for art and antique dealers."

7. *Statement.* The majority of bank ad headlines fall loosely into this category in that they consist of a statement about the bank that cannot really be called news but which does not fit in any of the categories above. In fact, many of them are not very interesting and do not offer any benefit to the reader.

Format

Format and layout elements, such as ad size, shape, color, and illustration also affect the ad's impact value. Generally speaking, the larger the ad, the more attention it will get, although the increase in attention may not be proportional to the increase in production and

Exhibit 13-10

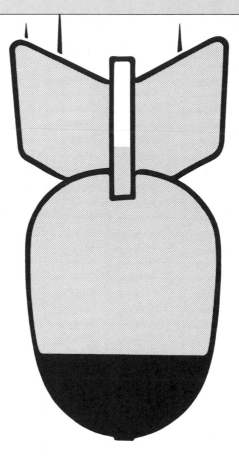

Has the cost of your third grader's college education hit you yet?

A degree at a private college 10 years from now could run you over $100,000. State schools as much as $50,000.

Which means it's time for parents and grandparents to be thinking about scholarships for the kids. And about Zero Coupon Bonds at Centerre.

Our Zero Coupon Bonds are government-insured U.S. Treasury bonds without the coupons you normally have to clip and bring in for payment. So there's no reinvesting your earnings or interest lost due to delays in reinvesting. Zeros simply grow and grow until the maturity date you pick.

The growth of your zeros is taxable yearly even though all interest is paid at maturity. Which is why, under current tax laws, zeros are especially suitable for a college fund in your child's name. Or even an IRA in yours.

So if you've got big plans for your little one, talk to us about Zero Coupon Bonds. Before someone drops another bomb on you.

Who knows, you might have twins on the way any day now.

Centerre Zero Coupon Bonds			
Investment	Maturity	Yield*	Value at Maturity
$11,727.25	10 years	7.65%	$25,000.00
$23,454.50	10 years	7.65%	$50,000.00
$ 7,658.02	15 years	8.00%	$25,000.00
$15,316.00	15 years	8.00%	$50,000.00

*Yields may vary. This graph is for illustration purposes only. Call for current yields.

CENTERRE BANK
One Centerre Plaza • St. Louis, MO 63102
(314) 554-6225

Member FDIC

media space costs. Similarly, the use of color, especially in a black and white medium (for example, a newspaper), will also increase an ad's chances of being seen and read. The use of color has a substantial impact on the cost of producing and placing a print ad.

Occasional departures from the usual ad size and shape can be very effective, especially when promoting a parity product (the same thing that every other bank is promoting). The ad might be long and narrow or 4 inches high, running across the bottom of a one-page or a two-page spread.

The fourth major format component is the illustration, or speaking more broadly, the ad's graphic design. A single bold illustration can be very compelling. Consider, for example, Marine Banks' series of loan ads (Exhibit 13-16). A striking photograph or a photo taken from an unusual perspective (Exhibit 13-17) may also be quite compelling.

There is no hard and fast rule about how much information or content to put in an ad. Ads that are mostly white space can be very arresting (Exhibit 13-18), but ads containing a great deal of information may be called for in situations in which the bank's primary communication goal is to increase comprehension of a difficult or misunderstood subject (Exhibit 13-19).

Measuring Advertising's Effectiveness

One of the reasons why bank advertising expenses are so vulnerable in times of economic uncertainty is that bank marketers seldom do a complete job of measuring the effectiveness of their advertising efforts. Evaluating advertising's effectiveness should be an ongoing process, with research being done in waves over time (that is, doing the same basic study every few months). This is necessary because changing consumer attitudes or opinions is a slow process, and it takes time to see substantial results. If marketers cannot make a strong argument for the value of their advertising, they have difficulty justifying the expense. Banks might conduct so-called advertising research studies, but unless they are measuring the communication effect against predetermined goals, they are not doing a thorough job.

Exhibit 13-11

WITH INTEREST RATES LIKE THESE, IS IT ANY WONDER THEY'RE CALLED CHARGE CARDS?

Institution	Rate*
Sears Discover Card	19.80%
Citibank MasterCard	19.80%
Fleet VISA & MasterCard**	16.70%
Hospital Trust VISA	17.04%

11.75% APR.

Charge cards are supposed to be convenient. At these rates, however, the only people they're convenient for are the institutions that issue them.

But right now, you can replace your old cards with a VISA or MasterCard from People's Bank at 11.75% APR.

A Better Rate.

People's 11.75% VISA and MasterCard are currently the lowest interest rates available in Rhode Island. (Just in time for all your holiday shopping, we might add.)

What's more, we'll hold the rate to 11.75% through June 30, 1987. (After June 30, the rate won't go up to more than 15.00%.)

And we'll even waive the annual fee until 6 months after you get your card.

*Rates based on a telephone survey conducted by People's Bank as of 10/15/86.   **Applicable with balance less than $1000.

A Better Deal.

People's low interest VISA and MasterCard can even save you money on purchases made on your old bank and store cards at higher rates. Tell us the name and balance of the accounts, and you can pay them off at the more manageable rate of 11.75%.

A Better Way.

Getting the cards is easy, too. Just fill out this mini-application and drop it in the mail. Or to apply by phone, call us at 1-800-233-1738, ext. 220, Monday through Friday from 9 a.m. to 9 p.m.

But do it today. Because until you do, you'll be getting overcharged for everything you buy with a charge card.

People's Bank

Member FDIC. A Federal Savings Bank.

PEOPLE'S BANK
Consumer Loan Department   P.O. Box 667   Providence, RI 02901
Yes, I'd like to apply for a People's Bank MasterCard ☐ and/or VISA ☐
PLEASE PRINT

Applicant Name — Home Phone — Social Security Number
Address — City — State — Zip
Previous Address (If Less Than One Year At Above Address) — Date of Birth
Employer — # of years — Position — Monthly Take Home
Previous Employer (If Applicable)
Other Source of Income — Monthly Amount
– COAPPLICANT (If Applicable) –
Name — Social Security # — Employer — Monthly Take Home
– PLEASE PAY OFF THE FOLLOWING CREDIT CARD –
Bank Name — Account Number — Amount of Payment
Applicant/CoApplicant Signature — Date
Note: Alimony, child support or separate maintenance income need not be revealed if you do not wish to have it considered as a basis for the repayment of the credit requested.

FOR PEOPLE'S 11.75% CREDIT CARDS, CALL 1-800-233-1738, EXT. 220.

Case E presents a study of a corporate banking advertising campaign. The term *advertising* is used rather than *promotion* because the primary promotional technique used was advertising. The bank's objectives for the campaign were to communicate to consumers and financial decision makers in middle market firms specific messages about the bank. The bank conducted research among both target markets before the campaign began and after its kickoff. The follow-up tests showed a marked increase in awareness of the bank and of those items that were specifically addressed by the advertising. If this campaign's effectiveness in its first 4 months had been judged on the basis of increased volume of commercial loans and deposits, it might have been deemed a failure. But the purpose of the campaign was to create an awareness and an image so that the commercial target market would be more receptive to the sales efforts of the calling officers. As the McGraw-Hill ad in chapter 12 demonstrates so well, a great deal of communication with prospects is necessary before the salesperson will be well received.

Advertising Research

Not all advertising research concerns itself with setting objectives and measuring the progress that is made toward them. Three other areas addressed by advertising research are ad pretesting, audience research (also called ad posttesting), and media research. These tools help the advertiser to design advertising and to select media to maximize audience attention, interest, impact, and retention.[9]

In **pretesting**, the interviewer shows the proposed ad to a representative audience before the campaign is run in order to evaluate its reaction. Ads representing alternative ways of executing the same basic message may be compared with one another. For example, one particular bank wanted to convey itself as the bank that gives truly personalized service. One of the ads proposed by the agency showed a mass of heads without faces with the headline, "The end of faceless banking." This ad was the favorite of the bank's management, but pretesting revealed that a large proportion of the people who saw the ad were repulsed by it; they found it eerie and unpleasant to look at.

Exhibit 13-12

NEW FRIDGE BY KELVINATOR. HOME IMPROVEMENT BY NORSTAR EQUITY RESERVE.

HOME IS WHERE

THE LOAN IS

NORSTAR
BANK

Before you say "YES" to a home equity loan from just any bank, you should know there's a better way to open a credit line. And it's called **Norstar Equity Reserve**. For starters, you can borrow money by simply writing a check. Anytime you want. For anything you want. Even better, there are NO POINTS. NO MAINTENANCE COSTS. NO FEES AT ALL for qualified applicants. Best of all, **the rate is one of the most competitive in Maine**. So improve your home. And still get the interest tax deductions you deserve. With Norstar Equity Reserve. Just call or visit us today.

Norstar Bank. Straight talk, good banking and you. Member F.D.I.C. Equal Housing Lender 🏠

Audience research surveys the people exposed to the media (radio, TV, newspaper, magazine) at the time the ad was running to measure their recollection of the ad without being prompted. In recognition testing, the bank surveys readers or viewers, showing or describing to them the various ads run in a specific magazine or on a specific time segment on television, and asks them to identify what they recognize seeing or reading and to what extent they paid attention to it.

Advertising pre- and posttesting are useful for measuring whether an ad is understood and for determining its attention-getting quality, but it does not address the extent to which the ad might affect consumer attitudes or behavior, which is the ultimate goal of advertising.

Media research analyzes the size and characteristics of the audience reached by a particular medium. Advertising agencies provide this information to help clients select the most efficient and cost-effective ways to reach a particular target market.

The Advertising Budget

Banks spend about one-half to two-thirds of their total marketing budgets on advertising, but how do they determine what the exact amount should be? There are at least four basic methods used by banks to determine what they will spend on marketing in general or advertising in particular: the percentage method, the task method, the parity method, and the incremental method.[10]

Percentage Method

This method bases the bank's advertising expenditures on the size of the bank. The percentage used may be, for instance, 1/10th of 1 percent of total assets, or some percentage of deposits. This method is quite popular, but it has several flaws. First, it is based on the bank's past performance rather than on objectives for the future. Second, it views assets or deposits as the cause of advertising rather than recognizing that increases in these variables might be, to some extent, the effect of advertising.

Third, it discourages aggressive advertising or advertising in periods of economic slowdown. As mentioned earlier, there is research

Exhibit 13-13

Ride the crest of higher rates at Atlantic and you could go all the way to Australia.

8.00%
Money Market Rate
guaranteed for two months

You'll make more money with a new Atlantic money market account – one of the highest yielding investments available today. Atlantic will pay an 8% rate (8.30% annual yield, compounded monthly) guaranteed for 2 months.* Plus, you'll get these additional benefits:
- access to your money through checks
- access to your money through a nationwide ATM network
- the coast to coast convenience of Atlantic's extensive branch network in Pennsylvania and affiliate branch networks across the country
- the security of FSLIC insurance

7.25%
Checking Account Rate
guaranteed for two months

Now you can make even more money on your checking account. Open a new Atlantic Checking Account and you'll earn up to 7.25% (7.52% annual yield, compounded daily) guaranteed for 2 months.** Plus, you'll get these additional benefits:
- an initial free supply of checks
- access to your money through a nationwide ATM network
- the coast to coast convenience of Atlantic's extensive branch network in Pennsylvania and affiliate branch networks across the country
- no monthly maintenance fee
- help in transferring your account to Atlantic
- high quality Atlantic service

Atlantic has a long history of being one of the most aggressive rate paying institutions in the country. Feel free to ask us about our rates. Visit our branch offices, mail the coupon application below or call our toll free number. Find out why investors as well as savers come to Atlantic and stay. Atlantic is a full service financial institution with complete lines of CDs, credit, brokerage, and other fine services.

1-800-4-ATLANTIC

Win a trip for two to Australia to see the America's Cup Finals.

Enter Atlantic's "Win Back the America's Cup Contest." Grand prizes are three trips for two to Australia to see the finals. Includes stops in Los Angeles, Tahiti, Sydney, Perth, Honolulu & San Francisco. Over 600 other prizes to be awarded.

To receive an official contest entry form, just add $5,000 to any new or existing Atlantic Financial account, or roll over an existing Atlantic Financial Certificate of Deposit before December 12, 1986.

Then print or type an essay of 100 words or less on "Why I Think the U.S. Should Win Back the America's Cup." All entries will be read by an independent panel of judges.

But hurry. Each entry must be different, mailed separately, and received no later than December 17, 1986.

AtlanticFinancial
We can make a difference

MEMBER
FSLIC

that indicates that firms that maintain or increase their advertising in recessions do better in postrecession periods. Since this research was conducted among a variety of firms, including banks, its findings are probably applicable to the banking industry.

Task Method

Using this method, the bank defines its marketing objectives and determines the cost of the level of advertising deemed necessary to attain those objectives. Then, that cost is weighed against the expected net benefit of the new business to be sure that the amount by which it reduces the profit margin on the newly acquired deposits or loans is within acceptable limits.

For instance, if a bank seeks to increase 1-year certificate of deposit volume by $5 million over and above its expected normal growth during the promotion period, and if the profit margin on those funds is, say 2 percent (or $100,000), then the cost of the promotion must be considerably less than $100,000.

This is the most rational budgeting method, but it has its drawbacks. While it works for specific promotions that have immediately measurable results, such as increased deposit or loan volume, it cannot be used to determine the level of advertising necessary to build awareness and the image of the institution. A bank that advertises only when it has a specific promotion to communicate may be out of the media for considerable periods of time. Most marketers agree that some maintenance level of advertising, either product or image-related, is a necessary investment, simply to keep the bank's name in front of its public.

Parity Method

This method might also be called "follow the leader." It involves determining what competitors are spending and then following suit. The assumption here is that the market responds in the same way to the same volume of dollars spent by different banks, which is, of course, erroneous. It denies the effects of variations in creativity, different uses of media, the timing of campaigns, and the pre-existing image and awareness level of the bank.[11] Furthermore, there is no

Exhibit 13-14

reason to believe that the competing banks use a more logical system for determining advertising expenditures than one's own bank.

Another example of the parity method is to base advertising expenditure decisions on the results of the annual survey, published by the Bank Marketing Association, of marketing expenditures by banks throughout the country. In addition to the aforementioned criticisms, this method disregards the fact that no two markets are identical and that, within the average expenditures shown for banks in a particular size group, there can be wide variation from bank to bank in actual expenditures.

Incremental Method

Through this method, the bank simply increases its advertising budget by a certain percentage each year. The percentage may take into account the rate of inflation or the growth rate of the bank, or it may be dictated by a planner or budgeter whose primary objective is to make the bottom line show a targeted return on assets.

Whatever the percentage increase, this method does not take into account the desired objectives of advertising and the most cost-effective ways to attain them. Adjusting for inflation assumes that next year's goals will require the same effort as last year's. This poses no challenge to the marketer to question the techniques being used or to take a fresh look at the objectives being sought.

In summary, the task method is the most professional method for arriving at an advertising budget. It may involve more effort than the other methods, but, like any planning effort, it helps to set direction and increase the value to the bank of its advertising expenditures.

The Advertising Agency

An **advertising agency** is "an independent company set up to render specialized services in advertising in particular and in marketing in general."[12] Advertising agencies provide creative talent in the form of artists and copywriters to help the bank put its communications into words, pictures, or music. They also conduct advertising and

Exhibit 13-15

Everywhere he went, Norman ran into a Sovran Bank.

When Norman found out about all the Sovran Bank locations near his new school, he opened a checking account at one.

He liked it so much, the next day he went back to open a savings account. He was told there would be no service charge on a balance of $100 or more. And he would earn 5½% interest. Norman's still trying to figure out what happens to the other 94½%.

SOVRAN BANK™

Exhibit 13-15   **continued**

Norman tried to use the 24-hour teller machine, but he couldn't stay awake that long.

Norman was really impressed with the Sovran Bank Cash Flow® machine. It could withdraw or deposit cash, transfer money between his accounts, even tell Norman his balance.

And with over 300 locations, all across Virginia, Maryland and Washington, D.C., Norman was sure he'd have no trouble finding one. Still he was disappointed to learn that Cash Flow machines were available for 24-hour use. Norman knew he'd never stay awake more than 23.

SOVRAN BANK™

media research, select media, place ads in the media, and provide other services, such as the development of promotional materials.

The term *advertising agency* is really a misnomer because a good agency helps the bank in its entire marketing program. During marketing planning and strategy sessions, agency staff can help the bank look at itself more objectively and generate creative approaches to solving old and new problems. A good agency will also want to help the bank set measurable objectives. The term *marriage* is often applied to the agency/client relationship, because in order for that relationship to be effective, the agency must be considered a partner. The bank's performance and concerns must be shared with the agency. Needless to say, it is a highly privileged, confidential relationship.

Many banks have an advertising department that maintains a liaison with the agency. Other banks with their own in-house agencies must maintain certain positions on the bank's staff, such as artist, copywriter, media analyst, and media buyer. Unless this talent can be kept busy full-time, it may be more efficient to use an outside agency.

The major source of income for an agency is generally the commission paid to them by advertising media. A newspaper, for instance, may quote a price of $1,000 gross or $850 net of agency commission. The agency paying the bill for the bank will pay $850, but the bank will be charged $1,000 by the agency. Thus, the agency will have earned a 15 percent commission on the media. An alternative arrangement is for the advertiser to pay the agency a fixed fee that covers both the creative talent used and the individuals servicing the account (for example, the account supervisor, the account executive, and secretarial help). The alternative is to set up some combination of fees and commissions.

Whatever the method for compensating the agency, the advertiser is paying for the time spent on the account. To reap the most value for those dollars, the bank must set clear-cut, measurable objectives for each ad and for each campaign. The bank should identify its target audience, indicate what communication goal it wants the ad to accomplish, and set an upper limit on expenses to be incurred. Without such guidelines, an agency can waste a great deal of time.

Bank Advertising Regulation

Over the years, regulations have been established by federal and state banking regulators to hold down abuses such as false, misleading, or deceptive advertising by banks. Also, the banking industry has itself established certain guidelines. The American Bankers Association's Statement of Principles on Financial Advertising sets the following guidelines for ethical advertising:

> An advertisement is ethical: (1) when it is truthful; and (2) when the intended audience can reasonably be expected to understand the message. Because of media physical limitations, it is not necessary for an advertisement to contain all the details about a service. However, any feature, any terms (including prices), or any purchaser benefits should be presented in a manner that does not mislead. The purchaser should not be misled by what is stated nor have false impressions created by what is omitted.

The statement defines when and how the word *free* may be used as it pertains to premiums, checking, and other services. It states that when free checking is offered, there must be no charge for integral parts of the service, such as regular statements or checks, and no monthly charges or charges if the balance falls below a certain level.

The Federal Reserve's Regulation Z governs the advertising of credit services. There are a number of terms that, if used in a loan ad, trigger the need to give further explanation. If the ad says, for example, "20 percent down payment," then it must also state the repayment terms and the annual percentage rate. Furthermore, if the loan in any way relates to housing (mortgage, home equity loan), the equal housing lender logo must be displayed.

In addition, the Federal Deposit Insurance Corporation regulates advertising for deposits. For instance, if the yield on a savings certificate is shown (for example, "7.00 percent yielding 7.25 percent annually"), the method of compounding must be stated (for example, "compounded daily") as well as any time requirement. On all ads for deposits, the words "Member FDIC" or "Deposits Insured by FDIC" must appear next to the bank's name.

Bank marketers must keep current on regulations affecting bank advertising since failure to comply might result in the imposition of fines.

Exhibit 13-16

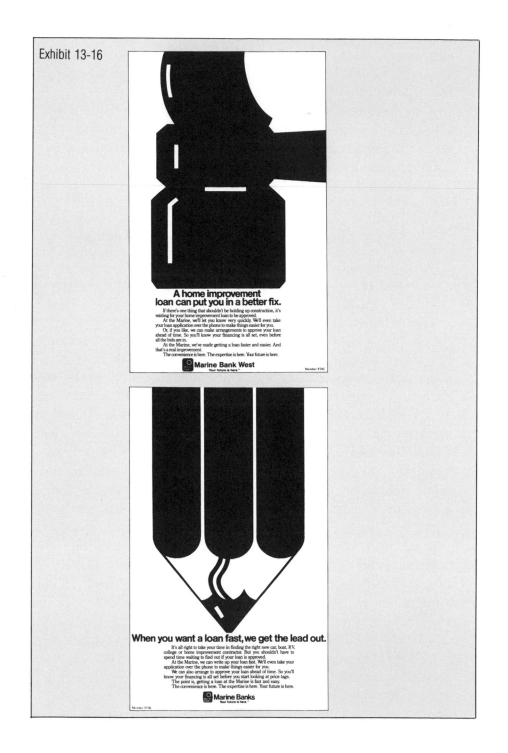

A home improvement loan can put you in a better fix.

If there's one thing that shouldn't be holding up construction, it's waiting for your home improvement loan to be approved.

At the Marine, we'll let you know very quickly. We'll even take your loan application over the phone to make things easier for you.

Or, if you like, we can make arrangements to approve your loan ahead of time. So you'll know your financing is all set, even before all the bids are in.

At the Marine, we've made getting a loan faster and easier. And that's a real improvement.

The convenience is here. The expertise is here. Your future is here.

Marine Bank West
Your future is here.™

Member FDIC

When you want a loan fast, we get the lead out.

It's all right to take your time in finding the right new car, boat, R.V., college or home improvement contractor. But you shouldn't have to spend time waiting to find out if your loan is approved.

At the Marine, we can write up your loan fast. We'll even take your application over the phone to make things easier for you.

We can also arrange to approve your loan ahead of time. So you'll know your financing is all set before you start looking at price tags.

The point is, getting a loan at the Marine is fast and easy.

The convenience is here. The expertise is here. Your future is here.

Marine Banks
Your future is here.™

Member FDIC

SALES PROMOTION

Another element in a bank's promotion mix is sales promotion. It includes those communications that do not fit into the categories of advertising, publicity, and personal selling. Some examples of sales promotion devices from consumer goods industries are cents-off coupons and the offering of merchandise for a low cost plus a proof-of-purchase. Some of the more frequently used sales promotion tools in banking are point-of-purchase displays, incentives, seminars, specialties, contests, and premiums.

Point-of-Purchase Displays

A bank's primary audience for new and existing services is that group of people who are already customers. The bank has a chance to communicate with them every time they come in to conduct a transaction. Furthermore, if the competition is advertising a new or different service, the interested customer will generally look to his or her own bank before going to the competition.

Some of the best ways to communicate with the customer are through posters, counter cards, and literature attractively displayed in the lobby of the bank. This type of promotional material (also called **collateral material**) is also useful when communicating with prospective new customers who come into the bank looking for information. In such a situation, they may feel more comfortable picking up information about the bank's services before approaching someone at a desk.

Effectively worded signs, displays, and other merchandising techniques can be used to support media advertising and to increase sales. Some banks that have tested the effectiveness of coordinated point-of-purchase displays have reported sales at the test branches to be 15 to 20 percent higher than at the traditionally decorated branches.

Many banks apparently do not understand the value of such support materials. The marketing director of a community bank reported that he visited the offices of his own bank and four competitors to

Exhibit 13-17

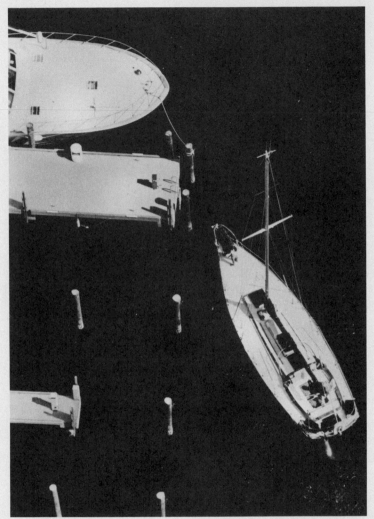

Riggs Can Help You Celebrate A New Berth In The Family.

When it comes to boat loans, there are certain advantages to being in the same boat with Riggs. Our rates, for example, are extremely competitive. Now they're even reduced for a limited period of time. Riggs also has 27 branches where you can answer the call of the sea. Or just call us at 835-4192 and we'll mail a loan application to you. What's more, Riggs approves boat loans in a mere 24 hours. So if you get underway now you could start celebrating tomorrow.

Exhibit 13-18

OUR
AUTO
LOAN
RATES
HAVE
SHRUNK.

We're offering some of our
lowest rates in years.
So apply now by phone. We'll
do the paperwork
and give you an answer
the next business day. Call
Mon.-Fri. 8 a.m. to 8 p.m.
(800) 233-1583.

Bank of America

BANK ON THE LEADER™

Exhibit 13-19

THEY CHANGED THE RULES IN <u>THIS</u> HOUSE.
WHAT CHANGES SHOULD YOU MAKE IN YOURS?

WHEN THE PRESIDENT SIGNED THE NEW TAX BILL BACK IN OCTOBER, IT CHANGED THE WAY MOST PEOPLE WILL HANDLE THEIR FAMILY FINANCES. WE HAVE SOME IDEAS TO HELP.

Tax reform has given us a new set of rules on IRAs, savings, loans, leases, and investments. And at the same time, falling interest rates have made old patterns of saving and borrowing obsolete.

The choices aren't always clear-cut. For example, loans are cheaper than before…but the interest won't be tax-deductible unless you're borrowing on a house.* How do you know what to do?

At BANK ONE, we think these changing times call for a change in financial strategy. You can't expect to succeed with the same old answers.

BANK ONE affiliate presidents met recently to discuss how we can answer customer concerns about tax reform and other money issues.

In times like these, what you really need are Money Solutions.

WE'VE BEEN LISTENING TO THE MARKETPLACE—AND HERE'S WHAT WE HEAR.

Tax reform has added to

Consult your tax advisor for specific conditions and details.

people's money-management concerns. Our customers are asking us about the best ways to borrow—not just for major demands but for everyday needs. And we hear concern about low interest rates from savers who want to improve their return these days.

These questions, and many others, went into the thinking behind our "Money Solutions"—a new generation of banking products and services we've developed especially for this new financial era.

MONEY SOLUTIONS MAKE YOUR MONEY WORK SMARTER.

Among our Money Solutions are such hard-working alternatives as *Preferred Checking* and *Preferred Savings*, interest-earning accounts which pay you increasingly higher rates as your balance increases.

And there's the *VISA*

Premier Card, a credit card with a substantially higher credit line—which gives you a chance to consolidate some of the cards now filling up your wallet.

Another Money Solution: *IRAs.* Despite their retooling at Congress's hands, we think tax-deferred interest still makes them a valuable investment.

Tax reform has made home-equity borrowing a particularly popular Money Solution these days, as homeowners arrange a tax-favored loan or credit line through our *Equity Money Service.*

WE'VE EVEN DEVELOPED A PRIME-BASED LINE OF CREDIT WHICH DOESN'T REQUIRE A SECOND MORTGAGE.

For customers who have established their credit over the years, we have a Money Solution which doesn't require

a home mortgage. It's our PrimePlus personal credit line…and in times like these, its versatility makes it a great money-management tool.

With PrimePlus, you can draw on your credit as you need it, and pay it back on a flexible basis. Borrowing is as easy as writing a check.

Best of all, your creditworthiness earns you a very low interest rate, based on our prime lending rate.** A benefit that more than makes up for the gradual phase-out of interest deductibility.

IN TIMES LIKE THESE, YOU NEED ALL THE BANK YOU CAN GET.

And at BANK ONE, we're working harder than ever to help our customers take advantage of change. From top management to tellers, we've put in countless hours mastering Money Solutions which didn't even exist a year ago.

So if you're considering how to develop better financial rules for your household, ask us to help. We're ready. And we think that just might make us the kind of bank you'd like to have on your side these days.

IN TIMES LIKE THESE, YOU NEED BETTER
MONEY SOLUTIONS

PRIME PLUS:	Our personal unsecured line of credit lets you borrow without coming into the bank.
PREFERRED CHECKING:	You earn interest every day—and the higher your balance, the higher the rate.
EQUITY MONEY SERVICE:	Our low-cost, tax-wise way to set up a line of credit or a lump-sum loan.
PREFERRED SAVINGS:	Our only savings account gives you higher interest rates as your savings increase.
VISA PREMIER CARD:	Our most powerful credit card offers you an increased line of credit.
IRA:	Since tax is still deferred on earnings, your savings grow faster…to help assure a comfortable future.

BANK☰ONE™

Ten thousand people who care.

An affiliate of BANC ONE CORPORATION, Columbus, Ohio
Member FDIC

**Prime is that rate announced as the prime rate from time to time by BANK ONE.

gather information for an annual marketing plan situation analysis. Only one institution—his own bank—provided material about the variety of the bank's services in a prominent display. Only one other bank had service literature, but it was kept behind the barrier separating the customer service area from the teller and lobby area and, thus, it was out of the public's reach. Another bank had a literature rack in a prominent position, but the only information in it was a brochure about FDIC insurance and other consumer-oriented pieces from the FDIC and other regulatory agencies. The other two had nothing to give to the customer describing the bank's basic services, so the "shopper" had to take his own notes from conversations with bank staff. In one case, it was necessary to call the bank later because the customer relations representative he spoke to did not know whether the bank offered a line of credit attached to a personal checking account. One wonders how many other industries would make it so difficult to get information about their products and pricing.

While the customer or prospect is in the stage of the buying process when he or she is comparing various offerings and looking for information, promotional materials and literature can play an important role.

Incentives

Employees can be motivated by incentives either to cross-sell the bank's products or to bring in business for the bank (see chapter 12). If properly conducted, with a commitment from senior management, these programs can be highly successful. One bank reported an increase in its accounts sold per customer from 1.07 to 3.00. Many banks have reported that significant new business was acquired as a result of rewarding employees who referred customers to the bank.

Seminars

Seminars are an excellent way to target in on a specific market. Some examples are fraud prevention seminars for merchants, economic forecasting for larger businesses, estate planning for senior citizens, and trust seminars for attorneys and accountants (who are excellent sources of referral business). Through this promotional tool, the bank communicates a specific message to a specific audience and, through follow-up contact, can generate new business.

Specialties

Specialties are the giveaways that banks provide, such as key rings, rain hats, calendars, paperweights—all bearing the bank's name and/or logo. Their purpose is to provide a constant reminder of the bank and its services.

Contests

Contests and sweepstakes are used as traffic builders—ways of getting people into the bank. They are especially effective when installing an automated teller in a new location. The bank might, for example, offer a sweepstakes in which everyone who participates in a demonstration becomes eligible for a certain amount of money or a trip. Building traffic is not an end in itself, however. There must be a program to guide the bank staff in precisely what to do or say to the individuals who come into the bank in response to the contest.

Premiums

A **premium** is cash or merchandise that the bank gives or sells at a discount to a customer in return for a deposit or loan. In the case of deposit premiums, the gift may be given either in addition to, or in the place of, the payment of interest. For years, banks and thrift institutions were among the leading users of premiums in this country. Premiums were a way of providing the customer with added value when competing in a regulated rate environment. Now that interest rates are deregulated, banks may compete on the basis of rate, and consumers are rate-sensitive and eager to get the highest return on their funds. Therefore, premiums have become much less popular as a merchandising tool. Nevertheless, cash bonuses and premiums are still used from time to time.

For example, First Tennessee used a computer as a premium in a long-term certificate promotion. The computer was given away in lieu of some of the interest. (See Exhibit 13-20.)

THE PROMOTIONAL CAMPAIGN

When the bank has an important message to communicate, it may use a promotional campaign to do the job. A campaign is "a coordinated series of promotional efforts built around a central theme and designed to reach a specific goal."[13] The theme of the campaign permeates all the bank's communication efforts. *Case D* presents a study of the development and execution of a total promotional campaign. There are six steps involved in the process of developing a campaign:

1. *Setting objectives.* Every campaign should have a predetermined goal stated in measurable terms (for example, to generate $5 million in retail savings and time deposits).

2. *Selecting the media.* Once the target audience has been identified, it is possible through published media research to determine the most effective ways to reach them, whether that be through television, selected newspapers, magazines, radio, or outdoor advertising.

3. *Creating the advertising.* The next challenge is to develop the theme of the program and the method of executing the theme, and to communicate the message in a way that will break through the clutter of competing advertising.

4. *Developing the sales promotion materials.* Media advertising alone cannot do the entire communication job. Literature explaining the offer must be available, and point-of-sale posters or counter cards should be used to help arouse customer awareness and curiosity.

5. *Marketing to the staff.* The most important element in the success of any promotional campaign is the support of the bank's staff. They must understand what is being done, why it is being done, and be encouraged to assist the bank in reaching its goals. Their enthusiasm

Exhibit 13-20

NOT ALL BANK PREMIUMS ARE STUPID.

Now when you open a First Tennessee Certificate of Deposit, instead of getting a silly premium you'll get something you can really use.

A sophisticated Apple IIc personal computer. Plus an Apple monitor and software.

Just deposit $3,000 in a 10-year CD, $5,000 in an 8-year CD, or $10,000 in a 6-year CD. You'll earn a high yield, plus get an immediate return on your investment. There isn't a smarter place to put your money.

1st FIRST TENNESSEE

First Tennessee's Certificates of Deposit.

Substantial penalty is required for early withdrawal. Offer does not apply to IRA accounts and is subject to change without notice. Other conditions may apply. ®Registered Service Mark First Tennessee National Corporation.
©1986 First Tennessee Member FDIC

can help assure the success of a promotion and, conversely, their lack of cooperation may diminish its effectiveness. Their behavior can make a bank's claims about itself ("accurate," "friendly," "competent") ring true or appear as sheer puffery.

6. *Measuring results.* One of the surest ways to negate the possibility of future promotions is to fail to demonstrate the effectiveness of past promotions. If the goals are clear and measurable, and procedures are installed for collecting the necessary data, this very critical step can be relatively simple.

SUMMARY

introduction

The purpose of a bank's promotion strategy is to communicate to the target market the bank's need-satisfying service. That communication takes place through the four elements of the promotion mix: advertising, sales promotion, publicity, and personal selling.

The five steps of the communication process can best be summed up as: "who . . . says what . . . in what way . . . to whom . . . and with what effect." Communication is most effective when the communicator (the bank) encodes its message in symbols that are interpreted by the receiver (the target audience) in precisely the way the sender meant them to be understood.

The goal of a bank's communication efforts is to move the target audience through the communication spectrum from a stage of unawareness, to awareness, to comprehension, to conviction, and ultimately, to the action desired by the bank. The various elements of the promotion mix have varying degrees of effectiveness at each of the stages in the communication spectrum. Advertising is most effective for building awareness and comprehension, while personal selling is more effective for developing conviction and obtaining action. The use and effectiveness of the promotion mix elements also depend upon the type of product being promoted, the nature of the market, and the life cycle stage of the product.

Advertising is paid mass communication that takes place through print, broadcast, and other media. The largest proportion of a bank's marketing dollars is spent on advertising, and newspapers are the medium most frequently used by most banks. Radio, television, newspaper, magazine, direct mail, and outdoor advertising all have strengths and weaknesses. These must be evaluated, generally with the help of an advertising agency, to determine the best media mix for reaching the target audience in a cost-effective way.

A bank should set specific, measurable objectives for its advertising program that correspond to, but are separate from, its marketing objectives. It is not fair to measure advertising's effectiveness on the basis of sales, since so many other factors combine to produce a sale. The objectives for advertising should relate to a specific communication goal, such as "to increase awareness by 30 percent." This type of objective setting requires the use of marketing research both before, during, and after the advertising program.

Media research and advertising pretesting enable banks to design and place advertising in a way that will maximize attention, interest, and retention by the target audience. Audience research measures audience recall and recognition of an advertisement.

There are a number of ways to arrive at an annual advertising budget, but the task method is the best. Using this method, the bank determines its advertising objectives, the most cost-effective strategies and tactics for accomplishing them, and the cost involved.

The bank may have its own internal advertising agency or it may use an independent firm, depending upon its needs. An advertising agency is really an arm of the marketing department, providing ideas to assist not just in promotion strategy, but in the other elements of the marketing mix as well. In all their advertising, banks must be aware of the various advertising regulations that are designed to prevent false or misleading advertising.

Sales promotion refers to all those communications efforts that do not fit into the categories of advertising, publicity, or personal selling. They include point-of-purchase displays, incentives, seminars, specialties, contests, and premium promotions. Each method has its place in the attainment of the bank's communication goals.

A promotional campaign involves the coordinated use of several promotional techniques by the bank when it has an important message to communicate. The process of developing a promotional campaign involves setting specific measurable objectives, selecting the media to be used, creating the advertising, developing the sales promotion materials, training the bank's staff, and measuring the results.

This chapter concludes the study of the fourth key element in the marketing planning process: the formulation of marketing strategy. The next chapter addresses the last two elements in the marketing planning process: implementation of the plan and evaluation of its results. (See Exhibit 3-2.)

POINTS FOR REVIEW

1. Define or briefly describe each of the following terms:
   - communications
   - advertising
   - sales promotion
   - publicity
   - personal selling
   - advertising agency

2. Think of a recent communication situation in which you were the communicator. What was your message, audience, medium, and feedback from the audience?

3. Using a recent communication you received from a bank through any medium (radio, television, direct mail, newspaper), explain how the bank used each of the stages in the communication process.

4. How would you respond to a bank executive who says that the purpose of advertising aimed at corporate financial executives is to sell commercial loans, cash management, and other corporate banking services?

5. Think of a significant purchase that you made recently. How did you first become aware of the product? How did you learn more about it? What caused you to decide to get it? What moved you to actually make the purchase?

6. How would you respond to the following statement by the bank president: "Next year's advertising budget should be 8 percent more than this year's, or the same as the rate of inflation, whichever is lower."

7. Provide examples of current sales promotion techniques being used by banks or consumer product companies.

8. Select three bank ads from current magazines and newspapers and critique them on their use of style, tone, wording, and format.

PART V OTHER TOPICS IN BANK MARKETING

Parts II through IV of this text have covered four of the stages in the strategic marketing management process. However, that process is not yet complete. As discussed in chapter 3, there are six stages in that process. The first four constitute planning; the last two are implementation and evaluation. These last two stages will be dealt with in chapter 14.

In chapter 13, product publicity was pinpointed as being part of the promotion mix, but the bank's nonproduct-related publicity and its public relations and corporate communications efforts are very important to the formation of the bank's image and position, and thus, very much related to the bank's marketing effort. Therefore, a separate chapter is devoted to this topic.

This text has focused largely on the marketing of retail banking products, as the nature of the retail market is such that it requires more products, more people, and more promotional activity per million dollars generated or loaned than does the commercial side of the business. However, that side of a commercial bank generally outweighs the retail deposit and loan side. Therefore, chapter 16 addresses the wholesale side of banking.

Finally, this study of bank marketing concludes with a discussion of a number of developments that are on the horizon in the world of banking and tells how they might affect the future of bank marketing.

14 ORGANIZATION, IMPLEMENTATION, AND EVALUATION

As discussed earlier, the marketing management process is a circular process that consists of three steps: planning, implementation, and evaluation. Up to this point, the planning process has been the major focus, but the best laid plan is of no use unless it is put into action. Implementation of a marketing plan is affected by how the marketing function itself is organized, how it fits into the bank's organizational structure, and how it works with other areas of the bank. Thus, this chapter looks first at the organizational aspects of bank marketing and at issues pertaining to the interrelationship of marketing with other line and staff departments.

A plan is not just a document; it must be a dynamic element—not just something that a bank develops and then puts on a shelf. Furthermore, the planning process is not completed until the objectives are achieved. The bank must not only implement the plan, but while doing so, must recognize that events probably will not proceed entirely as anticipated.[1] Murphy's Law (not just an amusing maxim, but an observation based on experience) says that if anything can go wrong, it usually will. Also, planned events tend to take longer than expected. To quote Joselyn and Humphries:

> The one absolute axiom of marketing planning is that the plan *will not* work as expected. Competitive reactions, changes in the economic

environment, and the operating problems of personnel within the bank will interact to bring about different results than expected. (Those results can be better or worse for your bank than your objectives had suggested.)[2]

Since conditions change and things rarely go as expected, a plan needs to be adjusted from time to time. The key planning element that enables this to occur is performance monitoring and evaluation. (See Exhibit 14-1.)

MARKETING ORGANIZATION

Besides being an organizational philosophy and a management process, marketing is also a function and department within an organization. This section considers the organizational aspects of marketing and how it relates to other departments.

Positioning of Marketing Within the Bank

In banking, as in other industries, the organizational placement of the marketing department says a great deal about the chief executive officer's attitude toward marketing and the overall level of marketing awareness in the bank. Generally speaking, there are three ways that marketing might fit into a bank's organizational chart. (See Exhibit 14-2.) These are:

1. *Type I organization:* Marketing is essential and necessary. In this type of organization, marketing is seen as fundamental to the business of the bank; its activities are regarded as mandatory and an essential part of staying in business. A bank organized in this way has achieved—or is well on the way to achieving—the highest level of marketing awareness. The marketing head reports to the president and/or chief executive officer and has the same status as the line division heads. In a large bank, it is not the title so much as the power of the person to whom the marketing head reports that is important. That individual might be a chief executive or a senior vice president. The important thing is that, either directly or through the chain of

command, the marketing head must be able to mobilize many line and staff areas of the bank (such as systems, operations, and branch administration) to support the marketing plan.

2. *Type II organization:* Marketing is necessary but nonessential. Here, marketing is seen as a necessary and unavoidable function, but not as essential to the operation of the bank. In such an organization, the marketing department head may report directly to the president, chief executive officer, or another senior executive but does not have the same status or title of the individuals who head the line divisions of the bank. In such an organization, marketing has not been fully integrated into all areas of the bank and is unlikely to be, because the attitude of the top management is communicated and expressed to the rest of the organization through the institutional structure.

3. *Type III organization:* Marketing is nonessential but expedient. In this type of organization, marketing is viewed as useful and contributing to the bank's self-interest, but clearly, not essential to the business. The marketing head is one step removed from the center of power and authority and obviously has a lesser status than in either of the other two organizational structures. The marketing department in this type of organization is especially vulnerable when budget and staff cutbacks become necessary.

These three descriptions are, of course, a simplification of the real world. The position of marketing within the organization is influenced by many variables, including the size of the institution. In all three types of organization outlined here, marketing is shown as a centralized activity that services the needs of the various divisions of the bank. But in very large institutions, marketing is likely to be decentralized, with separate marketing departments within the various divisions.

For bank holding companies, marketing may be either centralized or decentralized, and the particular form of organization structure depends on the size of the subsidiary banks. In a holding company with multiple small banks, marketing is likely to be centralized at the holding company level. In this way, the individual banks can take advantage of economies of scale in the production of advertising and promotional materials. For example, the cost of statement stuffers for

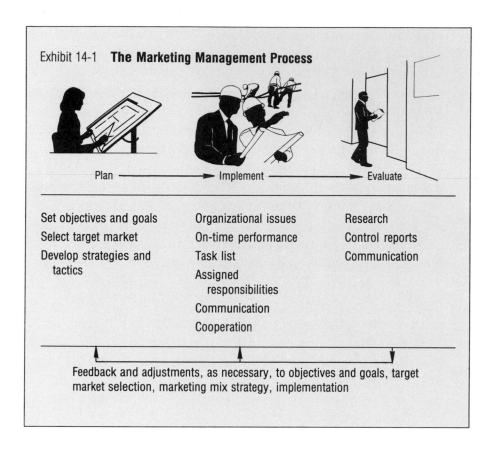

Exhibit 14-1 **The Marketing Management Process**

Plan ──────────────▶ Implement ──────────────▶ Evaluate

Set objectives and goals	Organizational issues	Research
Select target market	On-time performance	Control reports
Develop strategies and tactics	Task list	Communication
	Assigned responsibilities	
	Communication	
	Cooperation	

Feedback and adjustments, as necessary, to objectives and goals, target market selection, marketing mix strategy, implementation

a small bank might be several cents each. By consolidating and standardizing advertising efforts, the cost might be reduced to a cent or less.

Holding company subsidiaries also have the advantage of being able to draw upon research and other marketing expertise available from the holding company, which they would not be able to afford if they were independent institutions.

Another organizational alternative is to establish a centralized marketing function at the holding company level and then appoint marketing heads in each subsidiary institution. This option is more likely to be followed when the subsidiaries are medium- to large-sized banks.

Still another variation exists when holding companies do not have a separate corporate staff at the parent company level, but the marketing department of the lead bank services all the subsidiaries. This type of organization has the advantage of fostering economies of scale, but, in addition to possible operational difficulties, the small subsidiaries may resent being dependent upon the staff of the lead bank. They may feel that their interests are not being adequately represented or that they are not receiving their fair share of the marketing department's time. Clearly, each organizational alternative must be evaluated for its suitability to a particular bank or bank group.

In summary, the organization of the bank and the position that marketing holds within it tells something about the bank's orientation and the extent to which it has adopted the marketing concept. In addition, the way in which the marketing department itself is organized is critically important to the development and implementation of the bank's marketing strategy.

Organization of the Marketing Department

There are many ways to organize a marketing department, depending on the size of the firm and the nature of its business. However, two of the most common structures are the functional organization and the product management organization.

Functional Organization

In a department organized this way, specialists who supervise various functions of the department are coordinated by a marketing vice president.

This type of organization has the advantage of being simple to administer. However, it has an important disadvantage, especially as the number of products or numbers of target markets increases. If one reviews the four elements of the marketing mix, it may be noted that the essential elements of product and pricing are not represented in this type of structure. This issue raises two questions: (1) Where does the responsibility for the key element of product strategy and

Exhibit 14-2   **Positioning Marketing in the Bank's Organizational Structure**

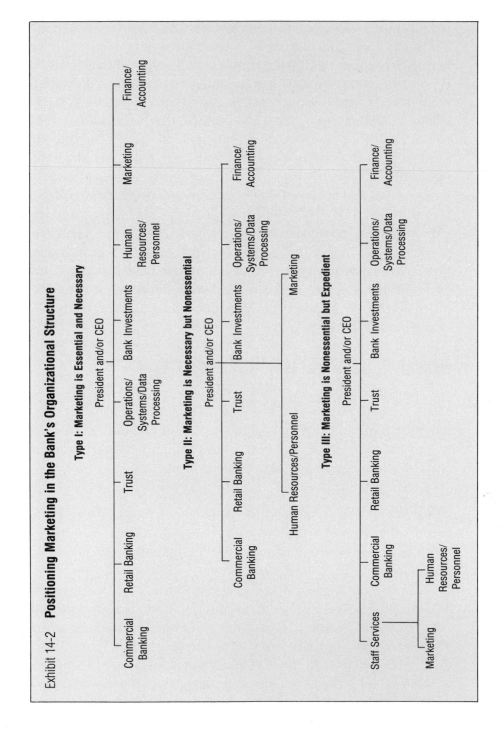

Type I: Marketing is Essential and Necessary

President and/or CEO

Commercial Banking | Retail Banking | Trust | Operations/Systems/Data Processing | Bank Investments | Human Resources/Personnel | Marketing | Finance/Accounting

Type II: Marketing is Necessary but Nonessential

President and/or CEO

Commercial Banking | Retail Banking | Trust | Bank Investments | Operations/Systems/Data Processing | Finance/Accounting

Human Resources/Personnel | Marketing

Type III: Marketing is Nonessential but Expedient

President and/or CEO

Staff Services | Commercial Banking | Retail Banking | Trust | Bank Investments | Operations/Systems/Data Processing | Finance/Accounting

Marketing | Human Resources/Personnel

new product development lie? and (2) How do those functions relate to the marketing department?

A marketing department as organized in Exhibit 14-3 is responsible for promotion (through the advertising manager) and distribution (through the sales training and research managers), but not for product development and pricing. This means that two important elements of the marketing mix will have to be conducted outside the marketing department.[3] In banking, this means that products are developed by the operating areas responsible for servicing them. For example, a new personal revolving credit line might be designed and developed by the consumer credit operations department. That department would work with the computer systems staff to make the programming modifications necessary to offer the product. The consumer credit department would also work with the funds management and accounting areas to determine how the product should be priced. The greatest potential problem with this approach is that the operations staff might have more of a production orientation than a consumer or marketing orientation in its product design. Then, the marketing department is in the passive position of having to successfully promote a product that may not be as competitive and marketable as it could have been.

Product Management Organization

This organizational structure is similar to that of the functional organization, but it includes another manager or group of managers with product responsibility. (See Exhibit 14-4.) These managers use the services of the other functional managers.

The concept of product management began in 1927 at Procter and Gamble. Its Camay soap was not selling well in the marketplace, so one man was given sole responsibility for marketing the product. He succeeded in improving Camay's market position and was later made president of the firm. The product management (or brand management) concept extended to other products within Procter and Gamble and eventually spread to other firms.[4]

A product manager's job is to develop and enhance products, establish and implement marketing strategies, and measure results. The functional departments (advertising, etc.) are a resource or staff

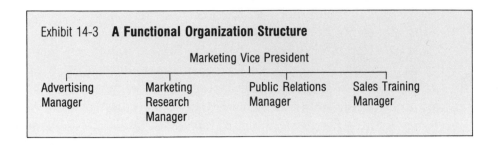

Exhibit 14-3 **A Functional Organization Structure**

Marketing Vice President

| Advertising Manager | Marketing Research Manager | Public Relations Manager | Sales Training Manager |

service available to the product managers. This type of structure is being found increasingly in banking today.

The principal shortcoming of the product management form of organization in banking is that the product manager has certain responsibilities with respect to a specific product, but generally no authority over the people on the line whose cooperation and sales effort dictate the success of the product marketing plan.

One way in which some banks have addressed this problem is to develop a form of matrix management in which the product managers report to two people: the marketing head and the respective division head. In other words, the retail deposit product manager reports to both the marketing manager and the head of the retail division. In this form of organization, the division head is specifically responsible for the development and enhancement of products as well as for the implementation of product marketing plans. The product manager's responsibilities are not changed, but there is a greater likelihood that product plans will be implemented.

No matter how the bank or its marketing department is organized, the four elements of product development and enhancement, pricing, promotion, and distribution must be addressed.

Relationship of Marketing to Other Departments

In the ideal marketing-oriented bank, all departments and divisions work together toward achieving the goals and objectives set in the marketing plan, and all have a basic customer orientation. In the real world, however, few banks have reached this ideal state. Generally, various bank departments are run by specialists who have their own particular concerns and ways of viewing their jobs and the business of banking. Often, they do not see their efforts as part of an overall marketing effort.

Yet the marketing department constantly interacts with other departments, and the implementation of marketing plans is dependent on just about every department in the banking organization, especially the following:

- data processing;
- systems and operations;
- human resources and personnel;
- accounting and finance;
- bank investments;
- legal services;
- auditing;
- line divisions; and
- branches.

Data Processing

Many bank products exist solely as electronic entries on a piece of magnetic material. Where exactly is John Doe's checking account? It is stored with thousands of other accounts on a computer tape that can be held in one hand.

Since most bank products are data based, the product specialist must be able to work and communicate effectively with data processing professionals. However, it is imperative that bank products be designed by the product manager and not by the data processing people. The objective of the data processing group is to develop systems that accomplish a desired end result. In contrast, marketing's objective is to see that all the steps along the way are customer-oriented. For example, a checking account statement could be developed by the data processing department that would technically do what it is supposed to do but which might be difficult for customers to

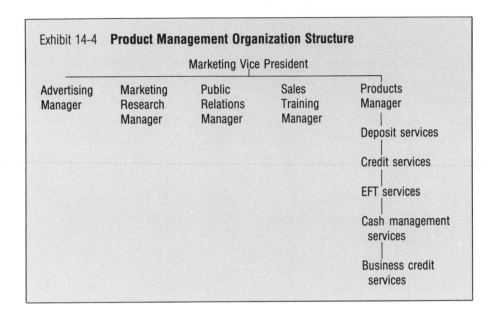

Exhibit 14-4 **Product Management Organization Structure**

Marketing Vice President

Advertising Manager	Marketing Research Manager	Public Relations Manager	Sales Training Manager	Products Manager
				Deposit services
				Credit services
				EFT services
				Cash management services
				Business credit services

understand. The responsibility of the marketing department would be to ensure that the product's primary advantage is ease of use.

The data processing department can also be the source of a vast amount of information for the research manager and the product manager. This information is essential in the evaluation stage of the marketing management process, but it will not be automatically available from the computer. It must be requested, and the format in which it is to be presented must be carefully specified.

Systems and Operations

As a product is being developed, someone must design the forms and write the procedures telling the branch staff how to set up and service the product. But operations officers are primarily concerned with the smooth, accurate, timely accomplishment of the day's work. For them, customer satisfaction is often secondary to the need to have proper documentation and checks and balances to avoid error, fraud, or other operational problems. Many officers would rather cause the customer some amount of inconvenience than to risk being found at fault by auditors or examiners. It is useful for marketers to have some experience on the front lines of the banking business in order to anticipate and minimize potential clashes in these areas.

Human Resources and Personnel

This department is responsible for recruiting and training employees, establishing salaries and benefits, and monitoring the performance appraisal system. In a truly marketing-oriented bank, the customer orientation is written into each customer-contact person's job description, and performance appraisals and salary increases reflect how well the individual has performed. A customer service representative's job description should indicate responsibility for instructing the customer about the bank's array of services. The job of the bank marketer is to provide the customer service representative with the tools (such as brochures) and training in sales and product information needed to enable the individual to do the job.

Accounting and Finance

To the bank's financial people, marketers are often seen as extravagant spenders who are not "bottom-line" oriented. The marketing concept seeks customer satisfaction at a profitable volume, so marketers must be profit oriented in order to do the job well. The more bank marketers do their homework (that is, plan, set measurable objectives, and report on their progress), the more credibility they will have with the accounting people.

It is essential that bank marketers understand how the bank makes money and know how to interpret the bank's income records and statements of condition. The marketing head should sit in on meetings of the asset-liability management committee so that he or she always fully understands the bank's present and anticipated objectives for deposit acquisition and loan volume and its current investment policy.

Bank Investments

As mentioned previously, the marketing manager must be aware of, and sensitive to, the bank's long- and short-term goals for its asset and liability structure as well as its cost of funds and rate of return on investments. Deposits that are brought into the bank through marketing efforts must be put to use on the asset side of the balance sheet and, similarly, new loans must be funded from the liability side. Therefore, marketing decisions that affect rate setting cannot be made in a vacuum. Examples include offering gifts or premium rates to consumers in order to attract new deposits, or lowering interest rates for a loan promotion. Rate information obtained from the manager of bank investments should be used to demonstrate that the difference between the cost of funds and the use of those funds is sufficient to generate a reasonable margin of profit for the bank, thus satisfying the second objective of the marketing concept.

Legal Services

The number of regulations affecting banks today is staggering and growing steadily. Banks are regulated by the Federal Deposit Insurance Corporation (FDIC), the Federal Reserve Board, the Comptroller of the Currency, state banking departments, and, if publicly held, the Securities and Exchange Commission. Many laws and regulations, such as the Equal Credit Opportunity Act, influence the delivery of bank services. Other regulations govern advertising. For example, the FDIC stipulates that the savings interest rate and yield must appear in the same size type in an advertisement. Bank marketers must be constantly informed about these regulations so that services and ads will be in compliance. In larger financial institutions, it is not unusual for an attorney to be involved in the product development process and to then review all advertising copy for the new service.

The marketing department, through its marketing research function, may also become involved in the preparation of applications for new branches, mergers, and acquisitions of banks. Since these applications are submitted to banking regulators, the legal department may either coordinate the preparation of these documents or at least review them for completeness.

Auditing

Marketing is less involved with the internal auditing department than with other bank departments. However, due to the substantial volume of billing for expenditures on advertising media, the marketing department may be audited periodically to assure that proper accounting and recordkeeping procedures are being followed. During the development of new products or services, auditing is involved in the review of plans to be sure that adequate controls are in place and that security is not violated in any way.

Auditors from regulatory agencies, such as the Federal Reserve, are paying more and more attention to bank compliance with consumer protection regulations, so they may ask to see a bank's marketing plan and samples of its advertising. It is important that the advertising manager maintain accurate records of what advertising has been produced, including when and how services were publicized (by keeping samples of newspaper ads and brochures, for instance).

Line Divisions

The marketing department provides a service for the corporate, trust, international, and other divisions of the bank. These are marketing's "clients," so to speak. The heads of these divisions must be involved in the marketing planning process because they will be responsible for implementing the plan. It is imperative that there is open and frequent communication between marketing and the line divisions of the bank.

Branches

The branches are the bank's principal retail sales and distribution outlets. There must be a constant flow of information moving in both directions between the branches and the functional areas within marketing. The marketing department gathers a great deal of information on the competition and on customer attitudes that can be useful to the branch staff in their dealings with customers. Similarly, branches have access to first-hand observation of customer reactions and behavior that they should pass on to the marketing department. The advertising department regularly sends point-of-sale advertising such as brochures, posters, and counter cards to the branches and relies on them to display them properly. The branches use the services of the marketing department to help them function in their local communities by providing advertising to run in local program books and community newspapers, or by planning local promotions, celebrations, or customer entertainment events.

Retail marketing is highly dependent upon the cooperation of the branch staff to support promotional campaigns, and there must be a very good working relationship between the various individuals who are instrumental in managing the branches and among the various functional managers in marketing.

Chief Executive Officer

The marketing head works with and requires the cooperation of all the departments in the bank but has no authority over them. For this reason, it is important that the president or chief executive officer be marketing oriented, and that this orientation be reflected in his or her communication with other members of the management team. Without support from the top, the organization cannot be marketing oriented in practice, and the implementation of even the best-planned marketing program will falter.

IMPLEMENTATION

Implementation is the process that turns a marketing plan into specific tasks to be performed and ensures that they ultimately accomplish the plan's objectives. As shall be seen in the next section, there are a number of factors that may impede achievement of the plan's objectives that are not the result of poor implementation. However, if the implementation process has been well executed, any failure to achieve objectives will be traced to a change in the bank's uncontrollable macro- or microenvironment, or to some problem in objective setting, target market selection, or marketing mix strategy—not to a problem in implementation. On the other hand, if the implementation process is not well thought-out and managed, the plan will not succeed.

Effective implementation is dependent upon many factors, one of which being the way the bank is organized to perform the marketing function and the way marketing fits into the overall organizational structure. Some other important factors are:

- *On-time and accurate performance by marketing staff, agencies, and vendors.* The product management, advertising and sales promotion staff, the bank's advertising agency, and any other vendors (such as check printers, premium vendors, printers) must deliver their services according to the specifications in the plan.

- *Clear delineation of responsibility for various elements of the implementation process.* An implementation task list showing each task that must be accomplished and naming the individual responsible is a useful, if not essential, implementation tool.

- *Communication of the plan's objectives, strategies, and tactics throughout the bank.* It is important that all areas of the bank, even those that are not directly involved, be aware of the bank's marketing efforts. Often a corporate banking customer will mention seeing a bank ad for a retail product to the calling officer. That officer is in an awkward position if he or she is not familiar with the ad. It can be very embarrassing to the bank staff if they feel that the customer knows something about the bank that they do not. Of course, any area of the bank that deals with customers who are responding to the marketing program (either in person or by phone) must be given the necessary training to deal effectively with those customers in order to accomplish the bank's sales goals.

- *Cooperation of all areas affected by implementation.* Cooperation is a function of communication and involvement. The establishment of an implementation task force consisting of representatives in every area that will be involved in the implementation will help to ensure a smooth implementation process. The individual who chairs the task force (the product manager or the marketing manager) must effectively steer the group toward the desired end.

- *Monitoring of results.* It is important to have a system in place for monitoring the implementation process and its progress toward achievement of the plan's goals. However, evaluation is one of the three elements in the marketing management process and deserves special attention.

EVALUATION

As mentioned earlier, since conditions change and things rarely go as expected, the marketing plan needs to be adjusted from time to time. The key planning element that allows this adjustment to occur is performance monitoring and evaluation. If a bank has an adequate system for monitoring results, when it falls short of its objectives and goals, it will immediately be aware of the situation and will be able to analyze causes, take corrective action, and carry on with a revised plan. Conversely, if the bank does not have an adequate system for monitoring results, and objectives are not being met, the underlying problems will not be detected, and the plan will fail to accomplish its objectives.

Such a failure usually means that the bank will not attempt a planning effort again. Management will recall that the planning effort did not work the first time, so they will be disinclined to make the effort again. Furthermore, the staff's morale will have been damaged—those individuals who met their objectives will have received no reward, and those who failed to meet their objectives will not understand the reasons for their lack of success. The result is that there will be little motivation to cooperate again. The only way to keep the plan relevant and on course is to continually monitor its execution in order to be aware of variations and to take remedial action. In other words, the plan must be controlled.

Monitoring the Plan

It is unfortunate that the word *control* has such negative connotations. The word is commonly used in the sense of exercising authority over someone or something. However, an alternative meaning in Webster's New World Dictionary, and the way it is used here, is "to regulate," or "adjust to a standard." The bank must use controls as a monitoring device to ensure the attainment of its objectives and/or to discover why objectives are not being reached so that corrective action can be taken.[5]

There are a number of reasons why a plan derails. It may be that the environment in which the bank is operating changes. Recall from chapter 2 that the market is an ever-changing entity, affected by the competitive environment and by the external environment of social, economic, technological, and political/legal factors. Or, the plan's failure to proceed as scheduled might be due to some situation within the bank. For example, there might be a lack of cooperation at the operating level, or certain departments may not have the resources they need to get the job done. In any event, these deviations should not be seen negatively or interpreted as a weakness in the plan. Problems should be viewed as opportunities for learning, growth, and improvement.

Careful analysis of the reasons for a failure to reach goals will generally indicate that corrective action needs to be taken or that changes need to be made to one or more of the four key planning elements: the situation analysis, the objectives and goals, the target market selection, or the strategy and tactics.

Changes in the Situation Analysis

The plan, based on a list of strengths, weaknesses, problems, and opportunities, was derived from a study of the bank's internal and external environments. If any of the major elements in the situation analysis changes, it will likely affect the execution of the entire plan. For instance, if the plan assumed that the competitive situation would remain unaltered during the planning period, but a new competitor unexpectedly enters the market, original deposit or loan projections may no longer be attainable. Likewise, the existing competition might introduce a new service that threatens to take away some of the bank's customers. The bank must respond to this new situation.

Similarly, the economic environment can change. If the plan assumed constant interest rates but, in fact, interest rates change dramatically, the bank's goals might not be attainable. Or, there might be a layoff in the area's major industry that would affect many customers and make it difficult for the bank to achieve its goals.

Another unanticipated change might occur in the social or political-legal environment, such as the mandatory development of a low-cost basic checking account. This would affect the bank's product, pricing, and promotion strategies.

In summary, any environmental situation that has the ability to affect the attainment of the plan should be part of the monitoring and control process. In this way, changes can be detected before they have an opportunity to seriously hamper the plan, and objectives and/or strategy and tactics can be adjusted accordingly.

Problems with Objectives and Goals

Objectives and goals may need to be changed either to reflect changes in the situation analysis or to bring unrealistic objectives and goals more into line with reality. If objectives are being attained ahead of schedule, the bank might want to adjust them upward for subsequent periods. If, on the other hand, objectives are not being reached, the bank should make every effort to understand the cause. There are several possible causes for the failure to reach objectives and goals. Some of the more common ones are as follows:

- *The initial assumptions were incorrect.* The bank should review the situation analysis and make adjustments as required. The bank's staff can help by providing input to help management understand what factors have changed, since the staff is generally closer to the customer and the problem.

- *The resources committed were inadequate.* If it turns out that the task cannot be accomplished with the existing resources (people and money), then the bank must decide whether to lower the objectives or increase the resource commitment.

- *The tactics were not specific.* If management failed to assign specific tasks geared to the attainment of the goals, objectives will not be met. The solution is to assign tasks, establish a timetable for their accomplishment, and evaluate employees on the basis of their performance of those tasks.

- *The objectives and goals were unrealistic.* This is a cause that is too easy to retreat to. Before deciding that the bank's objectives were unrealistic, there should be a thorough study of the strategy and tactics to determine whether they are ineffective. It may be that the bank simply lacks internal marketing expertise. This shortcoming can be supplemented by adding marketing talent to the staff or by using outside professional expertise. An advertising agency or bank marketing consultant can be very useful in helping to evaluate the effectiveness of existing strategies and to suggest alternative ones.

If it is clear, however, that the objectives and goals were unrealistic, then the bank must adjust them. The revised objectives and goals and the reasons for their revision should be communicated to all employees. The lesson learned from the experience will be useful input to the next planning experience.

Problems in Target Market Selection

The failure to achieve objectives might be due to a failure to follow the guidelines set forth in chapter 8 for target market selection. The bank might have failed to select a target market and may have followed an undifferentiated strategy, without adequately differentiating itself from the competition. As a result, its offer might hold no special appeal, causing response to be weak. Or, the bank might have aimed its strategy at a segment that it did not fully understand. For example, a bank might learn that the 20 percent of its savings customers who account for 80 percent of its balances are primarily people over 60, and it might develop a promotion to attract similar customers from other banks. Its research should have shown that this segment is also the least likely to switch banks.

On the other hand, the bank might have selected a target that is not consistent with its image or positioning. Take, for example, the small bank that advertised itself as the region's "leader" in business banking, or the large commercial bank that advertised itself as "the saver's bank" when that position was locked up by the giant local savings bank. The bank might have gone after a market that was not consistent with its resources, as when a small, newly established bank attempts to attract the mass market in a large city. Or, the bank might have targeted a market that leads to unprofitable volume, as when a bank's consumer loan strategy attracts a market that results in considerably increased application volume but doubles the turn-down ratio.

Finally, the bank might have targeted a market that was already saturated with competitors, as when the bank is the last one into a market with a product and promotes it as if it were something new. Many target market selection problems can be avoided by careful use of marketing research.

Problems with Strategies and Tactics

When the environmental situation is unchanged, and the objectives appear to be correct, and the correct target market appears to have been selected, the bank must study its marketing strategies and tactics as the possible source of the failure to attain objectives. The problem might lie in the product strategy, pricing strategy, promotional strategy, or the distribution strategy. Problems in these areas are generally not difficult to detect. If a product is not generating customer interest, or if the price is out of line with market conditions, this will be immediately apparent. If customers are having difficulty using the service, or if the target market is not being adequately reached by the bank, the bank will know it through direct feedback from the customers or the staff.

Weaknesses in promotion strategy, including personal selling, are more difficult to evaluate and are more likely to require primary research. The customer contact staff may be willing to sell the bank's services, but they may need training in how to sell. In such a case, a shopper study can be undertaken to determine what techniques are lacking. Or, perhaps the advertising program was developed without any attempt to measure its communication effect. Having failed to set measurable goals, management will have only subjective opinions to call on to determine whether the problem lies in the advertising. Just as advertising is highly vulnerable when management is looking for ways to trim the budget, so is it vulnerable when looking for a place to lay the blame for failure to reach goals—especially sales goals. The only way to avoid this situation is to set specific, measurable goals, whether in advertising or in other areas of marketing.

THE REPORTING PROCESS

During the development of the plan, the bank should (1) design whatever forms are required to develop internal secondary data on the attainment of objectives; (2) arrange a timetable for carrying out primary research to get feedback from the marketplace; and (3) identify the external secondary data needed to monitor changes in the economic, competitive, technological, and political-legal environments. Some examples of the kind of reports a bank might generate are:

- a semiannual telephone survey to determine banking habits and behavior, and share of new business being obtained by each bank in the market;

- a quarterly follow-up study to monitor changes in attitude toward the bank among the target market(s);

- an annual analysis of published data on market share;

- quarterly reports from department heads on progress toward attainment of their objectives;

- weekly reports of cross-selling activity by the customer service staff; and

- monthly reports to senior management on new account activity compared with prior month and prior year.

From this list, it should be clear that the frequency and distribution of reports will vary.

Frequency

While there is no strict formula for determining how often control reports should be prepared, there is a rule of thumb: the more tactical the object of control, the more frequent the need for reporting activity; the more strategic the object of control, the less frequent the need for reports.[6] The logic for this is simply that operating personnel responsible for the day-to-day tactical activities of marketing plans require more frequent checks of status.

For example, the branch manager might collect daily reports on cross-selling. In addition to providing information on a daily operating basis, this also helps stimulate the branch staff to achieve its goals. But the manager will compile less frequent statements of status with regard to operating objectives and strategies based on the daily cross-sell and other reports. He or she might send a weekly report, including data on cross-sell activity, to the branch administrator, who reports monthly on cross-sell activity of all branches as part of a larger report to the chief executive.

Distribution

Control reports flow upward through the chain of command. However, there are a number of other individuals who should see copies as well. The reports should also be distributed downward to the staff members involved in the activity that is the subject of the report. In this way, they can see how their activities fit into the larger picture and how the department is progressing toward achievement of specific goals. Additionally, the employees may be able to explain why performance was better or worse than expected. Sharing reports in this way ensures that the staff understands the importance of the marketing plan and identifies with it.

Finally, reports should be distributed horizontally so that managers can see how the bank as a whole is progressing toward its objectives. Summary reports can be substituted for the original detailed versions. The marketing manager should be on the distribution list for all reports in order to monitor the progress of the strategy and to identify areas needing corrective action.

Content

The control report should be structured to maximize communication. In other words, it should be clear, concise, and direct. It should begin with a statement of the objective involved, the time period, the specific goal, the results, and a statement explaining circumstances that caused better or worse results than anticipated.

Exhibit 14-5 shows a hypothetical marketing plan quarterly review prepared by Marlton National Bank's marketing director to report to management on progress toward the volume and outstanding goals for the introduction of the new home equity credit line. (For more information on Marlton National Bank's planning activities, see *Case B.*)

SOME COMMON PROBLEMS ENCOUNTERED IN THE PLANNING PROCESS

The processes of performance monitoring and evaluation are appropriate only after the bank has successfully completed the planning process and is into the implementation stage. However, there are any number of things that can go wrong either before or during the planning process. Some of the more common problems include the following:

- *Cooperation is lacking during the initial development of the plan.* This problem may be attributable to a lack of understanding of the importance of planning or to a fear of the performance evaluation that might result from the implementation of the plan. This can be overcome (1) if top management communicates to all employees its support of the planning process, and (2) by educating management personnel in how to plan. An antidote to the fear of measurement is to emphasize that the evaluation process will be factual and objective and not subject to whim or personal feelings; that good performance will be rewarded; and that the process affords an opportunity for improving one's job performance.

- *Staff is willing but unable to get started with planning.* The probable causes here are a lack of specific direction or a confusion about precisely what is to be done. This can be overcome by assigning specific tasks to individuals, and through internal education.

- *Planning process was started but never completed.* The most probable cause is lack of senior management commitment. Other causes

Exhibit 14-5 **Marlton National Bank Home Equity Credit Line Product Introduction**

Quarterly Review

Marketing Objective
Increase the ratio of interest-sensitive assets in our loan portfolio.

Goals	Three-Month Progress
600 accounts in 12 months	300 accounts
450 accounts (75% of total)	240 active accounts (80% of total)
Average outstanding per account $20,000	Average outstanding $22,000
Total outstandings in 12 months: $9 million ($6 million average for year)	Outstanding after 3 months: $5.3 million

Comments
At 3 months, we have attained 50 percent of our first-year goal for number of new accounts.

We are ahead of projection for:

- percent of accounts with line in use; and
- average dollar amount outstanding.

With outstandings at $5.3 million, we will clearly exceed our target for average outstandings for the year of $6 million.

Our advertising for this new product broke at a time when competitive banks were not promoting heavily, giving us a higher than normal share of voice in the media.

Our direct mail response rate appears to be running ahead of projection. Final results will be available next month.

---

might be a lack of understanding of what is required of the managers. This, too, requires education. Another cause might be that the plan has tried to accomplish too much. It is better to focus on one or two objectives and to accomplish them than to have far-ranging plans with no results.

- *Planning process was completed too late to be useful*. One must plan for planning. In other words, if the annual budget must be submitted in October, the planning coordinator must work back from that date and develop a timetable showing when each stage must be completed. For some banks, this means that the planning must begin in April. Others start in June, while some banks (those presumably preferring to operate under pressure!) wait until August.

- *Plan was developed but was then shelved.* This cannot happen if responsibility for implementing the plan and achieving the goals is assigned to specific individuals and if a control system is put into place.

- *Project stalls after situation analysis.* This may happen when the staff is unable to develop specific objectives because the data in the situation analysis are irrelevant, incomplete, or too general. On the other hand, the data might be adequate, but the staff may not know how to interpret them. In the former case, management must identify precisely what data are needed and arrange to collect additional data. In the latter case, marketing expertise will have to be sought either internally or externally.

- *Employee morale slumps after setting objectives and goals.* The three primary reasons for this reaction are that (1) the staff did not participate in the establishment of the objectives and goals, so they feel it has been imposed on them arbitrarily; (2) the objectives and goals are unrealistic, and the staff recognizes this and loses its motivation; or (3) the resources allocated are not sufficient to do the job. All these problems can be resolved by improved communication and by making some changes in either the objectives or the resources.

- *Bank failed to develop strategies and tactics for achieving objectives and goals.* One of the leading causes is likely to be a lack of creativity or marketing expertise on the part of those assigned the task of formulating strategy and tactics. This problem can be remedied by a program to update marketing talent within the bank or by contracting for such talent on a temporary basis.

- *Enthusiasm is lacking for further planning.* The probable causes here are twofold: (1) management did not take the time to recognize the contributions of the staff to the planning effort and to the results—if the chief executive officer does not give this recognition to the managers, they will be less inclined to make the effort again; and (2) the results of the planning effort were disappointing. If the bank took all the steps outlined in this text and yet results were disappointing, it may be that the planning effort was not adequate to the task. Ideally, the bank's management should gain further education in planning and/or call on outside expertise to help them through the process as a learning experience.

SUMMARY

The marketing management process consists of planning, implementing those plans, and evaluating the results. Implementation of the marketing plan is a critical element in that process, and it is a step that must be well thought-out and executed if a bank is to have any chance of realizing its plan objectives. One of the factors that plays a role in plan implementation is the way in which the bank is organized to perform the marketing function and the way that marketing fits into the overall organization of the bank. Effective implementation rests on a number of other factors such as on-time and accurate performance by marketing staff, agencies, and vendors; clear delineation of responsibilities in a formal task list; communication and cooperation throughout the bank; and the monitoring of results.

Marketing planning must be an ongoing process in order to be effective. The ingredient that assures that it will be continual is the element of performance monitoring and evaluation—the reason being that it is very rare that everything will proceed precisely as planned. Unless the plan can adapt to change, it will become meaningless.

By instituting a series of procedures to continually monitor the situation in which the bank is operating and its progress toward the realization of objectives and goals, the bank is in a position to revise and adapt the plan in order to adjust to changing external and internal factors.

If objectives and goals are not being met, the problem may lie in the situation analysis, in the strategies and tactics, in the target market selection, or in the objectives and goals themselves. The situation analysis may need to be revised to reflect changes in the internal bank environment or the external market environment. The strategies and tactics may not produce the desired effect due to inherent weaknesses or problems in the way they are being implemented. Or, the target market may not have been properly selected. The objectives and goals themselves might be unrealistic for any number of reasons. Whatever the problem area, the bank must have timely feedback to recognize the problem and take remedial action.

Control reports are an essential part of the monitoring process. Their frequency will depend upon the nature of what is being measured. Their distribution should be in three directions: (1) upward to senior management; (2) horizontal, so that all managers know how the bank is progressing toward its goals; and (3) downward within a department so that the staff can see how they and the bank are doing. The reports should be clear and concise. They should contain specific information about what is to be accomplished, by whom, and within what time frame, along with results and relevant comments to help management understand why goals have been reached, exceeded, or not met.

While there are many problems that might arise in the execution of a plan, there are also a number of problems common to the planning process itself. They generally revolve around several primary causes: lack of top management support; failure to set specific, realistic, measurable goals; failure to involve staff in the objective-setting process; failure to assign responsibility to specific individuals; failure to acknowledge and recognize performance; lack of marketing expertise; and failure to communicate results to staff members.

POINTS FOR REVIEW

1. How is your bank's marketing function organized?
2. Where does marketing fit into your bank's overall organization?
3. What are the responsibilities of a product manager?

4. What are some of the factors that can affect the implementation of a bank's marketing plan?

5. What is the meaning of the word *control* within the context of the marketing management process?

6. How might each of the following events affect a bank's plan? What part of the plan would require adjustment?

    • acquisition of the leading competitor by a large out-of-state bank

    • rapid increase in the prime rate

    • failure to meet goals for number of new accounts opened

7. What factors should dictate how often control reports are generated?

8. What are some reasons why reports should be circulated horizontally and vertically?

9. What are the elements that should be contained in a control report?

15 PUBLIC RELATIONS AND COMMUNICATIONS

While marketing is a relatively recent development in banking, the public relations function has been on the banking scene for several decades. A concrete example may be found in the history of the naming of the Bank Marketing Association, a professional association serving the bank marketing field. From the date of its founding until 1965, it was called the Financial Public Relations Association. In 1965, the term *marketing* was added to the name, and the organization's scope was narrowed from the financial industry in general to banking in particular. Its name was the Bank Public Relations and Marketing Association. Five years later, that title was shortened to its present designation, not to diminish the importance of public relations, but to reflect the emergence of marketing as a major force in banking. Since the organization also concerns itself with public relations, its name seems to communicate the belief that public relations is or should be part of marketing. This is a subject that is often debated and which will be addressed later in this chapter. The marketing and public relations functions should and must work very closely, but they perform very different functions.

The early awareness of public relations in banking, especially its community relations role, is understandable since banks have traditionally been community institutions, almost totally dependent on the communities they serve. Therefore, bankers have long recognized the wisdom of being good corporate citizens, that is, doing things for the welfare and growth of their communities.

However, the bank public relations function has matured over the years.[1] Community relations is its oldest function. As bankers felt the need to become more involved with the local and federal lawmakers who were regulating their business, government affairs was added to the list of public relations responsibilities. In the 1960s and 1970s, as consumer activists challenged the financial establishment, consumer relations became a priority for public relations.[2] Now the list of publics addressed by public relations has grown to include directors, shareholders, investment analysts, nonprofit organizations seeking contributions, customers, employees, and, of course, the news media. (See Exhibit 15-1.) With all these added responsibilities, a more appropriate title for the function, and one used by many financial institutions, is "corporate communications."

In chapter 13, promotion was pinpointed as being a form of communication—specifically, it communicates the benefits of the bank's need-satisfying product offerings. Speaking very generally, marketing communications are product related, or are oriented toward customer satisfaction at a profitable volume. The communications objective of the public relations department is oriented toward an enhanced image or improved relationship with the bank's public.

There is some overlap between the public relations and marketing functions, as Exhibit 15-2 illustrates. One of the promotional tools is publicity, and this is generally provided by the bank's communications department. Similarly, some public relations campaigns require the development and placing of image, advocacy, or institutional advertising, and this service is provided by the advertising area of the marketing department. However, as the exhibit illustrates, these joint responsibilities account for only a small part of the bank's public relations and communications task. For this reason, public relations is not treated as part of the marketing management process in this text, but rather as a very important field on its own, separate from, but related to, marketing.

To understand how public relations and communications is related to marketing, refer back to the definition of the marketing concept given in chapter 1: The objective of marketing is customer satisfaction, at a profitable volume, carried out in an orderly and efficient framework, and *in a socially responsible manner*. The department most concerned with enhancing the institution's corporate citizenship and taking action to demonstrate its social responsibility is the communications department. In an era of consumerism, environmentalism, conservation, inflation, and women's rights, the need for banks to be socially responsible is more acute than ever, and the internal watchdog is the public relations function. For these reasons, no marketing discussion would be complete without addressing this important function.

In this chapter, there will be a discussion of what public relations is and does. Then, its activities from the broader perspective of community involvement and social responsibility will be looked at.

WHAT PUBLIC RELATIONS IS

Public relations may be defined as: "the collective effort of any group to win the esteem of people; by its conduct to deserve that esteem; and by its communications to maintain it."[3]

This definition emphasizes two activities: communication and conduct. Public relations has been a communications-intensive activity with special stress on the securing of favorable publicity for the bank. The significance of this kind of activity derives from the reality that banks operate in a climate of opinion. To the extent that this climate is unfavorable, the bank may find plans thwarted, achievements stunted, costs distorted, operations hampered, and customers taking their business elsewhere. Public relations enters the picture due to the assumption that a favorable climate of opinion must not be left to chance.[4]

Today, there is increased emphasis on putting people first and things second—on organizations as servants of people rather than people as servants of organizations. The essence of this movement is a concern for the individual and the opportunity for the individual to experience life

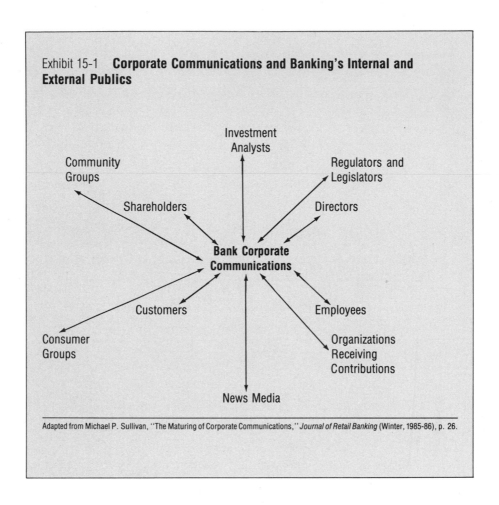

Exhibit 15-1 **Corporate Communications and Banking's Internal and External Publics**

Investment Analysts

Community Groups

Regulators and Legislators

Shareholders

Directors

Bank Corporate Communications

Customers

Employees

Consumer Groups

Organizations Receiving Contributions

News Media

Adapted from Michael P. Sullivan, "The Maturing of Corporate Communications," *Journal of Retail Banking* (Winter, 1985-86), p. 26.

to the fullest. In such an environment, it behooves banks to put less emphasis on isolated special events and more emphasis on continuing programs, community action, and leadership.

What Public Relations is Not

By now it should be clear that public relations has an identity of its own, but since there is often much misunderstanding about what public relations is, it is helpful to look specifically at what it is not.

Public Relations is not Advertising

Although advertising may well be part of a given public relations program, or public relations may be used to support an advertising campaign, advertising and public relations are not the same thing. By advertising, the bank buys space or time in the media and then uses it to convey messages.

Through publicity, though, coverage is never assured, and neither is content. The public relations officer uses press releases, press conferences, and other tools in the attempt to elicit a certain type of coverage but, in the final analysis, it is the news media that determines what is covered, how much emphasis it is given, and what the content of the communication will be.

Due to banking's role as a keystone of any community, the news media usually provide a fair amount of attention to banking news. The challenge to the public relations officer is to develop a relationship with news media personnel that permits the institution to receive positive coverage. In summary, advertising is directly paid for by the bank and, therefore, controlled by it; public relations is influenced by the bank, but controlled by the news media.

Public Relations is not Oriented to Specific Products

Public relations is generally concerned with the bank as a whole, not with regulating the demand for specific products of the bank. Public relations activity attempts to create a high level of esteem for the bank as an institution. It transcends the encouragement of demand for loans, ATMs, or savings accounts, for example.

This does not mean, however, that demand for the bank's services will not be affected because of public relations activities. A public relations effort may result in increased business for the bank, but its primary goal is not the sale of specific products.

The publicity for a new product being offered by the bank may be handled by the public relations staff, but that particular activity is part of the promotional strategy for the new product and is not, strictly speaking, public relations. It is product publicity. Again, public relations has to do with the climate of opinion surrounding the bank, not with the promotion of specific products.

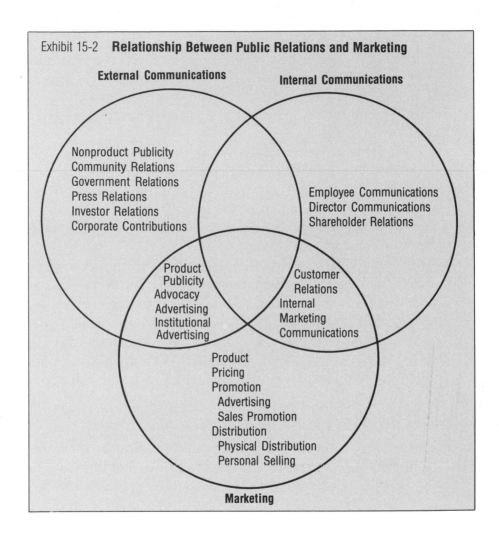

Exhibit 15-2 **Relationship Between Public Relations and Marketing**

External Communications

Internal Communications

Nonproduct Publicity
Community Relations
Government Relations
Press Relations
Investor Relations
Corporate Contributions

Employee Communications
Director Communications
Shareholder Relations

Product
Publicity
Advocacy
Advertising
Institutional
Advertising

Customer
Relations
Internal
Marketing
Communications

Product
Pricing
Promotion
   Advertising
   Sales Promotion
Distribution
   Physical Distribution
Personal Selling

Marketing

Public Relations, as a Whole, is not Part of the Marketing Mix

The marketing mix is the blending of product, distribution, promotion, and pricing strategies directed at a distinct target market. It does not pertain to the development and maintenance of a favorable climate of public opinion for the institution as a whole. Although proper execution of the marketing mix may add to a favorable climate of opinion, and poor execution may detract from it, the primary orientation of the marketing mix is to regulate market demand for a certain product or service.

Although marketing strategy and public relations strategy should be carefully coordinated in the bank, and although there are similarities in how they are developed (that is, through the planning process), public relations strategy, while it may support marketing strategy, is not part of the marketing mix and is not the same thing as marketing strategy.

THE POSITION OF PUBLIC RELATIONS IN THE ORGANIZATION

In many banks, the function of public relations reports to the director of marketing or of marketing and public relations; in other banks, to the chief executive officer (CEO). Exhibit 15-2 implies that public relations has a different scope from marketing, so theoretically, it should not report to the marketing director. Furthermore, marketing people and public relations people generally come from very different backgrounds. The former are more likely to have a business school background and a profit orientation, while the latter tend to be journalists with media skills and writing ability,[5] and, it is hoped, a concern for broad social and political issues. In reality, however, the public relations function often does report to, and is part of, the marketing department. In fact, in a community bank, all marketing and public relations tasks may be handled by one person.

A persuasive argument can be made, however, for having the public relations officer report to the chief executive for two major reasons. First, in order to do the job—especially the media relations part of it—the public relations director must be able to gain direct and immediate access to the chief executive. When the press is seeking the bank's response to a major turn of events or to verify a rumor heard in the market, the public relations person must be able to get to the top fast. Conversely, if the public relations director meets regularly with the chief executive and keeps informed on internal matters, he or she will be in a better position to respond intelligently to the questions from the press. If the public relations person is a professional and the bank is serious in its objective of being socially responsible, he or she should be involved in the decision process and have a chance to affect it.

Second, the chief executive officer sets the tone, image, or corporate personality that the public relations department is charged with projecting. The presence of a third party could muddy the waters and slow down the communications process. For example, when a CEO assigns a broadly defined task to a public relations person—such as "I want our bank to become known as the one that is really on the consumer's side"—the person given the task should have direct access to the CEO in order to seek approval for proposed strategies and to hear firsthand what the CEO likes or does not like about them.

THE ROLE OF PUBLIC RELATIONS

The activities conducted by the public relations department can most easily be described as communicating with the bank's publics.

The Bank's Publics

The bank's publics fall into two groups: internal and external. Publics are considered to be internal if the bank has some control over the reception of its communications to them (that is, the bank can control who gets the message, what the message will be, and when it is to be received). The bank does not have control over the reception of communications to external publics. It sends out its message but does not have precise control over who will receive it, when it will be received, or even, in many cases, what the final content of the message might be.

The bank's **internal publics** are its employees, directors, customers, and shareholders. The bank's **external publics** are the investment community, the community served by the bank, consumer groups, organizations receiving corporate contributions, and government officials and agencies. The public relations tasks revolve around communicating with these publics. Since some or all of them at one time or another may be reached through the news media, the press is treated here as another public—one with which the public relations person must establish and maintain a good relationship. (See Exhibit 15-1.)

Public Relations Tasks

The primary tasks of the public relations or communications department are media relations and publicity, investor relations (both internal among shareholders and external among the investment community), government relations, employee relations, customer relations, and community relations.

Media Relations

The news media (newspapers, magazines, radio, and public and commercial television) are the most important vehicles for the bank's communication efforts. Through the media, the bank can speak to each of its publics; therefore, one of the primary duties of the public relations practitioner is **media relations**.[6] The members of the news media determine whether a particular bank story is newsworthy or not. Being human, they are likely to have a more favorable attitude toward a story offered by someone they know, like, and trust. If the reporter's experience with a bank leads him or her to believe that the bank treats the media as adversaries, either telling them as little as possible or "stonewalling" on sensitive issues, the bank will be more vulnerable to adverse publicity. The investigative reporter will then seek the information from unofficial and less reliable sources within the bank.

There are other reasons for cultivating positive media relations. Reporters need sources of background information, and they appreciate being able to consult with a bank public relations officer or other spokesperson[7] as a source of such information. Furthermore, sometimes the news from the bank or from the banking industry is unfavorable (for example, a robbery, a defalcation, a bank failure). In such a situation, a reporter is likely to listen more favorably to

Exhibit 15-3 Sample Publicity Policy

Bank Publicity Policy

In order that all statements made to television, radio, magazine, or newspaper reporters are presented in the most accurate and authoritative manner possible, it is necessary that all inquiries be coordinated through the public relations office.

When any officer or other employee is contacted by the news media for a statement regarding bank policies or procedures, the following procedures should be followed:

- No immediate statement should be given. Rather, explain that you may not be the appropriate individual to respond to that inquiry and that the public relations office must make the determination.
- State that you will have the appropriate officer return the call immediately.
- Obtain the reporter's name, company, phone number, and deadline.
- Call the public relations office and convey the nature of the question, the reporter's name, phone, etc.

The public relations office will refer this information either to the appropriate department or division head, or the bank's public relations counsel, for immediate oral or written response.

In the case of a robbery, fire, or other emergency, where numerous inquiries are received in a short period, public relations, working with the appropriate department head, will formulate a single written statement to be read or delivered to reporters.

Although the above procedures are necessary safeguards, they should not be used to delay unreasonably the transmission of information. When we tell a reporter or other inquirer that we will call back, it is important that the call-back be made by the responsible bank officer within a reasonable time.

The only allowable exception to the above procedure will be prearranged periodic information inquiries made to department heads.

The switchboard and after-hours guards are all provided with the public relations director's home phone number in the event of inquiries made during nonbanking hours.

Source: This is the policy of the First National Bank of Denver as it appeared in "PR As A Marketing Tool," by Arthur J.L. Lucey in *American Banker*, February 7, 1977, reprinted in *American Banker's Marketing Management*, Volume 1, August 1976–April 1977.

someone he or she knows and trusts and to get the full and accurate story behind the potentially damaging news.

The bank should have a written policy that every officer notify the public relations director when an important story is about to break. In addition, the policy should make it clear that the public relations director is to be the only point of contact between the news media and the bank. Of course, this responsibility can be delegated to someone within the bank when another person is in a better position to give detailed information—but even in these cases, the public relations director should be present or at least cognizant of what takes place in the interview. Exhibit 15-3 is an example of such a policy. The bank should communicate it regularly to every employee in the bank, and it should be part of the new employee orientation program.

Effective media relations is a prerequisite for a related public relations task—**publicity**. Publicity is information with news and human interest value designed to promote a product, service, idea, or impression through the media in an effort to advance the cause of the bank. The principal difference between advertising and publicity is that the latter is not paid for, and the bank does not have control over the communication as it finally appears or is heard. Even the best-written press release might be cut down, rearranged, have new matter added, important information eliminated, or otherwise be changed by the media. In short, publicity is, to some extent, a gamble. However, a professional public relations person will know how to minimize the risks associated with publicity.

The primary fact to remember is that the publicity story must contain an authentic news or feature angle. Many of the events that banks seek to publicize are lacking in this area, and it takes considerable talent to write press releases about them in such a way that they will be used by the news media.

- *The press conference.* When a bank has a major announcement to make, regional economic facts to present, or has an important personality to introduce, it is appropriate to schedule a press conference. The public relations person should make certain that the press conference does not conflict with the deadlines of the various media. The announcement should be prepared in advance by the public relations office and presented at the press conference by someone designated by the bank to answer questions from the reporters. A kit containing a press release and any available back-up information helps to assure the correct transmission of the basic facts of the story.

For Immediate Release   **Contact: Jane Mason 201-555-6013**

United City Bank To Sponsor Pottery Demonstrations

If you'd like to see how pottery is made, United City Bank has arranged for members of the New England Potter's Guild to demonstrate their craft at some of its branches on November 21 and 28.

According to William L. Lamson, chairman of United City, pottery-making demonstrations will be given from 9 a.m. until 2 p.m. on November 21 at the Main Bank branch, 15 West Blackwell Street, Dover; the Panther Valley Branch, Route 517, Allamuchy; and at the 144 Main Street branch, Hackettstown. On November 28 the demonstrations will be held at the Roxbury Plaza branch, Route 10, Ledgewood; the Flanders branch, Route 206 and Deerfield Place; and at the Jefferson branch, Route 15 and Bowling Green Parkway, Lake Hopatcong.

The demonstrations, notes Lamson, have been arranged to highlight the bank's one-of-a-kind handcrafted pottery offer, which began November 15. "As an inducement for new deposits," he says, "we're offering customers an opportunity to save on a selection of original pottery handcrafted by members of the New England Potter's Guild." The selection includes vases, pitchers, candleholders, and hurricane lamps.

Customers depositing $250 or more in a new or existing savings account or in a new checking account can obtain a piece of pottery free or at a discount, depending on the amount of the deposit and the piece chosen. "The bigger the deposit," Lamson points out, "the bigger the gift or discount."

A collection of pottery, together with complete details on the offer, is on display at all branches of United City Bank.

- *The press release.* A press release calls for a very different writing style than that which is used for other bank communications. The lead sentence is crucial for two reasons: (1) it must catch the editor's and then the reader's attention and cause him or her to want to read further; and (2) it must contain the highlights of the message so that no matter how much of the article is cut out, as many of the major elements of who, what, where, when, why, and how will remain.

The wording and style of a press release used by one bank to launch a premium promotion is shown in Exhibit 15-4. Most releases are submitted with suggested headlines to help spark the news editor's interest. In addition, since newspapers generally compose their own, the presence of a headline in the press release alerts the headline writer to the main point of the story.

Another way to help assure that the press release is picked up by the news media and developed into a story is to use preprinted stock on which to type the release. Often the bank's logo is used in the design. This not only makes the release attractive and professional looking, but it also serves as an identifying mark that editors will come to recognize.

News releases may also be prepared electronically and sent to television or radio stations. Using a news service to transmit news releases instantaneously to many news media outlets is becoming more widespread. News services such as PR Newswire or Business Wire help convey an institution's message quickly and accurately.

Investor Relations

Investor relations encompasses communications with the bank's shareholders and with those who have the ability to affect the activity in, and price of, the bank's stock. These include institutional investors, brokers, and security analysts who specialize in the study of bank stocks. The major investor relations effort for most banks is the production of the annual and quarterly earnings reports and the holding of the annual meeting of shareholders. The annual report is a major communications tool and can be used to sell the bank's services as well as the bank itself.

The communications officer may be called upon to plan meetings in which the objective is to update stock analysts on the bank's financial situation and give them an opportunity to ask questions of the bank's senior management that enables them to do a better job of projecting the future performance of the bank. This is a very sensitive undertaking because, while it is desirable to present the bank and its management and performance in a positive light, there may be serious ramifications if problems or weaknesses are concealed. (The Securities and Exchange Commission has strict rules governing financial disclosure.)

The annual meeting of a bank's shareholders is a brief event that requires a great deal of planning and preparation. In addition to writing the speeches to be given by the chairman and others who might address the group, the communications director must arrange the time and place of the meeting, as well as work with the senior management in preparing answers to questions that are likely to be asked from the floor. He or she must also be prepared to deal with the occasional gadfly—a meeting-attender who makes a point of asking irritating or potentially embarrassing questions.

Government Relations

The laws and regulations that govern the banking industry and affect its operating environment can, to some extent, be influenced by developing relationships with those who make and enforce those laws. The legislative and regulatory arena ranges from local traffic and zoning ordinances affecting the physical operation of the bank to federal regulation of credit and deposit services.

At the state level, bankers should make a point of knowing and communicating with their state senators and representatives. These individuals frequently know very little about the business of banking. Through no fault of their own, but due to curriculum gaps in the schools, many of them have no understanding of how a bank makes money or how market rates of interest are determined. Yet, they are in a position to vote on matters that can affect the limits within which banks can operate. So, it is the responsibility of the bankers to be sure they understand the implications of banking legislation, and this is best done on a one-to-one basis. One of the responsibilities of state banking associations is to represent the banks in dealing with state legislators and banking departments, but the efforts of individual bankers provide a necessary adjunct to this activity.

State and local governments can also be important customers for a bank. They are often not only a source of large deposit balances, but they are also users of bank services (such as payroll services). As such, they should be the object of a bank's calling and sales efforts.

To be effective at the national level, it is necessary for bankers to combine forces in a unified effort, and this is done through the American Bankers Association (ABA). It has a professional staff that represents banking in governmental activities. The ABA also has a number of specialized committees of bankers who serve as a liaison between the banking community and the association. Other national banking associations have a more limited role and scope in national lobbying efforts.

Employee Communications

One of the most important publics for a bank is its own staff. To adapt an old adage: "Management proposes; staff disposes." The attitude and performance of the people on the front lines and behind the scenes make the difference between a smoothly operated, productive, accurate, personable, friendly bank, and its opposite. Of course, no amount of communication can overcome the effects of poor management. But if supervisors and managers are at least trying to follow good management practices, and if management has credibility among the staff, an internal employee communications program is a necessary tool for building morale and team spirit.

Some examples of internal communications are (1) regularly published communications about company news and job openings within the bank, and (2) periodically published communications informing the staff about new programs. The first type of printed internal communication, called the house organ, generally has long-term objectives, such as communicating management's philosophy and goals and acquainting the staff with the various people and departments within the bank in order to help them understand the bigger picture beyond their individual jobs. In addition, the posting of job openings allows employees to be among the first to apply for vacant positions for which they are qualified.

The objective of the second type of communication about new products, services, or marketing programs is to enlist the staff's support and cooperation. It is very damaging to the teller's morale and to the bank's marketing efforts when a customer comes in brandishing an ad about a new service that the teller has not yet heard about. The larger the bank, the more difficult it is to spread the word of new programs quickly, but it is so important that a way must be found to do it. A number of banking organizations are now using videotapes produced in-house to communicate with employees.

Customer Relations

Communicating with the bank's customers takes place largely at the point of sale (that is, in the main office or branch) and through the mail. Personal contact is largely the province of the branch administration and marketing departments. Mailings are the province of the marketing department since marketing is generally responsible for developing letters to customers to tell them about a new service or change in pricing.

However, every letter to a customer from the bank provides an opportunity to create a favorable or an unfavorable impression. In many banks, letters that tell customers that a loan has been approved or disapproved, or that a payment is overdue, or that a problem has been rectified, are written in a tone that implies an authoritarian attitude rather than one that recognizes the importance of the customer. Due to the demands of other tasks, many public relations officers do not take the time to conduct an audit of the bank's written communications to customers, but this needs to be done periodically.

Many banks develop newsletters on matters of general and financial interest to send to customers on a regular basis. This type of communication might be handled by the marketing department, especially if it has a sales orientation, but it might also be considered a public relations function.

One of the most important points of customer communication has to do with complaints. All banks get them, and how they are handled makes the difference between keeping or losing customers. Someone within the bank, possibly in the public relations area, should see that every complaint is addressed in a helpful and unemotional tone. In some banks, the public relations function is a contact point for consumer grievances.

In short, the public relations officer should be involved in all nonadvertising communications from the bank to its customers to assure that they are customer oriented, comply with management's overall communication goals, and are grammatically correct.

Community Relations

The majority of banks in this country are community-based institutions. Communities are, to some degree, dependent upon the banks that serve them (for example, for financing local business and providing mortgages and loans to consumers). But banks are almost totally dependent upon the communities they serve. Very few banks can get along without a community. Communities can change for the worse and the inhabitants can move away. But unless they move within the trade area, banks can rarely follow their customers. Therefore, it is not just for altruistic reasons that banks must play the role of good corporate citizens, intent on working for the welfare and growth of their communities, and striving in every way to keep their communities dynamic. If the community suffers an economic setback, the bank should work hard to bring about a rehabilitation.

A bank can influence the growth and development of a community through the provision of services (loans and financial counseling to struggling businesses, for example) and by the activities of its staff people. (See Example 2 in *Case G*.) Bankers can take on leadership positions in governmental units or industrial development committees, educational institutions, agricultural organizations, and in political affairs. An excellent example of a bank program that addresses a social and economic need is provided in Example 3 in *Case G*.

Through **community relations** activities, banks help in supporting the arts and in sponsoring athletic, educational, health, and human services through financial and voluntary support. Public relations in banking has been known largely for activities of this kind. But public relations has the potential to be something more. While these efforts have often been effective in winning the esteem of the public, many banks are now engaging in more powerful programs that respond to changes in society and its values. This is the subject of the next section.

SOCIAL RESPONSIBILITY AND THE BANK'S PUBLIC RELATIONS FUNCTION

So far, this chapter has described some of the principal functions of the public relations/communications department in a bank. All its functions are oriented toward communicating with various publics in order to enhance the bank's image or improve its relationship with those publics. But there is a vast difference between having an active public relations department and being a public-oriented bank.

Banking today is operating in an era in which the quality of life rather than the quantity of goods is paramount, and people—not things—come first. In this social environment, there is increased insistence that society's organizations truly serve people, and there is intolerance of those organizations that try to use people. Consumerism, environmentalism, women's rights, and the changing priorities of our young people and minority citizens are just some of the movements that reflect this adjustment in social values.

The word *responsibility* is derived from the Latin *responsum*, an answer, and *respondere*, to respond. **Social responsibility** means (1) that the organization is accountable or answerable to society for its actions and their consequences, and (2) that the organization must respond to the demands being placed on it by changing social values.

Manufacturers must be especially sensitive to the environmental and health effects of their operations. Banks are not generally in a position to be criticized for generating pollutants or wasting resources, but their actions in pricing and lending policies are subject to public scrutiny. Being answerable, however, is a passive position. Banks must take an active role in responding to changing social values. The bank's communications department is the most logical place for overseeing the bank's social responsibility. After all, communicating requires listening and answering, not just talking, and social responsibility involves those same skills.

Some might feel that the humanistic approach to life is anti-business, but this is not necessarily so. The current philosophy appears to be antibusiness when it is directed at specific firms or industries that have been perceived, because of their actions or lack of action, as not being sufficiently people oriented. In fact, these times provide an opportunity for aggressive, creative, responsive banks to take the lead in finding ways of responsibly offering people what they need and to create economic and social profit at the same time. (See Example 3 in *Case G*.)

Unfortunately, because of the past failure of the banking industry to be people oriented, the banking regulators have stepped in, and the industry now has laws and regulations to require banks to be consumer and community oriented. Because some banks in lower income or deteriorating communities were making loans and mortgages to higher-income individuals from outside their trade area neighborhoods, the Community Reinvestment Act (CRA) was passed. Now banks must make their mortgage and lending records available for public scrutiny and demonstrate that they are indeed meeting the credit needs of low and moderate income persons in their trade areas. Those who do not comply sacrifice their freedom to operate and expand. It is not unusual for the regulators to require that applications for permission to establish branches or to merge banks be accompanied by CRA and home mortgage disclosure information to demonstrate how they are serving their trade area's credit needs.

Similarly, the consumer movement has established the principle that consumers have certain rights: the right to be informed, the right to choose, the right to safety, and the right to be heard.[8] In banking alone, there have been numerous regulations imposed to protect consumers. Some of these are the Truth in Lending Act, Fair Credit Reporting Act, Equal Credit Opportunity Act, Home Mortgage Disclosure Act, Fair Credit Billing Act, Unfair and Deceptive Credit Practices Act, Financial Institutions Regulatory Act, and Community Reinvestment Act. These are designed to prevent banks from misleading and deceiving people about such things as interest rates, and from discriminating against certain groups in granting loans.

Consumer compliance examinations have become part of the regular bank examination schedule. Banks that fail to comply with these regulations risk losing some of their freedom to operate. The Federal Reserve Board has denied approval for a holding company to acquire a bank on the grounds that the applicant was doing a poor job of serving the consumer.[9] The bank had been cited repeatedly for violations of certain laws and regulations and had failed to take actions to correct them.

Until banks are truly public oriented and adopt an attitude of social responsibility, no amount of rules and regulations will be fully effective in preventing banks from occasionally developing misleading advertising or from doing other things that may harm consumers. Similarly, no amount of regulation or legislation can bring about a true consumer orientation. In fact, the very existence of regulations can retard the development of a consumer orientation. Regulations make it possible to adopt an attitude of, "Oh well, the regulations cover all that, so there's nothing more for us to do." This mentality leads to a strict adherence to the letter of the law but not to its spirit. However, observance of the law alone is not sufficient.

For example, does the fact that a mortgage agreement includes a provision that the bank can call the loan in 5 years (when rates are expected to be much higher) make it acceptable for the bank to take that action? At least one bank learned the hard way that it is not.[10] A savings bank in Buffalo, New York, had the "business sense" in 1975 and 1976, when mortgage rates were 8½ percent, to include such a call provision in the 900 mortgages it wrote. This meant that the bank could demand that the loan be repaid in 5 years or recast at a rate in line with current mortgage interest rates.

In 1981, when mortgage rates were 17 percent, the bank decided to take advantage of the provision and began demanding payment, offering new mortgages at the below-market rate of 14 percent. The public outcry was devastating, and the bank had to reverse its position. The irony of the situation is that when the bank made those loans, other local banks had stopped offering mortgages because the maximum allowable rate under state usury ceilings was not sufficient to generate a profit. But this bank made a short-term community-oriented decision that turned out to be a bad business decision plus a bad social decision in light of its impact on the individuals involved. Hundreds of people were faced with the threat of having to sell their homes because of the inability to meet the new mortgage payments. The local publicity was loud and negative: eight front-page news articles on the subject. A local attorney brought a class-action suit against the bank, and the local legislature took steps to examine the implications of callable loans. The bank rescinded the program and clearly suffered severe damage to its image.

Two morals from this story are: (1) no amount of fine print gives the bank the freedom to take action that is socially disruptive; and

(2) a bank had better have a good community-oriented image to help it weather the storm it creates when, even once, it makes a serious error in judgment.

A Broader Perspective for Public Relations

A situation such as the foregoing one illustrates the fact that the bank needs an internal "conscience" and a management that is open to listening and responding to it. The public relations department can perform that essential function. As Kotler has said, viewing public relations as simply a communications function will lead a lot of chief executive officers to miss some of its potential value. Such a view could even be counterproductive. Kotler quotes Harry Dreiser, an experienced public relations practitioner, from a private interview:

> Assuming the public relations director is a thorough-going professional, seasoned and skilled, this process wastes his talents and may give rise to real public relations problems. He ought to be in on the decision process early, and have a chance to affect it. He contributes his knowledge of the media and how they are likely to treat a corporate action, and his perception of the public and its attitudes. If he is to be fully effective, he cannot be simply handed a decision and told to go out and sell it. He must know the bits and pieces of fact and opinion that went into the making of the decision, and if it is a decision with profound public relations implications, he should have a chance to influence it as well.[11]

The public relations function has commonly been viewed from the multiple focuses of isolated and specific events (such as the annual Christmas party for children or the bank's anniversary celebration), for publicity stimulation (such as getting the CEO's picture in the paper regularly), and other communications activities (such as an investor relations presentation). A broader concept of public relations emphasizes continuing programs rather than specific events, and community action and leadership, rather than merely publicity and communications. This is not to suggest that specific events, publicity, and communications have no place in bank public relations. Rather, these types of activities, standing alone, do not typically represent the kind of activity that can serve to maximize marketing opportunity in the contemporary social environment.

Banks must pay more attention to their conduct and be continually involved in and committed to solutions to one or more important problems faced by the communities they serve. Although a donation to the local Boy Scout troop or the sponsorship of a concert are nice, such singular and unsystematic actions as these are likely to be much less meaningful to the welfare of a specific community (and to the welfare of the bank) than would be a well-planned, continuing, systematic commitment to a given problem area within the limitations imposed by resources availability. *Case G* provides examples of ways in which some banks have chosen to address local needs or have identified themselves with a cause—such as the education of disadvantaged youth, or the needs of community service agencies.

Benefits of a Broader Perspective

The profit-minded reader might ask what the bank stands to gain from this type of action. Specific advantages and benefits accrue to banks that adopt a broader view of public relations and community involvement. These benefits are felt in market results, employee recruiting and morale, image of the bank, and community impact. The examples in *Case G* demonstrate this principle.

- *Market results.* Just as it is difficult to attribute specific sales results to a specific promotional campaign, so it is difficult to claim precise market results due to a public relations program. Nonetheless, there is every reason to suggest that one benefit of well-executed, community-oriented public relations programs may be appreciable economic gain for the bank, particularly if long-term as well as short-term results are considered.

- *Employee recruiting and morale.* One of the most overlooked potential benefits of community-oriented programs is the effect on present and prospective employees. When a bank takes a stand on an issue and does something positive for the community, its employees often develop a feeling of pride in their bank. Programs that demonstrate the bank's social concern attract the attention of people within the community and foster an image of being "the kind of place I'd like to work."

- *Image and credibility.* Another potential benefit of a broader perspective of public relations is an enhanced sense of organizational credibility or aura of trust within the bank's market area. This kind of response, of course, can be a measurable objective of such a program.

- *Community impact.* A well-planned, cohesive program can have a significant impact on the community to which it is directed. In addition to being beneficial for the individuals and businesses in the community, it is also good for the bank, since a bank's financial well-being is inexorably related to the economic health of the community it serves.

SUMMARY

Public relations concerns all the efforts of the bank to win the esteem of its various publics: the news media, stockholders, securities analysts, legislators and regulators, directors, employees, customers, and the community. Public relations, unlike marketing, has been a part of banking for many years, although its role continues to evolve.

While public relations and marketing overlap, especially in the area of product publicity, the majority of public relations activities can be considered marketing only from the broad perspective of the marketing concept—namely, that all the bank's activities are aimed at customer satisfaction, at a profitable volume, carried out in an organized and efficient framework, and conducted in a socially responsible manner. The public relations function should be the social conscience of the bank.

There are many tasks that may constitute the public relations function. One of them is the development of good relations with the news media and the writing and placing of press releases. The investor relations function includes the preparation and publication of the annual and quarterly reports, arrangements for the annual meeting of stockholders, and development and presentation of programs aimed at investors and the investment community. The goal of these is to increase demand for, and ultimately the price of, the bank's stock. Government relations includes getting to know, and communicating with, legislators representing the bank's trade area, and working with state and national banking associations in the ongoing effort to obtain a favorable regulatory climate for banking.

Other public relations functions include internal communications with the bank's staff, which help to develop employee morale and enlist staff support of the bank's marketing and other programs. In addition, the public relations officer monitors or develops communications with customers to ensure that they are customer oriented and in tune with the bank's overall communications goals. A bank's community relations programs are also under the direction of the public relations function. Since banks are so dependent upon the vitality of the communities they serve, banks should take an active role in helping the community solve its most pressing problems.

These functions constitute the public relations role, but the mere involvement of the bank in a number of programs in these areas does not, by itself, assure that the bank is a public oriented institution. Banks today are operating in an era that is characterized by a reorienting of priorities: people are first; things second. In other words, the quality of life is paramount. Consumerism, environmentalism, women's rights, and the other popular movements of this era have their roots in that basic change in priorities. Public relations officers now have the opportunity to help their banks find ways of responding to these new values and to create an economic, as well as a social, profit. The rules and regulations governing the behavior of banks with regard to consumers' rights are not sufficient to ensure that banks will be truly people oriented. What is more significant, laws and rules will not necessarily protect those banks that fail to be sensitive to society and its values.

Due to these realities, the public relations function is in a position to take on a broader perspective: one that emphasizes continuing programs of community action and leadership rather than isolated events. The bank that does this can expect to realize benefits in terms of its performance in the market, employee recruitment, employee morale, enhanced credibility and image, and the good health of its community.

Since most of the previous chapters on strategy have dealt with the retail side of banking, the next chapter addresses the application of marketing strategy to wholesale banking.

POINTS FOR REVIEW

1. Define or briefly explain the following terms:
   - public relations
   - publicity
   - investor relations
   - social responsibility
   - internal publics
   - external publics

2. What are the major differences between public relations and marketing?

3. In what ways are public relations and marketing similar with respect to goals and activities?

4. Why does public relations consciousness predate the onset of marketing consciousness in banking?

5. Look at any piece of literature from a bank or a bank advertisement. How much of its text do you think is there because of a concern for consumerism?

6. What is the purpose of a written publicity policy?

7. Does your bank, company, or school have a regular publication? Evaluate it and describe its communication objectives.

8. Obtain a copy of an annual report from a bank. Look through it, reading the headlines and photo captions. What is the theme or the main message being communicated by the report? Read the letter to the shareholders. What positive information is being communicated to the investors by the chairman and the chief executive officer? What negative information is being communicated?

16 THE WHOLESALE SIDE OF BANKING

The wholesale side of banking refers to all banking products and services not aimed at the retail or individual consumer market. Therefore, the term *wholesale* can apply to corporate banking, government banking, correspondent banking, international banking, trust, and any other activities directed toward markets that consist of organizations rather than individuals.

Wholesale and retail banking are not mutually exclusive, however. There is some overlapping of services to the wholesale and retail markets. For instance, trust services may be marketed to individuals (personal trusts, estate planning) and to corporations (pension fund management). Some corporate banking services, such as demand loans, are offered to individuals in certain circumstances (for example, "bridge" loans for home buyers). Exhibit 16-1 shows a partial list of services for the wholesale market and indicates that, while some services are marketed only to that market, others apply to both the wholesale and retail markets.

The wholesale side of the business, and, in particular, the corporate banking effort of the bank, is extremely important to the success of a commercial bank due to the sheer volume of business (specifically, deposits, loans, and fee-based services) capable of being

Exhibit 16-1 **Some Services Provided to Wholesale Customers (Showing Overlap with Services for Retail Customers)**

	Wholesale	Retail
Deposit/Funds-Generating Services		
Checking	X	
Money Market Deposit Account	X	X
Savings Account	X	X
Certificates of Deposit	X	X
IRA/Keogh/401(k)	X	X
Treasury Tax & Loan Account	X	X
Credit/Funds-Using Services		
Term Loan	X	
Line of Credit	X	X
Mortgage Loan	X	X
Lease Financing	X	X
Acceptance Financing	X	X
Installment Loan	X	X
Credit Card	X	X
Overdraft Funding	X	X
Demand Loan	X	X
Export Financing	X	X
Equipment Leasing	X	X
Noncredit Fee-Based Services		
Account Reconciliation	X	
Balance Reporting	X	
Zero Balance Accounts	X	
Lockbox	X	
Concentration Account	X	
Depository Transfer Checks	X	
Payable Through Drafts	X	
Direct Deposit of Payroll	X	
Wire Transfer	X	X
Deposit of Credit Card Drafts	X	
Preauthorized Checks/Debits	X	
Controlled Disbursement	X	
Automatic Investment	X	
Investment Services	X	X
International Services		
Domestic & Foreign Collections	X	X
Letters of Credit	X	
International Funds Transfer	X	X
Foreign Exchange Service	X	X

generated. In a typical bank, it would not be unusual for commercial accounts to comprise about 20 percent of total demand accounts, but two-thirds or three-quarters of total demand balances. Similarly, on the asset side of the balance sheet, commercial loans may constitute one-half or more of the bank's total loans. Most of these loans are tied to the prime rate. When rates rise, the yield on these loans rises; when rates fall, it falls. It is desirable that assets be rate sensitive since the liability side of the balance sheet (deposits and borrowed funds) is becoming increasingly rate sensitive. The once huge core of low-cost, fixed rate savings deposits has disappeared as a result of deposit interest rate deregulation, and noninterest-bearing demand deposits as a percent of total deposits and borrowed funds is small and declining. They are being replaced by market rate deposits.

Another reason for the importance of the corporate side of the business is that it is less labor-intensive than retail. While large numbers of staff are required to service the small retail depositor, a few major corporate accounts might generate millions of dollars of deposits for the bank.

The trust area also has potential for sizable account relationships and fee income, but it is a highly specialized service about which there is much disagreement concerning its potential and value. Some banks excel in the trust area. Others have been in it for years with little to show for it on the income statement. Nevertheless, it is a specialized market with unique marketing challenges.

This chapter concentrates on corporate and trust marketing and the application of marketing principles to these wholesale banking areas.

CORPORATE BANKING

The basic objective of marketing remains the same regardless of the market being addressed. For corporate banking in medium to large banks, the concern is to meet the financial service needs of businesses of about $10 million in sales and more. Smaller businesses may be handled by the branch or retail system.

In chapter 6, there was a discussion of organizational buying behavior and the fact that the buying behavior of organizations is affected by a number of factors: environmental, interpersonal, individual, and organizational. Furthermore, the process involves several persons—influencers, users, deciders, buyers, and gatekeepers. Although the behavior of the organizational buyer is based more on economic logic than that of the individual buyer, personal and interpersonal factors play a very large part in the marketing of corporate banking services.

Identifying the Market and Assessing Its Needs

Even more than the retail banking market, the corporate banking market must be sought out. By merely putting a branch on a street corner, the bank will attract some retail customers for whom that office is the most convenient. But, it is not likely to attract any new commercial lending or noncredit business just by virture of its being there. The market needs to be identified through research and sought out by sales officers.

Secondary Research

The bank that wishes to develop commercial business must identify its prospects systematically. Through secondary data sources, including personal inspection of the trade area, telephone calls, information from the Chamber of Commerce, Dun & Bradstreet reports, and industrial directories, the bank must learn what firms are within the geographic trade area.

For each firm, the bank should note the line of business that it is in, its annual sales volume, the number of people it employs, and the names of the principal officers of the firm. An attempt should also be made to determine which banks the firm is currently using.

Most larger firms deal with more than one bank. Their primary bank is the one in which they have their demand account or from which they receive the most services. In most cases, they also have secondary banking relationships with institutions that provide them with one or two other services. For its own corporate customers, a bank should know (1) whether it is the primary or secondary bank; (2) if it is not the primary bank, which of its competitors is; and (3) with what other banks the customer has secondary relationships. The bank should attempt to gain such information for its noncustomer prospects as well.

The purpose of collecting this data is to be able to direct the bank's calling (or selling) efforts. The best potential for a bank lies in calling on firms with which it has secondary relationships—the objective being to turn them into primary relationships. Similarly, knowing the secondary banking relationships of customers enables the bank to assess its vulnerability to competition. For example, suppose Bank A knows it is the primary bank for XYZ Corporation and that Banks B and C have secondary relationships with XYZ. The calling officers at Bank A become aware that Bank C is making a major push to develop new business. Therefore, they would be wise to direct special attention to XYZ and to other customers who deal with Bank C in order to protect Bank A's relationships against Bank C's competitive efforts.

When trying to attract new customers, it is important to have knowledge about their existing relationships and to know as much as possible about the competition so the calling officer can prepare for the call. For example, Bank A's calling officer knows that TUV Corporation is using Bank B's account reconciliation service. The calling officer also knows that Bank A's account reconciliation service has several features that make it more efficient than Bank B's. These features would be points to cover when calling on TUV's financial decision makers.

Primary Research

As in the case of retail banking, primary research can be a useful tool in determining the bank's present situation in the market and the needs of corporate customers and prospects. However, it is much more difficult to identify and communicate with the corporate banking decision maker than it is to identify and contact the household banking decision maker. One reason is that the gatekeepers mentioned in chapter 6 effectively screen out mail and phone calls from banks or other firms that wish to interview the president or chief financial officer.

Exhibit 16-2 Some Key Differences Between Retail and Commercial Bank Services

	Retail Services	Commercial Services
Customers	Individual consumers	Businesses, institutions
Nature of product	Similarity within product lines, for example, consumer loans (car loans, home equity loans, lines of credit)	Wide product differences, for example, customized loans, customized product features for large corporate customer
Pricing	Published and applied to all customers (fees occasionally waived but not modified)	Published but negotiable; paid with fees or compensating balances
Promotional mix emphasis	Mass media advertising; point-of-sale promotion; in-bank personal selling	Personal selling supported by advertising and sales promotion
Promotional appeal emphasis	Combination appeal to emotions, economic logic	Appeal to economic logic
Distribution channels	Branches, ATMs, telephone	Account manager, account support staff, Automated Clearing House system, telephone and computer terminal, branches (for some services)

Since primary research is a specialized field, there are consulting firms that expertly conduct research among the middle market (sales of $10 to $120 million), the large corporate market, the correspondent banking market, and the corporate trust market, among others. A bank may share in the results of such syndicated research, or it may commission a study of its own. Among the information that can be obtained are names of banks used for credit and noncredit services, level of satisfaction with banks used, the ways corporate needs for various banking services are changing over time, the image and market share of the bank, and the strengths and weaknesses of the bank as compared to its competitors.

Adapting the Marketing Mix to the Corporate Banking Market

Since the corporate banking market is different from that of retail banking, the marketing mix must be adjusted accordingly. The product, pricing, promotion, and distribution strategies that are effective in the one will not necessarily be effective in the other.

Product Strategy

As Exhibit 16-1 illustrates, the product line for corporate banking is more diversified than for retail banking. Exhibit 16-2 illustrates some of the key differences between retail and corporate banking services. Within a retail product line, such as consumer loans, the various product items (car loans, home improvement loans, personal loans) are actually quite similar. Also, their terms are standardized. Conversely, within the product line of corporate credit, there are wide product differences. Loans are frequently tailored to a company's specific need, with terms (such as collateral, payback plans, length of time involved) arranged to fit the situation.

Traditionally, the bank's credit services are the key to its success in the corporate banking arena. By and large, a firm will deal with the bank that provides it with credit when needed. However, firms have now found ways to obtain financing from sources other than banks. As a result of this change in the market, it is essential that banks stay attuned to changing customer needs and adapt to fit them. As corporations stop borrowing directly from banks, some banks are putting themselves in the position of being brokers—that is, linking borrower and lender together for a fee.

Many banks use cash management products as a way to gain entry to a firm whose credit needs are satisfied. The larger the company, the more likely the bank will be to lead with its noncredit products. The cash management product line is shown in Exhibit 16-3. Generally speaking, cash management products are designed to speed up the company's collection of receivables, concentrate its cash, forecast its disbursements, slow down its cash outflow, and provide systems to give the company information and control over its cash position.

Fewer regulations govern the product line in corporate, as compared with retail, banking, so there is more competition and innovation. The product line in commercial banking also undergoes more frequent changes than in retail. Products have shorter life cycles, and new product introduction generally takes place more frequently.

As interest rates have become more volatile, corporate treasurers have become more sophisticated in the management of available funds in order to maximize return for the company. This phenomenon is making it increasingly difficult for banks to generate the high-balance, interest-free commercial demand deposits of bygone days. Technological advances have helped this to occur. Cash management has become one of the most important financial services in corporate banking. Using a computer terminal in the treasurer's office, the firm can assess its cash position at any time in order to make decisions about where to put its idle funds for the best return overnight, over the weekend, or until they will be needed. This trend is here to stay, and although only the largest banks and data processing suppliers have participated in developing sophisticated cash management services, any bank may purchase them and provide them to their corporate customers.

The market for corporate banking services is a dynamic one. The successful commercial banks will be those that monitor changing product needs and respond to them in a timely manner.

Pricing Strategy

Many companies pay banks for corporate banking services through compensating balances rather than fees—that is, the customer maintains certain balances in an interest-free demand account to which the bank applies an earnings credit rate that reflects the current cost of funds. The bank has a fee schedule for each service that the company might use—from basic checking service to lockbox service, bulk coin and currency services, and armored car service. On a regular basis, usually monthly, the account activity is analyzed, and the bank calculates the cost of the services used. The earnings credit on the company's balances should compensate for the provision of the services and allow for a margin of profit. If it does not, the bank requests the firm to increase its compensating balances, or pay the required fees.

When interest rates are high, however, the potential value of those idle funds to the company increases, and many corporate treasurers prefer to put their idle funds into short-term investments and pay a fee for the bank services they use. With corporate treasurers managing their cash positions to maximize income, there is downward pressure on demand balances, and it has become necessary for banks to move toward explicit pricing for their services.

A major concern is whether the charges and fees earned for services will, in the long run, offset the outflow of funds from the banks. In this sense, developments in pricing, specifically in interest rates (the price of money), have been the leading cause for changes in the marketing of corporate banking services. In the high-rate environment of the late 1970s and early 1980s, firms found nonbank sources of financing. The very largest companies have become increasingly self-sufficient in financial services. Since the trend among these firms is to assume many former banking services, such as performing acquisition studies, selling commercial paper, and making private placements, there has been a large push among banks toward the middle market and the lower end of the large corporate market (sales up to $200 million).[1] With many firms satisfying their financial service needs internally or through nonbank sources, competition for the corporate banking market is stronger than ever.

In short, the pricing of corporate banking services is a complex problem and one that must balance the pressures from the competition, both banking and nonbanking, with the pressure to maintain or increase earnings. Meanwhile, all this is taking place as buyers become more knowledgeable about, and sensitive to, interest rates and pricing.

Distribution Strategy

When discussing retail banking, physical location and personal selling are the two most important aspects of distribution for banking services. In corporate banking, physical location is less important, and personal selling much more so. For example, a commercial loan does not require the physical presence of a branch. Similarly, a deposit relationship does not necessarily require physical proximity since advances in technology enable the corporate treasurer to communicate with the bank over telephone and computer lines. A large company might have its primary demand account in a bank in New York City or San Francisco, with accounts in numerous, smaller local banks that are swept every night so balances can be concentrated in the primary account. The only reason for maintaining a relationship with a local bank that is convenient to the firm's offices is for the regular deposit of cash receipts or for the check-cashing convenience of the firm's employees.

The fact that physical proximity of a branch is not required in order to provide credit services is attested to by the fact that United States and foreign banks have many successful commercial loan production offices scattered throughout the country.

Personal selling, on the other hand, is an important ingredient in marketing corporate banking services. Research and experience in the middle market indicate that the quality of the bank's calling officers is of paramount importance to financial decision makers. It is imperative that the calling officers know their own products, know as much as possible about the company with which they are talking, and have the ability to get the job done—whether that be arranging a loan or providing some fee-based service. It is not possible to pick up an article or book about corporate banking without reading about the importance of developing a formal officer call program. Yet, there are a number of banks, both large and small, that do not have an organized, systematic method for both regularly calling on customers, and on prospects who have the greatest potential for becoming customers.

Another purpose of an officer call program, besides acquiring new customers, is to retain and develop established business. Firms that are satisfied with their present banking relationships are much less vulnerable to the competition than are dissatisfied firms. Meeting the corporate customer on his or her own territory is one way of assessing and maintaining satisfaction with the bank's services and learning about needs for other services.

Small- to medium-sized banks usually involve their entire staff in the calling effort. Others use only trained corporate banking officers, and others use a combination approach. To be effective, the bank must set goals in terms of number of calls per month per person. The calling officer should prepare for the call by reviewing the customer's present accounts, or if the call will be made on a prospect, reviewing whatever information can be obtained about the nature of the business and the name of the financial decision maker and its banking affiliations. The calling officer should have a goal for the call and be prepared to get a commitment and close the deal if the service does not require approval from a loan committee.

People have a natural reluctance to make calls, and there is a tendency to overestimate the amount of effort involved. For instance, consider the following example from the small business market. A branch manager received calls from two merchants inquiring about the bank's point-of-sale terminal service, which provides fast authorization of credit card transactions and guarantees checks. The branch manager made one appointment on each of two afternoons, although the merchants were not far from one another, and the visits could easily have been done in one afternoon. In each case, after describing the benefits of the service, the merchant was eager to sign up, but the calling officer did not have the necessary papers to close the deal. This lack of preparation wastes time and creates an unfavorable impression in the minds of prospective customers.

Promotion Strategy

Advertising in the corporate banking area is largely aimed at paving the way for the calling officer. (For a graphic illustration of this point, see the McGraw-Hill ad in chapter 12.) Since the target audience for communication about the bank's corporate banking services is a select one, a bank's promotional strategies for addressing this market will be quite different from its retail promotion strategy. Corporate treasurers and presidents of small- to medium-sized firms are not a mass market. Nevertheless, it is possible to use mass media selectively to reach this group.

Case E presents a study of a promotional program for a bank that wanted to communicate a specific set of messages to financial decision makers in the middle market. The media selected were television, radio, and newspaper. The television time slots selected were those programming hours that the target market would most likely be watching. The newspapers used were the New York Times business section and the Wall Street Journal. Case E illustrates how mass media can be selected to reach the bank's targeted audience—corporate customers.

An important promotional tool in the corporate banking area is literature describing the bank's people and services, which can be left with a prospect during a call. Generally speaking, this promotional literature should contain considerable product information, since its objective is to promote understanding of financial services. However, an equally important objective is awareness. Leaving something behind on a call is a good technique for reminding the prospect of the call, the calling officer, and the bank.

Direct mail can also be used effectively in the corporate banking market when a bank has a list of firms that it has identified as prime prospects. An attention-getting direct mail piece followed by a phone call to set up a meeting can facilitate the process of getting a date for a first call.

Another useful sales promotional tool in corporate banking is the presentation of seminars for business people and professionals, such as attorneys and accountants. The latter are in an excellent position to refer their corporate clients to a particular bank and, therefore, may themselves be the object of a business development program or advertising campaign.

Finally, entertaining commercial customers and prospects is an effective strategy that can be used as part of the business development effort. It provides an opportunity for financial decision makers to mingle with the senior and executive management of the bank. This type of top-level attention from the bank is especially important to businesspeople in the middle market.

TRUST MARKETING

The area covered by the broad term *trust* is another important wholesale banking activity. The trust department, however, services both retail and corporate customers. It provides management services for an individual's investments or an estate, as well as management services for corporate pension funds.

As with the market for corporate banking services, the market for trust services is a select one. The individuals who make up the market for trust services represent only a small percentage of the total population of a bank's market area—perhaps 5 percent or less. The market for the management of pension funds is made up of companies of all sizes that have pension funds to invest. Of course, the corporate banking calling officer can be an important source of referrals for the trust department.

Adapting the Marketing Mix to the Trust Market

Here again, product, pricing, promotion, and distribution strategies must be adjusted to serve the market for trust services. The marketing mix for trust services bears some resemblance to that of corporate banking services, but, in several important ways, it differs.

Product Strategy

Generally speaking, trust products revolve around the management of assets held "in trust" for another—an individual or a business. There is considerably less product innovation in the trust area than in the corporate banking area. Nevertheless, the more aggressive trust marketing banks find ways to repackage existing investment management services for new markets. Some banks, especially those in mature markets where the personal trust business is no longer growing, have developed services for individuals who have as little as $100,000 in assets to be managed. Other banks have developed investment services for individuals who want to invest in precious metals or collectibles.

The backbone of the trust department is its investment research and its resulting record for earnings on managed funds. The bank's ability to outperform some well-known indicator of stock earnings, such as the Dow Jones Industrial Average, is an accomplishment worth advertising.

Some aggressive trust departments sell their investment advisory services for a fee to others, such as insurance companies, brokerage houses, money market funds, and other banks. Although the basic product remains asset management, marketing-oriented trust departments are successful at finding new markets for old services and new ways to earn fees.

Pricing Strategy

The trust department is the only area of a bank that earns its income almost exclusively from fees. Its services do not, for the most part, generate interest income. As in retail and corporate banking, it is important that trust departments understand their costs and price accordingly. Generally speaking, the market for trust services is not highly sensitive to price because it is difficult for customers to place a value on the quality of the service provided, on the expertise of the investment advisers, and on the department's earnings record—all of which are of primary importance to the customer. Naturally, banks with the best track record are in a position to demand the highest price.

Distribution Strategy

As with corporate banking, the distribution of trust services is heavily dependent upon personal sales and service and less upon physical proximity (as with retail banking). However, for the management of personal trusts, the trust officer should be near enough to meet with the client at least occasionally. Some banks, having recognized this, establish trust offices in areas to which large numbers of their trust customers migrate in their retirement. It is not unusual to find a trust office of a northeastern commercial bank in Florida or Arizona. The motivation is more than simply serving existing customers, however. Retirement areas are often populated by a high concentration of individuals who are the best prospects for personal trust: senior citizens with substantial assets to be managed or disbursed after their deaths.

Promotion Strategy

Perhaps more than any other area of the bank, the trust department uses direct mail to communicate with its customers and prospects. Lists of customers who are potential personal trust prospects can be developed from the bank's records—for instance, by culling out high-balance customers and frequent visitors to the safe-deposit-box area. Lists of firms that might need employee benefit plan management services can be derived from various directories, published both by the federal government and by private sources, that list the names and sizes of all companies, unions, and other organizations with pension funds. Additionally, attorneys, accountants, and insurance agents can be valuable sources of referrals.

Some of the best prospects for a trust department are the businesses and executives of those firms on which the commercial banking officers call. Since these officers are focused primarily on credit, and secondarily on cash management, sales, trust services are often ignored in the calling process. Many banks, therefore, use ongoing incentive programs to motivate and reward calling officers for referring prospects to the trust department.

Once trust service prospects have been identified, the bank should develop a communications program to address them. For the retail trust market, even the smallest bank can buy preprinted brochures explaining the need for, and operation of, various trust services. Some banks offer personal financial planning courses through the mail, with each part of the course containing an exam that the prospect returns to the bank to be graded. At the end of the course, a computerized financial analysis is provided, and the prospect is encouraged to make an appointment for a consultation with a trust officer.

Some investment management services can be effectively marketed through print advertising in selected newspapers and magazines. Whether the bank has an exceptional earnings record, or is offering a special service (such as a personal financial analysis), or is simply trying to build up its image, an ad in the financial pages or in periodicals read by high-income individuals can be effective. Whenever possible, it is wise to include an offer to send some useful information and to include a clip-out coupon in the ad. This provides the department with specific leads to be followed. And, due to the potential size of trust accounts, even a low response rate can more than justify the cost of the ad.

Another effective promotional device for the trust area is the holding of seminars for individuals, businesses, and professionals such as attorneys, accountants, and insurance agents. Seminars enable the bank to demonstrate its expertise and provide an opportunity for staff to mingle with prospects and opinion leaders.

Point-of-sale advertising should be used within the bank, especially in the safe-deposit-box area, the new accounts area, and the corporate banking area, where it may be seen by business clients.

The officers in the trust department should be active in organizations that are likely to generate leads for new business—such as service and charitable organizations, municipal boards, cultural groups, and educational institutions. This type of activity provides positive publicity and visibility for the bank, as well as numerous contacts and business leads.

Speaking generally, bank trust departments do not have a highly favorable image. Many people react negatively to the fact that the bank earns a fee for its services regardless of how good or poor a job it does in managing other people's money. Many do not trust a bank to give objective advice, but rather expect them to offer only self-serving investment advice to the customer. Before engaging in an advertising campaign, therfore, it is wise to do some research to learn precisely what the image of the bank is. If the bank is perceived as being overly conservative, or is seen as an institution that only caters to high-income individuals, it will have its communication goals identified. Image research among corporate trust prospects is also useful to help establish objectives and strategy for increasing business in this area.

SUMMARY

Corporate banking and trust are two of the wholesale banking departments that might be found in a commercial bank. These departments and others (correspondent banking, government banking, international banking, and so on) must operate on the same basic marketing principles as outlined in this text for retail banking—namely, the satisfaction of customer needs at a profitable volume through a well-planned and executed strategy in a socially responsible manner.

Research, both secondary and primary, is the foundation for understanding the task to be accomplished in the corporate banking market. It is essential that banks identify and understand their best prospects and develop an organized plan for calling on them since it is primarily through personal sales that corporate services are sold.

The product line for corporate banking services is very broad and products tend to be customized to the needs of the customer. This market also exhibits rapid product development and frequent alterations brought on largely by changing technology and by competition from within and outside banking. As a result, there is pressure on corporate banking officers to keep abreast of change and to recognize areas where income can be generated through fees, especially as idle demand balances diminish due to the increasing sophistication of corporate treasurers.

The traditional bank practice of pricing corporate services on the basis of compensating balance requirements is losing ground as corporate treasurers recognize the value their idle funds could have in the money market. Bankers are in the position of having to provide cash management services that compete with, or rather cannibalize, their own demand deposits in order to retain and develop customer relationships. High prices (interest rates) for loans cause corporate borrowers to seek alternative sources of credit.

Advertising in corporate banking serves to prepare the audience for the selling effort of the calling officer and to build the bank's desired image in the corporate banking market. Personal selling and referrals are the leading sources of sales, so promotional efforts are geared to support these. Such promotional efforts can include media advertising, direct mail, informational material, seminars, and business entertainment.

The trust department serves a select market, and its services revolve around its ability to skillfully manage the assets of its customers, both individuals and organizations (profit and nonprofit). Product alterations and pricing are less volatile than in corporate banking, but the more aggressive trust marketers are finding ways to develop new markets for variations of their basic services.

In both corporate banking and trust, the distribution system relies more on the officer servicing the account than on the physical proximity of the bank. Advertising to these markets presents a challenge because the individuals who are decision makers for the trust and corporate banking services are a relatively small proportion of the total marketplace. Therefore, it is important to find efficient ways to communicate with them without wasting money on those who are not part of the target market.

In summary, the tactics involved in the marketing of wholesale banking services differ from those used in retail banking, but the broad approach of planning, objective setting, target market selection, strategy formulation, and control is the same. This chapter completes the study of the fields of marketing and public relations as applied to banking. To conclude this text, the next chapter looks at where banking may go in the years ahead and what this might mean to bank marketers.

POINTS FOR REVIEW

1. Explain how economic environmental factors have affected the product line for corporate banking services.

2. What competitive factors have affected the pricing of corporate banking services, and why did this happen?

3. Why is the corporate banking area so important to the commercial bank?

4. What are the similarities between corporate and trust marketing in terms of techniques for generating new business and for promoting the services offered?

5. Obtain and evaluate the following information from your bank's statement of condition or annual report:
   - Noninterest-bearing deposits as a percent of total deposits/borrowed funds, for the most recent year and 2 years prior.
   - Commercial loans as a percentage of total loans.
   - Commercial loans as a percent of total loans.

17 THE FUTURE OF BANK MARKETING

OVERVIEW

Good marketing means managing change—a statement that was elaborated upon in chapter 1. The future of bank marketing will be shaped by changes that are already underway or that are expected to take place in the external macro- and microenvironments in which banks operate. (See Exhibit 1-5.)

There are four important events in banking's microenvironment—specifically the competitive environment—that banks are already reacting to and will have to react to in the years ahead. They are:

- the deregulation of interest rates;
- the spread of regional and interstate banking;
- heightened competition from nonbank sources; and
- the increasing level of marketing expertise within banking.

In the macroenvironment, banks must deal with:

- the ever-changing complexion of society as it affects consumer values and lifestyles;
- economic cycles and change;
- advances in technology; and
- changes brought about by the political-legal system.

Exhibit 17-1 **Impact of Market Change on Marketing Mix Elements**

	Product	Pricing	Promotion	Physical Distribution	Personal Selling
Competitive Environment					
Rate Deregulation	X	X	X		X
Interstate Banking	X	X	X	X	X
Nonbank Competition	X	X	X	X	X
Increasing Marketing Expertise in Banking	X	X	X	X	X
Outer Environment					
Social Change	X	X	X	X	X
Economic Change	X	X	X	X	
Technological Change			X	X	X
Political-Legal Change	X	X	X	X	X

In the following pages, there will be a discussion of these changing realities and some of the ways in which they impinge upon the various elements of the marketing mix and the development of bank marketing strategy. As Exhibit 17-1 illustrates, changes in banking's competitive microenvironment and macroenvironment tend to affect the entire spectrum of the marketing mix—not just one or two elements. The implication is clear: more than ever, bank marketers must be capable of adapting to market change that is beyond their control with creative product, pricing, promotional, and distribution strategies.

CHANGES IN BANKING'S COMPETITIVE ENVIRONMENT

As mentioned above, the principal changes taking place in banking's competitive microenvironment are the deregulation of interest rates,[1] regional and interstate banking, nonbank competition, and growth in bank marketing expertise.

Deregulation of Interest Rates

The past several years have seen many changes in the competitive environment for commercial banks and for all banking institutions. One of the principal changes, which occurred in 1986, was the **deregulation** of deposit interest rates. Deregulation removed the ceilings on interest rates that banks were permitted to pay, allowing rates to reflect prevailing money market rates. Now, banks are able to price their deposits to reflect the income that will be generated when putting the funds to work as loans or investments. This fundamental change in the ability of banks to price their deposit products has had implications for bank marketers not only in the area of pricing strategy, but also for product development, promotion, and personal selling.

Effect of Rate Deregulation on the Marketing Mix

In the face of deregulation, bank marketers had to rethink their checking and savings product strategies. The checking product line had consisted primarily of noninterest-bearing regular checking, 5¼ percent NOW accounts, and market rate Super-NOW accounts. The savings product line consisted of 5½ percent regular passbook or statement savings, 5¾ percent 90-day notice savings, and a market rate money market deposit account. To add to the complexity of the situation, ceilings came off at a time when market interest rates were relatively low, and the 5½ percent regular savings rate was high in light of then-current money market deposit account rates. The combination of the low interest rate economic market environment and the savings interest rate deregulation led many banks to lower their regular savings rates and restructure their checking and savings product lines. (See Exhibit 17-2.) In essence, the ability to let all rates float with market conditions made the NOW account obsolete. The same was true of the 90-day notice savings account, which had been a way of offering a higher rate savings account in a regulated rate environment.

Rate deregulation's primary impact has been on pricing—not just the setting of rates, but also the establishing of fees and maintenance charges. With an increasing proportion of deposits floating at money

Exhibit 17-2 Example of Product Line Restructuring Due to Interest Rate Deregulation

	Before Deregulation	After Deregulation
Checking Product Line	Regular checking 5¼% NOW account Market rate super-NOW account	Regular checking Market rate checking account
Savings Product Line	5.5% Regular savings 5.75% 90-day notice savings Market rate money market deposit account	Fixed rate regular savings with provision to change rate with 15-days' notice Market rate money market deposit account

market rates, bank interest margins are under pressure. Therefore, it is more important than ever that banks price their products prudently in order to ensure the profitability of each account. Bank deposit product managers and accounting staff will be devoting more and more time attempting to measure the true cost of each product in order to be able to price more rationally. Gone are the days when the bank's earnings on its low-cost or no-cost, high-balance savings or checking customers offset losses on low-balance customers. The focus on customer profitability will lead to increased use of relationship pricing strategies whereby higher interest rates are paid to customers who have more accounts (that is, a broader relationship) with the bank. The old, and presumed dead, concept of service packaging is coming back with a new twist.

The principal effect of rate deregulation on promotion strategy has been the emergence of rate competition and the reduction in the use of premiums and giveaways. The latter had been a way of offering added value to depositors at a time when all banks paid the same rates. The deregulated environment has also led to broader use by banks of image advertising and positioning as a strategy to give customers a reason, other than rate, for banking with a particular financial institution. Increasingly, banks are talking about establishing "brand identity," something that has been going on in consumer packaged goods industries for many years. This strategy is wise, for no bank can afford to buy or retain market share by continually paying the highest rates in its market. The bank that creates an image and position in the consumer's mind as "a place where I'd like to do business" can use that strength to overcome modest differences in rate from the market rate leaders.

The elimination of ceilings on rates has and will continue to place increased demands on the personal selling skills of bank staff. New accounts staff must be skilled in responding to price objections (". . . but ABC Bank is paying a higher rate"). Furthermore, bank personnel must be able to communicate to customers and prospects the intangible reasons for doing business with their particular institution. In other words, they must be schooled in selling the bank, not just the bank's products, a task that will be a formidable challenge to the bank's training staff.

Regional and Interstate Banking

The gradual elimination of barriers to banking across state lines is a political-legal development, but one that has already started to affect the competitive environment within which many banks operate. The vast majority of states have passed reciprocal or **regional banking** compacts allowing bank holding companies from one state to acquire or establish banks in another state. Given this movement, the ability of a bank to establish branches across state lines is not far behind. **Interstate banking** affects all elements of the marketing mix and poses challenges to bank marketers, whether they work for the expanding banking organization or the banks that find themselves competing with the out-of-state organizations.

Generally, new market entrants from out-of-state are large regional banks that have considerable data processing and promotional resources putting them on the leading edge in terms of product strategy. Local banks faced with this type of competition will be forced to find ways to respond and to compete or risk losing valued customers.

The pricing of bank products, whether in terms of interest rates or fees and service charges, can vary greatly from one state or geographic market to the next. Banks that are operating in more than one market must carefully monitor prices in all their markets and be capable of dealing with nonuniform pricing. One of the strategies that might be used by a new market entrant to quickly gain or increase share is penetration pricing—paying above-market rates on savings deposits. This strategy puts the management of competing banks in a position of having either to respond and increase their costs (thus cutting into profits), or to find more aggressive, nonprice means of competing to retain market share.

Interstate banking poses challenges for both the new market entrants and the banks with which they compete in terms of promotion. The entrant faces the challenge of competing in a market where its name may have little or no recognition. It requires considerable expenditure in mass media to build awareness from such a level. Bank advertising staff will be required to have an understanding of the customers in the new market in order to develop an awareness campaign that will gain acceptance and not insult, offend, or bore the target audience. Advertising personnel in banks already operating in the market may find that they are being considerably outspent in advertising dollars, making it difficult for them to maintain their desired levels of awareness among the target audience. Since market share often moves to a bank that is spending heavily, especially on television, marketers in the competing banks will be challenged to find ways to compete and maintain awareness in cost-effective ways.

Interstate banking is, obviously, a **physical distribution strategy**. Banks that are crossing state lines have many choices to make about entering new markets: where to locate, whether to combine management and staff, whether to expand the newly acquired bank, and which products to distribute through the new channel. These are all choices that will challenge the marketing expertise of both the acquiring and the acquired banks.

Perhaps the biggest challenge to marketers of banks that are expanding across state lines, however, is encouraging all employees—especially those involved in personal selling roles—to accept, identify with, and feel part of the new organization. Disgruntled staff can negate all of the advertising dollars spent on establishing an image in a new market. Exhibit 17-3 presents an example of how one expanding banking organization met the promotional and staff-training challenges involved in acquiring two very different banks in an adjacent state in which they were unknown.

Competition from Nonbank Financial Institutions

In addition to competition from within the banking industry, commercial banks will continue to face competition in the financial services arena from nonbank financial service providers and from the so-called nonbank banks. According to the definition in the Bank Holding Company Act, a bank is an institution that both takes deposits and makes commercial loans. An organization owning a bank that does only one of those things avoids being designated as a bank holding company and is, therefore, able to engage in businesses that are forbidden to bank holding companies. By acquiring commercial banks and selling off their commercial loan portfolios, many companies, such as Sears, J.C. Penney, American Express, Dreyfus Corporation, Beneficial Finance, Merrill Lynch, and Gulf & Western, have entered the retail banking business. These nonbank institutions can offer a variety of products for their customers including:

- regular savings accounts;
- certificates of deposit;
- checking accounts;
- auto and personal loans;
- home equity loans;
- mortgages; and
- credit cards.

In this way, nonbank financial organizations (such as brokerage firms and insurance companies) can market bank products to their nonbank customers and to the market at large. For example, through Sears' retail bank, their Dean Witter subsidiary sells bank certificates and money market deposit accounts to its brokerage customers. The deposits of that bank grew from less than $11 million when Sears acquired it to nearly $2 billion in less than 3 years.[2] Additionally, Sears offers its Discover credit card through this bank, so its loan outstandings similarly grew from $12 million to $2 billion.

Brokerage firms and mutual funds themselves are stiff competition for increasingly rate-sensitive customers who are willing to accept some risk in order to earn a greater return than they can get at their banks. Money market mutual funds were the first major nonbank competition for consumer deposits. They grew from $74 billion in assets to more than $230 billion between 1980 and 1983. This phenomenon led banking regulators to authorize banks to offer money market deposit accounts in order to meet the competition and stem the runoff in deposits.

In the low-rate, booming stock market environment of the mid-1980s, mutual funds that invest in equities gained popularity with former bank depositors seeking higher rates and willing to accept some principal risk. Banks cannot compete with the historical rates of return that many of these funds have experienced, and they are precluded by law from managing and offering their own mutual funds. While changes in interest rates and in the stock market indexes will cause consumer funds to flow back and forth between banks and mutual funds and the stock market, competition for funds has forever changed because of the increased sophistication and reduced risk aversion of so many consumers.

The growth of nonbank competition affects every aspect of bank marketing. Nonbanks may offer financial products that banks are prohibited from offering their customers. Chief among these are mutual funds, insurance products, and real estate services. Unless and until regulations change, banks will be forced to find creative ways to offer similar but not truly comparable products in an effort to retain their customers. Mutual funds and insurance products can be offered indirectly through arrangements with providers of those services. However, banks can act only as conduits for such providers. Banks will also be required to design deposit products that have some of the variable rate characteristics of mutual funds and equities, while finding uses for those funds that will ensure profitability.

Nonbank competitors have made the consumer more rate savvy. The proportion of banking customers who are rate sensitive is increasing. This poses a challenge to bank marketers to price competitively without sacrificing profit. This is one of the greatest challenges that will face bank marketers. On the promotion front, bankers must get smart and meet the competition where they are strongest. Nonbank competitors are masters at direct mail and telemarketing. It will become increasingly important for bankers to use these tools, especially among their current customers, in an effort to retain customers and deposits. Banking's physical distribution system—the branches—must become sales outlets. With customers coming into the bank less and less, it is important that banks take advantage of every opportunity to make customers aware of the bank's services and of the fact that they offer a variety of services to meet financial needs. At the very least, this means the use of effective point-of-sale displays, but some banks are going even further, experimenting with totally new branch floor plans that eliminate the teller/platform distinction and create an atmosphere conducive to personal financial consultation.

Finally, personal selling will become more important than ever in the new competitive environment. Bank sales personnel will be required to discuss complex financial products with increasingly sophisticated customers and to actively sell the bank's products. Again, this strategy has major implications for the bank's training staff.

CHANGES IN BANKING'S MACROENVIRONMENT

As described in chapter 2, the macroenvironment for banks has four components:

- the social environment;
- the economic environment;
- the technological environment; and
- the political-legal environment.

These environments are in a constant state of flux, and their long-term trends will significantly affect the future of bank marketing.

The Social Environment

Society undergoes major shifts in values and lifestyles over time. In the 1960s and 1970s, the traditional values of the postwar years gave way to an era of hedonism and self-absorption. The late 1980s reflect a blending of the newer self-centered values with the more traditional values of home, family, heritage, patriotism, and belongingness.

One organization that measures social change described this new environment as **neotraditionalism**, a return to something similar to basic American values but with a difference.[3] While Americans are once again receptive to discipline, principles, responsibility, commitment, and social bonds, they are not willing to accept an externally imposed morality. Rather, they want to establish their own rules and structures.

This neotraditionalism has five major aspects that affect marketers of all types of consumer products:

1. Consumers are more strategic in their decision making.

2. They are looking for "anchors"—for identification with a broader group—and they are seeking to establish a moral focus.

3. Consumers are once again recognizing the value of authority—that one cannot be an expert in everything so one should look for reliable sources of information and guidance.

4. Consumers want to assume control over many aspects of their lives by setting priorities, minimizing risk, and ensuring the preservation of their lifestyles for the future. Their attempts to exert more control in the marketplace demonstrates itself in the "consumer power" thrust.

5. Consumers seek pleasure, fun, and excitement as a regular part of their lives, not just an occasional treat.

The implications for bank marketers are numerous. Consumer power and moral focus are the forces behind the movement toward the development of a new transaction product, the lifeline or basic checking account. It is also demonstrated in the heightened attention paid to the length of holds placed by banks on deposited checks. There are a number of instances where basic checking accounts, with no minimum balance and low fees and charges, have been mandated by community groups opposing bank mergers. As for check holds, many banks do not allow customers to draw against a deposited check until several days after the bank has received credit for the check. They do this to allow for the possibility of a deposited check being returned unpaid. This product feature will be brought into line in response to consumer reaction.

As consumers move toward consolidating relationships rather than fragmenting them, banks will move toward full relationship pricing. The consumer power focus will lead to the rationalizing of credit card fees and interest rates to more closely reflect market rates of interest.

Emerging social trends will also affect the way banks promote their products. Since many banks have been deceptive, or at least misleading, in their advertising of savings and certificate of deposit interest rates, the industry is sure to have truth-in-saving legislation imposed upon it. Just as the Truth in Lending Act has shackled banks in terms of what they can and must say in consumer loan advertising, so will this regulation complicate the business of advertising for deposits.

These social trends will influence not only what bank advertising can or may say, but will increasingly influence the style of bank advertising, especially that which is seen on television. Many banks will follow the consumer goods manufacturers in shifting their advertising strategies away from the "slice-of-life" execution and toward the depiction of "lifestyles." Rather than showing people within a setting in which they are using the product (whether it be cereal, shortening, or a personal loan), the ads might cut from one scene to another that suggests the lifestyle of the target audience and that subtly weaves the product into the scene.

Social trends can also play a role in the physical distribution strategy of banks. Failure of a bank to comply with the spirit and letter of the Community Reinvestment Act can impede that bank's ability to merge with other institutions—that is, to establish or assume a presence in a market that it seeks to enter.

The greater sophistication and the more strategic orientation of consumers will require greater sophistication and training of a bank's sales staff. Furthermore, increased emphasis on control coupled with the tendency to value relationships is behind the growing recognition of the importance of providing quality customer service in banking. Indeed, service quality will be one of the major bank marketing thrusts of the next decade. Some banks are employing consultants in the field of service quality and are putting considerable resources into systems and staff for dealing effectively with customer complaints, problems, and inquiries. There is a growing recognition on the part of banks that the way bank customers feel they have been treated during the attempt to resolve a problem, such as an error on a bank statement, is critical to their decision to stay with the bank and to tell others about their positive experiences. In fact, customers who have had problems resolved quickly and satisfactorily do more to spread positive information about the bank than those who have had no problems at all.

The Economic Environment

Bank marketers of the future will need to be able to cope with the problems inherent in various types of interest rate environments, with pressures on profit margins, and, in some geographical areas, with serious problems in the regional or local economy. The interest rate and profit environments are most likely to affect pricing and promotion of bank products. Local and regional economic slumps, of course, also affect bank profitability, which in turn, affects pricing and promotion strategies. However, a further effect of such economic problems is the acceleration of interstate banking.

The squeeze on bank profits, regardless of the source, will continue to challenge product managers to review their pricing to be sure that each product is generating a profit. The increased emphasis on fee income will continue for some time. Pressures on earnings also affect advertising and sales promotion strategy. The advertising budget is usually one of the first to be cut in a push for cost reduction. Bank marketers will need sharp minds and pencils to cost-justify the levels of promotion they believe to be necessary to do the job of bringing in deposits and loans for the bank, and it will be more important than ever to create advertising that works.

Physical distribution through out-of-state locations is a phenomenon that has been facilitated by economic factors. The number of banks failing and ailing, especially due to regional and economic slumps, has sped up the process of interstate banking as large financial institutions have been permitted by banking regulators to buy smaller problem banks and thrift institutions in other, often far-flung, states.

Technological Change

There have been great advances in technology in the past several years. They can be expected to continue and to result in greater affordability of advanced systems, making the technology available to a larger number of banks. The most important of these technological changes will take place in the broad area of computer technology. The marketing impact will be felt primarily in the distribution and promotion of bank products.

Home banking via personal computer hookup with the bank is a distribution strategy that has been tested by many institutions but which is slow to gain market acceptance. Costs are high, and the perceived customer benefits are not great, so only slow growth is expected in this distribution technique. More interesting to consumers, however, are direct telephone links with the bank, allowing customers to not only pay bills by telephone but to also access information about their accounts and to transfer funds between accounts without going to the bank.

Advances in technology are also leading many banks toward full branch automation, providing tellers with direct, on-line access to the customer's account information and eliminating the need for audio response systems. Customer service staff have administrative terminals at which they can see a customer's total relationship with the bank, change an address instantly, or open a new account and produce the required documents.

The increasing use of on-line loan application processing systems is changing the way many banks distribute their personal credit products. Loan customers will no longer have to come into a branch to apply for a loan. Rather, they will call a special telephone number, and a loan interviewer enters the application information directly into the computer. The application processing system automatically scores the application and taps into a credit bureau file for an updated credit report. Within minutes, the loan decision is made. The customer need only come into the branch to sign the documents and pick up the proceeds of the loan.

An example of the effect of technological advances on the promotion of bank services is the use of interactive video systems to make customers aware of the bank's products and to walk the customer through the early stages of the buying process (that is, through prepurchase search activity) in a nonthreatening, impersonal way.

Personal selling will also be affected as branch automation technology is expanded. The terminal screen can be used to help customer service representatives cross-sell by prompting them as to the next question to ask or statement to make. The challenge to marketers and sales trainers will be to keep the sales interview personal despite the intervention of the screen.

The Political-Legal Environment

The future of banking and bank marketing depends greatly on what happens to regulations affecting banks and nonbank financial institutions. The biggest issue on the legislative horizon, and one that is being spearheaded by large money center banks, is the expansion of bank powers to enable them to sell insurance, real estate, and mutual funds, and to deal in securities. The legislation that prohibits most of this activity originated in 1933 with the Glass-Steagall Act. Approximately 15,000 banks failed between 1920 and 1934. Responding to this situation, Representative Henry Steagall was the guiding force behind the creation of deposit insurance. Senator Carter Glass wanted to divorce the banking and investment businesses, arguing that financial institutions had put too much of their assets into securities underwriting and financing, leaving less money for the banking side of the business. With the stock market crash of 1929 and the ensuing Great Depression, bankers and brokers were experiencing a rather poor reputation, so it was not difficult for Glass to sell his proposal to Congress. He never demonstrated, however, that securities underwriting and brokerage were improper activities for banks. Furthermore, it was not speculation that had caused the failure of banks. Rather, it was a combination of a lack of liquidity and a run on the banks by customers wanting their deposits back. Banks were unable to collect on loans because of the collapse of prices and markets for their borrowers' products. Thus, the Glass part of Glass-Steagall was based on some half-truths and supported by the emotions of the times.

Those times are far behind us now. Today, there is no demonstrated reason why banks should not be allowed to do as one activity what they are allowed to do as separate activities: pool assets or commingle funds, act as managing agents for customers, and purchase stock for customers' accounts.[4] It is this restriction on banking that kept banks from being able to respond to the popularity of money market funds in the late 1970s and early 1980s and, more recently, to the popularity of equity-based mutual funds.

If the larger banks are successful in getting Glass-Steagall repealed, that will affect the products banks can offer, with consequences for pricing, promotion, and distribution strategies. Banks will face the challenge of developing expertise in the newly allowed businesses and in building an image as providers of services in which banks currently have limited experience. Being in an underdog position, banks will probably do as the retailers did when they entered the banking business: buy the outlets and the talent to enter the business. Bank branches may become broader-based financial outlets with a real estate, insurance, and brokerage department on the banking floor. Sales staff will need to learn about the new products or at least be able to recognize and refer prospects for the new services. This issue will become a major marketing challenge for banks that choose to enter these businesses.

What is the community banker to do while anticipating these developments? There have been many suggestions in the literature, and they all revolve around capitalizing on one's principal strengths, especially the bank's position in the local community and its relationship with larger correspondent banks. As one writer put it, local roots are a secret weapon. "The big bank can bring only a fraction of its attention and resources to bear on any given local market. The community banker can give that market his all, knows it intimately. . . . The community bank has a faster reaction time to local changes, more customer loyalty."[5] The smart community banker will get all the talent, expertise, products, and support he or she can from large correspondents. The combination of local talent, concern, and reputation with up-to-date products and services is a difficult one to beat. The number of new "boutique" banks that are springing up, especially in major metropolitan areas, demonstrates this belief.

THE CHALLENGE AHEAD FOR BANK MARKETERS

With these developments and more on the horizon, the years ahead will be exciting and challenging for bank marketers. Some of the strategies that banks can plan in order to position themselves for the challenge are:

- to hire people with sales aptitude and to train them in sales ability for customer-contact positions;
- to make a commitment to ongoing sales and product training;
- to upgrade the quality of service provided to customers after the sale;
- to develop a unique image and position among target audiences;
- to develop among noncontact staff the mentality that although they are not serving the customer directly, they are serving someone who is;
- to conduct research in order to understand the trends taking place in their own market;
- to keep abreast of political-legal issues and to respond when asked for comments by the regulators;
- to act responsibly in matters that affect customers in order to forestall consumer groups from initiating regulations to make responsible behavior mandatory; and
- to hire bottom-line-oriented marketing staff.

SUMMARY

In chapter 1, there was a discussion of the "Law of Slow Learning" and how it has taken banking a long time to realize that marketing means analysis, planning, and control. In many other industries, that period has been followed by a period of marketing success, after which the corollary, "Law of Fast Forgetting" takes over. The banking industry is positioned somewhere between adopting the marketing concept and struggling to experience or maintain a period of marketing success. If polled today, most bank marketers would say that it is very unlikely that their institutions might soon fall into the trap of forgetting the importance of having a market orientation. Things are simply changing too fast and competition is too great to be able to rest on one's laurels after any one particularly successful marketing campaign.

This new marketing dynamism in the banking industry is attested to by the number and quality of people who are expressing an interest in getting into banking in general and bank marketing in particular. The annual crop of college and graduate school alumni who are applying to banking institutions is growing. This bodes well for the future of the industry. New entrants to this business, as well as those professionals who have been in it for a while, will learn that it is not an easy job, but it should be fascinating for those who welcome hard work and a challenge.

POINTS FOR REVIEW

1. How did your bank modify its checking and savings product lines as a result of the deregulation of interest rates?

2. What is your state's position on interstate banking?

3. Give an example of a nonbank institution's marketing efforts (for example, through print advertising or direct mail) within your bank's market area.

4. Give an example of a lifestyle television commercial for a bank or a consumer product.

5. In what ways has your bank utilized technological advances to distribute, service, or promote its products?

NOTES

CHAPTER 1

1. *Marketing News*, March 1, 1985, p. 1.

2. Philip Kotler, *Marketing Management: Analysis, Planning, and Control*, 5th edition (Englewood Cliffs, N.J.: Prentice-Hall, Inc., 1984), p. 12.

3. *Ibid.*, p. 22.

4. J.B. McKitterick, *The Frontiers of Marketing Thought* (American Marketing Association, 1957), pp. 71–82.

5. Peter F. Drucker, *Management: Tasks, Responsibilities, Practices* (New York: Harper & Row, 1974), p. 62.

6. Kotler, *Marketing Management*, pp. 21–22.

7. *Ibid.*, pp. 27–28.

8. *Ibid.*, p. 28.

9. *Ibid.*

10. Theodore Levitt, "Marketing Myopia," *Harvard Business Review*, July-August 1960, pp. 45–56.

11. Lisabeth Weiner, "Changes in Lifestyle Spur Marketing Strategies," *American Banker*, September 1, 1987, p. 3.

CHAPTER 2

1. Kotler, *Marketing Management*, pp. 99–100.

2. *Ibid.*, p. 100.

3. *Ibid.*, p. 278.

CHAPTER 3

1. William J. Stanton and Charles Futrell, *Fundamentals of Marketing*, 8th edition (New York: McGraw-Hill Book Company, 1987), p. 40.
2. *Ibid.*, p. 12.
3. Kotler, *Marketing Management*, p. 14.
4. James S. Hensel, "The Essential Nature of the Marketing Management Process: An Overview," in Leonard L. Berry and L.A. Capaldini, eds., *Marketing for the Bank Executive* (New York: Petrocelli Books, Division of Mason-Lipscomb, 1974), p. 65.
5. This section, and especially the treatment of the benefits and prerequisites for planning, draws heavily upon Robert W. Joselyn and D. Keith Humphries, *An Introduction to Bank Marketing Planning* (Washington, D.C.: American Bankers Association, 1974).

CHAPTER 4

1. Sheshunoff & Company, Inc., P.O. Box 13203, Capitol Station, Austin, Texas 78711. The volume is entitled *Banks of (State name)*.
2. One of these is Decision Research Sciences, Inc., 300 Axewood East, Butler and Skippack Pikes, Ambler, Pennsylvania 19002. The volume is entitled *Branch Directory and Summary of Deposits*.

CHAPTER 5

1. Robert W. Joselyn and D. Keith Humphries, *An Introduction to Bank Marketing Planning* (Washington, D.C.: American Bankers Association, 1974). Much of the information contained in this chapter is based on this publication.
2. *Ibid.*, p. 28.
3. Kotler, *Marketing Management*, pp. 252 ff.
4. *Ibid.*, pp. 264–265.
5. There are FDIC regulations governing this type of promotion. For instance, the individuals responsible for approving the loan may not be given an incentive for generating loans since this could possibly result in lowered credit standards. The reader is advised to become familiar with these regulations, or to consult legal counsel, before implementing such an incentive program.

CHAPTER 6

1. B. Berelson and G. Steiner, *Human Behavior: An Inventory of Scientific Findings* (New York: Harcourt, Brace and World, 1964), pp. 239–40.
2. A.H. Maslow, *Motivation and Personality* (New York: Harper and Brothers, 1954), chapter 5.
3. Kotler, *Marketing Management*, pp. 139–140.
4. Richard P. Coleman, "The Continuing Significance of Social Class," *Journal of Consumer Research*, December 1983, pp. 270–272.
5. William D. Wells and George Gubar, "The Life Cycle Concept in Marketing Research," *Journal of Marketing Research*, November 1966, pp. 355–363.

6. Dan H. Robertson, Robert W. Joselyn, and Beverly Hadden, "Psychographics and the Automatic Teller," *Bank Marketing*, January 1974, pp. 19–23.

7. Arthur J. Lucey, "Maximizing Your ATM Network," *American Banker*, February 11, 1981, p. 4.

8. Frederick E. Webster, Jr. and Yoram Wind, *Organizational Buying Behavior* (Englewood Cliffs, N.J.: Prentice-Hall, Inc., 1972).

9. *Ibid.*, p. 188.

CHAPTER 7

1. Definition given by the American Marketing Association.

2. *Analysis of 1985 Bank Marketing Expenditures* (Chicago: Bank Marketing Association, 1986).

3. Luther H. Hodges, Jr., and Rolle Tillman, Jr., *Bank Marketing: Text and Cases* (Reading, Mass.: Addison-Wesley Publishing Company, 1968), p. 231.

4. *Ibid.*, p. 7.

5. *Ibid.*, p. 235.

6. Ronald Kurtz, *Strategies in Marketing Research*, revised edition (American Management Association Extension Institute, 1970), p. 114.

7. Robert W. Joselyn, *Designing the Marketing Research Project* (New York: Petrocelli/ Charter, 1977), p. 185.

8. Patricia J. Labaw, *Advanced Questionnaire Design* (Cambridge, Mass.: Abt Books, 1980), p. 87.

9. *Ibid.*, p. 65.

10. S. Smith, R. Brien, and J. Stafford, eds., *Readings in Marketing Information Systems* (Boston: Houghton Mifflin, 1968), p. 7.

11. Bertram Schoner and Kenneth P. Uhl, *Marketing Research, Information Systems and Decision Making* (New York: John Wiley & Sons, Inc., 1975), pp. 20–21.

CHAPTER 8

1. Kotler, *Marketing Management*, p. 260.

2. *Ibid.*, pp. 264–265.

3. Russell J. Haley, "Benefit Segmentation: A Decision Oriented Research Tool," *Journal of Marketing*, July 1963, pp. 30–35.

4. Stanton and Futrell, *Fundamentals of Marketing*, p. 158.

5. *Ibid.*, pp. 169–170.

6. *Ibid.*, p. 171.

7. Al Ries and Jack Trout, *Positioning: The Battle for Your Mind* (New York: McGraw-Hill, Inc., 1986), p. 2.

8. For additional positioning strategies, see Kotler, *Marketing Management*, p. 275.

CHAPTER 9

1. Kotler, *Marketing Management*, p. 463.

2. *Ibid.*, pp. 463–464.

3. Stanton and Futrell, *Fundamentals*, p. 496.

4. *Ibid.*, pp. 499–500.

5. *Ibid.*, pp. 220–222.

6. Ann N. Morrison, "The General Mills Brand of Managers," *Fortune*, January 12, 1981, pp. 98–107.

7. Joe W. Kizzia, "Free Checking Holds Firm in Two Big Markets as New Outbreaks Diminish," *Banking*, August 1973, p. 25.

8. Ronald J. Roderique, "Product Development—Not For Big Banks Only," *Bank Marketing*, May 1980.

9. Ralph W. Jones, "Management of New Products," *The Journal of Industrial Engineering*, September-October, 1958.

10. Josh Levine, "Test Marketing Vaults Into Bank Prominence," *Advertising Age*, January 12, 1981, p. 6.

11. For more information on the product management concept and why it is effective, see William J. Wichman, "Product Management: Lessons from the Package Goods Industry," *Journal of Retail Banking*, Winter, 1984, pp. 27–34, and "What Institutions Should Expect from their Product Managers," *American Banker*, February 7, 1986, pp. 4 ff.

12. Francis X. Shea and John H. Shain, "How Concept of Product Manager Works in Banking," *ABA Banking Journal*, October 1980, pp. 127–132.

13. For more details, see Peter F. Drucker, *Managing for Results* (New York: Harper and Row, 1964), especially Part I.

14. Charles H. Kline, "The Strategy of Product Policy," *Harvard Business Review*, July-August 1955, p. 100.

15. Richard T. Hise, *Essentials in Product/Service Strategy* (New York: Petrocelli Books, Division of Mason/Charter, 1976).

16. R.S. Alexander, "The Death and Burial of 'Sick' Products," *Journal of Marketing*, April 1964, pp. 1–2.

17. Hise, *Essentials in Product/Service Strategy*.

18. Kotler, *Marketing Management*, p. 371.

19. Alexander, "The Death and Burial of 'Sick' Products," p. 1.

CHAPTER 10

1. Philip Kotler, *Marketing Management—Analysis, Planning and Control*, 5th edition (Englewood Cliffs, N.J.: Prentice-Hall, Inc., 1984), pp. 505–506.

2. "Pricing Strategy in an Inflation Economy," *Business Week*, April 6, 1974, p. 43.

3. Jack W. Whittle, "Fundamental Truths About Pricing Financial Services," *Financial Marketing*, March 1979, p. 34.

4. Based on Joseph P. Guiltinan, *Pricing Bank Services: A Planning Approach* (Washington, D.C.: American Bankers Association, 1980), p. 12.

5. *Ibid.*, p. 72.

6. This and the discussion of skimming and penetration pricing are based on Joel Dean, "Pricing A New Product," *The Controller*, April 1955, pp. 163–164.

7. Benson P. Shapiro, "The Psychology of Pricing," *Harvard Business Review*, July-August 1968, p. 160.

8. Based on Alfred R. Oxenfeldt, "A Decision-Making Structure for Price Decisions," *Journal of Marketing*, 1973, p. 51.

9. Neil M. Ford, "Pricing Bank Services," a paper presented at the Seventh Annual Marketing Research Conference of the Bank Marketing Association, May 1974. This paper also appears in the proceedings of this conference entitled *Research as a Management Tool*, published by the Bank Marketing Association.

10. Kotler, *Marketing Management*, pp. 532–534.

11. For a thorough treatment of this subject, see Guiltinan, *Pricing Bank Services*, and G. Michael Moebs and Eva Moebs, *Pricing Financial Services* (Homewood, Ill.: Dow Jones-Irwin, 1986).

12. Guiltinan, *Pricing Bank Services*, p. 39.

13. *Ibid.*, p. 40.

14. *Bank Pricing Strategies* (Chicago, Ill.: Bank Marketing Association, 1985), p. 11.

15. "Pricing Bank Services: Theory and Practice," *ABA Banking Journal*, October 1980, p. 134.

16. Moebs, *Pricing Financial Services*, pp. 179–182.

17. Whittle, "Fundamental Truths About Pricing," p. 32.

CHAPTER 11

1. The majority of marketing texts devote little attention to the marketing of services. One notable exception is William J. Stanton and Charles Futrell, *Fundamentals of Marketing*, 8th edition (New York: McGraw-Hill Book Company, 1987), chapter 21. There are also two monographs devoted entirely to this problem. See Eugene M. Johnson, *An Introduction to the Problems of Service Marketing Management* (Newark, Del.: University of Delaware, Bureau of Economic and Business Research, 1964), and Donald D. Parker, *The Marketing of Consumer Services* (Seattle, Wash.: University of Washington, Business Study Series, 1960).

2. Any basic marketing book will have a complete discussion of the concept of a channel of distribution. For one example, see William J. Stanton and Charles Futrell, *Fundamentals of Marketing*, Part 5.

3. For those interested, there are three excellent publications devoted entirely to selecting bank locations. They are *A Guide to Selecting Bank Locations* (Washington, D.C.: American Bankers Association, 1968); James E. Littlefield, G. Jackson Burney, and William V. White, *Bank Branch Location: A Handbook of Effective Technique and Practice* (Chicago: Bank Marketing Association, 1973); and Rex O. Bennett, *Bank Location Analysis: Techniques and Methodology* (Washington, D.C., American Bankers Association, 1975).

4. See also L.H. Hodges, Jr., and Rollie Tillman, Jr., *Bank Marketing: Text and Cases* (Reading, Mass.: Addison-Wesley Publishing Company, 1968), pp. 95–101.

5. See *A Guide to Selecting Bank Locations*, pp. 39–46.

6. One of these is Decision Research Sciences, Inc., 300 Axewood East, Butler and Skippack Pikes, Ambler, Pennsylvania 19002. The volume is entitled *Branch Directory and Summary of Deposits*.

CHAPTER 12

1. "Bank Marketing Round Table," *Banking*, September 1971, p. 21.

2. *Analysis of 1985 Bank Marketing Expenditures* (Chicago: Bank Marketing Association, 1986).

3. David C. Casey, "Bank Management: Problems and Possibilities," *Business Horizons*, June 1970.

4. Robert W. Haas, "The Missing Link in Bank Marketing," *Atlanta Economic Review*, January-February 1974, p. 37.

5. While much research exists on this subject, the following can be considered representative examples: "Why Every Sale Must Have Two Parts," *Sales Management* (March 15, 1957), p. 90; D.L.A. Pym and H.D. Auld, "The Self-Rating As a Measure of Employee Satisfaction," *Occupational Psychology*, April 1965, pp. 103–113; and Roger Bellows, "The Weighted Application Blank Can Improve Retail Employee Selection," *Journal of Retailing*, Spring 1970, pp. 19–23.

6. David Mayer and Herbert M. Greenberg, "What Makes a Good Salesman?" *Harvard Business Review*, July-August 1964, pp. 119–125.

7. Philip Kotler, *Marketing Management—Analysis, Planning and Control*, 5th edition, (Englewood Cliffs, N.J.: Prentice Hall, Inc., 1984), p. 689.

8. Patrick Robinson and Bent Stidsen, *Personal Selling in a Modern Perspective* (Boston: Allyn and Bacon, Inc., 1967), p. 14.

9. For two important articles on this viewpoint see Franklin B. Evans, "Selling as a Dyadic Relationship—A New Approach," *The American Behavioral Scientist*, May 1963, pp. 76–79 and Frederick E. Webster, Jr., "Interpersonal Communication and Salesman Effectiveness," *Journal of Marketing* (July 1968), pp. 7–12.

10. Webster, "Interpersonal Communication," pp. 11–12.

11. For example, see L.H. Hodges, Jr., and Rollie Tillman, Jr., *Bank Marketing: Text and Cases* (Reading, Mass.: Addison-Wesley Publishing Company, 1968).

12. Robert M. Negri, "A Sales Training Program for Affiliates," *Bank Marketing*, December 1973, p. 25.

13. As an example, see *Selling Bank Services* (Washington, D.C.: American Bankers Association, 1988). The program consists of five books designed for tellers and written in a programmed learning format. The five books deal with checking account services, savings services, loans to individuals, safe deposit boxes and traveler's checks, and cross-selling.

14. For a treatment of the components that have contributed to the success of 10 banks that have built effective sales programs, see Leonard L. Berry, Charles M. Futrell, and Michael R. Bowers, *Bankers Who Sell* (Homewood, Ill.: Dow Jones-Irwin, 1985).

CHAPTER 13

1. These five questions were first suggested by H.D. Lasswell, *Power and Personality* (New York: W.W. Norton, 1948), pp. 37–51.

2. Russell H. Colley, *Defining Advertising Goals for Measured Advertising Results* (New York: Association of National Advertisers, Inc., 1961), p. 51.

3. Ralph S. Alexander, *Marketing Definitions: A Glossary of Marketing Terms* (Chicago: The American Marketing Association, 1960), p. 20.

4. Colley, *Defining Advertising Goals*, pp. 43–54.

5. *How Advertising in Recession Periods Affects Sales* (New York: American Business Press, Inc., 1979).

6. *Analysis of 1985 Bank Marketing Expenditures* (Chicago: Bank Marketing Association, 1986), p. 6.

7. This section is based largely on Colley, *Defining Advertising Goals*, chapters 1–4.

8. Philip Kotler, *Marketing Management—Analysis, Planning and Control*, 5th edition (Englewood Cliffs, N.J.: Prentice-Hall, Inc., 1984), pp. 643–644.

9. Colley, *Defining Advertising Goals*, p. 35.

10. Adapted from Kotler, *Marketing Management*, pp. 638–640.

11. *Analysis of 1979 Bank Marketing Expenditures* (Chicago: Bank Marketing Association, 1980), p. 3.

12. William J. Stanton and Charles Futrell, *Fundamentals of Marketing*, 8th edition (New York: McGraw-Hill Book Company, 1987), p. 474.

13. Stanton and Futrell, *Fundamentals of Marketing*, p. 468.

CHAPTER 14

1. The reader is directed to *An Introduction to Bank Marketing Planning* by Robert W. Joselyn and D. Keith Humphries (Washington, D.C.: American Bankers Association, 1974), upon which much of the information contained in this section has been based.

2. *Ibid.*, p. 25.

3. Kotler, *Marketing Management*, p. 719.

4. *Ibid.*, p. 720.

5. Joselyn and Humphries, *op. cit.*, p. 38.

6. Ibid.

CHAPTER 15

1. Michael P. Sullivan, "The Maturing of Corporate Communications," *Journal of Retail Banking*, Winter 1985–86, pp. 25–32.

2. Michael P. Sullivan, "PR and Marketing, Adversaries or Partners," *Bank Marketing*, April 1981, p. 23.

3. *Let's Consider Public Relations—An Occupational Guide* (New York: Public Relations Society of America, Inc., 1963), p. 3.

4. Robert L. Fegley, "The Organization and Its Publics" (Presentation to the Public Relations Course, Publicity Club of Chicago, Illinois, February 19, 1968), p. 2.

5. Philip Kotler and William Mindak, "Marketing and Public Relations, Should They Be Partners or Rivals?" *Journal of Marketing*, October 1978, p. 17.

6. Michael P. Sullivan, "Banks Should Manage Relations with the Media," *American Banker*, July 2, 1987, p. 4.

7. Michael P. Sullivan, "The Compleat Spokesperson Meets the Media," *American Banker*, March 26, 1986, pp. 4 ff.

8. William J. Stanton and Charles Futrell, *Fundamentals of Marketing*, 8th edition (New York: McGraw-Hill Book Company, 1987), pp. 598–599.

9. Jay Rosenstein, "Fed Issues First BHC Denial on a Consumer-Compliance Basis," *American Banker*, September 10, 1981, pp. 1 ff.

10. Karen Slater, "Local Uproar After Thrift Calls Loans," *American Banker*, September 23, 1981, p. 1.

11. Kotler and Mindak, "Marketing and Public Relations," p. 20.

CHAPTER 16

1. Charles P. Stetson, Jr., "The Reshaping of Corporate Financial Services," *Harvard Business Review*, September-October 1980, pp. 134–142.

CHAPTER 17

1. Deregulation, interstate banking, and nonbank competition might also be categorized as events taking place in banking's political-legal environment. However, because they so intimately affect the current and prospective competitive environment, they are categorized here for the purposes of this discussion.

2. Eric N. Berg, "Limited Banks' Giant Hurdle," *New York Times*, July 2, 1987, pp. D-1 and D-4.

3. Based on results of *Monitor 1987*, a subscriber service of Yankelovich Clancy Shulman, a marketing intelligence firm headquartered in Westport, Connecticut.

4. Joseph Asher, "Glass-Steagall: A Fresh Look," *ABA Banking Journal*, February 1981, p. 70.

5. Joseph Asher, "Survival Kit for Small Banks," *ABA Banking Journal*, September 1980, p. 51.

A · CONDUCTING MARKETING RESEARCH TO ASSIST IN A NEW PRODUCT PRICING DECISION

A	**CONDUCTING MARKETING RESEARCH TO ASSIST IN A NEW PRODUCT PRICING DECISION**

OVERVIEW

(For the purposes of this case, we asked the marketing research manager of the fictitious Marlton National Bank to review the steps she followed when conducting a recent marketing research project. That review follows.)

1. Defining the Problem

Our bank (Marlton National Bank) currently offers only one type of personal checking account:

> If the monthly minimum or average balance is $500 or more:
> No charge for checking
> If the monthly minimum or average balance is less than $500:
> Maintenance charge: $3.00
> Each check: $ .25

We recognized that there is a national consumerist movement requiring banks to offer a low-cost checking account for persons of limited means—that is, an account for individuals who write few checks and keep low average balances.

Exhibit A-1 Stratification of Personal Checking Accounts

Average Monthly Balance Range	No. of Accounts	Balances ($000)
0– 300	6,443	604
301– 500	2,761	966
501– 1,000	4,276	3,094
1,001– 2,500	4,238	6,549
2,501– 5,000	1,387	4,763
5,001– 10,000	560	3,819
10,001– 20,000	212	2,883
20,001– 50,000	90	2,674
50,001–100,000	21	1,436
100,001–250,000	8	1,194
250,001–500,000	2	675
500,001 or more	2	6,548
	20,000	35,205

Our marketing department, therefore, sought information to help design a new checking account that would appeal to that target audience and yet not reduce fee income so greatly as to be detrimental to the bank. We determined that research should be conducted to help us to:

A. establish a pricing structure that would

1. appeal to the target audience, both customers and noncustomers, and

2. minimize the loss of fee income to the bank.

B. estimate what percentage of our own customers might switch to the new account; and

C. estimate the number of new accounts that we might expect to draw from our competitors in response to the new product.

Since any pricing decision would surely result in a reduction in service charge income from existing customers, it was important to develop a product that would attract new customers to help offset that loss of income as much as possible.

2. Selecting the Sources of Information

A. *Secondary data*
From internal data, we learned that 46 percent, or 9,204 of our 20,000 personal checking accounts had average monthly balances of $500 or less. While these accounts provide only 4.5 percent of our total personal checking balances, they account for 100 percent of our personal checking service charge income of $51,750 per month. See Exhibit A-1.

B. *Primary data*
We wanted to measure the appeal of five alternative pricing schemes among low-balance checking customers. This type of information can be gathered only by surveying a sample of the target audience. The marketing research department worked with an outside research supplier in the design, implementation, and interpretation of the research.

3. Preparing the Data Collection Materials

It was determined that the telephone survey method would be most effective for this research. A questionnaire was developed to gather information on:

A. the type of checking account currently used by the respondent;

B. the number of checks written each month;

C. the respondent's stated likelihood of switching banks to save $1.00 per month in service charges;

D. reaction to five alternative pricing schemes; and

E. demographic information about the respondent.

We also determined that the best way to compare the relative appeal of each of the five pricing alternatives would be to use the trade-off analysis technique—that is, the potential pricing schemes would be paired, and the interviewer would ask the respondent to indicate which of the two pricing schemes he or she preferred. This would be done for five pairs of pricing schemes. The five pricing schemes to be tested were:

1. a $5.00 flat fee (no charge for checks written);

2. a $1.00 maintenance fee and $.35 per check;

3. a $2.00 maintenance fee; 8 free checks; $.50 each for checks written in excess of 8;

4. a $1.00 maintenance fee; 8 free checks; $.50 each for checks written in excess of 8; and

5. $.50 cents per check (no maintenance fee)

The respondents were asked to indicate a preference among the following five pairs: 1 or 2; 2 or 5; 3 or 2; 4 or 2; and 1 or 5. On the basis of this information, we were able to rank the five pricing schemes in order of appeal to the target audience.

4. Designing the Sample

We felt we could safely assume that our own low-balance checking customers were typical of low-balance checking customers in general. Furthermore, from our own checking account system, we could easily identify and draw the names and addresses of customers with balances under $500. Therefore, we decided to sample only our own low-balance checking customers.

We observed from our secondary data that the number of accounts with balances under $500 were not evenly distributed among the balance ranges from zero to $500. Rather, there were more than twice as many accounts with balances of $300 or less than with balances from $301 to $500. Since these groups were likely to be different from one another demographically and attitudinally, we decided to draw a large enough sample from each of these two balance categories that they might be analyzed separately.

In determining the size of our sample, we recognized that the larger our sample, the more statistically reliable our data would be, but also the greater our cost would be. We decided that interviewing a sample of 100 each of our customers with balances under $300 and between $301 and $500 would provide us with sufficiently reliable data for our purposes.

Drawing the Sample

Our goal was to obtain 100 completed interviews from each balance category. In drawing the sample, the following facts were taken into consideration:

- Many customers have unlisted telephone numbers.

- Those with listed numbers may be difficult to reach at home.

- Some customers will refuse to participate or will terminate the interview before it is completed.

Therefore, we made the following assumptions:

- Half of our accounts will have unlisted numbers.

- We will be successful in reaching only half of the customers called.

- Half of those reached will complete the interview.

On the basis of these assumptions, we required approximately 800 customer names and addresses from each balance category. If only half actually did have listed telephone numbers, we would be providing the research firm with four names and numbers for every completed interview desired.

Knowing that there were 6,443 customers with $300 balances or less, and 2,761 with balances of $301 to $500, we prepared instructions for the programming department to draw a systematic sample as follows:

- For customers with balances of $300 or less, draw every eighth account (6,443 ÷ 800 = 8.05; drawing every eighth will give us 805 names).

- For customers with balances from $301 to $500, draw every fourth account (2,761 ÷ 800 = 3.45; drawing every fourth will give us

Exhibit A-2 Age of Respondents

	No. of Respondents	Balance $0–$300	Balance $301–$500
Total	200	100	100
By Age			
25 or less	30	21	9
26–45	103	46	57
46–60	50	24	26
More than 60	13	6	7
Refused to Respond	4	3	1
Average Age	38.7	37.4	40.0

Exhibit A-3 Household Income of Respondents

	Total	Balance $0–$300	Balance $301–$500	Age 25 or Less	Age 26–45	Age 46–60	Age Over 60
Total Income	200	100	100	30	103	50	13
	100.0	100.0	100.0	100.0	100.0	100.0	100.0
Less than $15,000	24	20	4	9	4	7	4
	12.0	20.0	4.0	30.0	3.9	14.0	30.8
$15,000-24,999	29	19	10	6	19	3	1
	14.5	19.0	10.0	20.0	18.4	6.0	7.7
$25,000-49,999	96	36	60	8	55	25	7
	48.0	36.0	60.0	26.7	53.4	50.0	53.8
$50,000 or more	24	11	13	3	12	8	1
	12.0	11.0	13.0	10.0	11.7	16.0	7.7
Refused	27	14	13	4	13	7	—
	13.5	14.0	13.0	13.3	12.6	14.0	—

690 names, which is expected to be adequate given our conservative assumptions about unlisted numbers and incompleted interviews).

The sample was drawn by computer and sent to an outside firm that looked up the telephone numbers.

5. Collecting the Information

We instructed the research firm to conduct the interviews in the evening during the week (from 4 to 9 P.M.) and on weekends (between noon and 6 P.M.). We held a training session with the interviewers during which we reviewed the questionnaire and answered their questions about the study. Participants were not to be told that our bank was sponsoring the research, but rather that they had been selected at random to participate in this banking study. We felt that they might be more open in general, especially about their likelihood of switching banks, if they were not aware that they were speaking to a representative of their checking account bank.

6. Analyzing the Data

Much more data was gathered and tabulated for this project than is reported here. The tables that are presented covered the key issues and enabled us to see the differences in response to the key questions between the very low and moderately low-balance customers and between four different age groups of customers, as well as for the sample of 200 respondents as a whole. Through our analysis of the data we answered the 15 questions listed below:

A. *Demographics*

1. Looking at Exhibit A-2, is there a relationship between age of customer and average checking balance? If so, describe that relationship, making specific reference to both younger and older age groups. Which age group contains the largest proportion of customers with balances under $500?

2. Looking at Exhibit A-3, is there a relationship between level of household income and size of average balance? If so, what is that relationship?

Exhibit A-4   **Likelihood of Switching Banks to Save $1**

Question:

"If another bank in your area had a monthly fee for a checking account that was $1 less than your bank charges, and everything else was the same, how likely do you think you would be to move your checking account to that bank?"

| | | Balance | | Age | | | |
	Total	$0–$300	$301–$500	25 or Less	26–45	46–60	Over 60
Total	200	100	100	30	103	50	13
	100.0	100.0	100.0	100.0	100.0	100.0	100.0
Very likely	25	15	10	2	12	10	1
	12.5	15.0	10.0	6.7	11.7	20.0	7.7
Somewhat likely	41	25	16	6	27	7	1
	20.5	25.0	16.0	20.0	26.2	14.0	7.7
Not very likely	62	26	36	11	32	14	2
	31.0	26.0	36.0	36.7	31.1	28.0	15.4
Not at all likely	72	34	38	11	32	19	9
	36.0	34.0	38.0	36.7	31.1	38.0	69.2

3. Is there a relationship between age and income? If so, what reasons might there be for that?

B. *Likelihood of Switching Banks*

We recognized that asking people what they would do "if . . ." has only limited value. Asking such questions opens the door to conjecture and to influence by all of the factors that affect customer behavior. Generally, it is better to ask people questions based upon their actual past behavior than to ask what they "might" do. Nevertheless, the answers to this question were helpful in determining which groups of customers might be more likely to change banks in reaction to a cost saving.

Switchers were of concern to us because (1) they are our best prospects among noncustomers, and (2) among our own customers, they are the ones we would have the most difficulty retaining in the face of stiff competition from a comparable product.

4. Looking at Exhibit A-4, what percentage of total respondents indicated that they are very or somewhat likely to switch to save $1 in monthly fees?

5. Which age groups appear more likely to switch? Which least?

6. Which balance group appears more likely to switch?

7. Putting the answers to questions 5 and 6 together, how would you complete this statement?: "_____ customers who are in the _____ group are the ones who are most likely to switch banks to save on checking fees." Looking at Exhibit A-3, what proportion of the bank's customers with balances under $500 fall into that group? What percentage of customers in the $0–$300 balance range fall into that group?

C. *Checking Activity*

8. Looking at Exhibit A-5, what can we say about the number of checks written by those 25 and under and those 26–60?

9. Complete these statements: "The largest number of very low-balance customers write _____ checks per month; the largest number of moderately low balance ($301–$500) customers write _____ checks per month."

10. If you were asked to describe two typical customers in terms of number of checks written per month, how many checks would each of those two customers write? (Hint: look at the modal range for the two balance groups.)

D. *Pricing Preference*

11. What are the two sample customers, described in question 10, paying for checking today with Marlton National's current pricing? What would they pay at each of the five pricing schemes being tested?

Exhibit A-5 Number of Checks Written Each Month

		Balance		Age			
	Total	$0–$300	$301–$500	25 or Less	26–45	46–60	Over 60
Total	200	100	100	30	103	50	13
	100.0	100.0	100.0	100.0	100.0	100.0	100.0
1 – 3	9	9	—	5	—	3	1
	4.5	9.0	—	16.7	—	6.0	7.7
4 – 6	37	28	9	6	20	7	3
	18.5	28.0	9.0	20.0	19.4	14.0	23.1
7 – 9	29	12	17	5	15	6	2
	14.5	12.0	17.0	16.7	14.6	12.0	15.4
10 – 12	51	20	31	5	26	16	2
	25.5	20.0	31.0	16.7	25.2	32.0	15.4
13 – 15	28	12	16	2	16	6	4
	14.0	12.0	16.0	6.7	15.5	12.0	30.8
16 – 18	9	5	4	2	4	3	—
	4.5	5.0	4.0	6.7	3.7	6.0	—
19 – 24	17	8	9	3	13	1	—
	8.5	8.0	9.0	10.0	12.6	2.0	—
25 – 35	16	4	12	1	9	5	1
	8.0	4.0	12.0	3.3	8.7	10.0	7.7
36 or more	2	1	1	—	—	2	—
	1.0	1.0	1.0	—	—	4.0	—
Do not know	2	1	1	1	—	1	—
	1.0	1.0	1.0	3.3	—	2.0	—
Average	12.14	10.51	13.78	9.86	12.72	13.00	10.54
Median	11	10	12	9	11	11	10
Modal range	10–12	4–6	10–12	4–6	10–12	10–12	13–15

Note: In statistics, the *mode* of a set of numbers is that value which occurs with the greatest frequency. In the chart above, it is the range that contains the largest number of each segment of customers. The *median* is the middle value, or the average (mean) of the two middle values. In the above, where there are 100 customers in the group, the median is the average value for the 50th and 51st customers. Half fall above and half below that value.

	Checks ___ written	Checks ___ written
Charge at current pricing	___	___
1. $5.00 flat fee	___	___
2. $1.00; $.35/check	___	___
3. $2.00; 8 free checks; $.50/check over 8	___	___
4. $1.00; 8 free checks; $.50/check over 8	___	___
5. $.50/check	___	___

12. For each of our six customer groups (very low and moderately low-balance customers plus the four age groups), we wanted to rank the pricing schemes on the basis of the information in Exhibit A-6. Starting with the lowest balance group, develop the ranking of the five pricing schemes for each of the six groups. Enter these rankings in Exhibit A-7. Hint: look at the responses to the first pair of pricing schemes, and write the preferred scheme on a piece of paper above the less-favored scheme, leaving space between them. Then look at the second pair and position the $.50/check scheme on your paper in the appropriate position relative to the $1.00 and $.35/check scheme. Continue through all five pairs. If two schemes appear to have equal value, give each the same rank and drop down two positions in assigning the next rank. (For example, you may rank the five schemes for one customer group as 1, 2, 2, 4, and 5 rather than 1, 2, 3, 4, and 5 because two had equal appeal.)

13. Not only were we attempting to provide customer satisfaction with our pricing, but we were also concerned with the "profitable volume" component of the marketing concept. Therefore, we wanted to rank the five pricing schemes from the bank's perspective. Prepare two rankings, one for the customer who writes 5 checks per month and one for the customer who writes 11 checks per month. Using the grid developed for question 11, which shows the bank's service charge income at each of the proposed pricing schemes, rank

Exhibit A-6   **Results of Trade-Off Between Pairs of Pricing Schemes**

		Balance		Age			
	Total	$0–$300	$301–$500	25 or Less	26–45	46–60	Over 60
Total	200 100.0	100 100.0	100 100.0	30 100.0	103 100.0	50 100.0	13 100.0
A monthly fee of $5.00 and no per-check charge	113 56.5	44 44.0	69 69.0	18 60.0	58 56.3	30 60.0	5 38.5
A monthly fee of $1.00 and $.35 per check	87 43.5	56 56.0	31 31.0	12 40.0	45 43.7	20 40.0	8 61.5
A monthly fee of $1.00 and $.35 per check	147 73.5	70 70.0	77 77.0	21 70.0	76 73.8	39 78.0	8 61.5
No monthly fee and $.50 per check	53 26.5	30 30.0	23 23.0	9 30.0	27 26.2	11 22.0	5 38.5
A monthly fee of $2.00 and $.50 for each check over 8 with first 8 free	109 54.5	52 52.0	57 57.0	11 36.7	61 59.2	29 58.0	7 53.8
A monthly fee of $1.00 and $.35 for each check	91 45.5	48 48.0	43 43.0	19 63.3	42 40.8	21 42.0	6 46.2
A monthly fee of $1.00 and $.50 for each check over 8 with first 8 free	120 60.0	64 64.0	56 56.0	16 53.3	66 64.1	29 58.0	8 61.5
A monthly fee of $1.00 and $.35 for each check	78 39.0	35 35.0	43 43.0	14 46.7	36 35.0	20 40.0	5 38.5
A monthly fee of $5.00 and no per-check charge	116 58.0	48 48.0	58 68.0	16 53.3	61 59.2	30 60.0	5 38.5
No monthly fee and $.50 per check	82 41.0	51 51.0	31 31.0	14 46.7	41 39.8	19 38.0	8 61.5

the schemes from the bank's income perspective, and enter the results in Exhibit A-7.

E. *Developing a Pricing Recommendation*

14. Referring to the grid of eight rankings (six for our various customer groups and two for the bank), we used a process of elimination to narrow down to the recommended pricing alternatives. For example, the pricing scheme that is one of the most acceptable to the bank ($.50 per check with no maintenance fee) is the least acceptable to most customer groups. Work through the elimination process, indicating for each scheme that you eliminate your reasons for doing so.

15. Which two pricing alternatives would you recommend? If you were making the final decision, which pricing scheme would you choose? Defend your choice.

7. Reporting the Results

After analyzing the data and discussing their implications with our own staff and the research supplier, we wrote the research report. The format that we used is one that management finds most informative and helpful:

A. *The Executive Summary:*
This was a three-page summary of the key findings and resulting recommendations. The information was presented in bullet-point format rather than in lengthy narrative.

B. *Methodology:*
In this section, we set forth:

- our objectives for the study;
- the background to the questionnaire design;
- how we designed and selected the sample;
- our experience in the data collection phase (number of calls attempted and completed, length of interview, and completion rate); and
- information on statistical reliability of the results.

Exhibit A-7 **Rankings of Pricing Schemes**

	Customer Ranking						Bank Ranking	
	$0–$300	$301–$500	25 or Less	26–45	46–60	Over 60	No. of Checks 5	11
$5.00 + $.50 + 8 free								
$2.00 + $.50 + 8 free	___	___	___	___	___	___	___	___
$1.00 + $.35	___	___	___	___	___	___	___	___
$5	___	___	___	___	___	___	___	___
$.50	___	___	___	___	___	___	___	___

C. *Detailed Findings:*

In this, the largest section of the report, we addressed each of the key findings, in order, with the supporting tables and a detailed interpretation of the findings.

D. *The Questionnaire:*

A copy of the survey instrument is always included as an appendix to the research report so that the reader may see how the questions were worded.

**MARKETING PLAN FOR A NEW PRODUCT:
HOME EQUITY CREDIT LINE**

(This is a hypothetical case that demonstrates the steps used in developing a commercial bank's marketing plan for a new product.)

EXECUTIVE SUMMARY

This plan constitutes a recommendation for the introduction of an equity-secured revolving line of credit in March of next year. Some key features of the proposed product are:

Line limits	$10,000 to $100,000
Interest rate	Prime (our bank's) plus 1.75 percent, adjusted quarterly
Means of access	Checks and automated teller
Term/Minimum monthly Payment	10 years; $50 or 1/120th of outstanding principal plus accrued interest (whichever is greater)
Fees	Bank's cost for appraisal, recording of mortgage, other closing costs (maximum of $350)

We anticipate a first-year profit margin of 2.0 percent on average outstandings of just over $6 million. Year two's profit margin is expected to be 2.5 percent of average outstandings of $11.7 million.

Exhibit B-1 Home Equity Credit Line Financial Projections

	Year 1	Year 2
Applications received	1,000	600
Applications approved (60%)	600	360
Total accounts	600	960
Total volume of lines (at $30,000 average)	$18 mil.	$28.8 mil.
Number in use at 75%	450	720
Outstandings (at $20,000 average)	$ 9 mil.	$14.4 mil.
Average outstandings for year	$ 6.05 mil.[1]	$11.7 mil.[2]
Income		
Interest margin at 3.25%	$196,625	$380,250
Credit life insurance at 0.1%	6,050	11,700
Net income	$202,675	$391,950
Expenses		
Advertising & promotion	$ 45,375	$ 29,250
Operations (.6%)	36,300	70,200
Total expense	$ 81,675	$ 99,450
Net profit	$121,000	$292,500

[1]Assumes 400 new accounts within 6 months.
[2]Assumes new accounts are spread evenly throughout the year.

In year two and the following years, we anticipate a net margin of profit of 2.5 percent, based on the assumption that the bank's cost of funds continues at prime rate minus 1.5 percent, that no increase in staff will be needed in the Consumer Lending Division, and that revenues and expenses are as follows:

Net interest income	3.25%[1]
Insurance income	.10
Total income	3.35%
Operating expense	.60%
Marketing expense	.25%
Total expense	.85%
Net profit margin	2.50%

We project that at the end of year one, we will have 600 approved lines of credit with the average line being $30,000 and total lines approved being $18 million. We expect 75 percent of these lines to be in use, with average outstandings of $20,000, so that total outstandings at the end of year one will be $9 million. Net first year profit will be $121,000 on average outstandings of $6.05 million, rising to $292,500 in year two. (See Exhibit B-1.)

Introductory promotion of this new product will consist of newspaper advertising, direct mail with follow-up telemarketing to a selected sample of current credit and deposit customers as well as to targeted prospects within our branch trade areas, statement inserts, point-of-sale materials, and personal sales efforts by our customer service representatives.

At 1.75 percent over the prime rate, our pricing is highly competitive, while affording us a profit margin of 2.5 percent in year two. (Year one's profit margin is narrower because of the high initial cost of product introduction.)

We believe these plans and projections to be reasonable and conservative, and we fully expect to meet and exceed our projection of $9 million in outstandings within 12 months.

I. SITUATION ANALYSIS

A. Economic Data

Second mortgage lending, the foundation of this product, has grown considerably in the past 15 to 20 years due largely to the effects of inflation:

1. Inflation in the 1970s caused housing values to more than quadruple while mortgage debt grew at a slower rate. As a result, the total value of household equity in the United States grew from $876 billion to $3.5 trillion between 1970 and 1981.

2. Record high interest rates in the late 1970s and early 1980s caused a tightening of the housing market. Homeowners chose to borrow against the equity in their houses to make home improvements rather than move.

3. Also, during the late 1970s, banks found second mortgages more attractive than first mortgages because their shorter maturities were more desirable, while the cost of funds was high and the future of rates uncertain.

These factors were felt no less in our own trade area than in the rest of the country.

B. Demographic Data

Large increases in home ownership during the 1970s had their foundation in demographics: the post-World War II baby boom inflated the size of the generation that was ready to buy homes in the 1970s. At the same time, the divorce rate increased and the number of single people purchasing houses increased. These factors produced strong housing demand, which peaked in 1978. From 1970 to 1978, sales of existing houses rose from 1.6 million to 13.9 million nationally.

Research indicates that the demographic profile of users of equity-secured credit closely parallel the demographics of our own customer base. Users tend to be high-income heads of "full-nest" households, generally males age 35 to 49 years. Credit needs are high at this stage of life, while liquid assets tend to be relatively low. Applicants for this type of credit typically cite children's education and home remodeling as the purpose for which the funds will be used.

With regard to trends for the future, we can expect that the segment most likely to use equity credit lines will grow as the general population matures and as housing values in our trade area continue to escalate.

C. Political/Legal Considerations

A major factor that is expected to further stimulate the demand for equity-secured credit is the Tax Reform Act of 1986. Starting in 1987, borrowers will no longer be able to deduct from their taxable income all the interest they pay on most consumer debt. The only consumer debt interest that will remain deductible when the full effect of the law is in place (with certain limitations) is debt secured by the equity in a house. Many borrowers will use equity-secured credit lines and installment loans to pay off other forms of debt in order to retain the interest deductibility. With the large amount of publicity being given to this phase of the new tax law, and with more expected around tax time next year (when our promotion will be in full swing), the timing of this new product introduction could not be better.

D. Social/Cultural Considerations

The social and psychological stigma attached to putting one's home up for collateral for a loan has gradually diminished. Homeowners who are the primary target market for this type of credit, namely those with household incomes of $50,000 and more, with housing values in excess of $100,000, and in their peak wage-earning years, are not subject to this bias to the extent that their parents were.

E. Competitive Analysis

Most major area banks, as well as a number of nonbank competitors, are already offering this type of product. Three of them are being very aggressive in their promotional efforts, which is increasing market awareness of, and interest in, the product. Additionally, numerous competitors have blanketed our trade area with direct mail programs. Included among these are banks from neighboring states and two finance companies.

Exhibit B-2 compares our product features and pricing with our four major competitors. At prime plus 1.75 percent, ours is the best rate in the area. This feature helps offset the fact that we will lend only up to 70 percent of the available equity in the house, compared with 75 and 80 percent by our competition. With $50,000 in loanable equity, we would lend a maximum of $35,000 compared with $37,500 and $40,000 by our competitors.

A major competitive advantage of our product is the monthly payment: with a repayment period of 10 years and a minimum payment of 1/120th of outstanding principal, our monthly payment at any given loan amount is considerably less than all but 1 of our major competitors. At the average projected outstanding principal of $20,000, the amount of principal payment required monthly would be only about $167 compared with $278 to $400 by 3 of our major competitors. (See Exhibit B-3.)

Exhibit B-2   Equity Credit Line Competitive Comparison

	Marlton National	Statewide National	Peoples Savings	City National	First National
Interest Rate	Prime +1.75%	90-day T-bill plus 5.25%	Prime +3.0%	Prime +2.0%	Prime +2.0%
Frequency of Rate Adjustment	Quarterly	Quarterly	Quarterly	With prime change	Monthly
Minimum/ Maximum	$10,000/ 100,000	$10,000/ none	$5,000/ 50,000	$10,000/ 90,000	$10,000/ 100,000
Percent of Equity Loaned	70%	Not quoted	80%	75%	75%
Payment/ Repayment Terms	$50 minimum; 1/120th of principal plus accrued interest	$50 minimum; 1/50th of principal, plus accrued interest	$50 minimum; 1/72nd of principal, plus accrued interest	$50 minimum; 1/180th of principal plus accrued interest	$150 minimum; 1/60th of principal, plus accrued interest
Access Method	Checks/ATM	Checks	Checks-telephone transfer	Checks; premier credit card	—
Minimum to Access	$100	$100	$100	None	—
Fees/Other Requirements	Actual closing costs; may be funded from credit line	Actual closing costs; paid in cash	Actual closing costs; title insurance required	$300 closing costs; $25 application fee; $25 annual fee	$175 closing cost

Exhibit B-3   Competitive Comparison of Monthly Payments

Approximate amount of principal payment required at stated outstanding principal balance.

Bank/Principal Due Monthly	$10,000	$20,000	$50,000	$90,000
City National 1/180th	$ 56	$ 111	$ 278	$ 500
Marlton National 1/120th	**83**	**167**	**417**	**750**
Peoples Savings 1/72nd	139	278	694	1,250
First National 1/60th	167	333	833	1,500
Statewide National 1/50th	200	400	1,000	1,800

F. Self-Analysis

1. Good Experience with Equity-Secured Installment Credit
Our bank has been doing second mortgage lending for several years and currently has outstandings of $9 million in fixed rate second mortgage installment loans. The deliquency rate on this type of credit is low: 0.9 percent compared with 1.94 percent for nonequity secured installment credit. Furthermore, we have had no charge-offs in this portfolio within the past 3 years.

2. Success with Unsecured Revolving Credit
Three years ago, our bank offered an unsecured revolving line of credit to the market, and today we have the dominant share of this business in our trade area. This experience in selling, delivering, and servicing revolving credit will serve us well as we begin offering a secured revolving line of credit.

3. Need to Be Competitive
We will be the last bank in our trade area to offer an equity-secured credit line. Given the recent and projected popularity of this type of credit, we must offer this product in order to remain competitive.

4. Predominance of Fixed-Rate Credit in Portfolio
Even with the popularity of our unsecured revolving credit line, 75 percent of our consumer credit outstandings are at a fixed rate. In the current relatively low-rate environment, and in light of our corporate objectives, it is advisable to grow the variable rate component of our consumer credit in order to reduce the risk associated with future rate increases.

5. Current Penetration of Target Market
Our recent customer survey demonstrated what we believed to be the case—namely, that we have an above-average share of suburban households with incomes greater than $50,000 and with household heads in the 35 to 55 age range. This profile closely matches that of the likely equity credit line user, giving us a captive market to tap for this new product and providing us with an opportunity for product expansion.

6. Ability to Price Competitively
For a variety of reasons, we are uniquely positioned to price this product competitively and still realize or exceed the profit margin

required by the bank's corporate objective. We have an excellent computer software package that has been enhanced and tested through several years' experience with unsecured revolving credit. We have an experienced revolving credit operations department that is staffed to handle the expected increase in volume due to this new product introduction. We have lenders experienced in buying a high quality of equity credit. The better the credit quality, the lower the costs related to collection and servicing.

G. Summary of Problems and Opportunities

1. Problems
a. We are a late entrant to the market for this product.
b. Our consumer credit portfolio is still too heavily dependent upon fixed-rate assets.

2. Opportunities
a. The new tax law is expected to stimulate the market for equity-secured credit just as we are entering the market.
b. Our customer profile matches the profile of the target market.
c. Our consumer credit systems and operations are experienced in dealing with revolving lines of credit.
d. Our customer service representatives are comfortable selling revolving credit, and we can capitalize on this experience.
e. We have a proven track record of success in equity-secured lending.
f. Our new product is highly competitive in terms of rate and monthly payment amount.

II. OBJECTIVES

A. Corporate Objectives

Introduction of the proposed equity credit line is consistent with the following corporate objectives as set forth in the bank's 5-year master plan:

1. We will increase the ratio of interest-sensitive assets in the bank's portfolio.

2. We will achieve a profit margin of at least 2 percent on each of our consumer credit products.

B. Marketing Objectives and Goals

1. Increase the ratio of interest-sensitive assets in our loan portfolio.

Goal 1: Generate outstandings at the end of year one of $9 million in this variable rate product.

Goal 2: Generate a total of 600 equity credit lines in the first year, with 450 (75 percent) lines in use.

2. Price our products to reflect the cost of doing business and to generate at least a 2 percent margin on outstandings.

Goal 3: Generate net revenue in year one of $202,675 and year two of $391,950.

Goal 4: Achieve a net profit of $121,000 in year one and $292,500 in year two (or 2 percent and 2.5 percent, respectively).

3. Create and maintain an image of our bank as a provider of a full range of consumer banking products.

Goal 5: Achieve a 30 percent level of awareness among the target market of our bank as a provider of equity credit.

4. Train customer contact staff and provide them with the materials they need to be effective in selling our consumer banking products.

Goal 6: Conduct training for customer contact staff during second and third weeks of February.

Goal 7: Provide point-of-sale materials to branches during last week of February.

5. Develop an effective direct mail and telemarketing program to introduce the Home Equity Credit Line.

Goal 8: Achieve a 1 percent response rate to the direct mail campaign.
Goal 9: Achieve a 5 percent response rate to the telemarketing campaign.

Exhibit B-4	**Product Description for Equity Credit Line**
Definition	Variable rate revolving line of credit secured by equity in borrower's primary residence
Target Market	High income heads of full-nest households
Interest Rate	Bank's prime plus 1.75 percent Rate adjusted quarterly Periodic rate (rate divided by 365 days) charged daily against outstanding principal balance
Minimum Line	$10,000
Maximum Line	$100,000
Access Device	Checks Automated teller
Minimum Amount to Access Line	$100
Credit Review	Annual in-house performance review and updated credit bureau report Reappraisal of property every 5 years
Payment Terms	Higher of $50 or 1/120th of principal, plus applicable interest
Fees	Actual costs of appraisal, mortgage recording fee, property search, closing fee, and credit report fee (total up to $350) May be funded from credit line or paid in cash Charged only on approved lines
Insurance	Optional: credit life Required: fire
Late Charges	5 percent of entire billing amount if not paid within 15 days of due date

III. DETAILED MARKETING STRATEGY & TACTICS

A. Target Market

The principal target market for the Equity Credit Line is high-income heads of "full-nest" households—generally males age 35 to 49 years. Credit needs are high at this stage of life while assets tend to be relatively low. Research indicates that applicants for this type of credit line typically cite children's education and home improvement as the initial purpose for such credit.

We expect many existing customers to become users of this new product. With this product, however, we hope to attract many new customers to the bank meeting the profile of the target market.

B. Product Strategy: Product and Market Expansion

The Equity Credit Line recommended in this plan has been designed to offer features and benefits that meet consumer needs, to be competitively superior, and to comply with all legal and regulatory requirements. This section presents the features of the proposed product, lists the key features and the matching consumer benefits to be stressed in product sales, and describes our target market.

1. Product Description
For a complete description of this product, see Exhibit B-4.

2. Features and Benefits
A chart of features and benefits is presented in Exhibit B-5.

C. Pricing Strategy

We are recommending a penetration pricing strategy that both meets the financial objectives of the bank (2 percent profit margin on retail credit products) and positions us as the most affordable equity credit line in the city. The latter is due to our relatively low rate (1.75 percent over prime, compared with 2 percent or more) and our 120-month repayment period. We believe that this pricing will give us the competitive edge needed as a late entrant to this market.

D. Promotion Strategy

We propose a niche strategy, aiming at a carefully selected target audience from our own customers and from noncustomers within the trade area. Our tactics include advertising, point-of-sale promotion, and direct mail with follow-up telemarketing. While we will highlight the affordability of our equity credit line in comparison with the competition, we will not adopt a "bargain-basement" approach which would attract unqualified applicants.

1. Advertising Tactics (Responsibility: advertising manager)
We propose using limited print advertising in the principal daily

Exhibit B-5 **Equity Credit Line Features and Benefits**

Feature	Benefit
A revolving line of credit	You can use the amount of credit you want when you want it
	No need to reapply every time you need credit
	As you repay your loan, the funds become available to you again
Secured by the equity in the borrower's primary residence	The amount of credit available to you is limited only by the amount of equity in your house (and, of course, your ability to repay)
	The interest you pay is tax deductible
The interest rate is the bank's prime plus 1.75 percent, adjusted quarterly	Your interest rate is lower than the rate on unsecured credit lines and installment loans
	You pay interest only on what you use
	Your interest rate will fall when rates in general fall—you are not locked in to a fixed rate
	While the prime might change at any time, your rate cannot change more than quarterly
$100 or more may be accessed by writing a check and through our automated teller network	Obtaining the funds is as easy as getting cash out of your checking account
	No need to reapply every time you need funds
	It is confidential; the people to whom you write checks will not know that you are using credit
Customer may borrow up to 70 percent of the appraised value less the first mortgage (if credit review indicates ability to repay)	You can put the unused equity in your house to work for you
Monthly payment is $50 or 1/120th of outstanding principal, whichever is greater	Very low monthly payment because repayment is spread over 10 years
	You can pay the line off faster if you wish—there is no prepayment penalty

newspaper and in the weekly papers in upscale suburban communities. The objective will be to increase general awareness that our bank has introduced this new competitively priced product. We do not propose the use of radio or television because these media reach too broad an audience for this product.

2. Point-of-Sale Promotion (Responsibility: advertising manager)
Our in-branch lobby displays will include posters, counter cards with a "take-one" pocket for the announcement brochure, and rack brochures in the style of our other product brochures. These materials will be distributed to the branches following the kick-off and training sessions and coinciding with the first newspaper ad and the first wave of the direct mail solicitation.

Statement inserts describing the product will be inserted in all retail checking and savings' statements during the month of March. In addition, computer-printed statement messages will tell customers to "Ask about our new Equity Credit Line, the affordable way for homeowners to meet all their financing needs."

3. Direct Mail and Follow-Up Telemarketing Tactics (Responsibility: sales promotion manager)
A direct mail package will be sent to targeted and prescreened customers and noncustomers, as follows:

a. Over the 4 months of March through June, we will stagger our mailing to the following customer groups:
   - Mortgage customers
   - Secondary mortgage installment loan/former customers
   - Other installment loan and unsecured credit line customers meeting certain credit criteria

b. In addition, we will obtain a list of subscribers to national business publications and professionals at their home addresses.

Each of the names generated will be screened through the credit bureau according to criteria established by the consumer loan division.

E. Distribution Strategy and Tactics

We expect a large proportion of applicants for this product to be walk-ins to branches. An essential element of our program will be product knowledge and sales training specifically for the Equity Credit Line. We would accomplish this through tactics:

1. Develop a product manual consisting of product features and benefits, forms, and procedures for taking applications and handling loan closing after approval by central lending (responsibility: product manager).

2. Hold a kick-off meeting for all branch managers and assistant managers, regionals, and division heads at which the product plan will be reviewed. The product manuals for each customer service representative (CSR) will be distributed at this meeting with instructions to the managers that CSR's should be instructed to review the manual and that the managers should include discussion of the new product in a staff meeting (responsibility: product manager).

3. Half-day training sessions will be held for CSR's in groups of 12 to 16 over the 2-week period prior to rollout. Training results will be measured by means of a pre- and posttest (responsibility: training manager).

4. A special mailing will be done to all commercial account officers explaining the product to them and suggesting that they discuss it with the executives of the companies in their portfolios. (Responsibility: product manager)

Employee incentives are not being planned for the introduction of this product.

IV. MEASUREMENT AND EVALUATION OF RESULTS

In order to monitor the success of this new product introduction from the start and to measure our progress toward our stated goals, the following reports will be generated:

Goals 1 and 2: The consumer loan division will provide the product manager with a report showing as of each month-end:

- number of Equity Credit Lines
- number of lines in use
- dollar volume of lines approved
- dollar outstandings (amount in use)

Goals 3 and 4: The product manager will produce for the marketing director an interim revenue and profitability report (using information from the accounting department) 6 months after introduction (that is, report by 9/15 with data as of 8/31). Thereafter, reports will be produced at the end of each calendar quarter.

Goal 5: Questions to measure awareness of our Equity Credit Line will be incorporated into our quarterly advertising tracking research. First results will be available to the product manager from marketing research in early May.

Goal 6: The results of the pre- and posttests conducted during product and sales training will be provided by the training department to the product manager by March 15.

Goal 7: By copy of the memo that accompanied the point-of-sale materials sent to the branches, the marketing director will be informed by the advertising manager that these materials were distributed on time (before February 27).

Goals 8 and 9: To measure the effectiveness of our direct mail and telemarketing programs, the advertising manager will report to the marketing director on the response rates weekly. Furthermore, to better understand the market we are actually attracting with our strategy, we will do the following:

- *Marketing research department* will track income, occupation, county of residence, and stated purpose of loan from approved applications. The first report to the product manager is due May 1; subsequent reports are due quarterly.

- *Consumer loan division* will report weekly to the product manager on the ratio of approved applications to total applications received.

By the end of the first week of each month, the product manager will provide the marketing director with a memo reporting on the progress of the new product introduction and summarizing the information described above.

---

[1]Difference between cost of funds and yield on this product. With cost of funds at Prime minus 1.5% and the yield being Prime plus 1.75%, the interest margin on this product is 3.25% (1.5% plus 1.75%).

C SALES TECHNIQUES

Case C consists of three scenarios illustrating effective and ineffective selling techniques:

1. New checking customer (effective technique)
2. New checking customer (ineffective technique)
3. New savings customer (effective technique)

1. Effective Technique

New Accts: Good morning, may I help you with something?

Customer: Yes . . . I need to open a checking account.

New Accts: Fine, why don't you have a seat.

Customer: Okay, thanks.

New Accts: By the way, I'm Kathy Mayer, Assistant Manager.

Customer: Nice to meet you . . . I'm Jim Anderson. My wife and I just moved to the area.

New Accts: Oh really . . . from another part of Jersey, or . . .

Customer: No . . . out near Pittsburgh—Western part of Pennsylvania.

New Accts: Um . . . that's pretty country out there.

Customer: Yeah, sure is.

New Accts: Now, you're interested in checking. This would be a personal, household account?

Customer: Yes. This is our first try at getting some banking done. With the move and everything, things get so involved.

New Accts: I know what you mean, Mr. Anderson. We can offer you a number of different checking plans. The one that's best will depend on your checking activity and what you want from the account. Generally, what do your balances run each month?

Customer: Well, a lot of activity goes through that account. We tend to keep rather high balances . . . I'd say 12 to 15 or $1,600 a month. One thing I know, we don't want one of those line-of-credit accounts. We've had one . . . we just can't seem to keep it straight.

New Accts: I was thinking more of a way that you can earn interest on your checking and with the kinds of balances you're talking about, there's a good possibility that the account will be service charge-free. Sound interesting?

Customer: Yes, it does. You're talking about one of those checking accounts with interest, aren't you? I saw advertising out where we were, but we really didn't get into it.

New Accts: Our interest-paying checking account is popular with many of our customers. Take a look at this brochure.

Customer: Thanks.

New Accts: We call it Money Market Checking. It's designed specifically for people like you who maintain high checking balances. You earn a money market rate of interest on every penny of your unused funds each day.

Customer: You said something about possible service charges . . . what are we talking about?

New Accts: You mentioned your balances run between $1,200 and $1,600 a month. Your account will be free of service charges as long as your minimum or average balance for the month is $1,000 or more.

Customer: You're saying an *average* monthly balance of $1,000 or more . . .

New Accts: That's right, and I'm glad you mentioned that. Many of our local banks specify only a *minimum* monthly balance. That, of course, means that you are service-charged when your balance drops below the minimum even for one day. We like to think this is a benefit to you—that even if your balance drops below $1,000 any day, it's the *overall average* for that month that counts.

Customer: Um. I see.

New Accts: Here too, you'll be earning a market rate on this account. It's currently 5½ percent. Interest is based on daily compounding, and you'll get a statement each month listing all your transactions, plus interest earned. And should you have a monthly maintenance charge, that will show on your statement also.

(Pause)

It's a checking plan that would really benefit you. Shall we open one?

Customer: Yes, it sounds right for us.

New Accts: Now, to make it easier for you to get cash from and make deposits to your account, I'd like to suggest that we provide you and your wife with an automated teller card. We're part of the regional automated teller network, so you can use any of the 1,000 network machines in the tristate area to get cash from your account, and any of the hundreds of machines in New Jersey to make deposits. May I do that for you?

Customer: That sounds good. I'm on the road a lot, and I see those machines everywhere.

New Accts: I'd like to suggest that you start a statement savings account today also. If you like to put away a little money in a less accessible interest earning account, we can open one today with only $10, and you can add to it whenever you want. Then, the statement you receive each month will show both your checking and savings activity. It pays a higher interest rate than the Money Market Checking Account, compounded daily, and the dollars in your savings account also count toward your minimum balance requirement for the checking account. Would you like that?

Customer: Well, I guess I might as well do that now. I have a savings account back in Pittsburgh that I have to close out.

New Accts: If you'll give me the information, I can arrange to do that for you. I can contact your bank there and have them forward the funds directly to your new savings account here.

Customer: That would be a real help. Gee, thanks.

New Accts: We have an automatic savings plan that you might be interested in. It's a great way to build up your savings without even missing the money. We can arrange to have a fixed amount transferred from checking to savings every month, or every couple of weeks—whatever you prefer. It's amazing how fast money can accumulate when you set aside small amounts regularly. How does that sound?

Customer: Well, I get paid the 15th and 30th of each month. Could you transfer, say, $25 on the 17th and 2d of the month, for instance?

New Accts: No problem. That will start on the 2d of next month, and a year from now you'll have $600 plus interest that you hadn't counted on.

(They discuss the details.)

. . . and I'll take care of the rest . . . Just leave it up to us.

Customer: Thank you. You've been very helpful. It's nice to find a bank that's interested in me for a change.

New Accts: You're welcome. Thanks for stopping by.

2. Ineffective Technique

Our attention is on the teller, Nancy, who is processing customers in staccato-like fashion.

The next customer, Mrs. Benjamin, moves into place. Rather than offering a transaction, she starts to explain . . . she is new to the area, wants to open a checking account, and is looking for directions where to go . . .

Nancy, who has heard this scenario before, cuts in. Her voice trails off a bit as she recites, "Over there . . . you'll have to see someone on the platform."

Mrs. Benjamin starts to wander in the direction of "over there," hoping that a smile or wave will land her in the right place. As it turns out, there are no signs of recognition.

This case was originally provided by Mary Lee King, President, MLK Associates, Inc., Princeton Junction, New Jersey, and has been modified for this edition.

Mrs. Benjamin decides to settle for the nearest desk, so she moves within easy eyesight of the young man, Mr. Lincolf, sitting behind it. For a good 2 or 3 minutes, he seems oblivious to everything except the telephone conversation he is enjoying with someone named Dick.

Several minutes pass, Mr. Lincolf cups the receiver, glances towards Mrs. Benjamin and casually asks, "Is there something you need?"

At last given a wedge, she states her interest in a checking account and justifies her waiting there by "the teller said . . .".

Mr. Lincolf does not let her finish and proceeds to dismiss the importance of her request by offering his assistance in a minute or so. Back to his telephone conversation, the officer indicates he has "gotta go," but does not end the call until he has responded to a personal invitation to "get together with Dick and his wife . . . with their new motor home . . . over the weekend."

Meanwhile, knowing she has put up with a long day, Mrs. Benjamin takes it upon herself to settle into the chair next to his desk.

The customer gets his attention by suggesting the type of checking she and her husband want, only to be cut off again by the phone ringing.

Mr. Lincolf calls for time and picks up the phone. It is immediately clear that the caller is a former business associate of his. Mr. Lincolf appears totally devoted to discovering the when, the where, and for how long. Mrs. Benjamin might just as well not exist. She listens as Mr. Lincolf acknowledges that he is tied up right now, but it should not take too long. Mr. Lincolf says "Give me a few minutes, and I'll meet you at the pub just like old times!"

What a refreshing thought, Mrs. Benjamin remarks to herself.

With the reunion a matter of minutes away, Mr. Lincolf zeros in on completing the customer's request—a checking account. He fishes for signature cards and a service brochure he apparently has mislaid.

Not to waste time, Mr. Lincolf quotes the average monthly balance requirement for regular checking, followed by the maximum service charge that is possible for its maintenance.

Mrs. Benjamin changes direction entirely and indicates her particular interest in "something that offers a line of credit . . . does the bank offer anything . . .?"

Clipping her last question, Mr. Lincolf refers automatically to the cash reserve account. She responds with a puzzled look.

Condescendingly, he goes on to say that that particular service is really not for everyone.

Mrs. Benjamin looks shocked.

Trying to compensate for his customer's reaction, Mr. Lincolf decides to offer the brochure anyway with the suggestion that she can at least read more about it. He says, "You can fill out the information if you want."

Mrs. Benjamin turns him down flatly.

Reading this to be confusion, he plods along with the recommendation that she complete the signature card information and bring it back in with her deposit.

Dripping sarcasm, she manages to agree.

Feeling that he has apparently resolved the momentary confusion, Mr. Lincolf feels he must end on an agreeable note. He resorts to quoting the bank's image theme . . . "As we say—serving you is why we're here."

3. Effective Technique

New Accts: Excuse me, you look like you could use some help. Is there a problem?

Customer: Oh, I'm afraid so. I've been trying to understand these savings accounts, and I think I'm getting more confused.

New Accts: That's all right. We do have a number of them. Let's see if I can help. Why don't you sit here.

Customer: Thank you. My son used to help with my affairs, but he and his family just moved to Delaware. I've had some bonds come due, and this time I want the money in the bank so I know *exactly* where it is.

New Accts: I understand. Do you mind if I ask your name . . .?

Customer: Oh, of course not . . . I'm Mrs. Frazer. You probably know my son, Henry. He used to come here all the time.

New Accts: I'm sure I've met him. By the way I'm Nancy Stevenson. (pause) Mrs. Frazer, I think the key to our savings program is how you want your savings to work for you. You probably should be asking yourself some questions. For example: Do I want to be able to make deposits or withdrawals at anytime? Do I want to invest my funds and see them grow? Could I really use some additional income to live on?

Customer: All that's going to help me figure out what I want?

New Accts: Yes, it will. Once you tell me how you want to use your savings, and the amount of your investment, then I can help recommend a program that will be in your best interest.

Customer: Well, that sounds fine . . . well, I need an account to draw from . . . huh . . . and what person my age can't use some extra income?

New Accts: Isn't that true for all of us. Mrs. Frazer, what amount are you planning to deposit?

Customer: I have $25,000. You'll accept these checks, won't you?

New Accts: Absolutely . . . as a matter of fact that's the safest way of carrying a large sum. All right, let's see . . . (pause) Mrs. Frazer, we have many types of certificates that earn you high rates of interest. They all give you the option of having your interest drawn, providing you with additional income on a regular basis.

Customer: That would be nice.

New Accts: The first is our popular 6-month certificate. This guarantees you a good rate of interest for a short term. Are you familiar with this?

Customer: Not really.

New Accts: All right . . . you take some of your $25,000, deposit it for only 6 months and receive high interest. In your case, you wouldn't tie up your funds for too long; you could have monthly interest checks automatically deposited into a checking or statement savings account; and once the 6 months are up, you could have your original deposit automatically renewed at whatever the rate is then.

Customer: You mean to say the rate changes that quickly?

New Accts: Actually, rates go up or down each week, but your rate will be locked in and guaranteed for the entire 6 months.

Here's what it is this week . . .

Customer: Oh . . . Now you mentioned other kinds of accounts.

New Accts: That's right, I did, I was thinking of our 2½ year certificate. This also gives you an even higher rate of interest that's guaranteed for the entire term of the account.

Here, too, if you like, we can arrange to have interest mailed or credited to another account on a regular basis.

Customer: Now wait, let's see what we have here.

New Accts: To simplify things . . . the first certificate would give you high interest without tying up your funds for more than 6 months at a time. For additional income, you can have your interest credited monthly to checking or statement savings. The second also gives you high interest that's guaranteed for at least 2½ years. Here too you can have interest drawn regularly.

Customer: Umm. I think I'll have one of each. Ten thousand dollars in the first one you mentioned . . . and the rest for 2½ years.

New Accts: All right. If I may suggest, leave some money there to open a statement savings account. This will give you the deposit and withdrawal flexibility you also wanted, and we can credit your monthly interest directly to it.

How does that sound?

Customer: That will be fine. So, what are we doing now?

New Accts: We'll open the 6-month certificate for high interest over a short term. You've agreed on the 2½ year certificate, giving you a good guaranteed rate of interest. And a statement savings plan for crediting your interest monthly, if you like, and any other activity. Okay?

Customer: I think you've done well by me.

(They complete the paperwork.)

New Accts: That should take care of it. Mrs. Frazer, do you have your checking with us?

Customer: Oh, yes I do. We've been banking here for over 20 years.

New Accts: Ah . . . are you having your Social Security check deposited directly to the account?

Customer: As a matter of fact, I am. Before he left, my son suggested that I change over.

New Accts: That's good . . . he must have been very helpful to you.

Customer: He certainly was . . . and you have been, too. Thank you so much.

D DEVELOPING A RETAIL PROMOTIONAL CAMPAIGN

(The following is not a hypothetical case, but rather, is a true account of a cardholder activation promotion.)

OAK PARK TRUST & SAVINGS BANK'S CASH STATION® PROMOTION

Background

Oak Park Trust & Savings Bank is a $420 million bank with offices in Oak Park and River Forest, Illinois. The bank's four automated tellers are part of a statewide automated teller network that had more than 550 Cash Station® machines in the Chicago area at the time of the promotion. Oak Park was one of the first banks in its trade area to join the Cash Station® network.

In the spring of 1986, Oak Park Trust & Savings Bank had approximately 9,000 personal checking customers, 17 percent of whom had an ATM card. Although this proportion was relatively low, a more important statistic was that only 43 percent of cardholders were actively using the card. The bank recognized that it had a marketing opportunity: to increase usage by its cardholding customers and to make residents of its trade area aware of its Cash Station® machines.

Target Market Identification

The primary target audience for this promotion was the bank's existing cardholder base. Secondary targets were noncardholding Oak Park customers and customers of other banks holding Cash Station® cards of other banks. (When customers of other banks use one of Oak Park's machines, Oak Park receives a fee for providing that service.)

Objective

- To increase the percentage of active cardholders from 40 to 50 percent (a 25 percent increase).

Media Selection

The bank and its advertising agency chose to use only newspaper advertising for mass communication. Ads were run in the two local daily papers during a 3-month period beginning in June. To heighten impact, six small space ads were developed and run three at a time on three successive page spreads and located in the same position on each spread. For additional impact, a second color (green) was utilized for several insertions.

Message

Since recreational spending is at a peak during the summer months, the creative strategy was to focus on summertime uses for cash from the Cash Station®. Each ad was headed by the umbrella message, "Cash Station®—For Funds Under the Sun!" In each ad, the Cash Station® card was the dominant graphic element, creatively modified to illustrate the message. Short headlines focused on summertime reasons for needing cash: "Liquid Assets," "Cruisin' Cash," "Cold Cash," "Bleacher Bucks," "Sand Dollars," and "Cash & Carry."

Sales Promotion

To call attention to the promotion at the point of sale, the bank arranged to have a popcorn machine and balloons in each office. As a sales incentive, customers who signed up for the card were given a Cash Station® T-shirt.

Marketing to the Staff

Employees were motivated to cross-sell the card to existing and new checking customers. For each card sold, the employee received one

"Lucky Buck." At the end of the promotion, the "Lucky Bucks" were redeemable for gifts selected from a catalog.

Results

- Increased the proportion of active cardholders from 43 percent to 62 percent
- Increased the number of cards outstanding by 13 percent
- Increased the proportion of checking customers having the Cash Station® card by 12 percent

The entire promotion cost the bank less than $10,000 for creative, production, media, and sales promotion.

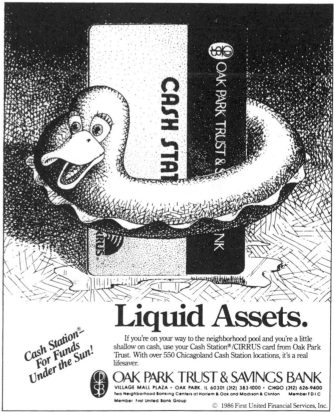

E   DEVELOPING AN ADVERTISING CAMPAIGN

POSITIONING CAMPAIGN FOR UNITED JERSEY BANKS: "THE FAST-MOVING BANK"

Background

At the start of its new positioning campaign in early 1984, United Jersey Banks (UJB) was a $3.6 billion (in assets) multibank holding company with 116 offices located throughout the state of New Jersey. It was and is the third largest commercial banking organization in the state, and its six member banks all bear the United Jersey name. Because of its locations throughout the state, its subsidiaries operate in two separate geographic and media markets: metropolitan New York and metropolitan Philadelphia. In these markets, the bank operates in the shadow of larger New York and Philadelphia banks that dominate the minds of United Jersey's prospects.

UJB's research had shown that the New Jersey retail banking market was highly fragmented, with one clear image and market share leader followed by 13 banks that were not truly distinguishable from one another in terms of market share or awareness. United Jersey was included among them.

On the commercial side, the United Jersey name was not known in that part of New Jersey that lies within the Philadelphia metropolitan area and, throughout the state, no one bank was seen as doing a particularly good job of serving the corporate market.

United Jersey had not conducted a major broadcast campaign in several years, and its management recognized that awareness of the bank in both the retail and commercial markets was not commensurate with their market position. They set about to correct that weakness in the summer of 1983. The campaign that resulted has continued and has been expanded, with excellent results in terms of awareness, image, and market share. Employee attitudes have also been affected: In addition to the pride that comes from being associated with a bank that has a positive and growing reputation, the employees have taken upon themselves the responsibility to help the bank live up to the claim that it is fast-moving.

This case deals only with the initial introduction of "The Fast-Moving Bank."

Situation Analysis

United Jersey began their planning with an assessment of their existing situation, answering the questions:

- What do our retail and commercial customers think about us?
- What is the current level of awareness and image of the bank among noncustomers?

In addition to the background information above, they learned that their commercial customers viewed the bank as being responsive. It also told them that responsiveness and efficiency are important to both commercial and retail customers.

UJB engaged Trout & Ries Advertising, Inc., an agency that had earned a reputation for finding unique positions for its clients. They believe that:

- to succeed in our overcommunicated society, a company must create a position in the prospect's mind, a position that takes into consideration not only a company's own strengths and weaknesses, but those of its competitors as well.[1]

This was to be accomplished by capitalizing on United Jersey's responsiveness and by positioning UJB as "The Fast-Moving Bank," against the imaginary "Lethargic National Bank."

Objective

The communication objective for the new campaign was:

- to communicate to consumers and to financial decision makers in middle market companies that United Jersey is the most responsive banking organization for their needs.

The bank's advertising management agreed that the *tone* of the television advertising should be humorous, and that the print advertising should be aggressive. Advertising *copy* would be written to present important news and facts to support the fast-moving claim. The *format* of the initial print ad would contain illustrations to support the copy points and would feature a tent card bearing the slogan, "Time is money." These tent cards were given to all UJB officers and customer service staff to display on their desks to reinforce the "fast-moving" message to both the customer and the employee.

Strategy

The broad strategy was to position UJB against its largest competitors by:

- exploiting their weakness, namely their slow reaction time; and
- ensuring that the bank delivered on the promise of the advertising.

In fact, the bank had already taken a number of steps toward being a responsive institution, so all that was necessary was to promote these facts and embellish them. They were:

- decentralizing commercial loan decision making by pushing authority down to the 10 commercial loan centers throughout the state;
- cross-training employees so that they are equipped to respond to a variety of customer questions themselves, without having to pass the customer along to someone else;
- continuing their commitment to electronic banking. The United Jersey automated teller system was the largest private network in New Jersey; and

Advertising copy

Date:	January 14, 1986
Client:	United Jersey Banks
Title:	"BUSINESS LOAN" (a/k/a/ **"Any Day Now"**)
Job number:	3645 Commercial Code UNJB-6301

Anncr:	When you need a business loan, does your bank seem to take forever?
Lethargic Banker:	It should be any day now. Any day . . . any day. . . .
Anncr:	At United Jersey, our bankers value your time as much as your money. We approve some commercial loans in three days, or less.
UJB Banker:	Mr. Gavin, you'll have the money in your account on Thursday. Yes, this Thursday.
Anncr:	If time means money to you, come to United Jersey, the fast-moving bank.

- providing speedy lockbox service. With their unique ZIP code and frequent postal pickups, customer receipts were processed and deposited quickly;

- providing FACT point-of-sale credit card authorization terminals. (FACT is an acronym for "Fast Authorization of Cashless Transactions");

- centralizing its headquarters—United Jersey's new corporate office building had been constructed in Princeton, the geographic center of the state, less than an hour away from any one customer; and

- being responsive to retail and commercial customers' needs in terms of product development and pricing.

These facts would be utilized as support for the "fast-moving" claim.

Media Tactics

The new message was to be communicated through television, radio, and print media. To maximize impact, the agency recommended that the bank launch the new campaign by airing its new television commercials during the January 1984 Super Bowl game. The campaign introduction ran for 4 months and consisted of three 30-second and one 10-second television spot, five radio spots, and one print advertisement.

Television

Exhibit E-1 shows the script for one of the most popular television commercials in the series. It contrasts United Jersey's speed in approving commercial loans with Lethargic National's slowness. The Lethargic banker's "a-a-a-ny d-a-a-y now, a-a-a-ny day" is in sharp contrast to the United Jersey banker's "You'll have the money in your account on Thursday . . . *this* Thursday." The spot concluded with the logo moving quickly across the screen with the voiceover: "If time means money to you, talk to the fast-moving bank. United Jersey."

The other 30-second spots dealt with delivering personal installment loans within 72 hours and with getting fast answers to questions about your account. The 10-second spot promoted the bank's ability to deliver car loans speedily.

Radio

The radio execution consisted of five spots, three aimed at the commercial market and two aimed at the retail. The commercial spots dealt with lockbox, international services, and loan decision making. The retail spots dealt with automated tellers and personal loans.

Print

The print ad is shown as Exhibit E-2. It was aimed at the commercial banking market and was run extensively in the *New York Times*, *Wall Street Journal*, and *Philadelphia Inquirer*.

The *media mix* strategy was that the bank would spend 80 percent of the introductory budget for the campaign on broadcast (TV and radio) and a significant proportion of the remainder in the *Journal* and

A simple idea that will revolutionize banking.

Time is Money.

Why are most bankers very careful with your money, but very casual with your time?

In today's fast-moving world, time is indeed money. We think it's high time the banking industry faced this fact and changed its ways.

That's why United Jersey is committed to being faster.

Faster in the way we handle your business needs. Faster in the way we approve loans. Faster in responding to your financial needs.

What have we done to speed up our service? That's a fair question, so read on.

We did away with our loan committee.

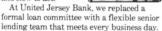

Old-fashioned loan committees can be a drag on your business. They're hard to convene and slow to act.

At United Jersey Bank, we replaced a formal loan committee with a flexible senior lending team that meets every business day.

That team has the authority to approve up to $10 million.

In Commercial Banking Centers throughout the state, United Jersey has other officers on site to make business loans quickly.

We train our people to have answers. Not excuses.

At United Jersey, we give our people training in all our banking services, not just their own specialties. So if a question comes up, they usually don't have to call an expert at the other end of the state. (But when they do, they know who to call.)

To date, more than 350 of our bankers and calling officers have gone through our cross-training program.

We cut out international red tape.

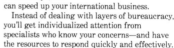

By eliminating a lot of the hassle and red tape, we can speed up your international business.

Instead of dealing with layers of bureaucracy, you'll get individualized attention from specialists who know your concerns—and have the resources to respond quickly and effectively.

The bottom line is that our international bankers, in many cases, can do in one day what can take other banks up to three days.

We speeded up our lock box service.

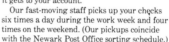

When you sign up for United Jersey's lock box service, your money never gets a chance to rest until it gets to your account.

Our fast-moving staff picks up your checks six times a day during the work week and four times on the weekend. (Our pickups coincide with the Newark Post Office sorting schedule.)

So we're emptying your lock box and filling up your account as fast as we can.

We're fast because we're fast. Not because we're small.

But just because we're fast, don't think we're small.

United Jersey Bank is a member of a $3.6 billion financial services organization with more than 125 offices throughout New Jersey. The holding company has lending capability in excess of $30 million.

So bring your account to a bank that values your time as much as your money.

For information on our banking services, please call Dan Haughton at (609) 924-8000, or Jim Holzinger at (201) 646-5140.

125 offices

$3.6 billion

▲ United Jersey
The fast-moving bank.

Member FDIC

Times, the papers most often read by corporate financial decision makers.

Performance Monitoring and Evaluation

In order to be able to measure the effectiveness of the advertising, United Jersey conducted benchmark research among both its target markets—retail and commercial—prior to the kick-off of the new campaign. The specific indicators measured were:

Retail

- Top-of-mind (that is, unaided) awareness of banks serving New Jersey
- Share of market held by each major bank
- Top-of-mind image ratings of banks for innovativeness, fast service, highest quality financial services, best rate
- Image of the bank among customers
- Believability of various advertising themes, including "Fast-Moving Bank"
- Interest in banks based on advertising statements
- How consumers define "responsive" and "fast moving"

Commercial

The commercial benchmark consisted of two studies conducted during 1983 among New Jersey firms with $4 million or more in annual sales volume. The indicators measured were:

- awareness of bank advertising and where seen;
- ability to relate specific advertising themes to the banks using them;
- credibility of various advertising themes;
- whether "fast moving" describes United Jersey; and
- meaning of "fast moving."

After the 4-month introductory period, follow-up research was conducted among both the retail and commercial markets. This research demonstrated the following results for the campaign:

Retail

The bank learned that its image had indeed improved. More consumers rated the bank as responsive and innovative than before the campaign. On several image factors, UJB was tied with the market leader. The bank nearly doubled the percentage of consumers who mentioned United Jersey when asked, unaided, to name banks that come to mind.

Through this research, the bank also learned that the "fast-moving" position had greater appeal to the younger (under 55) market than to the older market. The bank also saw a significant increase in market share for transaction accounts over this period. Additionally, while awareness of United Jersey had increased, the unaided awareness of its leading competitors had dropped.

Commercial

United Jersey's advertising was aimed somewhat more at the commercial market than the retail market, and this strategy was reflected in the results. Awareness of United Jersey among commercial prospects increased dramatically. The research also reinforced the meaningfulness of the fast-moving theme to this market segment. It further confirmed the wisdom of having spent such a large proportion of its budget on television and in the *Times* and *Journal*.

Other Feedback

While research results provided quantitative evidence of the value of the advertising, there were qualitative results reported as well. Many officers and employees of the bank reported ways in which they saw the advertising working. One subsidiary bank president reported receiving a number of commercial loan inquiries as a direct result of the advertising. The bank's telephone operators reported a significant increase in calls for information on products and locations. The public relations area reported increased coverage by the press and securities analysts, and several managers reported cases of lenders and employees trying to live up to the advertising by giving approvals faster and by simply not allowing matters to sit around unattended.

United Jersey continues to advertise itself as "The Fast-Moving Bank" and its reputation, image, and market share have continued to benefit from this strong position, which works so well in both its retail and corporate markets.

[1]Al Ries and Jack Trout, *Positioning: The Battle For Your Mind* (New York: McGraw-Hill, Inc., 1981), p. 28.

F DEVELOPING A MARKETING PLAN FOR CONSUMERS NATIONAL BANK

(This is a hypothetical case that demonstrates the steps in developing a marketing plan for a bank.)

INTRODUCTION

Consumers National Bank (CNB) is a hypothetical bank with assets of approximately $160 million. It is located in a rural county that has a population of 135,000. All eight of the bank's offices are located within Overland County.

The data presented in the situation analysis are not meant to be all-inclusive, but rather to illustrate the variety of information that might be gathered and how it might be used.

I. SITUATION ANALYSIS

A. Analysis of the Economic Market Environment

1. Employment Trends. Exhibit F-1 shows nonagricultural employment trends for the county. Not shown is the fact that the county has approximately 250 active farms, employing about 1,900 people, or

Exhibit F-1 **Nonagricultural Wage and Salary Employment Trends: Overland County**

	1978	1980	1985
Nonagricultural work force	54,700	54,300	52,600
Manufacturing	19,100	18,100	14,700
Durable goods	10,700	10,500	9,000
Stone/clay/glass	9,100	8,600	6,500
Other durables	1,600	2,000	2,500
Nondurable goods	8,500	7,600	5,700
Food	2,700	2,500	2,100
Apparel	2,500	2,300	1,800
Nonmanufacturing	35,600	36,200	37,900
Construction	1,700	1,800	1,800
Transportation/communications/public utilities	3,000	3,000	2,200
Wholesale & retail trade	9,100	9,000	10,500
Finance/insurance/real estate	2,200	2,400	2,700
Services	8,200	8,500	9,600
Government	11,500	11,500	11,200

Source: State Department of Labor and Industry.

Exhibit F-2 **Labor Force, Employment, and Unemployment**

Year	Civilian Labor Force (000)	Employment (000)	Unemployment (000)	Unemployment Rate (%)
1983	58.6	50.2	8.4	14.3
1984	56.8	49.3	7.5	13.2
1985	54.5	48.5	6.0	11.0

Source: State Department of Labor and Industry.

about 3.5 percent of the work force. Principal crops are soybeans, apples, and peaches. Exhibit F-2 shows total labor force (agricultural and nonagricultural), employment, and unemployment. On the basis of these tables and other information obtained during our research phase, we observe the following:

a. The nonagricultural work force peaked in 1978 and diminished through 1982. The work force in 1985 was greater than it had been during the prior 3 years.

b. The manufacturing sector continues to diminish, although the region is still more dependent upon manufacturing than the state as a whole. The industries suffering the greatest loss of jobs have been glass, apparel, and food processing.

c. The only manufacturing growth has been in the "other durable goods" category. This growth is primarily in the electronics components and aircraft-related industries.

d. While the manufacturing sector has been diminishing, the non-manufacturing sector has been growing steadily. The area of greatest growth has been trade, primarily retail, as shopping centers have opened in the outlying areas.

e. Job gains in the services industry are due largely to expansion of health care and medical facilities.

f. The unemployment rate, while declining each year, is still significantly greater than the state's rate of 5.7 percent.

2. Retail Activity. Exhibit F-3 shows the changes that are taking place in the retail sector of CNB's trade area. Some of the conclusions that can be drawn from this information are as follows:

a. From 1977 to 1982, the number of retail establishments in CNB's trade area declined by 10 percent. Hardest hit were businesses that were affected by oil price increases and energy conservation (for example, automotive, gasoline, and fuel dealers) and by the relatively low level of population and income growth (home furnishings, eating and drinking establishments).

b. Although total retail sales grew by 37 percent over the 5-year period, when adjusted for inflation, sales actually declined by 13 percent. Consumer prices increased at a 9.58 percent compound annual growth rate, while sales increased by only 6.46 percent.

3. Construction Activity. Exhibit F-4 shows residential construction for Overland County's three major cities, where all of CNB's offices are located, and for the county in total. In 1985, for the first time since 1978, the total number of dwelling units authorized in the county exceeded 300. The majority of units authorized were single-family

Exhibit F-3 Retail Trade Data

Kind of Business	Number of Establishments*			Sales ($ mil.)		
	1977	1982	Change (%)	1977	1982	Change (%)
Total	839	759	(10)	426.8	583.7	37
Building materials, hardware, garden supply, mobile home dealers	43	33	(23)	16.9	19.8	17
General merchandise stores	19	17	(11)	49.3	61.4	25
Food stores	114	112	(2)	120.4	165.4	37
Automotive dealers	82	62	(24)	85.0	104.7	23
Gasoline service stations	82	74	(10)	24.6	50.6	106
Apparel and accessory stores	87	80	(8)	22.9	30.3	32
Furniture, home furnishings, and equipment stores	57	44	(23)	16.8	17.8	6
Eating and drinking stores	180	157	(13)	29.4	37.8	29
Drug and proprietary stores	19	19	—	12.8	18.9	48
Miscellaneous retail stores	156	161	3	48.7	77.0	58
Liquor stores	21	26	24	8.0	13.2	65
Used merchandise stores	11	10	(9)	1.8	2.2	22
Misc. shopping goods stores	49	54	10	8.7	13.6	56
Nonstore retailers	17	12	(29)	5.1	6.4	25
Fuel and ice dealers	24	18	(25)	21.3	36.0	69
Florists	12	15	25	1.3	2.0	54

*With payroll.

Source: 1977 and 1982 Census of Retail Trade, U.S. Department of Commerce, Bureau of the Census.

units, and more than two-thirds were located in Plattville, where the bank has only one office.

The most significant commercial construction in the past few years has been in the health care field, as three area hospitals underwent major expansions. Other commercial construction has been limited to renovations and minor expansions.

B. Analysis of the Demographic Environment

Exhibits F-5, F-6, and F-7 summarize the more pertinent information regarding the population in CNB's trade area. Looking at numbers in isolation is neither useful nor interesting. Therefore, it is important to look at present data in comparison with past data (that is, to look at trends) or in comparison with present data for another area (for example, local data compared with state data). For the market served by CNB we can say the following based on these tables:

1. While the county's population showed good growth during the decade of the 1970s, the area was hard hit by the recession of the early 1980s. Natural increases in population due to the excess of births over deaths were offset by outmigration, causing total population to decrease in 1982 and 1983.

2. Population has been growing at roughly the same rate as the state for the 2 most recent years for which we have information.

3. Population is projected to increase slightly over the next 30 to 35 years, but at a rate considerably lower than that projected for the state as a whole.

4. Other data (not shown here) indicate that 85 percent of the recent gains in population are accounted for by growth in Plattville and Milltown, while population is declining in Bridgeboro.

5. During the decade of the 1970s, the population aged somewhat, with 57 percent being 25 years old or older. The educational level and family size also increased during this period.

C. Customer Analysis

1. **Customer Survey.** The following results are based on 276 responses to a questionnaire mailed to 914 randomly selected checking account customers of CNB. They show some effect from the recent price changes (that is, the service charge on low-balance savings and the increased minimum balance for no-charge checking), but that effect seems to be within tolerable levels.

Exhibit F-4   Dwelling Units Authorized by Building Permits

	1970		1978		1985	
	Single Family	Multiple Unit	Single Family	Multiple Unit	Single Family	Multiple Unit
Bridgeboro	4	—	5	—	1	—
Milltown	44	410	53	—	34	—
Plattville	315	448	113	103	181	102
County*	490	858	214	103	309	108

*Includes all 14 municipalities in the county.

Source: State Department of Labor and Industry.

Exhibit F-5   Population Trends: Overland County and the State

	County		State	
	Population	% Change	Population	% Change
1970 Census	121,374		7,171,112	
1980 Census	132,866	9.5	7,365,011	2.7
1981	133,900	0.8	7,408,000	0.6
1982	133,800	(0.1)	7,430,000	0.3
1983	133,000	(0.6)	7,468,000	0.1
1984	133,900	0.7	7,517,000	0.7
1985	134,900	0.7	7,562,000	0.6

Source: State Department of Labor and Industry.

Exhibit F-6   Population Projections for Overland County 1980–2020

1980	132,866
1985	132,900
1990	140,300
2000	151,500
2010	149,900
2020	142,400

Percentage change projected from 1980 to 2020:

Overland County:	7.2%
The state:	24.6%

Source: State Department of Labor and Industry.

a. About one in five of our present checking customers say they have closed some bank account relationship within the past year. Only 20 percent of these are reportedly due to our pricing changes. About one customer in four reports opening an account in the past year; and again, one in five gave our price change as a reason. In summary, it appears that about 5 percent of our present checking customers took some negative action in response to our price changes. Of course, those who left the bank entirely were not measured by this study.

b. The bank has a very large core of long-term customers. Over 57 percent have been with us more than 10 years; three-fourths more than 5 years.

c. While the bank got good ratings on many attributes, those rated lowest were our pricing, drive-in facilities, parking facilities, and speed of service. The physical problems at our two old drive-ins are causing service problems, and parking has long been a problem at two of our busiest offices.

d. There is a very high level of usage of other financial institutions by CNB checking customers: 45 percent have an account with a savings and loan, and 30 percent with another commercial bank.

e. One-fourth of checking customers opened some type of new account in the past year. Less than half of all new accounts opened by CNB checking customers within the past year were opened at CNB. However, one-fifth of these new accounts went to other commercial banks and one-third to savings and loans. No one reason for use of other banks predominates, with the exception of low-balance requirements at savings and loans.

f. Nearly two-thirds of our customers express interest in having automated tellers; 80 percent of those under 35 years of age said they would be very or fairly interested in this service.

g. Interest in telephone bill payment was highest among new and younger customers, but in total, only 39 percent expressed interest.

h. The age distribution of our checking customers is such that 28 percent are under 24, 33 percent are between 35 and 54, and 30 percent are over 55. Approximately 44 percent have had at least some college education. Median income is $31,000, with 15 percent making $50,000 or more. Fifty-nine percent of our

Exhibit F-7 Demographic Characteristics of the Population

	1970	1980
Total population	121,374	132,866
Percent nonwhite	14.9%	14.2%
Foreign stock	18.5%*	17.5%
Family income		
Total families	30,718	37,962
Mean family income	$10,407	$26,842
Median family income	$ 9,529	$21,223
Families below poverty level	9.2%	7.8%
Education		
% of population 25 or over	55.0%	57.0%
Median school years completed	10.7%	11.8%
% high school graduates	40.0%	45.0%
Persons per household	3.18	3.5
Housing characteristics		
Number year-round units	38,854	45,590
Built since 1960	21.7%	34.7%
% owner-occupied	57.3%	64.2%
% renter-occupied	30.4%	25.8%
Median value, owner-occupied	$13,700	$32,700
Median rent	$ 104	$ 225
Percent work inside SMSA	81.5%	82.5%

*36.3% Italian origin.

Source: Census of Population.

customers are married; 14 percent are single; and 22 percent are widowed, divorced, or separated.

i. Customers rate the bank very highly on most attributes—especially the friendliness of our tellers.

j. Checking account customers have, on average, 2.67 services with CNB, 0.6 with another commercial bank, and 0.7 with a savings and loan association.

2. Trade Area Household Survey. Because of last year's survey and the cost that would be involved in conducting an update this year, the management of CNB felt that this part of the self-analysis was not required this year. The study will be done next year, however, to enable us to measure the effects of our marketing strategies.

3. New Account Survey. This survey indicates that more than half of our new accounts are opened by people who already have some relationship with the bank. Of the totally new customers, two-thirds are new to the area, and the majority say they were recommended to the bank by a friend or relative. Records indicate that the average customer opening any new account is sold 1.3 accounts.

4. Closed Account Survey. Last year, the bank instituted a $2 service charge on savings accounts having a quarterly average balance of less than $100. This year, the bank increased its service charges on checking. These actions, of course, had an impact on account closings. The following are the results of the closed savings account survey for the first 6 months of the year.

a.   In 25 percent of the cases, the funds were consolidated with other accounts within the bank or used to open a new account or certificate of deposit at the bank.

b.   In nearly half of the cases (47 percent) the account was closed for reasons beyond the control of the bank (14 percent moved; 16 percent needed the money; 7 percent died, married, or divorced).

c.   One in five (21 percent) closed the account because of recent service charge changes.

d.   Only 2 customers out of 229 were critical of staff or service.

D. Analysis of the Bank's Competitive Environment

1. Operating Statistics. CNB competes with a number of banks in Overland County. However, because of merger activity, many of them have their headquarters in other counties. Because their operating statistics would reflect operations outside Overland County, these banks are not truly comparable to CNB. Therefore, Exhibit F-8 compares selected statistics for CNB and its two competitors who are headquartered and located only in Overland County. The spread sheet in Exhibit F-8 indicates the following:

a.   CNB is the largest bank headquartered and located only in the county (in asset size). However, if the current rates of growth

Exhibit F-8 Operating Results of CNB and Other County-Headquartered Banks: 1980 and 1985

	CNB		Merchants		Anacola	
	1980	1985	1980	1985	1980	1985
Total assets ($000)	97,085	160,906	73,850	148,000	42,395	103,987
Return on avg. assets	.69	.75	.79	.84	1.02	1.45
Total deposits ($000)	84,806	141,489	66,036	131,833	37,466	92,632
5-Yr. compound growth	4.6%	10.8%	4.6%	14.8%	9.5%	19.9%
Loans/deposits[1]	72.9%	74.3%	78.0%	77.6%	49.7%	48.5%
Total loans	62,887	97,447	46,485	80,917	17,736	46,921
As a % of total:						
Auto	17.2	18.5	22.5	23.0	4.4	5.5
Credit card	1.2	3.0	0	0	0.7	2.0
Mobile home	0.1	0.1	0.1	0.1	0.5	0.5
Other installment/						
revolving	16.9	17.5	5.5	5.8	5.3	8.2
Single payment	2.2	2.1	0.7	0.8	5.9	6.0
1- to 4-Fam.						
residential	22.8	20.2	12.1	11.8	19.6	17.6
Nonfarm						
nonresidential	18.0	15.0	23.6	23.5	33.0	30.4
Commercial/industrial	13.2	15.2	32.2	31.5	28.4	27.8
As a % of avg. assets:						
Net interest margin	4.38	3.76	4.26	3.87	4.78	3.84
Noninterest income:						
Svc. chgs. on						
deposits	.26	.24	.26	.28	.10	.10
Other svg. chgs.	.04	.05	.16	.18	.01	.10
Trust	.06	.07	.14	.13	—	—
Other	.07	.08	.03	.02	.05	.05
Total	.43	.44	.59	.61	.17	.25
Operating expense:						
Salaries/benefits	1.45	1.43	1.64	1.65	1.51	1.18
Occupancy	.89	.85	.64	.62	.49	.43
Provision for loan						
losses	.17	.20	.24	.25	.10	.25
Other	.94	.76	.83	.87	.78	.75
Total nonint. expense	3.46	3.24	3.35	3.39	2.88	2.36

[1] Net loans to total deposits less public funds.

continue, Merchants will exceed CNB in assets and deposits within 3 years.

b. The bank's 5-year compound growth rate for deposits is not keeping pace with the competition.

c. The bank has maintained a consistently high ratio of loans to deposits and there is little room for increasing this proportion.

d. The loan portfolio is skewed toward consumer loans. The competition is much more active in the commercial sector.

e. The bank has a very high proportion of mortgages. These low-yielding, fixed-rate, long-term loans are a disadvantage in a fluctuating rate environment.

f. CNB has an unusually large proportion of "other installment loans" due to its consumer banking service package, which includes a line of credit.

g. CNB is one of the leading automobile financers because of its dealer relationships.

h. Net interest margin as a percent of average assets is lower than the competition.

i. Noninterest income as a percent of average assets is well below Merchants', largely because of trust and "other" service charges.

j. CNB's noninterest expense ratio was the highest of the three banks in 1980 but has been reduced through reductions in the "other expense" category. Occupancy expense is the highest of the group.

2. Market Share. Exhibit F-9 shows deposit market share for CNB and its principal competitors. Analysis of these deposit market share statistics reveals the following:

a. With regard to transaction accounts, CNB's share has held rather steady over the period. At least two commercial competitors are losing market share.

b. With regard to certificates of deposit, CNB lost share over the 5-year period, as did most commercial banks.

c. The credit union is becoming an increasingly significant competitor.

Exhibit F-9 Deposit Market Share Data (Percent of deposits held each year)

	Transaction Accounts*		Certificates of Deposit		Public Funds		Total Deposits	
	1980	1985	1980	1985	1980	1985	1980	1985
Consumers National	**12.2**	**12.0**	**11.1**	**9.5**	**12.2**	**20.1**	**11.7**	**11.9**
County Federal S&L	13.3	24.1	20.3	20.5	0	0	15.8	21.8
Merchants National	10.3	11.1	5.1	4.2	29.7	48.0	8.9	11.1
Modern S&L	8.4	8.0	12.5	13.8	0	0	9.8	8.9
Traditional Bank	9.3	8.0	6.6	6.5	4.9	7.2	7.6	7.6
Peoples Trust	12.2	6.0	12.4	6.3	26.1	18.1	13.0	6.8
Patriots Bank	9.5	6.0	7.0	6.0	18.0	4.3	8.8	5.9
Anacola National	1.0	2.9	1.1	4.0	0	0.3	1.0	3.5
County Workers C.U.	0.5	3.3	3.9	3.0	0	0	2.0	3.0

*Interest- and noninterest-bearing transaction accounts, money market deposit accounts, and savings accounts.

d. Public funds share is highly volatile. These generally go to the highest bidder, so shares are not relevant. Merchants Bank now has nearly half of this business.

e. Patriot's Bank lost considerable share since being acquired by a large state-wide bank that changed local management and policies.

f. The inclusion of public funds in total market share masks the fact that Merchants' market share has risen from 7.45 percent to 8.8 percent, while CNB's share has fallen from 11.0 percent to 10.7 percent.

3. Competitive Marketing Strategies. Exhibit F-10 compares retail products and pricing of CNB and its competitors. Exhibit F-11 compares facilities and hours. Examination of this information by CNB suggests the following:

a. The bank's pricing of transaction accounts is among the more expensive. Thrift institutions have priced for volume.

b. CNB's interest rates on savings and time accounts are generally competitive and are compounded daily.

c. CNB offers longer daily banking hours than any competitor.

d. CNB is one of only four banks providing full-service banking on Saturdays.

e. CNB is one of only two banks that operate in all major cities of the county.

f. CNB is one of the few banks not offering automated teller access to accounts.

g. In random "mystery shopping" of competitors and CNB, we found our staff to be far better informed and more courteous than the staff at the other banks.

h. CNB's parking facilities are a competitive disadvantage.

i. The physical appearance of the bank's offices is neat but not particularly appealing in comparison with some competitors.

j. CNB has excellent locations except in the largest city, where the bank does not have sufficient coverage.

4. Subjective Factors. The following information is drawn from the experience of CNB's officers:

a. CNB's staff is at least equal to, and in many cases, superior to the competition's in terms of performance and appearance. There is good morale and low turnover among staff.

b. Patriot's Bank is having many problems. Many key people have left the bank, leaving many customers—especially business customers—vulnerable to sales efforts by other banks.

c. CNB has no formal sales training program for its retail and commercial customer-contact staff. To the bank's knowledge, none of the competition engages in sales training either.

E. Self-Analysis

CNB's self-analysis is contained within the analysis of our customers and our competitive situation. These sections provide information on how the bank is seen by its customers, how its customers compare with residents of our market, how our financials compare with those of the competition, and how our facilities, products, and marketing strategies compare with the competition.

Exhibit F-10 Competitive Comparison of Retail Products and Pricing

Institution	Interest Checking	Regular Checking	Overdraft Checking	Regular Savings	Money Market Account	Certificates of Deposit
CNB	$1,500 avg. = free $1,000–1,499 = $3 Under $1,000 = $5 Compounded daily	$500 avg. = free $400–499 = $1 $300–399 = $2 $200–299 = $3 $100–199 = $4 Under $100 = $5	Advances equal to overdraft amount	Compounded daily, paid quarterly; Under $100 = $2 charge	$2,500 = free Under $2,500 = $5 Compounded daily	$1,000 min. Compounded daily
Peoples Trust	$1,000 min. = free Under $1,000 = $5 Compounded daily	$250 min. = free Under $250 = $3	Advances in $50 multiples	Compounded daily, paid monthly	$1,000 = free Under $1,000 = $2.50 Compounded daily	$500 min. Compounded daily
Patriots Bank	$2,500 avg. = free Under $2,500 = no interest and $5 Compounded monthly	$500 min. = free Under $500 = $5	Advances in $100 multiples	Compounded and paid quarterly	$2,500 = free Under $2,500 = no interest and $5 Compounded monthly	$1,000 min. Simple interest
Merchants National Bank	$1,000 min. = free Under $1,000 = $3 plus 15¢/check Compounded daily	$300 min. = free Under $300 = $3	Not available	Compounded and paid quarterly	$2,000 min. = free Under $2,000 = $3 Compounded daily	$50 min. Compounded daily
Anacola National Bank	$1,000 min. = free Under $1,000 = $4 No interest if under $500 Compounded monthly	$200 min. = free $100–199 = $2 Under $100 = $3	Advances in $50 multiples	Compounded daily, paid quarterly	$2,000 min. = free Under $2,000 = $2 Compounded monthly	$100 min. Compounded daily
Traditional Bank	$1,000 min. = free Under $1,000 = $3 plus 20¢/check Compounded daily	$100 min. = free Under $100 = $1 plus 20¢/ check	Not available	Compounded daily, paid quarterly	$2,000 min. = free Under $2,000 = $3 Compounded monthly	Offer discounted CDs $100 min. Compounded daily
Modern S&L	$500 min. = free Under $500 = $2 Compounded daily	N/A	Not available	Compounded daily, paid monthly	$500 min. = free Under $500 = $2 Compounded daily	$50 min. Compounded daily
County Federal S&L	$500 min. = free Under $500 = $2 Compounded daily	N/A	Not available	Compounded daily, paid monthly	$500 min. = free Under $500 = $2 Compounded daily	$50 min. Compounded daily

F. Summary of CNB's Problems and Opportunities

- Population is growing, but much of that growth is in areas where the bank does not have adequate market coverage.

- CNB has a relatively low proportion of commercial loans and a high proportion of mortgages in its loan portfolio. This disproportion between fixed rate and flexible rate assets puts the bank at a disadvantage as the cost of funds rises.

- CNB's deposit growth rate is not keeping pace with its principal local competitor. At current rates, Merchants will outstrip CNB in deposit size within 3 years.

- While CNB's noninterest income ratio is high, it is still well below Merchants'.

- CNB's regular and interest checking prices are high for the market. The $1,500 average balance required for no service charge may be perceived as higher than the $1,000 minimum of other banks.

- CNB's minimum deposits required for certificates is higher than the competition.

- CNB's parking facilities are a competitive disadvantage.

- CNB is at a competitive disadvantage by not offering automated teller service.

- The bank's drive-ins are inadequate and noncompetitive and are a source of customer dissatisfaction.

- Customers are opening more new accounts (including savings, checking, certificates, and loans) at other financial institutions than at CNB. This is an unfavorable trend.

- CNB's cash reserve line of credit is the most consumer-oriented service of this type in the market. Other banks either do not have the service or advance in multiples of $50, which is detrimental to the customer.

- The bank gets very few complaints about the service given by its staff. In fact, many customers praise our staff very highly, and the level of referrals from customers indicates an excellent reputation.

- Patriot's problems are making their business and personal customers vulnerable to the sales efforts of other banks.

Exhibit F-11 Competitive Comparison of Facilities and Hours

Institution	24-Hour Banking	Daily Hours	Friday Evening Hours	Saturday Hours	Parking	Appearance of Offices	Locations
CNB	No				Poor at main office; fair at others	Aging but clean	One of only two institutions serving all three major cities; central business districts, except one location on fringe of largest city
Lobby		9-3	6-8	9-1			
Drive-In		8-5:30	5:30-8	9-1			
Peoples Trust	Yes				Limited at city offices	Cluttered with premium merchandise	Largest city; central business district; good locations
Lobby		8:30-3	3-8	9-1			
Drive-In		8:30-5:30	5:30-8	9-1			
Patriots Bank	No				Adequate	Modern, colorful facilities	All good locations in all three major cities
Lobby		9-3	6-8	None			
Drive-In		9-5:30	5:30-8	None			
Merchants National	Yes				Excellent	Beautiful new main office; others aging	Capitol city; central business district and major intersections; all good
Lobby		9-3	6-8	10-1			
Drive-In		8:30-5:30	5:30-8	10-1			
Anacola National	No				Adequate	Modern, neat	Good locations in largest city
Lobby		9-3:30	6-8	None			
Drive-In		8:30-5:30	5:30-8	None			
Traditional Bank	Yes				Limited in cities; adequate elsewhere	Old offices recently refurbished; pleasant	All good locations in two of three major cities (except capitol)
Lobby		9-3	5-8	None			
Drive-In		9-5:30	5-8	None			
Modern S&L	No				On-street or limited parking	Old offices looking rundown	Central business districts of capitol and smallest city
Lobby		9-3	6:30-8	None			
Drive-In		9-3	3-8	None			
County Federal S&L	Yes				Excellent parking facilities	Old offices well maintained	Excellent locations in central business districts and major intersections of largest city
Lobby		9-3	3-8	10-1			
Drive-In		9-5	5-8	10-1			

II. OBJECTIVES AND GOALS

A. Mission Statement and Corporate Objectives

1. CNB's mission is to provide quality financial service to individuals and businesses in Overland County. The bank will attempt to offer the complete spectrum of financial services to meet customer needs (as permitted by law), as long as the bank returns an adequate profit to its shareholders.

2. To the extent permitted by the economic characteristics of the market, the bank will attempt to achieve a balanced service approach between consumer and commercial segments of the market.

3. The bank will pursue deposit growth through product and/or market expansion but not through merger or acquisition.

4. CNB will attempt to achieve a growth rate in total deposits of 15 percent in the coming year and an increase in pretax profits of 12 percent.

B. Target Market Selection

On the basis of the situation analysis, the following markets should be targeted in our objective-setting and strategy formulation:
- higher income individuals, especially managerial and professional workers;
- newcomers to our geographic trade area;
- residents of Plattville, the fastest growing city in our trade area; and
- the business community.

C. Selected Marketing Objectives

1. To increase the bank's share of new services opened during the coming year

2. To increase the bank's penetration of higher-income segments of the market in the coming year

3. To increase average deposit size and profitability per customer

4. To achieve a greater proportion of professional and managerial workers in the bank's customer base

5. To increase the bank's share of newcomer accounts

6. To increase the bank's share of market for total deposits

7. To increase consumer and customer awareness of the services currently offered by the bank

8. To increase community awareness of the locations of the bank's offices

9. To increase the proportion of commercial loans in the total loan portfolio

10. To create an image among the business community that CNB is a strong commercial banking organization, and that its calling officers are innovative and have the expertise and authority to meet financial needs in a fast, responsive, and imaginative way

11. To improve customer service at the Bridgeboro main office

12. To increase the bank's presence in Plattville

D. Selected Goals

Related Marketing Objective	Goal	Achievement Level	Target Date	Responsibility
1,3,6,7	1. To increase number of accounts opened at new accounts desk	Raise accounts per customer from 1.3 to 1.75	6 months	Training department; new accounts staff; marketing officer
2,4	2. To achieve a greater than average share of accounts of			Personal banking officer and marketing officer
	• high income segments	Increase share by 25 percent	1 year	
	• professional and managerial segments	Increase share by 50 percent	1 year	

3	3. To raise average balance and profitability of personal transaction account customers	Increase average balance by 20 percent from $500 to $600	6 months	Retail products manager
		Increase income from personal transaction accounts by 50 percent	1 year	Retail products manager
5	4. To capture a share of newcomers commensurate with share of total deposit market last year	Capture 17 percent of all newcomers	6 months	Consumer accounts officer and marketing officer
6	5. To increase county share of deposits			Retail products manager and consumer accounts officer
	• CDs	Increase share from 9.5 percent to 11.0 percent	18 months	
	• Transaction accounts	Increase share from 12.0 percent to 12.5 percent	18 months	
8	6. To have a majority of county residents recognize CNB's name and logo and know it has offices in all three major cities	Achieve a 51 percent recognition level for logo and for locations	1 year	Marketing officer
9	7. To raise the proportion of commercial loans in the portfolio to more nearly reflect the market situation	Increase proportion from 15 percent to 20 percent	1 year	Commercial loan officer
10	8. To increase the proportion of corporate financial decision makers who think CNB has quality management and calling officers	Increase by 20 percent the proportion of target market expressing that opinion	1 year	Marketing officer

11	9. To improve customer service at Bridgeboro	Plan and execute drive-in and parking lot expansion in Bridgeboro	1 year	Properties manager
12	10. To increase the bank's presence in Plattville	Identify best sites for expansion in Plattville and file one branch application	1 year	Marketing department and properties manager
		Establish an ATM at Plattville office	6 months	Marketing department and properties manager

III. STRATEGY AND TACTICS (Action Plan excerpt)

Goal No. 1:

Increase number of accounts opened at new accounts desk

Strategy A:

Educate CNB new accounts staff on cross-selling the benefits and features of present retail services.

a. Responsibility for development and execution:
Training Officer Laura Brown
b. Date of initiation: January 1
c. Date of completion: March 1
d. Resource commitment: $1,000
e. Evaluation criteria: on-time completion of tactics

Tactic 1
Develop and conduct a 2-day cross-selling training session for all new accounts staff.

a. Responsibility:
Training Officer Laura Brown

b. Date of initiation: March 1

c. Date of completion: May 1

d. Resource commitment:
  1. $1,000 (refreshments, supplies, visual aids)

2. Two consecutive days for each new accounts rep. All to participate over a 2-month period

e. Evaluation criteria: completion of program within specified time frame

Tactic 2
Develop services guide in form of loose-leaf notebook describing each bank service, as a reference for all customer-contact staff.

a. Responsibility:
Consumer Accounts Officer John Smith

b. Date of initiation: January 1

c. Date of completion: March 1

d. Resource commitment
   1. $300 (binders, typing, printing, etc.)
   2. Half of John Smith's time for 8 weeks

e. Evaluation criteria: production of guide within specified time frame

Strategy B:

Inform and persuade existing CNB customers to use additional services.

a. Responsibility for development and execution:
Consumer Accounts Officer John Smith; tellers; loan officers; Advertising Director Jones

b. Date of initiation: March 1

c. Date of completion: ongoing. Target date for goal: December 1

d. Resource commitment:
   1. $10,000
   2. Consumer Accounts Officer Smith: 1 day per month; Advertising Director Jones: one half-day per week

e. Evaluation criteria: weekly report showing for each employee performance relative to goal

Tactic 1
Initiate personal cross-selling to customers making deposit/withdrawal. Each teller to cross-sell three new services per week.

a. Responsibility:
Tellers

b. Date of initiation: March 1

c. Date of completion: ongoing; begin December 31

d. Resource commitment:
   1. $500: reprint existing brochures explaining service for teller handouts
   2. Time minimal

e. Evaluation criteria: weekly report form

Tactic 2
Promote one service each month via weekly newspaper ad, one-third page every Tuesday.

a. Responsibility:
Advertising Director Jones

b. Date of initiation: February 1

c. Date of completion: ongoing

d. Resource commitment: $8,500

e. Evaluation criteria: tear sheets of ads circulated to Smith

Tactic 3
Develop in-bank displays related to service featured each month.

a. Responsibility:
Advertising Director Jones

b. Date of initiation: February 1

c. Date of completion: ongoing

d. Resource commitment:
   1. $1,000
   2. One day per month: Jones

e. Evaluation criteria: copy of memo instructing branches to display signs

G EXAMPLES OF BANK COMMUNITY RELATIONS ACTIVITIES

We have said that marketing is customer satisfaction at a profitable volume, carried out through an integrated and efficient framework *in a socially responsible manner*. The public relations or corporate communications function is generally the area within the bank that deals with the latter element in the marketing of the bank. The three examples in this case demonstrate a wide range of ways in which banks can win the esteem of their various publics while making a contribution to the society in which they operate. Our examples include a one-time public relations campaign that touched several of the bank's publics, an ongoing community service program, and a joint program in which a number of banks are addressing a major social and economic concern.

EXAMPLE 1: USING AN ANNIVERSARY CELEBRATION AS THE FOCUS OF A MULTIFACETED PUBLIC RELATIONS CAMPAIGN

Jackson National Bank is a community bank with six offices in Jackson, Tennessee. Jackson, a city of about 50,000 people, is located midway between Nashville and Memphis. The bank is the largest and only locally owned bank in the city.

During 1986, Jackson National celebrated its 100th anniversary with a coordinated program of advertising and special events that

Celebrating A Heritage Of A Hundred Years

1931

OH, SAY, CAN YOU SEE

THE CITY TRUST CO.

BANK

CLOSED

JACKSON NATIONAL BANK
UNDER EXPANSION

The Star Spangled Banner becomes the national anthem. Casinos in Nevada open their doors as gambling again becomes legal. Al Capone is found guilty of tax evasion. The bank panic increases as 800 banks are closed in two months. Jackson National expands its facilities and undergoes a complete renovation and rebuilding.

1886 · 100 · 1986
YEARS

Jackson
National Bank
Member FDIC

We were Jackson's bank then. And we're Jackson's bank now.

reached most of the bank's principal publics: customers, employees, directors, the Jackson community, and the local news media.

The celebration began in June with a 5-month advertising campaign and culminated at the end of October with a week-long series of events. Working with their advertising agency, the bank researched significant local and national events of the preceding 100 years. They selected 20 event-filled years between 1886 and 1986 and developed a series of 20 print ads and radio spots to be run sequentially over a 20-week period. Each ad told of the major events of that year and of what the bank was doing in that year. For example, one ad focused on the events of 1931, a Depression Era year. (See Exhibit G-1.) In that year, the Star-Spangled Banner was named the national anthem, gambling resumed in Nevada, Al Capone was convicted of tax evasion, and 800 banks closed within 2 months. But, Jackson National was renovating and rebuilding its offices. The radio spots used period music as a background in the retelling of the events.

During the final celebration week in October, there was a series of activities involving the bank's various publics.

The staff of each of the branches was given $100 to use in any way they chose, to participate in a branch decoration contest. Each branch selected and executed its own theme and the customers were asked to vote for the most creative ideas. The directors and senior management were invited to a dinner party in a restored home that had been the residence of the bank's fourth president, Thomas Polk. Customers were recognized with a Customer Appreciation Day. In each office, refreshments were served, and officers were on hand to greet and thank customers for their business.

Finally, the bank handed over to the city the deed for a new park. The bank had purchased a parking lot and converted it into a landscaped and well-lighted park where office workers might relax at lunchtime. (See Exhibit G-2.) The park was named in honor of a former chairman of the bank, Ridley Alexander. At the conclusion of the dedication ceremonies, balloons were released by fourth graders from the Alexander Elementary School, the school "adopted" by the bank as part of another community relations program called "Partner in Education."

This bank's anniversary celebration obtained considerable favorable publicity for the bank, demonstrated its pride in its community, and elicited a positive reaction from its various publics.

Exhibit G-2

EXAMPLE 2: A COORDINATED PROGRAM OF COMMUNITY SERVICE

The management of Union Planters National Bank, Memphis, Tennessee, believes the bank should be actively involved in its community and recognizes that its employees are a powerful resource in that effort. They demonstrate this with a program called IMPACT. IMPACT is an acronym for Individuals Making Progress and Changing Tomorrow, and it is an incentive program that motivates employees to donate their time, in the name of the bank, to more than 200 community service agencies in Memphis.

Essentially, the program uses bonus paid vacation days to reward employees for giving their time. The number of bonus vacation days that an individual can earn is directly related to the number of hours volunteered. In 4 years, the program grew from about 40 volunteers to more than 700.

An employee who is willing to commit to a minimum of 10 hours per year signs up for the program and completes a questionnaire that helps identify his or her specific interests. This information is loaded into a computer data base that helps match people with projects. The employee then receives an IMPACT license plate, which is a sign of membership in this respected program. It also provides the bank with hundreds of little traveling billboards for the program.

After the first 10 hours of service, the employee receives a T-shirt bearing the Union Planters IMPACT logo. Employees wear these shirts while working at their various projects. The program gives the employees 1 day of paid vacation for every 25 hours volunteered, up to a maximum of 5 days for 125 hours. So, at 25 hours, the employee receives his first vacation day memo. At 30 hours, he receives a golf shirt, again bearing the IMPACT logo. The golf and T-shirts complete the volunteer's "uniform."

Some examples of the types of work done by the employees are working at fund-raising foot races and phonathons, hostessing at hospitals, delivering meals to shut-ins, visiting nursing homes, or being a Big Brother or Big Sister. The community relations manager reports that many employees give 75 hours or more to the program. Special efforts are recognized at an annual awards banquet. One employee logged in 354 hours during 1 year. Some employees choose not to take the vacation days, demonstrating that they are more motivated by the desire to be of service than by the extra vacation time.

The program's director believes that for a relatively small annual investment, the bank receives about $2.5 million worth of free advertising and publicity. The IMPACT program is an excellent example of a bank conducting itself in a socially responsible manner and, in doing so, earning the esteem of its local community and its staff.

EXAMPLE 3: ADDRESSING A FUNDAMENTAL SOCIAL AND ECONOMIC PROBLEM

In many urban areas, banks face the prospect of an ongoing shortage of high school graduates for entry-level positions such as tellers, clerks, and computer assistants. Recognizing this problem, the New

York State Bankers Association joined forces with a private coalition to develop a 4-year program that guarantees jobs in participating banks to qualifying high school graduates. A number of New York City's largest banks, as well as at least one community bank, are participating in the program, which has the benefit of helping the community while also helping the banks.

The program is called the Nehemiah II Schools/Work Program, and its objective is to improve the performance of students in five schools in east Brooklyn. In order to participate in the program and obtain a bank job, the students must:

- obtain a high school diploma;
- possess basic entry-level skills; and
- have no more than five unexcused absences from school during their senior year.

As a result of this program, many disadvantaged young people are given the hope of a full-time, well-paying job. With the prospect of a job, many seniors are motivated to perform up to the required standard. Students in lower grades are also motivated by the prospect of participating in the program when they become seniors.

As part of the program, bankers visit classes to talk about banking careers, and students visit banks to learn about training programs and to see work situations first-hand. The students receive training in job interviewing skills, how to dress for business, and how to complete an employment application.

In its first year, 100 young men and women began careers in banking, school attendance increased, and many students received instruction in interviewing techniques. In addition, much was learned about preparing students for entry-level job examinations, and alliances between the banks and the community were formed.

This program demonstrates the dependence of a financial institution on the economic and social well-being of its community and the fact that it is in the bank's self-interest to work for the betterment of that community.

GLOSSARY

advertising Any form of paid communication by a sponsor about goods, ideas, or services for the purpose of informing and persuading consumers to buy. By using advertising, an organization can control what is said about its products, and when and where the information appears.

advertising agency A company that specializes in delivering the services required to design, execute, and place advertising messages in the various print and broadcast media. Ad agencies may also serve as consultants in developing marketing strategies.

AIDAS process An acronym for the five successive stages of consumer responsiveness in the selling process. The letters of the acronym stand for awareness, interest, desire, action, and satisfaction.

audience research The process of surveying consumers for their recollection of and reaction to an advertisement delivered in print or through a broadcast medium.

bank elasticity The likelihood that customers will change banks in response to a change in the price of services.

behavior modification pricing Setting a price that encourages consumers to alter their buying behavior.

channel of distribution The means through which goods and services move from seller to buyer.

collateral material   Information in the form of brochures, counter cards, and posters that describes to a customer the range of available products.

community relations   Active participation in and financial support of community projects by an organization for the purpose of fostering goodwill and gaining public esteem.

competitor   A rival business selling identical or similar products in the same market.

concentrated marketing   The practice of designing a single product and marketing strategy to appeal to one market segment.

concept testing   The process of trying out a new product or marketing approach on a selected group of consumers. Concept testing measures reactions to an idea and, unlike test marketing, not actual buying behavior.

consumer buying behavior   The actions individuals take in deciding which goods and services to purchase.

consumerism   A movement originating in the early 1960s to protect the consumer from bad products, poor service, and misrepresentation by businesses about their products and warranties.

corporate objective   A broad statement that gives direction to the business decisions taken to strengthen an organization's long-term financial position.

credit card   A card issued by a financial institution or company that, when used to make purchases or withdraw cash, debits a line of credit established for the customer.

cross-selling   The practice of promoting financial services in addition to the one currently being used by a customer.

cue   Information that arouses interest. An advertisement, unusual packaging, or a product display are examples of cues.

customer profile   A description of the distinctive attitudes and personal characteristics of the typical consumer who buys a product.

customer relations   The policies and practices for the handling of all customer contacts, including one-on-one transactions with employees, complaint resolution, and written communications, in a professional manner that results in a favorable image of the organization.

debit card   A card issued by a financial institution to its customers that, when used to make purchases or withdraw cash, debits a customer's personal account such as checking or savings.

demarket   To act to decrease demand for a product or service.

demographics   The study and analysis of population characteristics such as age, income, education, occupation, sex, and race.

deregulation   The removing or liberalizing of legal restrictions to promote competition. In recent years, the financial services industry has experienced price deregulation (removal of interest rate ceilings), product deregulation (regulatory approval to offer more diversified products and services), and geographic deregulation (expansion across state lines).

differentiated marketing   The practice of designing unique products and specialized marketing strategies to meet the needs of two or more market segments. A variation is to offer one basic product but distinctive marketing strategies to appeal to each segment.

direct marketing   The promotion and selling of goods and services through the mail, over the phone, and in advertising that provides a customer response mechanism (e.g., a coupon or application).

distribution   The process of moving goods and services from seller to buyer.

diversification   The development and sale of new products to new markets.

early adopter   Those consumers who, after innovators, accept and use a new product. Early adopters tend to be opinion leaders and from higher income and social status groups.

early majority   Consumers who are deliberate and cautious in their willingness to accept and use a new product. The early majority responds only after innovators and early adopters have found the product satisfactory but before it has established mass appeal.

elastic   A condition where demand changes quickly and dramatically in response to a change in price.

external public   The people outside an organization who have an indirect impact on its ability to do business and achieve its objectives.

Community organizations, the general citizenry, and the media are examples of external publics.

family life cycle   The progressive stages of a typical family's spending and investment behavior. Although descriptions may vary slightly, the basic cycle begins with a single person and progresses to young married couple, young married couple with children, older married couple with older children, older married couple with no children at home, to widow or widower.

fixed costs   Expenses incurred regardless of the volume of goods produced or services provided.

focus group   A group of people brought together in an informal, pleasant setting to be interviewed for their opinions of specific products, services, and marketing ideas. Because the number of participants is small and not scientifically selected, responses are not representative of a larger population.

goal   A statement of the specific, measurable result to be achieved in pursuit of an organization's corporate and marketing objectives.

heterogeneity   The degree to which quality of service varies. Unlike tangible goods where production is standardized, service quality can vary according to who provides what level of service, in what manner, and at which location.

hierarchy of needs   The theory, developed by psychologist Abraham Maslow, that five levels of need motivate human behavior. Once a lower level need is satisfied, an individual is then motivated to satisfy the next higher. The five needs in order are physiological, sense of security, need to belong, sense of esteem, self-actualization.

implementation   Putting a plan into action.

incremental cost   The change in expenses as a result of increased production or added services.

inelastic   A condition where demand either changes slowly or not at all in response to a change in price.

innovators   The small number of consumers who are the first to risk accepting and using a new product. Innovators tend to be younger and from higher socioeconomic groups.

internal public   The people within an organization who have a direct impact on its ability to do business and achieve its objectives.

The internal public consists of employees, directors, and shareholders.

interstate banking   The establishment of a banking presence in another market across state lines for the purpose of taking deposits.

investor relations   The preparation and presentation of financial reports and programs by an organization for the purpose of fostering goodwill with and gaining esteem from its stockholders and the investment community.

laggard   The small number of consumers who are among the last to accept and use a new product. Laggards tend to be from a lower socioeconomic standing, older, and more conservative.

late majority   Consumers who are likely to accept and use a new product only after the majority of the population has found it satisfactory. The late majority is skeptical and responds to social and economic pressure to accept a new idea.

macroenvironmental factor   A major trend or force in society that influences market conditions. Macroenvironmental factors, such as the economy, the political situation, and the current state of technology, are beyond a company's control but must be monitored and responded to.

management   The process of planning, staffing, organizing, allocating resources, initiating action, providing leadership, and evaluating performance in the pursuit of specific objectives.

market   All the potential customers for a product.

market aggregation   See undifferentiated marketing.

market elasticity   The speed and degree to which total demand for a product will change in response to a change in price.

market expansion   Finding new markets for existing products.

market penetration   Selling more of existing products to present markets.

market profile   A description of the geography, housing, population, and economic activity in the primary (the densest concentration of customers) and secondary (a sparser concentration of customers) areas where a product is sold.

market research The process of gathering and analyzing factual information about a specific market—its geography, customers, and competitors—to understand better one's own position.

market segmentation The process of dividing a market into subgroups, each identifiable by its specific preferences or needs, so that distinctive products can be developed and sold profitably to each.

market share One seller's portion of the total sales of a product, usually measured as a percentage.

marketing "The process of planning and executing the conception, pricing, promotion and distribution of ideas, goods and services to create exchanges that satisfy individual and organization objectives." (American Marketing Association, *Marketing News*, 3/1/85, p. 1.)

marketing concept The philosophy that marketing programs can be designed to satisfy consumer needs in a way that is both socially responsible and profitable for the seller.

marketing information system The people, computers, and procedures in an organization that are responsible for the collection and analysis of market data and the subsequent distribution of this intelligence to marketing management for use in planning and decision making.

marketing intermediary A third party that helps the seller promote and distribute the product to the consumer. Often known as a middleman.

marketing management To plan, implement, and evaluate programs that sell goods and services in a way that both satisfies a consumer need and results in a profit for the seller.

marketing mix The combination of four marketing activities—product development, pricing, promotion, and distribution—aimed at creating demand among the target market.

marketing objective A broad statement giving direction to an organization's short-term product, pricing, promotion, and distribution decisions.

marketing plan A written statement of the product, pricing, promotion, and distribution strategies that will be implemented to achieve long-range goals.

marketing research To gather and analyze factual information about products, prices, promotion, distribution, and consumers for use in marketing management and decision making.

mass market A market that has not been differentiated on the basis of geography, demographics, psychographics, or other form of segmentation.

McFadden Act A federal law enacted in 1927 that prohibits banks from establishing branches across state lines.

media Means of communication that carry advertising; i.e., newspapers, television, radio, magazines, outdoor boards, and direct mail.

media relations A coordinated program of policies, procedures, and written communications to foster good working relations with and favorable news coverage by the media.

media research The process of identifying the number, characteristics, and buying behavior of consumers who are regularly exposed to a particular advertising medium, such as consumers who read the city newspaper every day or who regularly listen to a specific radio station.

microenvironmental factor A key player or other factor in the immediate marketplace that affects a company's ability to do business. Microenvironmental factors are "controllable" to the extent that a company can make business decisions about them, for example, which suppliers of raw materials will be selected, which middleman will be hired to help promote products, and what strategy will work best against a competitor.

middleman See marketing intermediary.

mission statement A statement of common purpose that explains why an organization exists and what it hopes to accomplish.

motivation An inner need that causes a person to act, usually toward a specific goal.

multiple segmentation See differentiated marketing.

neotraditionalism The blending of traditional American values—adherence to principles, discipline, patriotism, and the importance of family, friends, and community—with the ethic of the 1980s that emphasizes the importance of self—making one's own decisions, choosing one's lifestyle, and needing leisure and self-fulfillment.

new product development   The process of taking ideas for new or enhanced products and developing them into actual goods and services that can be sold profitably. The basic steps in this process include (1) idea generation, (2) screening to weed out ideas that are not viable or likely to succeed, (3) a business analysis to forecast sales and profitability, (4) development of a sample, (5) market testing to determine consumer acceptance, and (6) introduction or commercialization of the new product.

objective   A broad statement that establishes a common purpose and a sense of direction for all future activities.

observation   A marketing research method where data are collected by physically observing how consumers use goods and services rather than by questioning them.

organizational buying behavior   The decision-making process used by firms to evaluate and select suppliers of goods and services.

penetration pricing   Setting a low initial price in order to attract quickly a large market share.

perception   The process by which we receive, organize, and interpret sensory information.

personal banker   A program where a bank employee is assigned to provide personalized customer service to a valued customer. Personal bankers are professionals who understand the unique financial needs of each customer and have the authority to handle their nonroutine banking transactions.

personal selling   One-on-one contact between a seller's representative and a potential buyer for the purpose of arousing interest and convincing the buyer to purchase products. Personal selling lays the groundwork for long-term relationships between buyer and seller.

physical distribution   The planning, handling, and delivery activities that result in the movement of goods and services from seller to buyer.

place   A synonym for distribution, or the ways in which products move from seller to buyer.

planning   The process of deciding in the present on objectives for the future and strategies for achieving them. Planning is deciding now where you want to be in the future and how to get there.

positioning   The art of promoting a product in such a way as to make a distinctive impression about the product in the consumer's mind.

premium   Cash or merchandise that a business gives away or sells at discount as an incentive to purchase a product.

pretesting   The process of evaluating the likely effectiveness and acceptance of a new advertising campaign by presenting it first to a representative group of consumers.

price   The amount of money one must pay to own a product or use a service.

price sensitivity   The degree to which changes in price will affect the demand for a product.

primary data   Data collected directly from their source. Questionnaire results are an example of primary data.

product   A tangible good that has both physical and psychological characteristics that make it desirable to the consumer. Often this term is used in a more general sense, as it is in this glossary, to refer to anything (goods, services, places, people, events, or ideas) that satisfies a consumer need.

product expansion   To increase demand by selling new products to current markets.

product item   A specific version of a product.

product life cycle   The successive stages of a product's sales volume. The four stages, which vary in length from product to product, include introduction (low sales), growth (rapid growth in sales), maturity (constant level of sales), and decline.

product line   A group of products that have similar characteristics or serve related functions. In banking, the savings product line would include passbook, statement, and money market savings accounts.

product management   The assignment of an individual or department to be responsible for introducing, marketing, and assuring profitable sales of a product or product line.

product manager An employee who is given responsibility for successfully introducing and managing the profitable selling of a product or product line.

product/market expansion See diversification.

product mix The complete lineup of goods and services offered for sale by a company.

promotion Activities that increase customer awareness and demand.

promotion mix The unique combination of four promotional activities—advertising, sales promotion, publicity, and personal selling—that results in a profitable demand for products.

promotional material See collateral material.

psychographics The study and analysis of the attitudes, interests, and opinions (AIO) that influence buying behavior.

public relations A coordinated program of policies, conduct, and communication designed to foster goodwill and gain esteem.

publicity Any form of unpaid communication about goods or services that informs and persuades consumers to buy. The media reports publicity at no cost to the seller because it is judged to have news or human interest value. As a result, consumers find publicity a more credible source of information than paid advertising. For the issuing organization, the disadvantage of publicity is the loss of control over how the information is edited, and when and where it appears.

qualitative research A research method where information is collected by in-depth, interactive interviewing of a small number of consumers. This method is effective for determining basic needs, desires, and reactions to new product concepts and for identifying issues to be measured with quantitative research.

quantitative research A research method where data are collected by presenting a sizable sample of consumers carefully prepared questions, either verbally or in writing. The result is statistical data about consumer attitudes and buying behavior.

reference group One or more persons whose attitudes and opinions influence the actions of others.

regional banking   The establishment of a banking presence in nearby states either by merger, acquisition, or new charter. Regional banking occurs when reciprocal laws are passed allowing bank holding companies in one state to acquire or establish a bank in another.

Regulation Q   A Federal Reserve Board regulation that prohibits the paying of interest on demand deposits, sets rules for advertising deposit accounts, and until recently set the maximum rate banks could pay on savings and time deposits. The Monetary Control Act of 1980 mandated the gradual phasing out of interest rate ceilings over the period 1980 to 1987.

relationship pricing   To set prices that provide an incentive for consumers to use multiple products.

sales promotion   Any activity, other than advertising, publicity, and personal selling, that provides incentive to the consumer to purchase goods or services. Cents-off coupons, premiums, and in-store displays are examples of sales promotion.

sample   A small number of individuals, scientifically selected from the general population, whose opinions, preferences, and characteristics are representative of the group as a whole.

secondary data   Data collected by a third party and made available for others to use. The *U.S. Statistical Abstract* is an example of secondary data.

segmentation   See market segmentation.

selective distortion   A tendency to alter or interpret information so that it is consistent with prior beliefs.

selective exposure   A tendency to notice only the information needed, expected, or that exceeds expectation.

selective retention   A tendency to remember only the information that supports current attitudes or beliefs.

selectivity   The process of filtering information from the environment so that only what is important is received and retained.

service   An intangible activity or benefit performed by a business that satisfies a consumer need. In banking, this term is often used interchangeably with "product."

service packaging   The practice of marketing a group of services as one customer product.

service shopping A marketing research method for collecting information about competitors' products and services by having an employee pose as a potential customer. This same technique can be used to measure how well an organization's own employees understand and market services.

single-segment marketing See concentrated marketing.

situation analysis The process of evaluating one's position in relation to the internal and external environments to identify strengths, weaknesses, and future courses of action.

skimming pricing To set a high initial price for a product in order to attract the "cream" of the market—consumers who will buy no matter what the price.

social responsibility The obligation of a company to conduct business activities in a way that does not adversely affect its customers or the community as a whole and to devote a portion of its resources to civic improvement efforts.

source market The market that provides the raw materials that enable a company to make and offer products to another market. In banking, consumers who deposit funds in checking or savings accounts are a source market because they provide the funds that can be loaned to or "used" by other customers known as the use market.

specialties A small, useful novelty that carries an advertising message and can be given free of charge to a customer. Calendars, pens, and matchbooks are specialties.

spread The difference between the income earned in using funds and the cost to the bank of those funds. The goal is to maximize that spread, also called the net interest margin.

strategic marketing planning The process of identifying an action plan for attaining long-range marketing goals, of implementing that program, and then of measuring and evaluating its success.

strategy A plan for achieving a desired result.

survey research A marketing research method where data are collected by asking consumers a series of questions, either verbally or in writing, about their attitudes and buying behavior.

systems selling Selling products and the associated services that support them as a comprehensive response to multiple customer needs.

tactic   A specific action taken to attain a goal. Tactics determine who will do what, when, and at what cost.

target market   A preselected group of buyers for whom a product is created and to whom a marketing campaign is directed.

telemarketing   Promoting and selling products by telephone.

test marketing   The process of selling a product on a limited scale in several representative markets. The feedback from consumers, dealers, and competitors enables the marketer to predict acceptance of both the product and the marketing campaign in national markets. Unlike concept testing which measures consumer opinion, test marketing measures actual buying behavior.

undifferentiated marketing   The practice of designing a single product and marketing strategy to appeal to the greatest possible number of customers.

use market   The customers who use a company's end product when they buy goods and services. This term distinguishes from the "source market" that provides the raw materials that enable a company to offer products. In banking, consumers who apply for personal loans are "using" the resources supplied by the source market, depositors.

value pricing   To set a price for a product based on its perceived value to the consumer, not on the basis of cost to the producer.

variable costs   Expenses that vary in amount depending on the volume of goods produced or services provided.

INDEX

specialties, 352
Sales techniques, 493. *See also* Case C
Sales training, 298–307
Sales training program, 301–7. *See also*
  Selling program
Sales volume, 185–86
Salesperson, 293–98
Secondary data, 158, 160, 242–43, 465
Secondary research, 418–19
Segmentation, 185–86
Segmentation strategies, 179–86
Selectivity
  selective distortion, 127–28
  selective exposure, 127
  selective retention, 128
Self-analysis, 75–78, 483–84, 529
Selling orientation, 22–23
Selling program, 299–306. *See also* Personal
  selling
Seminars, 351–52
Service packaging, 215–17
Service shopping, 93
Services
  client relationship, 268
  heterogeneity, 204, 267
  inseparability, 203–4, 267
  intangibility, 203, 266
  perishability and fluctuating demand,
    204–5, 268
Single-segment marketing, 191
Site location, 270–75
Situation analysis, 57, 73–78, 377–78, 479–84,
  508, 517–32
Skimming pricing, 244–45
Slow growth, 13–15
Social class, 131
Social factors
  family influence, 128–29
  reference group influence, 129
  roles and status, 129–30
Social responsibility, 11–12, 405–9
Social/cultural environment, 39, 81, 444–46,
  481
Source market, 44
Specialties, 352

Spread, 234
Strategic marketing management process
  model, 54
Strategic marketing planning, 31–32, 47–49,
  51
Strategy, 100, 107, 536–38
Strategy formulation, 105–13
Survey method, 161–64, 465–76
Survey research, 93
Survey research process, 158–70
Systems and operations, 370–71
Systems selling, 201, 215–17

Tactics, 100, 110, 536–38
Tangible product, 199–200
Target audiences, 16
Target market selection, 59–61, 106, 186–91,
  379–80, 486, 504, 533
Task method, 339
Technological environment, 41–43, 81,
  448–49
Telemarketing, 322–23
Telephone banking, 277
Telephone bill payment, 277
Test marketing, 221–22
Trading up or trading down, 209
Trust marketing, 427–31
Truth in Lending Act, 407, 446

Undifferentiated marketing, 188–89
Unfair and Deceptive Credit Practices Act,
  407
Use market, 44
Users, 145

Value pricing, 245–46
Variable costs, 249
Volume segmentation, 183

Whittle, Jack, 255
Wholesale banking, 415–17